About the Editors

Dr. Komol Singha (1972) teaches at the Institute for Social and Economic Change, Bangalore (India). He earned his Master and Ph.D. in Development Economics. Before joining the present position, he was teaching economics at Don Bosco College, Maram (Manipur); St. Joseph's College, Jakhama (Nagaland) and Royal University of Bhutan (Gedu, Bhutan). His areas of interest are—Institutional Economics, Social Capital, Human Capital, Rural Development, and Development Issues of North-East India, etc.

So far, Dr. Singha has authored three and edited four books and contributed 45 (forty-five) research papers in different journals of repute and contributed to edited volumes (31 in referred journals and 14 in edited volumes) till 2012. Also, he has completed three major research projects and three more major research projects are at the verge of completion. He has travelled extensively for different academic interactions in India and abroad. Besides, he was the Chief Editor of an interdisciplinary journal *Orient Vision* published by the National Research Centre, Manipur.

Dr. M. Amarjeet Singh (1974) currently Associate Professor, Centre for North East Studies and Policy Research, Jamia Millia Islamia, New Delhi earlier he taught sociology at the National Institute of Advanced Studies, Indian Institute of Science Campus, Bangalore (India). He holds a doctorate in sociology from North Eastern Hill University, Shillong (India). His research and teaching interests include sociological theory, Indian democracy, conflict studies, conflict and livelihoods, development and displacement, and migration studies. Singh has published widely on a variety of topics on identity, politics in India, conflict, and migration. E-mail: amarjeetdelhi@gmail.com

Identity, Politics and Economic Development in North-East India

Edited by

Komol Singha
and
M. Amarjeet Singh

CONCEPT PUBLISHING COMPANY PVT. LTD.,
NEW DELHI-110059

ISBN-13: 978-93-5125-040-1

First Published 2014

Published and Printed by

Concept Since 1974

Concept Publishing Company Pvt. Ltd.
A/15-16, Commercial Block, Mohan Garden
New Delhi-110059 (India)
T: 25351460, 25351794, *F*: 091-11-25357109
E: publishing@conceptpub.com, W: www.conceptpub.com
Editorial Office: H-13, Bali Nagar, New Delhi-110 015, India.

Cataloging in Publication Data--*Courtesy:* D.K. Agencies (P) Ltd. <docinfo@dkagencies.com>

Identity, politics and economic development in North-East India / edited by Komol Singha and M. Amarjeet Singh.

p. cm.

Contributed articles.

Includes bibliographical references and index.

ISBN 9789351250401

1. India, Northeastern—Scheduled tribes—Government policy. 2. India, Northeastern—Scheduled tribes—Economic conditions. 3. India, Northeastern Scheduled tribes—Education. 4. Microfinance—India, Northeastern. 5. Rural development—India, Northeastern. 6. Ethnicity—India, Northeastern. I. Singha, Komol, 1972- II. Singh, M. Amarjeet.

DDC 305.8009541 23

Preface

India's North-Eastern Region (NER) consists of eight States and is a 'mixed bag' of several ethnic groups. Around 200, out of 635 tribal groups of the country, are found in this region. The region covers an area of approximately 263 thousand sq. km. (8% of the total geographical area of the country) and its population is about 39 million (3.9% of the country's total population) as per 2001 Census. Around three-fourth of the region's geographical area is covered by hilly terrain and majority of the population (around 85%) live in villages, rural areas in poverty, in the midst of abundant resources.

Despite several years of affirmative action on the region's development that have been taken up by the successive governments and other institutions since the country's independence, it remains an underdeveloped region till today and becomes a catchy word of the politicians, leaders and policy makers at the podiums and public platforms. Therefore, the issue of development of NER requires greater attention and re-look from different angles.

Keeping the urgent needs of development initiative of the region in mind, the present volume entitled "Identity, Politics and Economic Development in North-East India", consists of 23 essays/articles contributed by scholars from different academic institutions of the region and beyond tries to explore some ways and means of ending the prolonged underdevelopment. In totality, the volume focuses the broader issues of ethnicity, tribes, empowerment of women and weaker sections, structure of social sector and public policy towards the development of NER.

Definitely, the volume will give reflection of the region's weakness and opportunities for sustainable development to some extent and help the policy makers in redesigning the policy initiatives of development of the region. For the effort, we want to express our heartiest gratitude to all the contributors for their ongoing support in the completion of this work. Last, but not the least, our special thank goes to Mr. A.K. Mittal of Concept Publishing Company Pvt. Ltd., New Delhi for his keen interest in bringing out this volume.

December 2012 Editors

Contents

Part V
Institutions and Rural Development

List of Contributors

Achintya Mahapatra, Department of Tourism and Management, Royal University of Bhutan, Gedu, Bhutan, Email: achintya4you@gmail.co.in

Bhagat Oinam, Centre for Philosophy, School of Social Sciences, Jawaharlal Nehru University, New Delhi, Email: bhagatoinam@gmail.com

Bidhu Kanti Das, Department of Management, Mizoram University, Aizawl, Email: bidhukantidas@mzu.edu.in

C. Vanlalkulhpuia, Department of Management, Mizoram University, Aizawl, Mizoram.

Damodar Nepram, Department of Economics, Manipur University, Canchipur, Manipur.

Elangbam Nixon Singh, Department of Management, Mizoram University, Aizawl, Mizoram.

Govinda Prasad Bhandari, Department of Management, North Eastern Hill University, Tura Campus, Chandmari, Meghalaya.

Gautam Patikar, Department of Commerce, Nagaland University, Kohima, Nagaland.

Indraneel Bhowmik, Department of Economics, Tripura University, Agartala, Tripura.

J. U. Ahmed, Department of Management, North Eastern Hill University, Tura Campus, Chandmari, Meghalaya.

Jayeeta Sen Department of Sociology, Ramkrishna Nagar College, Karimganj (Assam) Email: jayeetarknc@yahoo.co.in

K. Muktasana Singh, Department of Economics, Manipur University, Imphal, Manipur Email: cmmanimukta10@gmail.com

Komol Singha, Institute for Social and Economic Change, Bangalore, Email: komol@isec.ac.in

Marchang Reimeingam, Institute for Social and Economic Change, Bangalore.

Md. Samsur Jaman, Department of Economics, Jiri College, Jiribam, Manipur, Email: jamanms@yahoo.com

M. Amarjeet Singh, Centre for North East Studies and Policy Research, Jamia Millia Islamia, New Delhi. Email: amarjeetdelhi@gmail.com

Maila Lama, Department of Economics, Rajiv Gandhi University, Arunachal Pradesh.

Md. Abdul Rashid, Department of Commerce, Don Bosco College, Tura, Meghalaya.

Natalie West Kharkongor, Rajiv Gandhi Indian Institute of Management, Shillong, Meghalaya.

N. Shanta Singh, Johnstone Higher Secondary School, Imphal, Manipur.

Pradip Chouhan, Department of Economics, Tripura University, Agartala, Tripura.

Pritam Bose, Department of Economics, Tripura University, Agartala, Tripura.

P. Guha, Department of Economic Studies and Planning, Sikkim University, Gangtok, Sikkim.

Ruma Kundu, Department of Economic Studies and Planning, Sikkim University, Gangtok, Email: rumakundu76@gmail.com

R.K.P.G. Singha, Department of Commerce, Pachhunga University College, Aizawl, Mizoram.

Ram Krishna Mandal, Department of Economics, Dera Natung Government College, Itanagar, Arunachal Pradesh.

Subhendu Dutta, Department of Economics, IBS, Hyderabad, Andhra Pradesh, Email: subhenduiim@gmail.com

Samir K. Mahajan, Department of Economics, Mount Olive College, Kohima, Nagaland, Email: samirkmahajan@yahoo.co.in

Part - I
Identity, Contestation and Development

1

Dilemmas of a Receiving Community: Negotiating with Historicity and Projection

Bhagat Oinam

Introduction

There are few challenges that are perennially faced by the receiving communities—the communities who have been pushed to the fringes in the inter-regional or inter-civilisational politics, driven by historical contingencies. The fate of the receiving communities is driven by the fact that either they have remained isolated from the rest of the world due to their self-exclusive isolation or were marginalised by a more powerful military or cultural might. Communities of North-Eastern Region of India (NER)[1] face this plight of being pushed to the fringes by historical contingencies not totally of their making. The issue is not so much about these receiving communities *actually lacking* on different spheres of life, but of a lack being *projected* by the protagonists of power narratives. One of the challenges before these receiving communities obviously is to negotiate with the changing situations and the (colonial/global) forces that emerge from time to time. This chapter tries to engage with such issues taken up largely the case of Manipur as a point, where such sites of contestation are visible at different layers and the negotiations follow in various forms.

Negotiation often comes in the form of a dialogue. The assumption that participants in a dialogue are equal partners seems to be a misnomer since dialogue mostly turns out to be between the unequal parties. In the face of such a situation, what is generally missed out is the inalienable tension between the Life-World of the receiving communities and the forces from outside. The space for negotiation is historically twined that cannot be displaced, yet are constantly in surge with contest and adaptation. The ideas of modernity and globalisation have created such tensions for the receiving communities.[2] Colonialism is supposed to have brought into the underdeveloped worlds of Asia and Africa the sceptre of modernity, a changed vocabulary with the same spirit that has come in the post-colonial world. Globalisation as the new terminology brings the sceptre of modernity to the developing world. As the older sceptre changes from *colonial power* to *global power*, the receiver also changes from *underdeveloped* to the *developing* world order. While the change in vocabulary is witnessed, the spirit continues to remain.

The crisis of the receiving communities with the sceptre of modernity has remained problematic throughout. Interestingly, this fate of the receiving community does not seem to be a unique fate of the North-East region and its people, but a trend that every receiving community encounters with overarching and impending external forces. Import of modernity along with colonialism has created existential and intellectual anguish among the elites of the receiving communities. While at few historical moments response of these elites was of accommodation and assimilation, at other, it was of protest and denial. These responses have been marked by the politics of the time. Negotiation on power and control was not merely between the receivers and the advocates, but also among the receivers, some among them playing the role of second fiddle advocate. The marginal communities are not homogeneous either, and do not show similar forms of response to the forces of modernity. While variation in responses depends largely on several historical and social factors, role of collective consciousness and subjective interventions serve as significant causal factor.[3] The contest of modernity and tradition is not about two phenomena in alterity[4], but of negotiation within the self, for a space of identity and assertion.

For the North-East India, like many other colonised worlds, it is of wearing a permanent garb of a 'receiver'. The 'bundles of contradictions' that the colonial rule brought during the first-half of the 19th century, has created fractured self/selves with several ideational and ideological divides. A longing to discover or invent a 'past', through which the self could be recovered, not merely for functional deliberation but for providing a paradigmatic account, has become a self-generated task of many communities in the region.

This chapter is an indicator, not in the sense of measuring a standard, but as hinting at a possible methodology for studying the marginal communities. Its engagement, more than the interpretation of events, is of enacting a discursive framework. While historical narratives of the North-East have brought out rich information about kings, communities and their rule. These have remained partial with many communities being absent in these narratives. Pluralism, transparent representation, and objectivity are what are strongly called for a future historiography of North-East India.

Modernity and Colonialism

Like many parts of the Indian sub-continents, modernity's entry into North-East India was by proxy. It is a well-established thesis by several eminent scholars[5] that modernity did not emerge in the developing world in the way it appeared in the West, particularly in Europe. It was brought to the colonised world by the European colonial power in most cases. Entry of science, technology and education took a place that suited the colonial rule. Freedom, human rights, right to speech, etc., which were the major focus of modernity in the West, did not quite figure in the modernity programme in this part of the world. My difficulty is not so much with the critique that modernity 'while being rational within its confine, refused to be rational about accepting other traditions of knowledge'.[6] Enlightenment programme had been equally harsh with its own traditional values. It was by breaking the cultural foundation of the medieval Europe that modernity emerged. My concern is of the hypocrisy with which colonialism operated its modernity programme when it travels elsewhere in the world. It was inconsistent and driven by imperial design.

Modernity was packaged with many other forces that were inherently opposed to its own programme. Take for instance, the Church. It was against the Church and Catholicism that enlightenment programme stood on its ground. But the two antithetical poles happily mingled in the colonial frame of operation. As much as Hume saw 'reason as the slave of passion'[7], modernity in the colonized world became one of the tools for exploiting the receiving communities. Even it opens up the question if those were modernity at all. The contradictions that constituted colonialism not only made it internally unstable but also made scattered selves out of the receiving community. Take the case of several ethnic communities of North-East India where impact of Christianity has been immense. Often the gospel of Christ and sermon of the clergy is so overwhelming that pre-conversion state of these communities is 'revealed' as a state of barbarism—'people hunting down heads as trophy'. Christianity is supposed to have brought modernist values to these native receivers.[8] Contrary to such revelations, political discourse in many of these communities projects a contrary tale: 'of their unique history, of village republic, of their living independently from time immemorial'.[9] Different domains of the same self varyingly assert itself, sometimes eulogising certain past and sometimes disowning certain other past. Such a complex articulation highlights the impact of colonialism in the garb of modernity and subsequent internalization of external values by the colonized minds. An interesting part of this internalization is about 'discovering' the past in an unendingly varied ways. Nehru's *Discovery of India* is one among many forms of this internalization.

Unfortunately in most cases, this discovery does not seem to critically evaluate the covert designs of these colonial administrations in general. What the victim-subject often misses out is an eye towards seeing colonialism's overarching and prevalent characteristic in its policy of 'divide and rule' operated by forging unity and inventing new identities. This trend, as can be witnessed elsewhere in the developing world, Manipur[10] has had its share of experience—the seed of structural conflict in the region was sown by this policy. The case of Manipur explains quite explicitly the layers of impact that has been given by colonialism. To begin with, British colonial master's division of Manipur into hills and valley, and altering the boundary of the State was to serve the colonial interests by creating drastic changes not only in the socio-cultural lives of the people but also affected inter-community harmony. The aftermath of the post-1891 Anglo-Manipuri War witnessed not only a new Manipuri king being installed by the British, the administration of the hills by and large came under the direct control of the British. Installing a king reduced the colonial power of the day-to-day administrative responsibility, though the British political agent took major political decisions by proxy. Subsequent policies introduced in the Manipur valley showed naked economic exploitation of British colonialism. The British did not interfere much with the village administration of the communities in the hills except for a few additions like introduction of *Lamboos.*[11] Hills were left as playfield for evangelising activities. Even the space of operation between the Baptists and Presbyterians showed distinctive marks of boundary in their respective jurisdiction of operation. The entry of the missionaries in the hills enabled influence on the cultural/spiritual domain of the hill people leading to clear divide between the hills and the valley. Since administrative division made the valley and the hills as two segments in the administrative domain, entry of Christianity in the hills sharpened the division in the cultural domain. It made the division between the two segments complete. Formalization of categories like Naga and Kuki,[12] even though for administrative purposes, later helped in consolidation of identity in the cultural domain. This aspect of colonialism—of dividing the natives (the receiving communities) was indeed a tool through which colonial rule was sustained in a foreign soil, so much so is the success story that discovery of a barbaric history of the self and encounter with a novel worldview from outside was increasingly told and retold by the natives themselves. This is indeed the plight and irony of a receiving community. This trend witnessed in the North-East India, though widely prevalent, is not a unique phenomenon. Similar trend was witnessed in other parts of India, one of which was briefly witnessed in the Young Bengal Movement.[13]

I shall miss out the point if I do not bring in the fact that colonial administration had been focused more than imparting modern values, towards the control of economic resources. This of course is an obvious fact. But mentioning this is important to locate the colonial power and its agenda in proper place. In brief, British administration's focus had been, as elsewhere, the control of the material forces of the receiving communities. Though administrative changes were made in the field of revenue, trade and economy in general, its impact was indirectly felt in the cultural domain as well. For instance, in Manipur, the shift from the *Lallup* to the *patta* system[14] enabled the British to control the revenue of the State. In order to enhance trade, cartable road was developed from Moreh to Dimapur. In fact, British's interest in Manipur, in addition to creating a buffer State, was marked by need for a free trade route between Indo-China and British India. Colonial administration also brought about a more structured form of market economy. These changes led to 'dual government' that was witnessed in Bengal during 1757–1764. The British enjoyed all the power without responsibility while the king was given responsibility without economic power. This compelled the king to look for revenue in the cultural domain. New taxation such as *Chandan Senkhai, Mangba Sengba*[15] was introduced to increase royal exchequer, which in turn led to consolidation of orthodox Brahmanism in the valley. Never before in the history of Manipur was untouchability witnessed as during the colonial period. This is against the background that Hinduism arrived at Manipur during fifteenth century AD. The episode is blown out of proportion by few vested interests that Meiteis practised untouchability against the hill communities. More than the hill communities the Meitei subjects, particularly the marginalized and the underprivileged, were the real victims. Emergence of *Sanamahi* movement[16] as a protest against such atrocities, which later contested the control of the cultural space, serves as an important historical marker.

What have been witnessed as a whole are several contradictions with which colonialism operated. While the British administration projected an image of a benevolent master bringing about transformation in each sphere of life, modernity has been selectively used. Though modernity's characterisation lies in the primacy of reason and self-criticism that operate in each sphere of human life, either towards capturing the knowledge about the physical or the life worlds, or understanding the intricacies of human reality, the same do not get reflected in the lives of the people in the region. This is an area where not only the colonial rule failed, but the present 'liberated' State equally fails to address to the need.

Making Narratives of the Past

The 'past' often juxtaposed along with the idea of 'modernity' shows presence of modernity as an alien phenomenon. Then tradition as a legacy of the past is seen from the prism of the present even if conceived as a process. Our past does not remain independent in isolation in pure form. All that we know or claim to know is about what we perceive. And what we perceive is through a prism already construed and formalised. Tradition is thus perceived through a prism, and is not divorced from the present and a desired future. And that prism could be the 'prism of modernity'.

A complex nature of the juxtaposition is that the relationship projected between tradition and modernity lies with the fact that modernity has already crept in the tradition. The two are no more exclusive, at least for the receiving communities. The inseparability of the two, even though often seen as mutually exclusive, can be illustrated through several instances. Many of the protests that sporadically came up in Manipur in the name of preserving traditional values and heritage, such as 'script movement' and 'traditional dress code for girl students', have nothing so traditional about them. The image of a tradition that these movements project has already incorporated the modern political ideas such as 'right to culture', 'civil disobedience and courting arrest', 'language and script as vehicle for inculcating nationalism', etc. Even the idea of a denial of Westernisation or Indianisation has already incorporated the image of that which they wish to deny. Though images of a past heritage are projected, these images do not only seem to be very modern but also the mode of agitation is equally so. For instance, take the writings of Atom Bapu Sharma, Wahengbam Yumjao Singh, Asangbam Miniketan Singh and many others who engaged in the process of discovering a past that was close to Vedic lineage. Migration of *Kiratas* was thrown up to make the Meiteis closer to Vedic Bharata. The other group, *Meitei Marup*, completely rejected such a narration of the Hinduised Meiteis seeing it as concocted myth. Kangjiya Gopal's book *Adungeigi Manipur Kangleipak Natte* (The Distant Manipur is not Kangleipak) rejected the myth of locating the present Manipur (then Kangleipak) in the *Mahabharata*. While the two hold opposing positions, both look for traces of the past through the discourse of modernism. Linearity in modern historiography guides their perceptions that both fall back on constructing a long past heritage of 2000 years old history. More than the validity, or invalidity of the narration what becomes important is the mode of narration of construing a tradition from the modernist perspective.

Anxiety of having a genuine tradition or a modernity of the indigenous kind is based on two criticisms: one, of an encompassing and homogenising tendency of modern science; and two, of an anxiety of being a part of the colonized self. Both are factitious, faced by the receiving communities. But the world has witnessed tremendous change in the last few decades. Enlightenment programme has undergone drastic changes. Positivism, for instance, is no more fashionable. But problem with the receiving communities, to my mind, seems to be arising from encountering and fairing the complex 'bundles of contradictions', which colonialism brought. The dilemma and the anguish are not confined to the academia alone but also visibly witnessed in the day-to-day life world of the receiving communities. Complexity and paradoxes do not stop the ongoing journey of life. We continue to live with these bundles of contradictions.

Discovery of tradition among these communities is more about manifestation of anxiety of a scattered self. The failure at the material domain led to resurgence at the spiritual.[17] Defeat from the colonial rule gave birth to this new programme. The resurgence specifically tends to look towards a past. The nationalist movement in Bengal, for instance, in order to reject the colonial rule started looking at superior image of the natives in their pre-colonial time. Siraj-ud-Daula, for instance, became the hero and Mir Zafar a villain in Bengali theatre and plays. Apart from the recovery, the attempt was also a search for an alternate space. What came quite natural was search for a political space in the cultural/spiritual domain. This was projected to counter the British onslaught that had already overtaken the receiving communities in the material domain.[18] Discovery of Ramakrishna in the Bengali middle class[19] enabling assertion of middle class hegemony in Bengal was a case in point. This trend got reflected in Manipur through educated Manipuri middle class, who, from their education in Bengal, brought the spirit of nationalism. Introduction of print technology, inception of Nikhil Manipuri Maha Sabha, etc., were manifestations of the trend.

Similar cases had been witnessed in Manipur during the post 1891 colonial rule. Manipuris, unable to reconcile with the defeat in the Anglo-Manipuri War, looked for areas where the natives' supremacy could be recovered. Loss in the war meant loss of control over military, political administration, economy, and trade. The defeat in the political and economic sphere led the traditional Manipuri elites to look into the private domain. British were projected as impure and the 'dirty other'. There had been cases where houses entered by the British officials were destroyed and new houses were built.[20] These were collectively sanctioned and performed. It was a fight, more a protest, to a dominating power. It was not a direct fight as the domain of operation for the two were different. It was a judicious and selective move by the traditional elites not to directly confront the British yet register their protest differently.

Responses to modernity showed a complex phenomenon than a homogeneous archetype. Differences in the responses of these communities were shaped not only by the varying administrative policies of the colonial rule but also by the dynamics of power struggle among the receiving groups. In fact, complexity is shown by the varied and multi-layered character of these responses. Manipur, for instance, showed an interesting trend of elite formation. First was the traditional Brahmins and royal clan who still carried the legacy of a pre-colonial state authority. These were the priestly and feudal classes who were not very cordial, if not hostile, to the British. Slowly, this class was co-opted by the new state, took to English and Bengali education, leading to the formation of new elites. Some members of this class with the addition of a few other sections of the society formed a new group—the middle class. This second group was mostly educated at places like Sylhet, Dacca and (then) Calcutta. These emerging new elites were progressive, but used traditional idioms to register and propagate their political aims. They were the brands of middle class 'intelligentsia' as witnessed elsewhere in India. A case of Hijam Irabot could throw light into the trend and exceptions.[21] The third group emerged out of an existential crisis of being left out, took contrary positions to the ones held by other elite groups. This traditionalist *Meitei*

Marup (Pre-Hindu Sanamahi sect) took to indigenous pre-Vaisnava values and life style. Impressions of the trend still find traces in many of the organisations of the present.

Contemporary Manipur experiences have two most popular narratives: 'merger of Manipur to the Indian Union' and 'unique history of the Nagas'. In the former, annexation of Manipur by the newly independent India on the 15th October, 1949 is highlighted as the black day in the history of the state. To strengthen the narrative, pre-merger state of Manipur from 14th August, 1947 to 15th October, 1949 is projected as 'a temporal space' of free and independent Manipur. The real duration of the period was not considered important. State of freedom as a temporal concept was shown in continuity by bracketing the consciousness of temporality. This was made possible because the immediate preceding évent was the Anglo-Manipuri War of 1891 where Manipuris fought a losing battle with pride and glory. Projection of Manipur as an independent kingdom before the British invasion, and an independent state after the British left, has been successfully made as continuity in the minds of the people. But the protagonists of the narrative ignore the importance of colonial regime (1891–1947) as a basis of nationalist historiography. They downplay the fact that Manipur not only lost many parts of its territory in the treaty of 1834, but also gained several parts. During the span of a century, the territory of Manipur fluctuated to a considerable degree. When territories are lost inhabitants too are lost, and when territories are gained new populations are added. The experience of Manipur falls within this trend. Perhaps, the India-Pakistan experience of partition was among the exceptional few. Further, the protagonists fail to see that nationalism is built not merely by projecting geographical space and past heritage of a few, but by accommodating the world views of all. In a similar tone of 'Merger' narrative, Nagas (particularly of Manipur) come out with an equally exclusive narrative. The projection is of a unique history: of village republic, an unconquered Naga territory even during the height of British imperialism. This narration though initiated by Naga National Council (NNC), has been given a new direction in recent times by the NSCN (IM) as the protagonist of the Naga cause. The direction of freedom has changed, so much so has the concept. Just as the notion of 'sovereignty' is talked in terms of a 'special federal relation' with India, freedom from 'Indian imperialism' has shifted to freedom from 'Meitei imperialism'! There is nothing new about such a concept. 'Right to Self-determination' has varied layers of interpretation.

The present case is about discarding one concept and appropriating another.

The crisis is of contradicting narratives that seem to have become a trend than exception. This can be witnessed not only between the Meiteis and the Nagas of Manipur, but also between the Bodos and chaste Assamese in Assam. Similar is the case found in Meghalaya where the Bengalis and the Assamese struggle to get a place in the historical narrative of the State, which tends to selectively erase certain past memories involving their origin in the State. While the Assamese, Bengalis and Manipuris (particularly Meiteis) are being charged of denying possible spaces to other communities in the region in their long drawn historical narratives, the new trend by the protesting communities to carve a space for themselves through a new historical narrative rather denies than supplements the existing narratives. At the end, it turns out to be a contest for the control of space among different communities.

A Note on Historiography

The above narratives take us to a site of contestation. Narrating the pasts, these traditions end up with contesting claims. While each community goes on 'totalising' its goal and identity, each act of narration ignores the other narration, so much so the goals (as 'totality')[22] are mutually exclusive and opposed. In principle, two totalities cannot be realized simultaneously. A nation cannot have more than one 'totality' at a time unless it suffers from split personality. Even if the narratives (totalisation) differ, as in the case of a dialogue, the goal (totality) ought to be corresponding. The projection of the Nagas in Manipur narrating an alternative totalisation and totality shows that there is more than one nation in the present State of Manipur. And 'totality' is of an independent Naga inhabited land. Another version of the totality, largely held by majority Meiteis, is seeing the entire people of the State as one nation in evolution. A careful study will reveal that totalisation as present has deeper philosophical underpinning. Jean Paul Sartre's formulation that 'totalising present is conditioned by totalised and totalising past of the process of human development' could serve as a point for reflection. Totalisation projects a 'cultured' man (including illiterate societies) who totalises through centuries of history, through experiences.[23] In fact, each act of totalisation projects a long trace of historical origin of the people. The often-used phrase in these narratives is 'from time immemorial'. Through the phrase, legitimacy is sought for a narrative to become historical. Two options clearly emerge: one, whether to see multiple totalisations and totalities as prelude to smaller nation-states, or two, that these are the voices of a fractured self. The problem is not only unique to the State of Manipur. This is witnessed at every level of political discourse, whether one looks at North-East India as a whole or the Indian nation State as one.

Concluding Note

The challenge before the contesting narratives is of drawing mutually corresponding and admissible narratives. This has remained a daunting task in the region. To have narratives that not only corresponds with one another, but also mutually encouraging, will overcome the limitations of exclusivist narratives. The present political crisis in the region is largely because of the gap that exists in our knowledge of the other. It is the lack of what Ricoeur calls 'pairing' (*paarung*) of individuals' temporal fields, which form a historical field of experience that correlates gaps in our perception of the surrounding.[24] It is the exclusion of the other as well as non-recognition of the claims of the other that pairing is most urgently called for.

To draw a comprehensive history of the North-East fulfilling representation, there is strong need to go back to the colonial period. This is not to denounce the already existing narratives. Chronicles, such as *Buronji*, *Cheitharol Kumbaba* and *Rajmamala* will continue to have their own significance. But there is need to be critical of the narratives that project a mere imaginative fantasy[25] without pairing. It needs to be clearly shown that arrival of modernity in the package of colonialism shaped the consciousness of the communities in a particular direction. It was the colonial rule that paved structural changes to almost all the communities in the region. North-East was physically bridged and spiritually distanced by the British colonial power. A narrative that comprehends the historical fields of experiences of the region with a comprehensive rationality seems to be the most reasonable approach to understand the region – of its past and future, through an accommodative present.

NOTES

1. North-Eastern Region (NER) of India encompasses eight States – Assam, Arunachal Pradesh, Manipur, Meghalaya, Mizoram, Nagaland, Sikkim and Tripura.

2. However, it should be noted that essentialising modernity or globalization is to make it (as an idea and process/act) stagnant which would be self-contradictory. Modernity characteristically is self-critiquing, and its goal lies in the act/process. It is in our performing the act(s) that modernity is envisaged and accomplished.
3. Collingwood's 'free and deliberate act of a conscious and responsible agent' as a historical cause needs a special highlight. See, R.G. Collingwood, *An Essay on Metapnysics*, (Oxford: The Clarendon Press), 1962 (first published 1940), p. 290.
4. "Alterity" is about 'those' outside the self. But what is outside is not free from the actor who is an 'inside'. The conception goes closer to the ideas of Levinas where the outside gets meaning through the inside. See Michael B. Smith, *Towards the Outside: Concepts and Themes in Emmanuel Levinas*, (Pittsburg, Pennsylvania: Duquesne University Press), 2005.
5. Scholars like Ashis Nandy, Partha Chatterjee, etc., have been working on the theme, and it is well established thesis that modernity as it came in India had colonial tinge, some calls it as 'colonial modernity' (Nandy). So is modernity not a singular phenomenon even in Europe?
6. Ashis Nandy, *The Intimate Enemy*, (New Delhi: Oxford University Press), (first published 1983) 2002, pp. 2-3.
7. David Hume, *A Treatise of Human Nature*, L.A. Selby-Bigge (ed.), (Oxford: Clarendon Press), 1978.
8. This is not to ignore the 'liberation theology' that has come from Catholic fraternity.
9. This has been largely witnessed in the Naga narratives.
10. Manipur is the most North-Eastern State of India, bordering Myanmar in the east.
11. Roles of *Lamboos* were traditionally the intermediary between the king and the tribal chieftains. The same post was retained by the British administration who engaged them for collecting taxes from the villages in the hills.
12. Gangmumei Kamei (then Kabui) highlights 'common place' of origin of several tribes who are now clubbed within the category of the 'Naga' primarily to left the earlier period of origin of the term as well as identity of the group. This is not, however, left the present day expanse of tribes subsumed in the category as have existed during the pre-colonial or colonial period. What was known as 'Naga' to the Assamese before the advent of the British were limited to a few tribes inhabiting in the hill ranges south of the Brahmaputra valley. Further, many tribes of Kuki-Chin linguistic group today claim themselves as 'Naga'. The term was formalised by the colonial administration, and later internalised during the post-colonial period. The strength of identity formation lies not in merely tracing the origin but in futuristic engagement in the present. Naga identity formation precisely does that. To continue the debate, see

Gangumei Kabui, 'Genesis of the Ethnoses of Manipur', in Naorem Sanajaoba (ed.), *Manipur: Past and Present*, Vol. 3, (New Delhi: Mittal Publications), 1995, pp. 21-25.

13. I am referring to Young Bengal Movement initiated by Henry Derozio in Bengal.
14. Lallup is a form of military, administrative and civil services rendered by the subjects to the State. The subject in lieu of his service is entitled to hold land for cultivation. The practice was abolished to bring in patta system which enabled the British to have direct control of the revenue. See N. Joykumar Singh, *Social Movements in Manipur*, (New Delhi: Mittal Publications), 1992, pp. 29-30. Also see N. Lokendra Singh, *Unquiet Valley*, (New Delhi: Mittal Publications), 1998, pp. 29-30.
15. Chandan Senkhai was a form of taxation against the use of **chandan** as tilak on the Vaisnava population. Mangba-sengba was the purification fee paid by those ostracised as impure either by the king, king's brother, or the Brahmin. Purification fees varied depending upon the nature of the declaration. New forms of taxation made the king increasingly unpopular, but substantive revenue could be gathered through these ill practices.
16. Sanamahi movement aims at reviving the indigenous religious and cultural practices of pre-Vaisnava Meiteis.
17. Partha Chatterjee, *The Nation and Its Fragments*, (New Delhi: Oxford University Press), 1993, p. 26.
18. Ibid., pp. 26.
19. Ibid., pp. 36-37.
20. B.C. Allen, *Assam District Gazetteer: Naga Hills and Manipur*, Vol. IX, Part 2, (Calcutta: Baptist Mission Press), 1905, p. 61.
21. Leaders like Hijam Irabot, who were co-opted by the king, did not succumb to the pressure but genuinely worked for the people. He stood for the modernization of economy, social reforms and justice that shakened the existing feudal structure. He believed that Meitei society could be regenerated by rectifying the evils in the Hinduism itself. Activities of such middle class leaders were influenced by the dominant ideology of Indian freedom struggle. For instance, Irabot interacted with many leaders of Indian freedom struggle in Sylhet and Cachar. See, Yambem Sanamani, 'Nupi Lan: Women's Agitation, 1939', *Economic and Political Weekly*, Vol. XI, No. 8, February 21, 1976, p. 327. Also see, Karam Manimohan Singh, *Hijam Irabot Singh and Political Movements in Manipur*, (New Delhi: R.B. Publishing Corporation), 1989, pp. 153-54.
22. For Sartre, 'totality' and 'totalisation' refer to goal of praxis and act of praxis respectively. Human praxis is narrating and asserting about oneself, which is about creating history. The difference between the two is that totality is totalized and the totalisation totalises itself. While the former is projected as 'become', the latter is 'becoming', which suggests that it is locating in time and, as such, totalizes itself. So totalisation as an act in

the present encompasses the past acts as well as the future goal. If history is totalisation which temporalises itself, culture is itself temporalising and temporalised totalisation. Although one totalises individually, one's culture cannot be treated as mere subjective accumulation of knowledge as 'my own', but is conceived as specific participation in interiority in the objective culture. See J.P. Sartre, *Critique of Dialectical Reason*, tr. Alan Sheridan-Smith, ed. Jonathan Rée, (London: Verso/NLB), (first published 1960) 1982, pp. 53-56.

23. *Ibid.*, p. 54.
24. Paul Ricoeur sees 'imagination' as an individual action. Each individual imagines independently in isolation that creates a flux. It is through the idea of 'pairing' that one temporal flux accompanies another. This leads to a higher order temporality that categorises isolated events and actions. The formulation largely explains intersubjective understanding of imagination as an act of constructing history. However, it remains to be seen how far it successfully explains inter-community understanding of imagination. See, Paul Ricoeur, 'Imagination in discourse and in action', in Gillian Robinson & John Rundell (eds.), *Rethinking Imagination: Culture and Creativity*, (London & New York: Routledge), 1994, p. 127.
25. To illustrate the point, take the case of Meities as descendants of mythic figures of the *Mahabharata*. Such attempts are manifestation of a desperate self to equate with an imagined superior race and tradition.

2

Migration and Ethnic Identity: Insights from North-East India

M. Amarjeet Singh

Introduction

North-East India, consisting of eight States, namely Arunachal Pradesh, Assam, Manipur, Meghalaya, Mizoram, Nagaland, Sikkim and Tripura, occupies about eight per cent of the country's total geographical area; and has about four per cent of the country's total population. It is ethnically diverse, inhabited by a large number of ethnic groups. Geographically, it consists of both hills and plains. This land is connected to the rest of country by 22 kilometres long land corridor passing through Siliguri, the sub-divisional town in the State of West Bengal, hence almost surrounded by Bangladesh, Bhutan, China, Myanmar and Nepal. The density of population varies from 17 persons per sq km in Arunachal Pradesh to 397 persons per sq km in Assam, as per 2011 Census. A large number of people speak languages closely related to the South-East Asian languages. This borderland is relatively little known, both within and outside the country. Further, it has poor communications and transportation infrastructures. Almost all consumer goods are imported from other parts of the country; and in all these States, non-government employment opportunities are almost non-existent; and hence the government is the principal employer. Thus, this borderland gets special financial assistance from the country's Central government. Any Indian national who wishes to visit Arunachal Pradesh, Mizoram and Nagaland (except Dimapur town) require a permit known as Inner-Line Permit issued by the competent State officials to enter those territories. Implemented under the East Bengal Frontier Regulation Act 1873, during the days of the British, its intention is to prohibit any subject living outside the area from living or moving therein so as to keep the demographic profile of those territories intact. North-East India also happens to be the location of the longest-running armed conflict in India, started in the then Naga Hills of undivided Assam (now Nagaland) demanding increased autonomy to secession, or of reclaiming control of ancestral lands. Down the line, similar conflicts have spread over to different parts of the region. This is a political problem primarily linked to the issues of migration, geographical separateness, underdevelopment and lack of political integration.

Beginning of the Conflict

The borderland began increasing contact with the rest of India, just few centuries ago, mainly after its incorporation into the British Indian Empire in the nineteenth century. The advent of the British brought far-reaching transformation of its society, economy and polity. Since then it has become one of the great destinations of migration. Initially the educated Bengali Hindus were recruited to work in the new administration. Then since the demand for labour was high due to the rapid expansion of tea plantation, coal mining and oil exploration, the labour recruitment, especially from the present-day Jharkhand, Odisha, etc, was also started. The migrants worked as tea garden labourers, skilled labourers, manual labourers, cultivators, clerks, small traders and livestock farmers.

In addition, the territorial boundary of Assam, then constituted a large part of North-East India, was redrawn. It was initially administratively incorporated into Bengal, from 1826 to 1873, and then became a separate province of British India in 1874, in which the Bengali-speaking areas of Cachar, Sylhet and Goalpara respectively were administratively incorporated. The boundaries of Bengal and Assam were once again redrawn in 1905 to facilitate the formation of the provinces of (1) East Bengal and Assam, and (2) Bengal, respectively. This was reversed in 1912.

Apart from the territorial changes, the Bengali language was introduced in place of Persian language as the court language of Assam in 1831 on the ground of difficulty and cost involved to find replacement whenever a Persian scribe went on leave or left the service (Barpujari, 1963: 46)[1] and then as the language of school education in 1836. Thus, the Bengalis became indispensable in education since school teachers were not available in adequate numbers to impart lessons in Bengali language. But the dominance of the Bengalis was against the interests of the Assamese who wanted the introduction of their language as the language of education and administration. Subsequently, the Assamese language was introduced in 1872 as an official language and the language issue gave a fillip to the growth of Assamese sub-nationalism.

When the British rule came to an end, the empire was divided. In doing so, Bengal was divided in which the eastern part was allocated to East Pakistan (it later became Bangladesh in 1971), while Assam, Manipur and Tripura (now North-East India) were allocated to India. The allocation of territories triggered religious riots causing forced migration of hundreds of thousands of refugees (about 14.5 million Muslims and Hindus) defying the newly-created border. In the 1960s, the alleged religious persecutions and the construction of Kaptai hydroelectric dam across Karnaphuli river in East Pakistan forced several thousand Chakmas to move towards India. Further, during the Bangladesh liberation war of 1971, hundreds of thousands of refugees moved towards East and North-East India, put up in refugee camps and the relatives. Some of them permanently settled down in India. Besides, there has also been considerable movement of people into India in the hope of improving their livelihoods.

In the post-partition period, migration became more controversial. However, the total migrant population is never known, and the available estimates give confusing figures, from few lakhs to over 15 million. In 2001, the Government of India appointed a committee which estimated that as much as 15 million Bangladeshis, 2.2 million Nepalese, 70,000 Sri Lankans and about one lakh Tibetan migrants living in the country. The report maintained that "illegal migration" in the past five decades have led to demographic changes in West Bengal, Bihar, Assam, Tripura and Meghalaya. The report further stated that "such large scale migration has obvious social, economic, political and security implications. There is an all-round failure in India to come to grips with the problem of illegal immigration. Unfortunately, action on this subject invariably assumes communal overtones, with political parties taking positions to suit the interests of their vote-banks. The massive illegal immigration poses a grave danger to our security, social harmony and economic well-being" (Government of India, 2001: 60). However, the Census of India of 2001 shows that about 60 per cent of the 5.1 million migrants (by their last residence outside the country) came from Bangladesh alone, with West Bengal having the maximum, of about three million. It further reported that in terms of the share of migrants in the total population, Tripura is on the top with more than 9 per cent or 0.3 million of its total population. In 1965, Bimala Prasad Chaliha, the then Chief Minister of Assam, claimed that about one million "illegal Pakistani infiltrators" had entered India between 1951 and 1961 (220,961 in Assam, 459,494 in West Bengal, 297,857 in Bihar and 55,403 in Tripura) (quoted in Schendel, 2005: 204). India also claimed that thousands of Bangladeshis who came to the country with valid documents have been missing.[2] However, Bangladesh has all along denied the presence of their citizens in India. It even accused India of evicting Bengali-speaking Muslims by branding them as 'Bangladeshis'. Some of the frequently quoted complaints by the Indian officials are: "illegal migration is affecting our national security", "illegal migration has become a serious problem for India", "they are eating into the economy of the country", "it is a security threat", and so on. By contrast, the familiar statements of denial by the officials of Bangladesh are: "there are no Bangladeshi refugees in India any more", "there is no question of our taking any people back", "it is an internal problem of India", "under no circumstances accept any of the evicted persons", and so on.

One wonder, why it was, and has been primarily one-way flow of migrants and refugees. With a total population of about 142 millions in 2011, Bangladesh is one of the most densely populated countries in the world having a population density of about 964 persons per sq km. The land-man ratio in 2010 was .06 ha. It is also one of the poorest countries in the world. Further it is highly prone to natural disasters such as flash flood, riverbank erosion and landslide. Millions of people were left homeless each year due to these natural disasters. For instance, flooding has been a regular feature destroying lives and properties almost every year. One-fifth of the country used to be flooded every year, and in extreme years, two-thirds of the country (Agrawala *et al.,* 2003: 9-70). Moreover, it is almost surrounded by India, sharing about 4096.7 km long land border.

On the other hand, India is also a poor country, yet it is over 22 times the area of Bangladesh, and it has an average population density of 382 persons per sq. km in 2011, far below that of Bangladesh. The density of population is further less in its North-East borderland. The people of North-East are less mobile, and also not so familiar to work in new residential areas and communities. They are also not used to do certain occupations such as hair-cutting, shoe-repairing, tea-plucking, rickshaw pulling, etc. In such situation, these migrant workers usually do such jobs. The migrant workers also provide cheap labour, and are said to be hardworking and loyal. In short, the migrants are largely poor and illiterate, and are ready to do jobs that are rejected by the native workers. The aforementioned factors encourage migration into North-East India. Furthermore, the shared culture and history of the sending and the receiving places also provide crucial social networks for migration.

Proliferation of Identities

The introduction of Bengali language as the language of administration and school education in Assam, from 1837 to 1872, clearly marked the beginning of ethnic conflict. As Sandhya Barua (1978: 66-74) noted, "the polemic between the Bengali and Assamese languages since then had been fairly continuous and symbolises in many ways the fight between the interests on the one hand of a migrant and comparatively advanced middle class, and on the other hand an indigenous and suppressed middle class." Being one of the largest ethnic groups in Assam, the Assamese wanted due recognition of their language in the education and administration. The fear of losing their cultural autonomy started when Bengali language was introduced as the language of education and administration, and their historical narratives typically refer to the period as a dark period of Assamese language, literature and culture (Baruah, 1999: 59).

After independence, the Assamese, in place of the Bengali Hindus, retained control over the State government. The reorganisation of States on linguistic lines in the country in 1956 also considerably influenced the Assamese to consolidate their language and culture in the State. In 1960, the Assam Government made the first major step to make Assamese language the official language of the State for official communication at the State level.[3] The decision was taken despite opposition from other communities, leading to the outbreak of violent confrontations. In 1972, the oldest university in North-East India, the Gauhati University, decided to use Assamese language as the medium of instruction in the educational institutions under its jurisdiction amidst opposition by other communities. The non-Assamese condemned such steps as "the chauvinistic move on the part of the Assamese community." These developments gave a fillip to the demand for the creation of new States out of Assam. It is, therefore, evident that ethnic groups viewed the State government as an instrument by which to extend, consolidate and transform their position in the economy and social system (Weiner, 1983: 284). In the nineteenth and early twentieth centuries the Bengali Hindus used their dominance in the government to consolidate their position in the educational system and administration. In the 1930s and 1940s, when electoral politics were introduced, the Bengali Muslims won control over the government, and attempted to facilitate the Bengali Muslims migration into Assam. After independence, the Assamese won control of the State government, and used that control to consolidate their cultural identity. In these competitions ethnic coalitions were formed and dissolved. Initially the Bengali Muslims aligned with the Assamese in the campaign to make Assamese language the official language and medium of education. The alliance did not last long because the Assamese were worried of both Bengali Hindus and Bengali Muslims coming together to undermine their dominance (Weiner, 1983: 279-292).

In post-independent period the focus gradually turned towards the Muslim immigrants of East Bengali origin. India being a Hindu-majority country the Muslims immigration was never encouraged and even projected as the main concern. There were narratives of Bengali Muslims being labelled as illegal migrants and the Bengali Hindus as the refugees. The Bengali Muslims immigration has been projected as the primary cause of higher growth of population in Assam. Further, there were allegations of the manipulation of the voters' lists in Assam to enrol the Muslim migrants. When the Election Commission of India, the agency which supervises the conduct of periodic elections in India, decided to revise the voters' lists of Assam's Mangaldoi Assembly constituency in 1979 it received complaints against the inclusion of Muslim migrants in the rolls. That was investigated by a Tribunal appointed by the Assam Government. The Tribunal upheld 45,000 complaints out of a total six lakhs electorates. This was sufficient enough to kick-start the anti-immigration movement between 1979 and 1985. Popularly known as the Assam Movement, it was one of the most popular mass movements in the country. The agitators demanded recounting of the citizenship of those living in Assam on the basis of the country's National Register of Citizens (NRC) prepared way back in 1951. It concluded with an accord popularly known as the Assam Accord between the Government of India and the leaders of the movement in which the former promised to take actions to identify and deport all non-citizens, officially refer to as "foreigners". The government also promised to take actions to protect the cultural identity of the "Assamese people." The movement had its impact felt in other parts of North-East India. But most promises remain largely unfulfilled. The All Assam Students' Union (AASU) which led the said movement stated that: "The movement of the Muslim immigrants from

East Bengal (now Bangladesh) to Assam commenced in the early decades of the last century. At first, the Muslim settlers occupied 'Char' land of Goalpara district and only a few migrated further inland into Kamrup and Nowgong districts. The tempo of this movement of population gradually increased by a combination of circumstances during the independence and post-independence days" (All Assam Students' Union 2005). Interestingly, the AASU has been silent on Hindu migration.

Furthermore, the incidents like the killing of 1,819 people, mostly Muslim peasants of East Bengal origin, in an attack by rival communities at Nellie village during the Assam Movement in 1983 for voting in the Assam Legislature elections of 1983 defying a poll boycott called by those demanding the holding of the election on the basis of a revised voters' list have polarised the people along religious lines. Such incidents not only caused insecurity among the Muslims but halted, for the first time, the process of their assimilation with the Assamese society (Ahmed and Yasin, 1997: 148). Nevertheless, the Assamese Muslims had actively participated in the movement. The Muslims, including the Assamese Muslims, were often mistaken as foreigners by the vigilant groups. This led to their alienation from the Assamese society in which they coexisted for years. The immediate political fallout was the emergence of ideologically polarised political parties. The leaders of the movement formed the Asom Gana Parishad (AGP), and their opponents formed the United Minorities Front (UMF). Both came into existence in 1985. The former wanted the implementation of the Assam Accord, whereas the latter wanted that accord be scrapped. Although the AGP won the Assam Legislative Assembly elections held in 1985 and 1996 respectively, it failed to strike a consensus on the vexed issue.

When the Assam government started consolidating the Assamese language in the educational system and administration, the non-Assamese communities have also shown due apprehension. When the Assam Official Language Bill 1960 was introduced in the Assam Legislative Assembly in 1960, they interpreted the step as an attempt to suppress their language and culture. The Bodos, the largest plain tribes of Assam, soon started a movement for the inclusion of their language as the medium of education, followed by the demand for their own script. Subsequently, the Assam Government accorded the Bodo language as an associate official language of the State.

One of the terms of the Assam Accord which promised to protect the culture, social and linguistic identity of the "Assamese people" alienated the non-Assamese which had adverse impact on the future politics of the

State. The term Assamese people has created controversies because the non-Assamese refuse to be treated as Assamese people, and hence they felt that the accord might give legitimacy to the imposition of Assamese language and culture to them. They soon started the movements in the name of protecting and preserving their cultures, including the demand for the division of Assam to facilitate the formation of new States. For example, the Bodos started a movement for the creation of a separate State along the north bank of Brahmaputra. The policy of Assamisation, the policy of consolidating the Assamese language and culture, was termed by the non-Assamese as an attempt to assimilate them culturally. The Bodos and others resented the campaign of assimilation and felt that they have no chance of preserving their own cultural heritage in that atmosphere, dominated by the Assamese culture. The All Bodo Students' Union (ABSU), a students' body that spearheaded the Bodoland movement, often termed the general attitude of Assamese people as "anti-tribal", following the policy of expansionism and empiricism to capture and dominate all "corners" of Assam including the tribal areas (All Bodo Students' Union, undated: 43-45). It stated that anti-tribal Assam government, anti-tribal administration and bureaucrats were the number one factor for demanding a separate State (All Bodo Students' Union, undated: 46). The ABSU-led movement led to the granting of increased autonomy to the Bodo-inhabited areas of Assam and the Bodoland Autonomous Council (BAC) was constituted in 1993. In 2003, those areas were reconstituted as the Bodoland Territorial Area District (BTAD), an autonomous region under the constitution, to be governed by the Bodoland Territorial Council (BTC). This arrangement was intended to fulfil the economic, educational and linguistic aspirations of the Bodos and other ethnic groups. However, this policy has also opened a Pandora's Box for the creation of more States and autonomous regions.

Large scale immigration is generally perceived to be threatening to the people of North-East India. The reasons are obvious. First and foremost, immigration can be a potential demographic threat for the numerically smaller communities inhabiting the region. Second, the local residents are the weak contenders in the competition for the control of modern professions. Hence, the migrants were accused of taking away jobs from them. Finally, the trade and commerce is also controlled by the recent migrants. Immigration is, therefore, a potential threat to them. Pradip Phanjoubam, a journalist based in Imphal once remarked: "In the eye of the locals, among others, they (the traders from mainland) represent the agents of change that have intruded into their lives to dislocate and dismantle their old world. In the beginning they were welcomed guests, as they brought in new comforts from the outside world. However, not long after, when they started controlling the entire economy of these places, they came to be despised as usurpers" (Phanjoubam, 2001: 23-24). In a survey of the employment in unorganized sectors conducted in three towns of Nagaland in 2006, Dimapur has the largest migrant workforce of 32,700 persons, followed Kohima (10,900 persons) and Mokokchung (2,215 persons), respectively. The migrants dominated construction, loading and unloading, trading and entrepreneurial activities, plying of handcarts and rickshaws and catering industry (Government of Nagaland, 2007). States such as Meghalaya has been demanding the introduction of temporary work permits system for migrants working in the State to prevent them from settling down permanently. Talking to media persons in New Delhi on 11 December, 2003, the then Meghalaya Chief Minister, D.D. Lapang noted, "We cannot afford to allow outsiders to outnumber the indigenous population or let a situation arise when we will be totally helpless."[4] The "outsiders", in this context, are the Indian nationals from other parts of the country living in North-East. Under the Meghalaya Land Transfer Regulation Act 1973 (amended in 2001) those tribes which officially are the domiciled of the Statae are eligible to purchase and sell land in the State. Influential organisations like AASU wanted a law whereby "outsiders" cannot become owners of land in Assam. The "outsiders", in this context, are those who were not the permanent residents of the state prior to March 1971.[5] The North-East Students' Organisation (NESO), a coalition of student organisations, has also been demanding a special recruitment policy which provides 100 per cent reservation of jobs for the local youths in all Central government offices in the region.[6]

The insecurity caused by immigration was the root cause of armed conflict in Tripura and the emergence of United Liberation Front of Asom (ULFA) led armed conflict in Assam. Those who supported the armed conflict have the impression that the Government of India would listen to their grievances if they resorted to violence. Thus in the words of Samir Kumar Das (2007: 8), "although immigration remains at the heart of most conflicts in the region, the transformation of these conflicts into insurgencies, particularly in Nagaland, Mizoram, Manipur, Assam and Tripura coincides with a radical reinterpretation of their respective histories in which the Indian State is considered as external agent, and often a colonial power."

The influx of refugees at the time of partition had reduced the tribes of Tripura into the minority position. In the words of the Tripura

Government: "The partition of India in 1947 was a defining event in the history of Tripura, and had an enduring effect on the process of social and economic development in the State. The partition was perhaps the largest movement of evicted people in modern history. It witness a heavy influx of refugees into Tripura from erstwhile East Pakistan, who arrived with little wealth in hand ... The large scale immigration has not only placed a tremendous burden on resources of the State, but also upheaval in the social composition of its population. Tripura was a tribal-majority State before partition. Today, the tribal people constitute only 31 per cent of the total population (Government of Tripura, 2009: 22). Between 1947 and 1971, an estimated 0.6 million refugees came from East Pakistan, and were resettled under various rehabilitation schemes sponsored by the State government. These schemes facilitated the transfer of land owned by the tribal people to the recent migrants (Bhaumik and Bhattacharya, 2005: 216-241). The lands originally reserved for the backward tribal people were taken over by the government to construct refugee colonies. Soon the recent migrants established control over the State administration, and tried to consolidate and transform their position in the economy and social system. In 1964, Bengali language along with English was recognised as the official languages of the State, whereas Kokborok, a tribal language, got the second language status only in 1979. Around this time, the tribal discontentment started political mobilization for securing increased autonomy and the restoration of the lands that were once belonged to them. The State soon faced violent confrontation between the government and the insurgent groups. Some of their specific demands are (a) expulsion of Bengali-speaking migrants who entered Tripura after 1956; (b) restoration of land to tribal people; (c) removal of names of migrants who entered Tripura after 1956 from the electoral rolls; and (d) to establish a sovereign and independent Tripura through an armed struggle.[7]

Tripura was a princely state until its merger into Indian Union in 1949. Thereafter, it passed through several administrative status—became a territorial council in 1956, a Union Territory in 1963, and finally a State in 1972. In response to the massive influx of refugees a resistance movement against the policies of the government began in the late 1940s. It was initially led by the Tripura Rajya Mukti Parishad (renamed in 1967 as the Tripura Upajati Gana Mukti Parishad). It also coincided with the setting up of the All Tripura Upajati Juba Samitee. The former alleged that the Tripura Rajya Mukti Parishad had failed to protect the their interests. Subsequently, a political party known as the Tripura Upajati

Jubu Samitee (TUJS) was formed with the demand for the deportation of refugees and the constitution of an autonomous region for the tribal people. It also demanded the extension of inner line regulations and introduction of Kokborok as medium of education in Roman script. Around this time, an armed group known as the Sengkrak came into existence, but it was short-lived. In 1978, Bijoy Kumar Hrangkhawl then the leader of the TUJS set up the Tripura National Volunteers (TNV). The demand for the creation of autonomous region was opposed by the non-tribal Bengalis who perceived a threat to their landholdings and other rights. Thus the Amra Bangali was set up to launched a counter campaign against the demand of the autonomous region. For the first time in Tripura communal rioting involving the tribal and the non-tribal peoples broke out in 1980 killing several hundreds people. It left deep scars on the social fabric of the State. Following this riot, the TNV leaders went underground. Between 1984 and 1987, there was an escalation of violence directed against political opponents, State officials and security personnel. The army was subsequently deployed and the entire State was declared a 'disturbed area'. After the February 1988 State Legislative election the Congress (I) and TUJS assumed power after having dislodged the Left Front (comprising CPI(M) and CPI) from power. During this time, the TNV enjoyed almost free run. Meanwhile, the TNV signed a peace agreement with the State government in August 1988. The peace was, however, short-lived. The next phase of violent conflict began around 1990 with the formation of other armed groups like All Tripura Tribal Force (ATTF) and National Liberation Front of Tripura (NLFT). Down the line, several peace agreements have also been signed between the government and the insurgent groups on the issue of checking immigration, economic development, and the like. However the problem is far from over.

The Assam Movement also coincided with the birth of ULFA-led armed conflict, which was said to be the armed wing of the said movement with a secessionist agenda (Sinha, 2011: 27-37). They also felt that unabated migration was a threat to the demography of the State. It accused the Government of India of encouraging migration into Assam, for what it calls, "a population base having ethnic affinity with mainland India is always favourable to their long term security perspective."[8] According to Sanjib Baruah (2009: 17-18), "the most enduring legacy of the failure of the Assam Accord is the ULFA. Its position on the issue of the foreigners is more accommodative, but it views the failure of the Assam Accord as one more piece of evidence that India's political leadership is uninterested in addressing issues the Assamese public cares deeply about." In the past it selectively targeted migrants from mainland India to scare them away from the State. It also claimed that Assam was never a part of India at any point of time in history and wanted to set up a sovereign and independent homeland.

Response of the Government

As the response to the pressure from the local people mounted, the Government of India started implementing different measures in the name of checking migration from across the borders. In 1983, the country's Parliament passed the Illegal Migrants (Determination by Tribunals) Act 1983 (IMDT Act) which came into force in Assam alone instead of the Foreigner Act 1946 applicable in other parts of the country. Its stated objective was to identify and deport the non-citizens, officially known as "foreigners". It defined foreigners as those who illegally settled down in Assam after 25 March, 1971, and the onus of proof shall lie with the complainant. The Foreigners Act puts the onus on the accused to prove his/her Indian nationality. Two decades later in 2005, the IMDT Act was overturned by the Supreme Court of India on the ground that it acted as the biggest hurdle in the identification and deportation of the foreigners. Hence, the Foreigner Act was reintroduced in Assam. In addition, the policing along the Indian side of the India-Bangladesh border have strengthened with the construction of border fence, roads and floodlighting in order to check further migration and other criminal activities. But, the Assam Government claimed to have deported only 219 foreigners from the State back to Bangladesh between 2001 and 2010, while over Rs. 330 million was said to have spent for maintaining over 40 Tribunals set up for the purpose of their identification and detection.[9] It is, therefore, important to understand the main constraints.

First, the border traverses through forested hills, lowlands, river-line areas and human settlements thus making the construction of border fence and roads difficult. Movement of people between Bangladesh and India has always been easy because of the open border, compact geographical nature and socio-cultural continuity. In the past the migration from Bengal to Assam was also encouraged as there was shortage of labour. The migrants had also immensely contributed to agricultural development and tea industry in Assam. Second, there are unsettled border issues between the two young nations. Many people who were affected by the unfortunate partition questioned the validity of the border because they claimed that the partition took place without their consent. This is indeed a peculiar example of a conspicuous discrepancy between the cultural and the political borders. The partition uprooted their livelihood since the international border divided villages, towns, relatives, homes, markets and paddy fields. Many families who owned paddy field on either side of the border were forced to part away their valuable lands. This has been reason why they challenged the legitimacy of this border. Third, since people on both sides of the border share historical, religious and linguistic ties it is natural for some of them to shelter the would-be migrants who they consider as their kith and kin. Moreover, the registration of citizens was not properly done both in India and Bangladesh. Thus, the distinction between the citizens and the non-citizens is actually blurred in this part of the world. Fourth, Bangladesh denies the presence of their citizens in India. This makes India's effort extremely difficult. In this connection Willem van Schendel (2005: 199) stated "to the Bangladeshi elite acknowledging this would reveal the inability of their State to control the movement, or worse, suggest its complicity." Fifth, the issue is highly politicised in India in which political parties accused each other of indulging in vote-bank politics. It has also divided the local people along communal and religious lines. For instance, when the IMDT Act was overruled in 2005, some citizen groups expressed fear of possible harassment of Muslims by the local police in the name of detection of foreigners. By contrast, other groups welcomed the verdict because they felt that the said Act was useless. Further there were differences of opinion at the highest level of the government. For instance, a report on migration authored by then Governor of Assam, Ajai Singh, in 2005 was labelled as a "worthless document based on hearsay" by Chief Minister Tarun Gogoi. The latter alleged that the report caused confusion among the people. Finally, administrative corruption has all along posed one of the biggest challenges to the existing laws and schemes. The officials of the State usually helped the would-be migrants in fraudulently acquiring identity documents such as ration cards, birth certificates, domicile certificates and voters' identity cards. When someone possesses such documents they can establish the Indian nationality status. In this regard Willem van Schendel (2005: 222) remarked: "India could not implement the laws and the schemes that it devised because its registration of citizens was inadequate, it employed too few border guards to monitor the schemes, it could not trust those guards and other State personnel to put the interest of the State before their self-interest, and it failed to check Indian citizens who encouraged illegal immigration and registration."

In Tripura, the government has responded to the concerns of the tribal people by giving limited autonomy under the Constitution of the country. The Tripura Tribal Areas Autonomous District Council (TTAADC) was established under the Seventh Schedule of the Constitution (it later became under the Sixth Schedule of the Constitution from 1985). The Sixth Schedule provides for autonomous district and autonomous regions within those districts with elected councils which enjoy powers to levy taxes, to constitute courts for the administration of justice involving tribals and law-making powers on subjects including land allotment, occupation or use of land, regulation of *jhum* or other forms of shifting cultivation, establishment and administration of village and town committees, appointment or succession of chiefs, inheritance of property, marriage and social customs. Further, several peace agreements have been signed in the recent past between the government and the armed groups. A peace agreement popularly known as the TNV accord was first signed in 1988 in which the government promised stringent measures against immigration, reservation of up to 20 seats for the Scheduled Tribes in the Tripura Legislative Assembly and restoration of land once belonged to the tribal people.

Conclusion

Human migration takes place due to a number of reasons. The context could differ from an individual to another or from a place to another. Today migration has accelerated than ever before, in which an estimated 740 million people migrated inside their own country in 2009, while another 214 million did so across national borders (King *et al.*, 2010: 13-14). Now almost all countries are affected by migration either as the countries of origin, transit or destination for migrants, and increasingly are all three simultaneously (International Organisation for Migration, 2003: 4). Thus the division between sending and destination countries is no longer relevant because the distinction between the countries representing push factors and the countries representing pull factors become questionable, since most countries simultaneously display both (Duvell, 2010: 289-310). Migrants reportedly have higher income, enjoy better access to education and health care, and better prospects for their children (United Nations Development Programme, 2009: 9). Meanwhile, migration has also come under severe restrictions than ever before. For many sending countries the outmigration of their high-skilled workers has been portrayed as brain-drain and national loss, whereas the unskilled ones were encouraged so that they could send back remittances and brought new skills. On the other hand, the high-skilled workers were welcomed in many receiving countries, while the unskilled ones were not so. Thus certain categories of migrants are usually accepted, and hence the context of their reception in the receiving places could be of low receptivity; permitted but not actively encouraged; and privileged reception (Portes and Borocz, 1989: 606-630). Migration is a self-sustaining diffusion process (Massey *et al.*, 1993: 431-466) that depends on, and creates, social networks. These networks are the sets of interpersonal ties that connect migrants, former migrants and non-migrants in sending and receiving places through the ties of kinship, friendship and shared community origin. These networks help in providing initial adaptive assistance such as housing, money, information and emotional support. Then when a significant number of migrants were recruited into certain occupations, they became socially undesirable for the native workers. The native workers will be less inclined to do such occupations. Migration can, therefore, change the social definition of work, causing a certain occupations to be defined as stigmatizing, and viewed as culturally inappropriate for the native workers. This stigma came from the presence of migrants, not from the characteristics of the occupations (Bohning, 1974: 155-163). In such situation, the main assets the migrants bring to the receiving places are cheap labour, willingness to work harder and loyalty.

Those who could not fulfil the requirements to migrate legally across national borders resorted to irregular means, including entering a country with fraudulent documents and overstaying a legally obtained visa. This type of migration has become prominence in public discourse with the emergence of the nation-states because the political processes of State building define the extent of the State's territory, its national space, and so nationality and membership. Hence, the State migration control becomes a tool of demarcation and of enforcement of its crucial means. Yet, several countries reported irregular migration thereby defying their self-contained autonomy (Morris, 1997: 192). Indeed this has become an inherent aspect of global migration (Duvell, 2005: 16), their policies to control or reduce migration were influenced not only by the nature and the characteristics of the migrant population, but by the political, economic and social situations (Brennan, 1984: 409). Moreover, Ayelet Shachar (2007: 257-281) identified three acute inconsistencies in resurrecting the national borders. Firstly, the gap between open borders for trade and information *versus* closed borders for the movement of people have refrained most governments to adopt the fortress like mentality. Second, most countries have not adopted a zero tolerance immigration policy rather they sought to admit those they think will be useful. Third, since many countries failed to provide their citizens with access to democracy, freedom from poverty and other basic needs, it will be unwise to do nothing under such circumstances to ameliorate the pressure of global inequalities. There are two inadequacies: on the one hand, globalization is giving rise to greater interdependence and overlapping spheres of influence and jurisdictional authority, and on the other, the local and regional forces are making demands for State resources, cultural rights and devolution of governing power (Valadez, 2007: 303). Therefore, what appears absolutely rational at the global or perhaps the national level cannot be so at the local level. Thus, if global economic integration is to benefit people, ways have to be found to give local people a powerful voice in decision which affects them. Market mechanism is inherently incapable of doing this, while countries including the democratic ones often neglect the local in favour of overriding national interests (Castles, 1998: 186). Thus the migrants became the target because they are the most visible symbol of these changes, while the real causes are invisible, complex and difficult to influence.

In a nutshell, migration has been one of the key factors of ethnic conflict in North-East India, particularly in Assam and Tripura, forcing the Government of India to take up several measures to check large scale immigration from across the border. Ethnic groups in North-East India have been accusing the government of taking the issue lackadaisically thereby contributing to their further alienation from the country's national mainstream. This has further helped sustain the armed conflict to a certain extent. It is also true that the ethnic groups of North-East India are affected by large scale immigration in varying intensities, as evident in Tripura where the small ethnic groups were outnumbered by the recent migrants. Thus large scale immigration is a threat to them. Yet the anti-immigration movements had caused ethnic rift and polarisation leading to the proliferation of exclusive identities which in turn led to the separate movements for the control of political power. Thus the issue of migration is highly politicised now, seen differently by different groups. Each of them has their own interests. Initially the ethnic groups believed that the Government of India could take care of their concerns. When that did not happen, they started putting pressure on the government. As a result government took up several measures. However, these actions came too late, and did not consider the shared histories and geographies of the sending and the receiving places. Timely actions taking into account the shared histories and geographies could have better serve the interests of both the migrants and the non-migrants. This is so because migration cannot be stopped.

NOTES

1. Persian was then the court language of Bengal. For further see, H.K. Barpujari, (1963) *Assam in the Days of the Company*, Gauhati: Lawyer's Book Stall, p. 46.
2. For instance, in 2007, about 25,712 out of the five lakh Bangladeshis who came to India did not return after the expiry of their visas while in 2006 more than 24,000 went missing from the 4.84 lakh. India claimed that about 12 lakh Bangladeshis who had entered the country between 1972 and 2005 with valid documents have not gone back. It claimed to have deported about 15,000 of them in 2005, 12,000 in 2006 and 11,500 in 2007. See "More than 70,000 Bangladeshis missing: India", *Indian Express* (New Delhi), 4 February, 2009.
3. The Assam Official Language Act 1960 is an Act to declare official language of Assam. This is in accordance to the Article 345 of the Constitution of India that provides that the legislature of a State may by law adopt anyone or more of the languages in use in the State as the language to be used for official purposes of the State. This Act extends to the whole of Assam.
4. See "Meghalaya mulls pass for 'outsiders," *Telegraph* (Guwahati), 12 December, 2003.
5. See "AASU all set to form Asomiya Sena," *Assam Tribune* (Guwahati), 18 December, 2004.
6. See "*Bandh* paralyses life in North-East," *Assam Tribune* (Guwahati), 6 October, 2004.
7. For more information see: South Asia Terrorism Portal at www.satp.org.
8. See "Influx poses demographic threat to ULFA," *Assam Tribune* (Guwahati), 5 March, 1999.
9. See "Rs. 33 crore for deporting 219 foreigners", *Assam Tribune* (Guwahati) 11 February, 2011, p. 1.

REFERENCES

Agrawala, Shardul *et al.*, (2003). *Development and Climate Change in Bangladesh: Focus on Coastal Flooding and the Sundarbans*, Paris: Organisation for Economic Co-operation and Development.

Ahmed, A.N.S. and Yasin, Adil-Ul, (1997). "Problems of identity, assimilation and nation building: A case of the Muslims of Assam," in *Politics of Identity and Nation Building in North-East India* (eds.), Grin Phukan and N.L. Dutta, New Delhi: South Asian Publishers.

All Assam Students' Union (2005). *A Brief History of Illegal Immigration in Assam: An Overview of the Last Hundred Years*, Guwahati: All Assam Students' Union.

All Bodo Students' Union, (undated). *Why Separate State of Bodoland: Demand and Justifications,* Kokrajhar: All Bodo Students' Union.

Barpujari, H.K., (1963). *Assam in the Days of the Company,* Gauhati: Lawyer's Bookstall.

Baruah, Sanjib, (1999). *India Against Itself: Assam and the Politics of Nationality,* New Delhi: Oxford University Press.

Baruah, Sanjib, (2009). "Introduction," in *Beyond Counter-Insurgency: Breaking the Impasse in North-East India* (ed.), Sanjib Baruah, New Delhi: Oxford University Press.

Bhaumik, Subir and Bhattacharya, Jayanta, (2005). "Autonomy in North-East: The Hills of Tripura and Mizoram," in *The Politics of Autonomy: Indian Experiences* (ed.), Ranbir Samaddar, New Delhi: Sage Publications, pp. 216-241.

Bohning, W.R. (Summer 1974). "Immigration Policies of Western European Countries," *International Migration Review*, 8:2, pp. 155-163.

Brennan, Ellen M., (Autumn 1984). "Irregular Migration: Policy Responses in Africa and Asia," *International Migration Review* 18:3, pp. 409-425.

Castles, Stephen, (1998). "Globalization and Migration: Some Pressing Contradictions", *International Social Science Journal*, 156, pp. 179–186.

Das, Samir Kumar, (2007). *Conflict and Peace in India's North-East: The Role of Civil Society,* Washington: East-West Center.

Duvell, Franck, (2010). "Irregular migration: A global, historical and economic perspective," in *Migration: Critical Concepts in Social Sciences*, Volume 1, ed. Steven Vertovec, London/New York: Routledge, pp. 289-310.

Duvell, Franck, (2005). "Irregular Migration: A Global Historical and Economic Perspective," in *Illegal Immigration in Europe: Beyond Control* (ed.), Franck Duvell, Houndmills: Palgrave/MacMillan.

Government of India, (2001). *Report of the Group of Ministers on National Security,* New Delhi: Ministry of Home Affairs.

Government of Nagaland, (2007). *Evaluation Study on Employment Opportunities Forgone by Nagas and Employment of Non-Nagas in the State*, Publication No. 52, Kohima: Directorate of Evaluation.

Government of Tripura, (2009). *Economic Review of Tripura 2008-2009*, Agartala: Directorate of Economics & Statistics.

King, Russell *et al.*, (2010). *The Atlas of Human Migration: Global Patterns of People on the Move,* Brighton: Earthscan.

Massey, Douglas S., (1993). "Theories of International Migration: A Review and Appraisal," *Population and Development Review,* 19, pp. 431-466.

Morris, Lydia, (1997). Globalization, "Migration and the Nation-State: The Path to a Post-National Europe?" *The British Journal of Sociology* 48:2, pp. 192-209.

Phanjoubam, Pradip, (2001). "Insurgency and its Impact on the Development of Manipur," in *Constraint in Development of Manipur* (eds.) Gopalakrishnan, R. *et al.*, New Delhi: Regency Publication.

Portes, Alejandro and Borocz, József, J. (Autumn 1989). "Contemporary Immigration: Theoretical Perspectives on its Determinants and Modes of Incorporation," *International Migration Review,* 23:3, pp. 606-630.

Sandhya, Barua, (1978). Language Problem in Assam, *Social Scientist* 6:12, pp. 66-74.

Schendel, Willem van. (2005). *The Bengal Borderland; Beyond State and Nation in South Asia,* London: Anthem Press.

Sinha, S.K. (2011). "Security and Development in the North-East: A Case of Assam," in *Perilous Journey: Debates on Security and Development in Assam* (eds.), Rakhee Bhattacharya and Sanjay Pulipaka, New Delhi: Manohar Publications, pp. 27-37.

Shachar, Ayelet (2007). "Against birthright privilege: redefining citizenship as property", in *Identities, Affiliations, and Allegiances* (eds.), Seyla Benhabib, Cambridge: Cambridge University Press, pp. 257-281.

United Nations Development Programme (2009). *Human Development Report 2009: Overcoming Barriers: Human Mobility and Development,* New York: United Nations Development Programme.

Valadez, Forge M. (2007). "The continuing significance of ethnocultural identity," in *Identities, Affiliations, and Allegiances* (eds.), Seyla Benhabib *et al.*, Cambridge: Cambridge University Press.

Weiner, Myron (1983). The Political Demography of Assam's Anti-Immigrant Movement, *Population and Development Review*, 9:2, 279-292.

3

Highway Politics and Economy of Manipur: A Perspective of Behavioural Science

K. Muktasana Singh

Introduction

Generally, the development of a country, region or State depends on infrastructure, such as irrigation, power, transport and communication, etc. Of which, transport plays a vital and indispensable role in the process of regional economic development. In recent years, with the rapid growth of the economy, the importance of and urgency of removing infrastructure constraints have increased. Among the major sectors of infrastructure development, transport infrastructure development is considered as one of the major components. Because, the present day society which involves large scale production, regional development and product specialization and international trade along with the new wave of globalization, liberalization and privatization. All these rely heavily on the transport and communication development. In fact, a sufficient, developed and efficient transport system becomes an integral part of the overall economic, social and industrial development of a country. In other words, transportation is an effective catalyst in meeting the current demands of an economy and in facilitating the exploration of unutilised and underutilised resources mostly found in remote areas. In addition to this, with the changing demographic structure, urbanisation has been taken place throughout the world rendering the need for effective and sufficient transport system for social development and economic growth. So, deficiencies in transport system can lead to social tension and economic unrest which can, in turn cripple the life of the society (or city). Thus, transport influences economic growth and development, population distribution, the shape and structure of the city, energy consumption, access to markets and the quality of life and so on. It contributes substantial amount to the GDP, absorbs large investments and provides employment for millions of people. In a general view, developed countries have greater and better transport system than underdeveloped and developing countries. Therefore, adequate of transport infrastructure is a dynamic factor to achieve nation's endeavours. In the developed countries, transport sector accounts for between 6.0 per cent and 12.0 per cent of the GDP and provides million of jobs. For instance, in 2002, transportation accounts for 10.0 per cent of the United States' GDP and 9.0 per cent for Denmark and 10.5 per cent for Japan. But, the World Bank estimates that the transport sector accounts for an overall average between 3.0 per cent and 4.5 per cent of the GDP of a country. Again, an average between 10.0 per cent and 15.0 per cent of household expenditure has been spent on transportation in developed country (Muktar, 2009). Among various mode of transport, road transport plays the most pivotal role for movement of men and material because of its flexibility, connectivity, and accessibility. In addition, roadways have also connected railways, airways, and waterways and also provide door-to-door service. The basic functions of road transport is to link residence with employment and producers of goods with their users including shopping, recreation, access to health, education, and other social and cultural services. It also provides connectivity for remote areas with towns, cities and market centres. In this respect, highways acted as the primary road system in terms of economic, social and political development and the integration of a country; most significantly in strategic and national defence. For instance, roads are the dominant mode of transportation in India of which national highways carry 40.0 per cent of total road traffic although their road length is only 2.0 per cent out of the total road length. But, road transport carries almost 90.0 per cent of the country's passenger traffic and 65.0 per cent of its freight traffic (*Economic Survey of India*, 2009-10). The Indian transport systems developed to a great extent after independence to cope up with the demands for changing, uplifting and modernising the nation. Currently, with rapid industrialisation programmes and the liberalisation policy of the economy, the main objective of development planning in India is higher growth in GDP. India is now considered to be one of the fastest growing economies in the world. Prior to 1990s, it was a closed economy with a low rate of growth. Transport sector contributes significantly to India's GDP of around 6.4 per cent, employment of around 40 million people in 2007 and Foreign Direct Investment (FDI) inflows at around 13 per cent of the total inflows (Mukherjee, 2009).

Manipur, one of the India's most north-eastern States, is one of the most economically backward States in the country. The backbone of its economy has been relying entirely on the earmark budget (amount) from the Central government. Keeping in view of the tough geographical features of Manipur, the means of transport and communication are inadequate, difficult and expensive whereby road transport acts as the most important means of transport and communication of the State. Though, air transport also connects the State with the rest of the country, it is affordable only by a lesser percentage of the population. Therefore, transport system in Manipur is considered to be synonymous with road communication. The State's capital can be primarily connected by the National Highways 39 and 53 with the rest of the country. Further, these highways also link the State highways and major district roads as well as village roads. Hence, these two highways are considered to be its lifelines, especially the Highway Number 39 due to its commendable roles in the State's transportation endeavours in the absence of railways and waterways. In addition, the National Highway 39 is also a part of the proposed Asian Highway Network. Regrettably, at present, these two highways are located conveniently for sectarian and ethnic political lines. Their shabby conditions, frequent *bandhs* (blockades) and economic blockades in National Highways, illegal taxes by State and non-State actors are some of the critical transportation problems in the State. Due to such transportation problems, the people of the State suffered from acute shortage and adulteration of essential commodities, artificial price rise, and non-availability of life saving drugs during month of economic blockades along the National Highways. In this article, impacts of frequent *bandhs* and economic blockade on the general economic conditions of the State are discussed. Further, what behavioural sciences say during such transportation problems is also discussed.

Bandhs, Blockades and the Growth of Economy of Manipur

In the beginning, a *bandh* (forceful closure) used to be a true weapon to ventilate the wrath of the people particularly against the anti-people policies of the government. It was considered the last resort of a political party or organization to compel the government to reconsider its decision.

On the other hand, *bandhs*, strikes (*hartal*) and blockades were the symbols of strength in the history of the Indian freedom struggle which was full of *bandhs* and blockades or similar mass agitations. The people of India who were suppressed by the 'colonial forces' were made to live in the tune of the colonial rule of laws. But, to change the conditions, the people had to move against to resist or to defy the imposed laws. For instance, in 1921, when the Prince of Wales came to India on an official tour, Mahatma Gandhi called upon the public to observe general strikes wherever he went, as a peaceful protest against the colonial rule (Narendra, 2008). This form of agitation was growing gradually with a number of *bandhs*, blockades, rallies, demonstrations and lockouts. These 'collective' disobedient actions revitalised the mass people for developing a new sense of nationalism as well as in accepting a new role of building a new India. Indeed, the strength for calling a *bandh* or blockade at that time was the full tide of nationalism. Till today, many political organisations, trade unions and other associations use *bandhs*, strikes and blockades as effective tools to express their political aspirations and groups' personal benefit. In Manipur, the relationship between the discontent of different ethnic communities and bandhs/blockades has also become more complex. Earlier, *bandhs* were meant to press government for getting certain specific demands. But, these days, they are of several colours; and it was systematically analytically described by Arun (2008) as:

- For the larger demands related with administrative units;
- Ethnic, language or group assertion in the political space of the State or region;
- Separatist demands or politics;
- Small interest group assertion; and
- Counter insurgency related issues.

Bandhs and blockades are not homogeneous in nature which is having different goals to draw the attention of the government to their demands. In some cases, the demands for calling a *bandh* or *blockade* are of limited interest for some small individuals such as failure of power transformer, demand for science teacher in the hill districts and the demands for DPC (Departmental Procedure Committee) result of primary teacher and so on. Demand for a separate district of Sadar Hills and Jiribam sub-divisions are also other issues for calling frequent *bandhs* and economic blockades. Other organizations which imposed frequent *bandhs* and blockades during the same period are Senapati District Students' Union, Autonomous

Districthood Demand Committee, Sadar Hills District Demand Committee, Jiri District Demand Committee, Zoumi Students Union, IT Road Development Committee, Kuki Students Union, Action Committee Against Tipaimukh Dam, Apunba Lup, Manipur Forward Youth Front, Meetei Eyek Erol Loina Sinai Apunba Lup and the so called Joint Action Committees from time to time. Moreover, the National Socialist Council of Nagaland-Isak-Muivah (NSCN-IM) and Kuki National Front (KNF) have also used to impose blockades along the National Highways at some stage in Kuki-Naga ethnic tussle in the State during 1991-1994. There are some insurgent groups who often call *bandhs* and blockades in protest against the country's dominance in the State. These types of *bandhs* or general strikes called on by different organisations are often not directly related with their 'demands' but of showing their existence and of proving 'national contradiction' (as they call them). Yet another set of *bandh* is there to mark protest—may it be against State action or militant action on civilian population. Here, it can be noted that if the Government had taken up certain remedial measures on people's grievances in time many *bandhs* and blockades of the last decades could have been avoided.

In fact, the State of Manipur is flooded with numerous pressure groups, armed opposition groups, students' organisations, and voluntary organisations and the so called Joint Action Committees from time to time. The National Highways in the State have befallen as one of the most convenient tools for these organisations to achieve their political goals by blocking the lifelines of the State. In recent years, the political issues comprising of ethnic, language and State's political issues which should have been materialized politically were brought down into play along the National Highways connecting the State with the rest of the country, mainly by the tribal organisations in the hill. Initially, strike, boycotting of class in educational institutions, closing of government offices, mass rally or sit-in-protest were the forms of agitation in some State's rare issues like student's movements demanding for statehood during 1960s to early1970s, foreigners' issue in 1980s and other issues like killing of innocent persons (students) by the security personnel in the name of counter-insurgency operation from time to time. During those periods, *bandhs* or general strikes were very limited and restricted to some genuine issues in the State. But, calling general strike on Independence Day (15 August) and Republic Day (26 January) had begun since mid-1960s by the All Manipur Students' Union and then followed by armed opposition groups during the late 1980s.

From the early 1970s, the effect of *bandh* has been commonly felt in the State. However, the severe impact was felt from the early 1990s in numerous forms as – general strikes, *bandhs*, road blockades or blockades on the National Highways by the valley as well as hill-based civil and armed organizations to express or articulate their existence and potential or to pursue their demand. The term 'road blockade' further transformed into a new expression of 'economic blockades' since mid-1990s in a wide scale. In February 1991, the first ever longest (28 days) days road blockades was called on by NSCN-IM along the Imphal-Moreh section of the National Highway No. 39 as a reprisal to the Indian Army for helping Kuki armed groups during which Naga-Kuki ethnic tussle had taken place. Subsequently, the maximum number of *bandhs* and blockades were launched by the Sadar Hills Districthood Demand Committee during 1992, 1996, 1998 and 2011; and also by valley-base civil organisation, United Committee Manipur in 2001 in protesting against the extension of ceasefire into Manipur's territory (Bangkok Declaration 2001) between the NSCN-IM and the Central government. Again, by the religious revivalist organisation, MEELAL demanding the conversion of Meitei indigenous script in the school's text book of the state; and the Manipur Forward Youth Front (MAFYF) in 2004 and 2005 followed by the hill organisations, All Naga Students Association, Manipur (ANSAM), the United Naga Council (UNC) and All Tribal Students Union Manipur (ATSUM) during 2005 to 2010.

During June-July 2005, altogether 52 days long economic blockade was imposed by the ANSAM in protesting against the inclusion of the 18 June in the State's general holiday list. Again, in 2010, a total of 68 days long (starting from 11 April, 2010) economic blockades on the National Highways imposed jointly by the ANSAM, UNC and Naga Students Federation (NSF), opposing the autonomous district council's election in the hill districts of the State which fall in line with the State's government pronouncement to prevent NSCN-IM's leader Th. Muivah's proposed visit to Ukhrul district of Manipur on 24 April, 2010. Again, in 2011, Sadar Hills Districthood Demand Committee has launched indefinite economic blockades on National Highways since 1 August, 2011 demanding the elevation of Sadar Hill to a district; while the UNC again called on counter economic blockade since mid August 2011 to defy the demand of Sadar Hill by Kuki community. The number of days of blockade lasted for 121 days and became the ever longest economic blockade in the State and in the world perhaps. In fact, the matter of Sadar Hills district is a decades old issue which is purely an ethno-political and administrative subject matter and many a time this district demand committee has imposed numerous *bandhs* and economic blockades along the National Highways. In other words, this issue seems to have brought out into light by the Kuki elites usually before State assembly elections in order to catch the attention of the Kuki ethnic people. In the same manner, the Naga elites have so long been opposed the issue since its inception to influence the Naga ethnic people. Not only Sadar Hills, formation of Jiribam, Tengnoupal and Phungyar sub-divisions into a full-fledged revenue district are also impending district formation issues in Manipur. The key reason for this is that the districts alignment in the State has been made erroneously in the ethnic line and hill-valley divide policy for administrative convenience. To resolve this issue in the long run, the State government needs a fresh district reorganisation in the course of purely administrative convenience. These are still many excellent examples of language, sectarian, and ethno-political issues being played along the National Highways, the lifelines of Manipur.

Economic Losses due to *Bandhs* and Economic Blockades

For the first time in 2007, an attempt was made by the Directorate of Economics and Statistics of the Government of Manipur to calculate the economic loss due to *bandhs* and blockades in Manipur during 2004-07. It was an approximation made in order to have a rough idea of the volume of loss accrued to the State due to aforesaid eventualities. The study did not explain how the figures have been derived at. However, in the course of arriving at the estimates, a number of assumptions were made to give a new light to people of the State about the economic loss incurred due to frequent *bandhs* and blockades in the State. And, the economic losses due to *bandhs* and blockades have been estimated in the following manner:

Table 3.1 depicts the economic loss per day of *bandh* or blockade in Manipur. While estimating the economic loss due to *bandhs* and blockades, the primary sector is not affected to the tune of those disadvantages caused in the secondary and tertiary sectors. Therefore, the primary sector which covers agriculture, livestock, fishing, forestry and mining is not taken into consideration. But, on an average, the organised sector of manufacturing constitutes only about 2 per cent in the State's economy, is also faced difficulties when there is Manipur *bandh* but the lost is considered to be negligible. The activities of the unorganised sector are affected to the tune of 80-85 per cent per day in the case of Manipur *bandh* and to the tune of 36 per cent when there is economic blockade.

Table 3.1: Sectoral Loss per day due to *Bandh* and Blockades in 2007 (in Per Cent)

Sector	*Loss due to Bandh in Valley*	*Loss due to Economic Blockades in NHs*
Unorganised Sector	82.50	36.00
Construction	78.74	27.00
Transport, Storage and Communication	76.92	100.00
Trade, hotels and restaurant	100.00	84.00
Public Administration	40.00	—
Banking and Insurance	100.00	—
Other services	69.45	44.00

Source: Reported by O. Biren Singh, Former Director, Directorate of Economics and Statistics, Government of Manipur

Construction sector is the major contributor to the NSDP of Manipur which covers public sector, rural-urban residential buildings and non-residential buildings and residuals. When there is economic blockade in the National Highways, the commodity flow from outside the State is disturbed and the loss in the construction sector is estimated to be 27 per cent per day of blockade. Constructions of all kinds are assumed to be affected when there is Manipur *bandh.*

The tertiary sector comprising of transport, storage and communication; trade, hotel and restaurants; public administration, banking and insurance and other services have also affected in such a way that the share of transport by other means is estimated to be 60 per cent and this 60 per cent is considered loss when there is economic blockade in the National Highways, while its volume of loss is estimated to be 76.92 per cent when there is Manipur *bandh.* Share of private unorganised trade (trade, hotel, restaurants) is estimated to be 84 per cent and is taken as loss when there is economic blockade but when there is Manipur bandh, the loss in trade, hotel and restaurant is taken as 100 per cent. For public administration, the loss is estimated to be 40 per cent when there is Manipur *bandh* but no loss is accounted in the case of economic blockade. The loss in banking and insurance is estimated to be zero in the case of economic blockade but it is estimated to be 100 per cent in the case of Manipur *bandh.* In the case of other services like business and legal services, the loss is estimated to be 44 per cent in the case of economic blockade and 69.45 per cent in the case of Manipur *bandh.*

Using the aforementioned assumptions and the available data, the Directorate of Economics and Statistics of the Government of Manipur studied the impact of *bandhs* and economic blockades on the economy of the State and quantified the loss to the economy during 2004-05, 2005-06, 2006-07 and 2007-08 respectively.

Table 3.2: Loss to the Economy due to *Bandhs* and Economic Blockades (Rs. crore)

Year	No. of days of bandh	Loss per day due to bandh	Total loss due to bandhs	No. of days of blockade	Economic loss per day due to Economic Blockade	Total loss due to blockades	Total loss due to Bandhs & Blockades
1	2	3	4	5	6	7	8
2004-05	20	5.57	111.40	60	2.17	130.20	241.60
2005-06	48	6.38	306.24	97	2.44	236.68	542.92
2006-07	94	6.84	642.96	77	2.62	437.54	1080.50
2007-08	52	7.35	382.20	43	2.84	122.12	504.32
Total	—	26.14	1442.80	—	10.07	926.54	2369.34

Source: Same as Table 3.1.

From the Table 3.2 we can further verify that the number of days of *bandhs* during the estimated years of 2005, 2006, 2007 and 2008 are 20, 48, 94, and 52 days respectively. On the other hand, the number of days of economic blockade in 2005 was 60 and 97 in 2006 but it declined to 77 and 43 in 2007 and 2008 respectively. It can be seen that the total loss incurred to the economy due to *bandhs* during the year 2005, 2006, 2007 and 2008 were Rs.111.40 crore, Rs.306.24 crore, Rs. 642.96 crore and Rs. 382.20 crore respectively. The per capita loss per day (estimated at 365 days) was calculated as Rs. 23, 25, 27 and 28 respectively during the years. On the other hand, the total loss incurred due to economic blockades to the economy during the year 2005, 2006, 2007 and 2008 were estimated at Rs.130.20 crore, Rs.236.68 crore, Rs. 437.54 crore and Rs. 122.12 crore respectively. Also, the average loss per capita per day is calculated to be Rs. 10 during the years. Thus, the total loss to the economy of Manipur due

Table 3.3: Number of Days of Bandhs and Blockades in Manipur and the Growth Rate of NSDP and Per Capita Income at Current and Constant Prices (1999-00)

Year	No. of days of Bandh	No. of days of economic blockade	Growth rate of NSDP at Current Price	Growth rate of NSDP at Constant Price	Growth of PCI (%) at Current Price	Growth of PCI (%) at Constant Price	Growth of PCI (%) at Current Price (India)	Growth of PCI (%) at Constant Price (India)
1999-00	38	33	—	—	—	—	—	—
2000-01	63	53	(–) 4.76	(–)6.39	(–) 6.72	(–) 8.32	5.08	1.83
2001-02	43	42	7.12	6.23	4.86	3.98	6.56	3.69
2002-03	29	45	4.24	(-)0.56	2.16	(-) 2.55	6.20	2.03
2003-04	31	43	13.45	10.93	11.15	8.69	10.52	6.97
2004-05	20	60	13.86	9.25	11.58	7.06	11.15	5.62
2005-06	48	97	10.32	4.35	8.15	2.31	12.09	7.95
2006-07	94	77	6.91	3.92	4.83	1.90	13.54	8.20
2007-08	52	43	8.25	6.91	6.17	4.86	12.73	7.60
2008-09	45	63	8.53	7.40	6.48	5.37	12.64	4.94
2009-10	35	78	—	—	—	—	—	—
2010-11	27	135	—	—	—	—	—	—

Source: Author's Compilation from Local Dailies and *Economic Survey of Manipur 2009-10*, Directorate of Economics and Statistics, Government of Manipur, pp. 26. 28.

to *bandhs* and blockades during the same years are estimated at Rs. 241.60 crore, Rs. 542.92 crore, Rs. 1080.55 crore and Rs. 504.32 crore respectively.

Bandhs/blockades and its implications to the economy can be perceived from two propositions. First, it can be observed that there is an opposite relationship between economic growth and *bandhs* and economic blockades in such a way that when the number of *bandhs* and blockades increases, the growth of the NSDP and the Per Capita Income has decreased and *vice versa*. For that reason, imposing frequent *bandhs* and economic blockades can be considered as stumbling block to the economic growth of the State. But on the contrary the per capita income on national average has gradually been rising (see Table 3.3). During the year 2001 and 2003, growth rate of NSDP (at 1999-00 constant prices) of Manipur were –6.39 and –0.56 respectively while –8.32 and –2.55 accounted for the Per Capita Income of the State. These negative growth rates were considered partly due to frequent *bandhs* and blockades along the National Highways and roads of Manipur. However, besides *bandhs* and blockades, there were many other factors responsible for negative or low growth rate of the economy of the State like law and order condition, lack of resources and lack of necessary infrastructure to exploit unutilised resources, rainfall, non-existence of large and medium scale industries, failure of power and irrigation sector as well as the traditional attitude of the Central government of keeping the development issues of the State at lowest priority. For instance, by looking/observing the present condition of the National Highways in Manipur with pathetic conditions, it even seems to have adopted a regional exclusive policy. Generally, the economy of Manipur is considered to be a highways economy as the national highways plays the most important role in the State's transportation endeavour. Therefore, the importance of road transport facilities, especially national highways in the development of Manipur is multidimensional and thereby manifested as the basic amenity to perform the ordinary business of life. Second, the economic data do not support the view that the State's economy has suffered a lot due to frequent *bandhs* and economic blockades only. Because, despite numerous *bandhs* and blockades the growth rate of the per capita income and the NSDP have been rising during the years 2003-04, 2004-05 and 2005-06 but again declined in the following years (see Table 3.3). In addition, the NSDP at constant prices rose from Rs. 2,954 crore in 1999-00 to Rs. 4,408 crore in 2008-09 registering an annual exponential growth rate of 4.45 per cent (*Economic Survey of Manipur 2009-10*: 26). The growth of NSDP does not mean that the State was developing. In this respect, it can be said that every hazard has a winner. So, sections of people in the State are making huge abnormal profits out of *bandhs* and blockades (Bijoykumar, 2008). Thus, it leads to redistribution of wealth from the people to hoarders and businessmen, especially to black marketeers of energy sector and consumer goods brought in from outside the State.

Going little deeper into the changes in sectoral contribution of the State's economy that since 1980s, the construction sector and service sector have emerged as the most dominant sector in the NSDP. For instance, during 1960-80 (at 1980-81 constant prices), shares of small scale manufacturing units contributed between 73.2 per cent and 74.8 per cent to the secondary sector, while construction sector accounted for at an average of about 20.0 per cent only. However, since 1980-81, the major sectoral contribution to secondary sector shifted towards construction sector at an average of 76.0 per cent but inclined to 60.2 per cent in 1990, while small scale manufacturing sector was turned down to about 20.0 per cent only. Again, in 2006-08, construction alone constitutes between 87.46 per cent and 78.0 per cent of the secondary sector along with 36.83 per cent and 24.9 per cent of the NSDP of Manipur. But, share of secondary sector to the State's economy was only 10.0 per cent in 1960 and 8.0 per cent in 1970 at 1980-81current prices. On the other hand, there was a reversal role between primary and tertiary sector of the State's economy has been seen in the post-liberalization period. During 1960-80s, primary sector contributed at an average of about 65.30 per cent to the Manipur's economy as compared to about 33.03 per cent for tertiary sector. But, in 1991, the figures are 42.0 per cent and 45.0 per cent respectively. From the above assessment, it can be observed that the share of NSDP was increased mainly to construction and service sectors. In this respect, it will be worthwhile to mention that when performing the activities of these two sectors, it has to depend entirely on available transport facilities (Muktasana, 2012). Above all due to non-existence of large scale manufacturing industry in the State, 75 per cent of the consumer goods as well as the raw materials of small scale industries are imported from outside the State of Manipur through road communication network. So, if there were no transportation problems like *bandhs* and blockades in Manipur, the economy of the State would have been grown faster.

What Common People Get from *Bandhs* and Blockades"

If truth be told, the frequent *bandhs* and blockades becomes a social menace beyond the acceptable norms of tolerance. It is a temporary stoppage of normal activity undertaken as a protest against a policy, event, occurrence, etc. During such *bandh*, all economic activities are affected and there is sizeable amount of loss in the production of goods and services. Moreover, investors are reluctant to invest their hard earned money in an uncertain environment thereby vitiate the investment environment in the State. Infrastructure and resources are also lying underutilised due to such environment. In this respect, a poll on Kangla online (2006-07) on the question Do you support the frequent *bandhs* called by various organizations for different reasons in Manipur? And, the verdict was 69 per cent of the respondents said – No. In fact, certain issues definitely deserve to be discussed with approaches incorporating the type of *bandh* and blockade as they are not identical event as well as not unjustified all the times. But, during economic blockade, the prices of all essential commodities increased up to 2-3 folds. In reality, during the three months long economic blockades in 2011, the price of foodgrains and other household items has escalated to two to three folds. Prices of some selected items before, during and few days after economic blockades are shown in the Table 3.4.

Table 3.4: Prices of Selected Items before, during and after Blockades in 2011 (in Rs.)

Items	*Price before blockade*	*Price during blockade*	*Price after blockade*
Rice per kg in hill districts	18-20	50 to 100	25 to 30
Rice per kg in valley districts	16-18	27 to 28	20 to 25
Petrol per litre	50	100 to 150	100
Diesel per litre	36	90	70
Cooking gas per cylinder	500	1500 to 2000	1000 to 1200
Bus fare:			
Imphal to Sugnu (75 Km)	45	100	90
Imphal to Thoubal (25 Km)	15	30	25
Imphal to Guwahati (Air)	2500 to 4000	8000 to 13,000	8000 to 10,000

Source: Author's Compilation from Local Dailies.

Normally, the price of rice was Rs. 16-18 per kg in the valley districts while it was Rs. 18-20 in the hills districts (as per 2011 market price). But, it increased up to Rs. 27-30 per kg in the valley and even Rs. 50-100 in some remote areas of the hill region during the *bandh* and blockades. Economic blockades caused extremely difficult to survive for the common and poor people of the State. Another major issue of serious concern during blockades in the State is energy crisis like unavailability of petrol, diesel and cooking gas which gave a serious threat to the livelihood of common people. In this respect, it will be worthwhile to mention that the agencies of the said petroleum product have usually closed down as early as when any organisation imposed economic blockade saying that the stock has already finished. However, in the black market, plenty of such products are available in higher prices which are beyond the affordable limit of the poor common people but forced to purchase them as there were no alternatives to be substituted. Once the prices are hiked during the blockades, it usually takes time to come down to normal and during which, businessmen and hoarders were taking advantage of and earned abnormal profit. Nevertheless, the main trouble is that every two or three months or sometimes every month perhaps, there were *bandhs* or blockades for one or the other reason. However, the State government was unable to take up any stern action against those who imposed one or two month's long economic blockades.. Nonetheless, there has also been a habitual attitude of the State government that the public grievances will not be undertaken sooner or later without extreme forms of agitations or actions were launched. Above and beyond, it can also be pointed out that the State government does not show any strong interest in tackling the abnormal price hike in the State during and after the blockades because of the fact that some high profile politician and bureaucrats of the State even from police department seems to have linked with trade activities and enjoy the abnormal profits earned during and after the blockades. In this connection, it will be worthwhile to mention the comment by Prof. Amar Yumnam (Director, Centre for Manipur Studies, Imphal):

> In Manipur, we are now have a situation where those running the government move in tandem with the market players in order to earn abnormal profits at the cost of the common people. In other words, we now observe a kind of situation wherein there is an unwarranted transfer of income from the common men to the businessmen and the decision makers in the government; and it is the systematic disease which would kill the State in the long run rather than periodical blockade.

Therefore, it can be concluded that imposing frequent *bandhs* and economic blockades becomes a threat especially to the day-to-day bread earner and poor common people of the State. And, it can also be assumed that Manipur has the dubious distinction of recording the highest number of *bandhs* and blockades. As mentioned earlier, the economy of Manipur is considered to be a highways economy as 75.0 per cent of essential commodities including construction material were brought into the State through the National Highways network. Therefore, the importance of adequate transport facilities, especially National Highways in the development of Manipur is multidimensional and thereby manifested as the basic amenity to perform the ordinary business of life. Here, the tragedy is that it is not the first time that Manipur has faced a crisis of transportation problems in such a magnitude. All the time, the end results and suffering of the innocent public are untold miseries. Therefore, politics on National Highways must stop immediately so as to lead the State to the path of growth and development. In view of the above observation, everyone can see in their mind's eye that if such transportation problems happened or economic blockades for five days along the National Highways which connects Delhi-Amritsar, Delhi-Kolkata or Delhi-Agra; what would have been the response of the Government of India? In fact, by observing the past and present realities in terms of the political-economic setting in the State, the Central government seems to have adopted a regional exclusive policy to keep Manipur out of the present tendency of development realm attributed to various politico-historical circumstantial reasons, either to annihilate or made redundant to grow.

What Behavioural Sciences Tell about Transportation?

A conference on the application of behavioural sciences to transportation problems was held in Charleston, South Carolina, jointly sponsored by Secretary of Transportation, US Department of Transport and the University of Illinois, Chicago on October 31 to November 2, 1978. In this conference Mr. Danial Brand (a behavioural scientist) in his paper entitled "Transportation Policies and Problems for Study in the Behavioural Science" mentioned as:

> In transportation (planning), knowledge of personal and political behaviour is more important than knowledge of the engineering of these facilities. For example, a politician will exploit the public paranoia and fear of the unknown when an innovative approach in solving a particular transportation problem is undertaken. The objective of the politician is to become known in public, to become, perhaps, even a household word in the state/city. The impression to be left with the electorate at election time is that

the politician is a fighter of government excesses and, therefore, doing something right.

The above statement becomes quite relevant in the existing current state of affairs of Manipur if we little dig on to the behaviour of the local politicians in particular and the national politicians in general, also those who tries to attain political triumph during the course of highway development and its related problems instead of trying to resolving the existing impasse. This is in view of the behavioural sciences contributions to transportation problems that it will be no-nonsense to say that, for the time being, the politicians of the country and Manipur in particular, were hectic in trying to fortify their political reflection by making heroic and dramatic statement only during economic blockades instead of finding out a permanent resolution of this type of transportation problems. And, whatever, the politicians of the state (country) has so far done in dealing with the transportation problems of Manipur is nothing but to become known and to bestow sweet lip services only as a part of their exercise to achieve political ends and to minimise criticism from public. For instance, extremely shabby condition of National Highway No. 53 is a half century old transportation problem in the State. It has been a really wonder and doubtful thing that in this high-tech globalised era, the condition of the highways and some of the bridges along this route have still in pre-World War II vista. Due to this extremely shabby state, everyone would really surprise where to embark on and finish in narrating the suffering of taking a journey on these deplorable and dilapidated conditions of the State's lifelines. In fact, the present condition of National Highways in Manipur does not deserve to be called National Highways and is filled with large number of potholes, puddles and uneven surface inflicting every possible calamity. In this respect, the development and maintenance of the National Highway No. 53 was undertaken by Border Road Organisation (BRO) and Border Roads Task Force (BRTF) since 1964. For the last five decades what the BRTF was doing? Secondly, what is the politics behind in keeping these highways still in rough condition? Thirdly, why the State government did remember the highways only when there were *bandhs* and economic blockades. Lastly, during 2006-10, the Central government had constructed 135 km long Tamu-Kalaewa road into double lane in Myanmar to connect National Highway No. 39 at Moreh town. But, in the last sixty years, why did the Central government still keeping Pallel-Moreh portion of the National Highway No. 39 into a single lane with a shabby and deplorable condition which is only about 60 km to connect Manipur valley.

Or, is there any geo-political compulsion which critically needs to be assessed?

Concluding Assertion

In fact, frequent disturbances in the name of *bandhs* and blockades give a negative feedback to the society. It is the development of a sense of uncertainty in the collective psyche. This shows that people do not want frequent *bandh* and blockade, but while demanding the public grievances, the people do not find any suitable means to draw attention of the authorities. The general feeling of the people about frequent *bandh*/blockade is that they are fed up of such political means which seriously affect the State's economy as well as domestic economy of each household in the State. This line of argument is expressed by several persons in the columns of *Letter to Editor* in different newspapers. These means are more often perceived as anti-laymen or anti-poor political tools. But, this point of argument is well understood by the *bandh* caller but the critical issue in this case is that making loss to the government by calling *bandh*/blockade is the only key to success of a strike in the State mainly due to the arrogance attitude of the government towards public grievances. Curing of this chronic disease of *bandh*/blockade is in fact a distant dream at present but it can be controlled to a reasonable extent if there is good governance ensuring social justice, political will, appropriate legislation and its effective implementation. Risk management programmes should be given priority. The government should keep a network which can be made operational at short notice for distribution of essential commodities including petrol, diesel and cooking gas. *Bandh*/blockade is not the only wastage in the economy of the State but also violates human rights of the State. Besides, the loss due to corruption, extortion and poor governance are equally wasteful. Lastly, it is the time to wake up and start thinking about the future of Manipur; otherwise we will be very late in every aspect of growth and development and we should stop playing politics in the highways in the larger interest of the people by the non-State and State actors. And, for a permanent resolution, the people of Manipur must start thinking to be self-reliant, if not self-sufficient and to stand in our own.

REFERENCES

Arun, M.C. (2008) 'Bandh/Blockade and the Manipuri Society' Paper presented at the State Level Seminar on *Bandh* and Blockade in Manipur, Directorate of Information and Public Relations, Government of Manipur, Imphal (6-7 September).

Amar, Y. (2010) 'Dangerous than Blockades: Long Term Stunting of System Growth' *The Imphal Free Press*, Imphal (11-07-2010).

Bijoykumar, Singh E. (2008) 'Economic Impact of *bandhs* and Blockades in Manipur, Paper presented at the State Level Seminar on *Bandh* and Blockade in Manipur, Directorate of Information and Public Relations, Government of Manipur, Imphal (6 -7 September).

Biren, Singh O. (2008) 'Loss of State Economy due to Bandh/Blockade', Paper presented at the State Level Seminar on *Bandh* and Blockade in Manipur, Directorate of Information and Public Relations, Government of Manipur, Imphal (6 -7 September).

Brand, D. (1980) Transport Policies and Problems for Study in the Behavioural Sciences' in Micheal R.M.(ed) *Transportation Planning and Policy Decision Making*, p. 16. USA, Praeger Publishers, New York.

Indian Road Congress; Road Development Plan Vision: 2021, Ministry of Road Transport and Highways, Governmnet of India, New Delhi, 2001, p. 32

Ministry of Road Transport and Highways 'Road Development Plan Vision: 2021' Indian Road Congress; (2001), Government of India, New Delhi, pp. 1-8, 32.

Ministry of Finance, Government of India, *Economic Survey of India 2009-10*, New Delhi, pp. 213-215.

Muktar, M. (2009) 'Impact of Transportation on Economic Growth: An Assessment of Road Transport System' 2002, pp.1-6, http://www.org/paper/1223 html. Retrieved on 12/3/2009

Mukherjee, A. (2009) 'Social Impact of Globalizing Transport Services: The Case of India, Paper presented in the International Transport Forum, Paris (6-9 July).

Muktasana, Singh K. (2012) 'Transport Sector and its Role in the Economic Development of Manipur with Reference to National Highways' Unpublished Thesis, Department of Economics, Manipur University, Imphal.

Narendra, Ch. (2008) '*Bandh* and Blockade: A Legal Point of View' Paper presented at the State Level Seminar on *Bandh* and Blockade in Manipur, Directorate of Information and Public Relations, Government of Manipur, Imphal (6-7 September).

4

Tribal Uprising and Development: A Sociological Study of Reangs in Barak Valley of Assam

Jayeeta Sen

Introduction

India is proud to be a land of heterogeneous communities. Being the largest democracy in the world, it ensures justice, liberty, equality and dignity to all its citizens irrespective of caste, class, religion or sex so that the rights of the disadvantaged groups are not adversely affected in a competitive milieu. In order to provide safeguard to all, the Constitution of India not only provide individual's fundamental rights to life, freedom of expression, association, movement, belief and worship but also to provide for their material needs.

Tribals are considered as one of the backward communities in India. Development of the tribal people is considered as constitutional obligation. The constitution contains as many as 20 Articles and two special schedules (Fifth and Sixth) specifying the provisions for their development and welfare. In order to secure the socio-economic and cultural rights of tribes' different provisions are made in the Constitution. Article 46 entails the State to promote special care especially educational and economic interests, for Scheduled Castes (SCs) and Scheduled Tribes (STs) and to protect them from social injustice and all forms of exploitation. Further, in recognition of the fact that tribes constitute a distinct political and socio-cultural category with long history of independence and autonomy in their respective territory, Article 244 of Constitution of India provides special arrangement for the administration of tribal areas in the form of Fifth and Sixth Schedules.

Conceptual Framework and Objectives

Tribal development has been accorded an important place in India's strategy for national development. In pursuance of the policies of protection, integration and development, the government has formulated a number of development programmes and schemes for the development of the tribal and tribal areas to ensure a better quality of life and also to protect them from exploitation. The objective of the tribal development has been to 'level up' the underdeveloped tribals by bridging the socio-economic gap between them and the non-tribals so that they could be ensured of a better standard of living and come at par with the rest of the people. But over the years, it has been experienced that the efforts to draw the tribal people from subsistence economy into a wider economic framework of the country through legislative protection and progressive socio-economic programmes have not met with much success. Instead of the governmental assistance going to the tribal communities, the old entrenched exploitative elements have usurped them. The increased investment and change induced by numerous tribal development programmes through the successive plans. The 'Tribal Sub-Plan' have helped the tribes, but marginally.

Laws are made to protect the rights of the tribal people over their lands and prohibit transfer of their lands to the non-tribals. But many of these laws have, however, in-built loopholes that have been very judiciously manipulated by the non-tribal to concentrate land on their hands. Losses of land and land alienation, restriction on access to forest products, and the lack of opportunities for reasonable wage employment, have caused immense hardships to them. Consequently, developmental inputs for the benefit of these people have made little impact. Significantly the development process has, in many cases, interfered with traditional tribal institutions and ethos, and has produced negative results. Further poverty is a hindrance to the prosperity elsewhere, the abject poverty in which the tribal live may ultimately drag the economic advancement of a country down. Moreover, India cannot afford to develop at the cost of the poverty and ignorance of 67 millions of its tribal band. Further, continuous neglect of a particular segment of society may result, either in stagnation in economic progress or violent reversal of the existing social order. Acute poverty, malnutrition and starvation death of India have already contributed to the disgruntlement among the tribals. Besides, uninterrupted social and cultural discrimination leading to secessionist activities and the demand for separate statehood and self-government. This not only poses danger to the polity, but also impairs the peace and progress of the society. In view of the above situation at home on the one hand and the growing international concern for the cause of the indigenous people on the other, development of tribal people assumes much more importance than it was ever before. The rise of ethnicity and political activism among tribes in India including North-Eastern region owe their origin largely to this process. South Assam has been witnessing tribal unrest since last two decades and this chapter aims to highlight the primary causes.

Tribe and Tribal Culture

In general, the term tribe was applied to people who were considered primitive and lived in the backward areas of remote forests and inaccessible hill-tracts. Sometimes it was considered synonymous with the term race, which in scientific usage has an entirely different meaning. In the beginning, in the evolutionary perspective, it referred to a social form intermediate between the band and the nation. In this sense, it represented a territorially defined social group.

In modern parlance, a tribe is characterised by small-scale grouping that displays cultural continuity as well as unity. Its members have a self-conscious image and recognise affinity with one another. In current usage, it lacks precision and can cover several societies that are not recognised as tribal while anthropologists, sociologists, economists and administrators have adopted different approaches in defining the term, and there exists no universally acceptable definition of tribe. This is mainly because of different social, economic, political and cultural characteristics of different groups of tribe on the one hand, and the very process of their transition and transformation. In the Indian context, the term has been used and is being used somewhat indiscriminately. Oxford English Dictionary defines the tribe as "a group of people in a primitive or barbarous stage of development acknowledging the authority of the chief: and usually treating them as having a common ancestor". As the origin of these people can be traced back to the earliest stages of human evolution, some scholars refer to them by the term '*adivasis*' which means the original inhabitants on the land.

Anthropologically, tribe is defined as a social group the members of which lives in a common territory, speaks a common dialect, have uniform social organisation and possess cultural homogeneity having a common ancestor, political organisation and religious pattern (Dube, 1977). Here, the tribe is considered as a social group with common dialect, purpose, name and culture. Culture is often perceived as something that is associated with the aesthetic and refinement, the end product of human behaviour that is nurtured and transmitted by tradition. Culture is that entity which enhances the quality of life by endowing it with meaning of a beauty, truth, and goodness. In sociology, culture is used in a broader sense, not restricted to things of aesthetic values only, but also includes various aspects of material and social life. To quote Tylor (1898), "Culture is the complex whole which includes knowledge, beliefs, art, morals, laws, customs and other capabilities acquired by man as a member of society". Culture is viewed as crystallised phenomena of man's life activities (Bose, 1953). Individuals in society have knowledge about physical and social world and also have capacity to adopt a mechanism to conquer the physical as well as social odds. Culture is the essence of people. It reflects both the ideological and material base of a society. On the other hand, while culture is an abstract quality that shapes the subjective identity of a people, it is tangibly related to the social structure. This makes an important element in the process of social change. It not only defines our relationship with others but also shapes the way in which we react to external interventions. Put simply in a multi-cultural world, culture not only mirrors people's distinctive identity and consciousness but also serve as a medium through social contradictions and conflicts are handled.

Tribal culture is not a monolithic one, as each tribe or ethnic group is equipped with their own custom and tradition shaped according to their own intellectual genius and experiences with other. It is only when we view tribes within the Indian civilisational context that an entity could be designed as tribal culture, emerges which stand apart from the dominant tradition of Indian culture. In this regard, Unnithan, *et al.*, (1965) have brought to light in their book towards sociology of culture in India that tribal cultures are separated from each other. However, the folk tradition of Hinduism cannot be conceived in isolation from other. Tribal cultures are essentially whole in themselves.

One cannot speak of a universal tribal culture. Tribal societies are highly heterogeneous and manifest wide variations in the external representation of their arts, crafts and beliefs. Despite this overt variations, Indian tribal communities share close similarities with each other in their modes of subsistence social organization, world view and ethos. Central to this commonality is the tribal's relationship with nature. Over the millennium tribes have learnt to live and evolve with nature, adapting to its varied moods and judiciously drawing from its bounties to meet their material and spiritual needs. Indeed, for most tribes nature is not only a source of subsistence but also a source of their identity. In this common dependence on and respect for nature we find manifestations in the veneration of natural objects such as sun, moon, mountains and rivers and the concept of sacred species that distinguished tribal culture from cultural tradition of dominant Hindu society.

Tribal Development

Seen in the above perspective, tribal development can be defined as upliftment of the tribal communities, which are at different stages of socio-economic and cultural realms of growth. It implies social and economic development of the tribal people through phased manner and time-bound integrated area development and other programmes suiting the genius and the economic situation of the people, ensuring progressive elimination of all forms of exploitation and ensuring a move towards the goal of equality and social justice. It could be done by bringing about a positive change in the quality of life of the tribals through programmes on health, education, employment, transport and communication, technical manpower, etc., with a view to bring them on par with the general population. While the problem of tribal development in India is primarily linked with the backwardness of tribal areas, poverty of the tribal people and the issue of integration of tribals with rest of the population, the concept of development in tribal situations pose a number of difficulties. Even a good definition of tribal development may undergo scrutiny. Belshaw (1972), however, observed that "development should be looked upon as an organised activity with the aim of satisfying certain basic needs and to psychologically orient the tribals to adopt new skills, attitudes and life styles, so that they build up the inner strength and appropriate social and cultural infrastructure to stand the pressure of the new situation and acquire benefits from the new programmes and maintain higher levels". Belshaw (1972) considers development as a positive change, which provides an increase in the capacities of a society to organise for its own objectives and to carry out its programmes more efficiently.

According to Vidyarthi (1975), development means growth and change which includes both material and human, the socio-cultural factors which are an integral part of the dynamics of growth. He argues that "while striving for the development of a group or an area, due emphasis has to be given to their traditional values and historical experiences". Development activities particularly in the context of tribals, remarked Roy Burman (1986), should be concerned with (a) satisfaction of minimum needs; (b) control and management of productive resources; (c) employment optimisation; (d) broad based participation of the population in the development process; and (e) socio-cultural and political aspect of national integration.

The profit maximizing model of development has placed tribes at the receiving end of the process. It has not only disturbed the symbiotic relationship that they have traditionally mentioned with the natural environment but has also given rise to forced displacement and violent eviction from their habitat, putting their very survival and continuity as a species at stake. The extent of trauma experienced by tribes can be gauged from frequent stories brought out by national newspaper and other report on the inhuman atrocities faced by tribal communities at the project site of the dams, irrigation, canals, etc. Added to the sufferings meted out by State sponsored development, the tribes had contended with, land prospectors, tourism promoters and agricultural businessmen who together perpetuated and intensified their exploitative condition. The entry and functioning of the outsider-exploiter dyed either privately through corporate houses into the tribal areas may have provided with some short term benefits. On the whole, the processes have permanently scarred the tribal economy and undermine their knowledge system and intangible heritage acquired through centuries of intimate interaction with nature.

Reang and their Issues

Assam's Barak valley comprises the districts of Cachar, Karimganj and Haillakandi. Till 1983 these areas were part of the erstwhile Cachar district. Cachar, once a part of Kachari Kingdom had been the homeland of various tribal groups from pre-colonial period. When the British colonial rulers extended their hegemony, they called these areas as tribal backward tract. The valley is inhabited by tribes such as Barmans (Kacharis), Hmars, Mizo, Kuki, Khasi, Jaintias, Nagas, Chakmas and Karbis who are also the officially recognized Scheduled Tribes. Other tribes like Reang, Tripura Hrankhol, Chorei, Sakchep, Saihriem, Aimol, Khawchung, Chiru, Vaiphei, Ranglong, Halom, Rupini (Barman) are subjected to discriminations. Social discrimination is the offshoot of many tribal uprising including the Reang uprising.

The Reangs are one of the tribes in North-Eastern region. They migrated from Chittagong Hill Tract of Bangladesh. They belong to Tibeto-Burman tribes. They are closely resembled to Bodos and Tripuris. They have the larger concentration of population than the other smaller tribes and came to occupy an important position in the hilly areas of Hailakandi district. Majority of them presently inhabit in Mizoram. They practice Hindu religion along with some specific tribal rituals. There are 122 tribal villages, and out of which only 15 villages are recognised as forest villages of which six villages are dominated by Reangs.

Reangs are victim of socio-cultural and economic exploitations. Women atrocities in the form of rape and physical assault are common phenomenon. Reang male are alleged to be victimized as criminals of false cases. The Reangs who considered themselves marginalized sections have discontent regarding government's apathetic attitude to promote their culture. Since Cachar, Karimganj and Hailakandi districts are the plain districts. Reangs of these districts do not enjoy the Scheduled Tribe status. Barun Chherra and Kuki Cherra, are the two Gaon Panchayat of Hailakandi district predominantly inhabited by them but controlled economically and politically by others. Problems of land grabbing and act of swindling by village money lenders mounted the problems and annihilate their peace of life. It has been reported that the members of this marginalised community have no other alternative but to take loan from village moneylenders who charge high interest. In case of failure they have to sacrifice their standing crop. In this way they continued to be a soft prey of non-tribal population. And hence a sense of insecurity, lawlessness, and deprivation created in their psyche.

The United Liberation Front of Barak Valley (ULFBV) was reportedly formed in 2002 with the objective of creating a separate homeland for the tribal population in Karimganj and Hailakandi districts of Assam. The outfit has an estimated strength of 50 cadres, and all of them are tribals. Karimganj and Hailakandi districts remain their areas of operation.

Conclusion

From the above discussion it reflects that tribal uprising in this locality is due to self-assertion and protection of their identity. Each ethnic group is demanding limited autonomy which they feel can help protect their language, culture and enhance livelihood. The demand of Barak Valley Hill Development for the elevation of the autonomous council in the valley hints the fact that they are politically deprived because of the disadvantageous delimitation in assembly constituencies of the State. While their fellow schedule tribes have reserve seats in other States.

It is unequal distribution of power and autonomy which is responsible for tribal uprising. The policy makers who are not only numerically larger in number but their economic, political and cultural superiority also give them advantage to deprive the tribal people. This practice is not common among tribe-non tribe relation but in inter-tribe relation too, i.e., tribes who are numerically and socio-politically well off they also try to exploit their fellow groups. Moreover, there is always an attitude on the part of dominant communities that tribal are simple. This simplicity is taken as their inferiority. In this regard, Nongbri (2003) has put forward the Brahmmino-centric character of Indian scriptures. She added that in *Rig-Veda* and *Ramayana*, people of non-Aryan origin are presented as being of lesser God, unattractive colour and appearance and lacking in social and moral quality. Many of the highly derogatory term such as *dasyu*, *rakshas* (demons) and *vanaras* (monkey/apes) assigned to non–Aryan population and others.

Thus, in order to improve the situation following steps can be taken up. It should be specific to consider the tribe-non tribe equation while taken into account the planning for tribes. Erosion of tribal economy in the name of market economy and depletion of natural resources should be strictly handled. Aspect of tribal development should reach to common people. Dubious attitude by government officials, contractors and other people should be restricted. A change in people's attitude towards them from assimilation to a healthy respect for their cultural tradition and knowledge system is highly demanded.

REFERENCES

Belshaw, C.S. (1972). *Development: The Contribution of Anthropology, International Social Science Journal*, Vol. 24, No. 2.

Bhuyan, B.C. (1992). *Political Development of the North East Part II.* Delhi: Omsons Publication.

Borthakur, R. (2006). *Potentialities and Possibilities of Confidence Building Measures in South Asia: A Case Study in the Context of India-Pakistan Relationship*, Unpublished Ph.D Thesis, pp. 273-280.

Bose, N.K. (1953). Cultural Anthropology and other Essays. Calcutta: Indian Associated Publishing Co. Ltd.

Dube, S.C. (1977). Tribal Heritage of India. New Delhi: Vikash Publication, p. 2.

Roy Burnan, B. K. (1986). *Challenges of Tribal Development and Tribal Women in India*. Report of the National Conference on Tribal Women and Development: Problems and Perspective, MLV Tribal Research and Training Institute, Udaipur.

Tylor, E. B. (1898). *Primitive Culture*. New York: Harper Torch Books.

Unnithan, T.K.N., Indra Deva and Yogendra Singh (1965): *Towards Sociology of Culture in India*. New Delhi, Prentice-Hall of India.

Vidyarthi, L.P. (1975). *Strategy for Tribal Development in India*. Paper presented in the seminar on *Tribal Development*, Bhubaneswar.

Part - II
Education, Empowerment and Human Rights

5

Educational Development and Educated Unemployment in Sikkim

Marchang Reimeingam

Introduction

Education is considered as the means through which knowledge and skills can be developed. It also helps a person to get a job and perform the same with a fair degree of competence. It has been regarded as the determining factor for the level of economic prosperity and welfare of the people. According to Shingi, *et al.* (1988), education is "treated as a business proposition with all those investing in it wishing returns on it". Despite the many efforts, in a labour surplus economy like India, many people remain unemployed and continue to search or to be available for employment. Blaug, *et al.* (1969), pointed that "all the general factors that tend to inhibit market clearance for specialised skills in poor countries help to contribute to the creation of educated unemployment". While the increase in population and literate persons in general and educated people in particular amidst the limited job opportunities suitable with their acquired education itself originated the problem of educated unemployment in the State of Sikkim (one of the States of India's North-Eastern Region). The State being a developing one with a modest economic growth even in the era of globalisation is unable to generate adequate employment opportunities particularly in the organised public sector amid rising higher educational attainment. The expanding and growing number of educational institutions including higher educational institutions in the State is catering largely to improve the human capital and a mechanism to curb educated unemployment.

This chapter pertains to Sikkim and examines some aspects of population growth phenomenon based on Census data followed by a study on educational development based on Census and National Sample Survey (NSS) data. The state of educational institutions is briefly presented using the State government data. It is followed with the analysis of consumption expenditure on education based on NSS data which is discussed on employment perspective. Further, the problem of educated unemployment using NSS data is discussed before making some concluding remarks.

Concept and Definition of Educated Unemployed

The NSSO defines the unemployed as persons who, owing to lack of work, had not worked but either sought work through employment exchanges, intermediaries, friends or relatives or by making applications to prospective employers or expressed their willingness or availability for work under the prevailing conditions of work and remuneration, were considered as those 'seeking or available for work' (or unemployed). NSS provides three different estimates of unemployed as in the case of employed namely:

- Number of persons usually unemployed based on usual status approach (principal status, and principal status and subsidiary status together);
- Number of persons unemployed on an average in a week based on the weekly status approach; and
- Number of person-days unemployed on an average during the reference period of seven days preceding the survey.

The first estimates the magnitude of persons unemployed for a relatively longer period during a reference period of 365 days and approximates to an indicator of the chronic unemployment. Some of the unemployed on the basis of this criterion might be working in a subsidiary capacity. One can, therefore, get another estimate of the unemployed excluding those employed in a subsidiary capacity during the reference period. The former is called as the usually unemployed according to the principal status, the one that is used in the present study, and the latter, the usually unemployed excluding the subsidiary status workers (usual status adjusted) which admittedly will be lower than the former.

Educated are those "persons who have attained an educational level of secondary and above" and attained "age of 15 years or above" (NSSO, 2011). Unemployed are those persons who "sought work or did not seek but was available for work (for usual status approach)" (NSSO, 2011). Educated unemployed are persons who have obtained an educational level of secondary and above and are seeking or available for work.

Population Growth: Some Picture from the Census

Sikkim became a State of Union of India in 1975. The State with a geographical area of 7,098 sq. km is home to multifarious social, ethnic and linguistic groups of population numbering about 0.6 million (2011 Census). About 5 and 21 per cent of the State's population are Scheduled Castes and Scheduled Tribes respectively. Sikkim contributes only 0.22 per cent in the total geographical areas of India. However, only 0.05 per cent of India's 1.21 billion people reside in the State. Sikkim's population density has substantially increased from 57 in 1991 to 86 in 2011. Eventually, population was growing rapidly at 32.98 per cent, a decadal growth rate, during 1991-2001, however, it has slowed down to a considerable rate at 12.36 per cent during 2001-2011. The same trend was prevalent at the national level (or national average or country is used interchangeably here onwards) that the growth rate has declined from 21.34 to 17.64 per cent during the same period respectively. The decline in Sikkim is too drastic as compared to the national level. Is it because of the dearer cost of living in Sikkim? The period of 1991-2001 that showed a high growth might have caused by migration into the State, because of industrial as well as developmental work expansions in the State. Possibly, it might have also greatly enthused by the liberalisation, privatisation and globalisation policy.

The slow growth of population in the latter decade is due to the changes in migration pattern, educational development and economic growth. It is also attributed by an increase in outmigration for higher education and in search of jobs. Moreover, the increased in educational level and decline in infant mortality rate reduces the birth rate thereby reducing the family size and population growth.

The latest census figure showed a slight improvement in the sex ratio touching at 889 from the previous decades, however, very much below the national average of 940. It shows that male child preference is gradually but at a very slow pace losening from the existing social system; as females are slowly coping up in the educational arena in line of their male counterparts. Moreover, more number of females could have migrated in the recent decade towards Sikkim due to marriage to the previously migrated males. Moreover, it is not astonishing to observe, in the recent decade that the growth rate of females was slightly greater as compared to the male population counterpart in Sikkim, and also at the national level.

Educational Development

Education which is one of the development indicators is an integral part of human resources. Economists and educationists would agree that it is the human resources not its capital or material resources that ultimately determine the character and pace of its economic and social development. The growth of education plays an important role in altering the structure of employment. Sikkim has witnessed and experienced a rapid educational development over the recent decades. It is evident that literacy rate has rapidly growing at a more impressive rate in the State as compared to the national level. The educational attainment measured in terms of literacy rate has grown by about 23 per cent from 34.05 per cent in 1981 to 56.94 per cent in 1991 as presented in Table 5.1. It has further increased in the following decades touching 82.20 per cent in the year 2011. The increased in the educational development is sharper after the State merged with the Union of India. The rate of literacy at the national level has increased by about slightly less than 9 per cent points during 1981-91 attaining 74.04 per cent in the most recent decades. It is obvious that the pace of spread and growth of education in the State is relatively faster when compared to the national level. Only after nineties, which coincide with the era of liberalization, privatization and globalization, the level of educational attainment in the State surpassed the national level.

Table 5.1: Literacy Rates of Sikkim and India

Year	Sikkim				India			
	Male	Female	Person	Male-female gap	Male	Female	Person	Male-female gap
1971	25.37	8.90	17.74	16.47	45.95	21.97	34.45	23.98
1981	43.85	22.20	34.05	21.65	56.50	24.97	43.67	31.53
1991	65.70	46.76	56.94	18.94	64.13	39.29	52.21	24.84
2001	76.04	60.40	68.81	15.64	75.85	54.16	64.80	21.69
2011	87.29	76.43	82.20	10.86	82.14	65.46	74.04	16.68

Source: Census of India 1981 to 2011.

The level of growth rate has increased for both the gender at both the State and the national level. However, the rate continues to be lower for females than the males which generate a gender gap, that is measured as the difference between the rate for males and females. The gender gaps in attaining the literacy rate were lower for the State than for the country. For instance the gap was about 22 percentage points for the State as compared to about 32 percentage points at the national level in 1981; and about 11 and 17 percentage points for the State and the national level respectively in 2011. It has narrowed down indicating that education is increasingly delivered for females as much as for males for both the State and the country. And also females are increasingly opting for education rather than catering household obligation in the recent years. Yet, it remained higher for males than females. It implies that the pace of the female's literacy level would determine the speed towards reaching the goal of full literacy of the economy. Consequently, population growth will slow down and human development will improve.

The prevalence of high level of literacy does not necessarily mean to have attained higher level of education. This can be explained with the NSS data, as presented in Table 5.2. It shows about 11 per cent of the population have completed secondary and above education in Sikkim that is significantly higher than the figure for the national level of about 7 per cent in rural areas in 1993-94. Persons who have completed secondary and above education could be considered as educated. The educated consist "not only of graduates but of all those who have completed at least eleven years of schooling and are matriculates or above" (Blaug, *et al.*, 1969). The share was slightly higher in Sikkim than the national level throughout the periods. It has gradually increased to a record of about 16 per cent for the State against a level of close to 15 per cent at the national level during 2009-10. In urban areas, the attainment of education in secondary and above was prevailing at much higher level because of the better availability of educational infrastructure and institutional development. It was about 32 per cent and 37 per cent for the state and the country respectively during 2009-10. In the nineties the share of population who have attained secondary and above was higher for the State than for the country. However, afterward, the situation has reversed. It substantiates the argument that high prevalence of literacy attainment is just mostly a mere literate not an educated. For both the genders the share has increased in both the areas throughout the periods because of the rise in the level of enrolment, expansion of pre-secondary education, increased in government subsidy on higher education, implementation of

Table 5.2: Per 100 distribution of persons by general education for Sikkim and India

General education level	Year	Sikkim						India					
		Rural			Urban			Rural			Urban		
		Male	Female	Person	Male	Female	Person	Male	Female	Person	Male	Female	Person
Not literate	1993-94	32.2	48.9	39.6	16.1	20.4	18.0	45.5	67.9	56.4	24.1	38.4	30.9
	1999-00	26.8	40.5	33.2	13.9	23.9	18.4	41.2	61.5	51.1	21.6	34.3	27.7
	2004-05	21.2	31.0	25.8	11.0	26.0	18.0	36.4	55.0	45.5	19.5	30.7	24.8
	2009-10	12.8	21.1	16.7	5.7	18.1	11.3	29.4	46.7	37.8	16.4	26.4	21.1
Literate & upto middle	1993-94	54.6	43.4	49.6	51.4	57.6	54.2	44.6	28.6	36.8	47.7	42.8	45.4
	1999-00	60.9	52.2	56.8	57.3	50.1	54.0	46.8	33.5	40.3	46.5	43.1	44.7
	2004-05	66.4	59.2	63.0	60.3	49.1	55.1	50.1	38.2	44.3	46.0	43.8	44.9
	2009-10	68.2	65.6	67.0	54.8	58.1	56.3	51.7	42.9	47.4	42.4	40.6	41.5
Secondary & above	1993-94	13.1	7.7	10.7	32.5	22.0	27.8	9.8	3.4	6.7	28.1	18.7	23.6
	1999-00	11.4	7.1	9.4	28.7	25.8	27.5	11.7	5.0	8.3	31.7	22.5	27.3
	2004-05	12.3	9.9	11.2	28.7	24.9	26.9	13.4	6.7	10.2	34.5	25.5	30.2
	2009-10	18.6	13.3	16.1	39.6	23.2	32.2	18.8	10.3	14.7	41.1	32.8	37.1

Source: NSSO, 1993-94, 1999-00, 2004-05 and 2009-10.

right to free and compulsory education and as a result of which, educated unemployment rate has increased significantly in the State.

However, it continues to be higher for males indicating that the tendency to acquire higher education is greater for males. In general, the secondary and above educational attainment is more prominent in urban areas than in rural areas. For instance, it was about 5 per cent in rural areas against about 16 per cent in urban areas of Sikkim in 2009-10. It is also more prominent for the males than for females indicating the males' dominance in the field of higher education. It is interesting to observe the narrowing down of gaps of the share between males and females in the nineties in Sikkim. Afterward, it is surprising that the gap has considerably widened particularly in urban areas indicating that females are either not interested in pursuing higher education at the rate of their male counterparts or entered into family institution at early age. The gap was larger for the country in rural areas, however, it was lesser for the country in urban areas when compared to Sikkim in 2009-10. The gap for the country was more or less stable till 2004-05, however, the gap slightly widened in rural areas and slightly narrowed down in urban areas in the latter period.

In terms of educational institutions, in 2008, there were 784 numbers of government schools in Sikkim. These schools include from lower primary schools to senior secondary schools. Twelve colleges and research institutes were also recorded. As much as five universities including one central university existed. There are few institutions for teachers training and technical education. Vocational training is imparted in almost all the senior secondary schools in the field of horticulture, information technology application, travel and tourism management, dairying, automobile technology, hotel management and catering technology among others.

Consumption Expenditure on Education: Perspective on Employment

The increase in educational level relates with the rise in the investment and spending on human capital. The human capital theory ascertains that earning increases as the years of schooling increases (Borjas, 2005). In the study of Azad (1991), it is found that the "demand for wage employment increases as the level of education enhances". The expenditure on education is increasing over the years due to the rise in income level as well as due to the increase in educational level apart from dearer cost in accessing its infrastructure. The increase of expenditure on education can be substantiated by a factual figure on household consumption expenditure on education of NSS. According to the NSS, 2.32 per cent of the total monthly consumption expenditure was spent on education per person/household in 1999-00 (55th Round) which has significantly increased by slightly less than 2 percentage point to 3.97 per cent in 2004 (60th Round) in rural Sikkim; and, the increased in urban areas was more prominent by slightly less than 3 percentage point from 4.97 per cent to 7.52 per cent during the same period.[1] The higher level of expenditure on education in urban areas as compared to rural areas is due to the higher and expensive living cost in general and more expensive in educational cost including tuition fees, hostel fees or house rent and transportation expenditure.

In India, it has increased by slightly less than one percentage point from the level of 1.93 per cent to 2.86 per cent in rural areas; and it has increased by slightly more than 2 percentage point from 4.33 to 6.52 per cent in urban areas during the same period. The increasing share of consumption expenditure on education is partly due to the unmatched increased of cost on education and non-educational cost and partly due to the growing importance of education or higher demand for education in the household in order to enter into formal employment sector. The higher demand for education are mostly an induce demand in a sense it exerts demonstrative effect. The demand for an education sufficient to qualify an individual for entry into modern jobs appears to be related to the "wage differential between jobs in the modern sector and the traditional sector; probability of success in finding modern sector employment, direct private costs of education and, opportunity costs of education" (Todaro, 1991). Disposable income are less expended on education in rural areas as compared to the urban spending patterns on it, as expected, generally due to the wide differences in the cost of education as well as prevalence of lower level of education in rural as compared to urban areas. Consumer's expenditure of the State is relatively higher than the national average both in the areas. This can partly be explained by the growing importance of education as well as parents motivations and incentives to educate quality education might have led to higher spending. Most importantly, inflationary factor which induces to higher cost of education might have driven to higher spending. Moreover, it is due to the larger students' enrolment in private educational institutions which normally incurred higher cost compared to government institutions which give subsidies for social benefit[2], and the high cost for financing education, financing for higher education outside the State, inadequate availability of government or subsidies educational infrastructure and a higher proportion of household members going for school in the State. On the other hand, the lower level of household consumption expenditure on education at the national level are due to lower level of literacy and due to the generalization for all the States and Union Territories of India where some States or Union Territories have lower spending on education.

Education is a function of employment in the modern job market. People invest on development of human resources in order to yield some product for future economic well-being and for better welfare of society among many other purposes. Education is a means for development of morality and personality, accumulation of knowledge and skills, and for employability in the modern labour market in particular among many ends. Educating and motivating for prosperity through learning is widespread yet education remains a dream for large section of the people. At present education is considered as the most necessary commodity, therefore educational attainment is ever rising irrespective of the type of household job and income level. This is largely contributed by the nature of competitive structure of demand for labour with extra qualifications in the existing job market. The demand for education is in reality a derived demand for high-wage employment opportunities in the modern sector. This is because access to such jobs is largely determined by an individual's education. Most people especially the poor in less-developed nations do not demand education for its intrinsic non-economic benefits but simply because it is the only means of securing modern sector employment. These derived benefits must in terms be weighed against the costs of education. On the supply side, the public supply of the quantity of school places at the primary, secondary, and university levels is "fixed by the level of government educational expenditures" (Todaro, 1991).

The increasing spending on education is also a concern for the planners and policy-makers because each additional increment on educational expenditure is an outcome of factors like unemployment and the demand for higher educational qualification for particular job. Fostering on higher education is often argued as a mechanism to curb unemployment in short-run by enabling to accommodate more number of people in higher education through subsidy on education. As Marga (1974) has pointed that "educational expansion served to delay the entry of young job-seekers into the labour market by keeping them for increasingly longer periods in the educational cycle".

Expanding and instituting various higher educational institutions including distance education is a vivid example. Nevertheless, the growth of population also demands for more number of the institutions. In an existing trend of spiralling consumption expenditure on education a proper direction or guidance or course content that are in demand at present and in near future and applicable and adaptable in the local economy and environment are seemingly lacking. Expenditure on education should be made for employability, to enter in formal sector or to establish an establishment within existing economy. This will definitely lead to a reduction in unemployment level as well as save a wasteful money resources and time and use in other productive or developmental work.

Moreover, present job seekers are quite informative about the scarcity of vacant organized jobs in which extra qualification becomes necessary condition in search for job. On the other side, the employers are highly aware of the situation of the excess supply of the overqualified job seekers, which enhances employers bargaining power of wage particularly in the private sector. In the process job seekers' bargaining power is dwindling due to the increasing number of qualified applicants. Even though higher qualification is not a necessary condition where minimum qualification is prescribed; people possessing higher educational qualification seems to have advantages in getting a job. It is also a prevailing fact that many unemployed are seeking jobs where prescribed educational qualification is much lower than their own qualifications. It is due to a higher competition across the type of available job and also due to a high prevalence of unemployed people. Persons with an extra qualification are preferred so that same person can execute several types of jobs namely multitasking and also spend less resource in training. Technically, minimum prescribed qualification has risen. However, at present situation in many cases higher qualification is by and large a contributing factor for getting employment particularly in private sector. This induces to the growth of demand for higher education; thereby, resulting to an increase in amount of expenditure on education.

In exploring the possible means for all the educated unemployed to be employed the commonly called self-employment is the only way. Various schemes for educated unemployed are available, however, in reality the amount is meagre and less viable for execution. Further, it has lots of limitations like the knowledge of schemes, its amount, the terms and delivery norms of the scheme of finance to mention some examples. It can be argued that employment with a lower educational qualification could have benefited more than acquiring higher education and then experiencing a long period on waiting for the aspired job; had the present high unemployment level been foreseen. In other words, the opportunity cost for education is very high particularly among the poor. Job preference, high expectation and aspiration resulted to voluntary unemployment among the educated. However, education is not only for private benefit, i.e., earning but also for social benefit. Little education which the earlier generation has acquired propels the present generation to acquire higher than them so as to develop, realize and uphold the rich heritage, culture and values.

The decline of job vacancies in the labour market and the increase in demand for higher education resulted to steady growth of employment. Educated people are rapidly growing in the State which will result to a serious problem of unemployment in near future as at recent time most situations in rural Sikkim are discussed in the following section. Many remain voluntarily unemployed due to the non-fulfilment of their aspiration for job which commensurate with their acquired educational qualification. It is also threatening with the sluggish pace of job creation particularly in government sector. Government should add more amicable socio-economic environment and encourage and invite more private jobbers to generate adequate employment. Educational system should be restructured, delivered and acquired on the basis of quality and quantity of job available or likely to be available and for employability.

Problems of Educated Unemployment

The existence and growth of educated unemployed is attributed to the much higher growth rates in the population of educated (secondary and above) than the rate of growth of employment in the organized sector, in which the matriculates and college graduates seek to be absorbed. Parthasarathy, *et al.*, (2000) ascertained that the "educated seek employment mainly in the public/private organized sector" suggesting that the supply of labour to this sector comes largely from the educated. According to Puttaswamaiah (1977) the educated unemployment is presumably a consequence of the general impression among the public that investment in education by an individual should yield a return in terms of remunerative job; search of job suited to the particular type of education received, and decline in acceptance of job other than office jobs.

The educated unemployment problem in Sikkim has become severe in the recent years. It is more problematic than the general unemployment which has empirically proved that the educated unemployment rate is usually higher than the general unemployment rate. It is simply because the educated person makes a general impression that investment in education should yield a return in terms of salaried job; seeks or prefers organised, formal, salaried or white collar jobs, specific kind of employment; capability of affording unemployment; and their aspiration are increasing resulting in a serious mismatch between the supply of educated job seekers and the demand for them in the labour market causing rise in unemployment.

Educated unemployment problem was very severe in both rural and urban areas at the national level as well as in Sikkim in the post-reform period in the nineties. In Sikkim it was milder in terms of the problem as the rate of educated unemployment was lower for the State than the national level. According to the NSS, the educated unemployment rates (usual principal status) for 15 years and above of age has increased from 4.6 per cent in 1993-94 to little over 12 per cent in 1999-2000 against the declined at the national level in rural areas as shown in Table 5.3.

Table 5.3: Unemployment Rates (Usual Principal Status) for the Educated (15 years and above) for Sikkim and India

State/ India	Year	Rural			Urban		
		Male	Female	Person	Male	Female	Person
Sikkim	1993-94	2.0	15.5	4.6	3.4	12.5	4.9
	1999-00	13.4	10.1	12.3	9.0	17.2	12.1
	2004-05	7.4	8.3	7.7	6.4	6.3	7.3
	2009-10	11.3	6.0	9.8	0.1	0.0	0.1
India	1993-94	8.8	24.9	10.3	6.9	20.6	8.9
	1999-00	6.8	20.4	8.2	6.6	16.3	7.9
	2004-05	5.9	23.1	8.5	6.0	19.4	8.2
	2009-10	4.1	15.7	5.6	3.8	13.9	5.4

Source: NSSO, 1993-94, 1999-2000, 2004-05 and 2009-10.

The rate sharply declined to 7.7 per cent in 2004-05, however, it has increased to about 10 per cent in 2009-10 in rural Sikkim. At the national level it has slightly increased in 2004-05 but declined in the latter period. A similar trend that prevailed in rural areas also prevailed in urban areas at the national level. In Sikkim the trend differs from rural to urban areas. In urban Sikkim in the nineties the rate has significantly increased experiencing a severe educated unemployment problem. However, in the following years the rate sharply falls and continued to fall to a negligible level of 0.1 per cent in urban Sikkim. This sharp decline is due to the expansion of institutions for higher education, increased in self employment as employability increases with the large base of vocational programmes background and outmigration. Generally, according to Shingi, *et al.*, (1988), "there is an inverse association between the proportions of children or youth participating in economic activities and of those enrolled in educational institutions". Sikkim is the only State in India which recorded educated unemployment rate below one per cent in urban areas in 2009-10.

Unemployment has declined for males in both the areas at the national level throughout the period. Similarly, for females, it has declined throughout the period, except during 1999 to 2004 where it rose to some extent. This period is the economic reform period and boom period for private investors where many private job opportunities were in the process of generation in the country.

In Sikkim, it has declined throughout the period for rural females from 15.5 per cent in 1993-94 to 6 per cent in 2009-10. For both the genders in urban areas, it has increased during the nineties, however, it has considerably declined afterward reaching the negligible rate of unemployment in 2009-10. Educated unemployment rate touching the negligible level implies an increased labour's employability, flexibility in choosing a job, capability to adapt any working environment, acceptance of existing wage rate and also the high mobility of the workers among the urban workers in the State. Further, it would be explained by the fact that sometimes after spells of unemployment the educated unemployed after experiencing greater difficulty in finding work often "obliged to 'trade down' and accept second or third best" (Roberts, 1985) job; also it is assume that the educated unemployed are more informative which leads to outmigrate in search for job resulting to the declined of educated unemployment rate in Sikkim.

In case of rural males, it has sharply increased in the nineties and then decline in the following period, however, it has increased to a considerable extent to slightly more than 11 per cent in 2009-10. The existence of educated unemployment is attributed to the too literary character of education, too theoretical, lacking aptitude and techniques and largely not job oriented or employable in the present labour market structure which demands mostly specialised skills and knowledge resulting to the increase of educated unemployed people. Puttaswamaiah (1977) has pointed out that the "educational system in this country [India] is defective owing to its excessive theoretical bias". The system resulted to most of the "educated job-seekers having very little aptitude and technical qualifications for various types of works". As per Watson (1983) the system is of much speculation that schools have "failed to build bridges with employers" and or have "failed to produce youngsters who are employable".

Moreover, the formal jobs which are mostly sought by the educated are concentrated in urban centres resulting to higher unemployment prevalence in rural areas. In the recent decades various job oriented vocational courses have been dramatically introduced across the country including Sikkim. The question of employability possibly depends not only to the type of labour supply irrespective of acquired type (theoretical or practical) of education, but on the nature of market structure as well as the level of economic development of the country. In the developing nations, "each worsening of the employment situation calls forth an increased demand for [and supply of] more formal education at all levels [primary, secondary or university]" (Todaro, 1991). However, "the nature of formal schooling in India is not particularly job oriented and hence more and more educated end up unemployed" (Nair, *et al.*, 1989).

The problem of unemployment is more severe for females at the national level as the rates were considerably higher for females than that of males in both the areas throughout the period as presented in Table 5.3. The higher rate for females is because they possibly find a specific job in a place of proximity and they are less mobile in comparison with the male counterparts. Whereas, males are more responsive as the society is a patriarchal one and considered as family bread winners. The educated unemployed attempt to access employment market information to their fullest to get the appropriate job suitable with their acquired educational level. The high unemployment rate prevalence is also due to the unemployed unwillingness to take up work that is available, and unable to obtain the work they desire with their formal schooling. The "educated persons look for specific kinds of employment opportunities and remain unemployed till they get such work" (Gumber, 2000). Moreover, Azad (1991) has pointed out that majority of the educated personnel prefer to work in government departments rather than in any other sectors presumably because of the lure for white collar jobs with all sorts of facilities and leisurely place of work.

Further, the educated remain unemployed because of their limited flexibility and lack of adaptability to the changes in working and living conditions and income expectations. An educated prefer to stay unemployed until the right job has been found seems to be a "perfectly sensible one" in the light of his attitudes to income and status (Callaway *et al.*, 1973). On the demand side, Todaro (1991) and Blaug *et al.*, (1969) have ascertained that the employers tend to strengthen and upgrade hiring standards.

In Sikkim the picture of unemployment is somewhat peculiar. Its prevalence was inconsistent. The problem of educated unemployment was more severe in Sikkim as compared to the national level among the males and in rural areas in particular till recently. It is clearly visible that unemployment rate was prevailing at about 11 per cent in Sikkim as compared to about 4 per cent at the national level for rural males in 2009-10. Among the females, the problem was more severe at the national level as compared to Sikkim. The mobility of labour, flexibility in seeking a job and the employability of labour determine the differences in the degree of unemployment problem. Most importantly, unemployment rates differential between males and females has narrowed down in Sikkim over the years. It is not the case at the national level.

The prevalence of high unemployment level is because many job seekers' expectations exceed the emerging realities of the labour market and they prefer to remain unemployed for some time rather than accept a job which they feel lower to their status. This creates the inverse relationship between educated unemployment and educational attainment. Due to above mentioned various reasons the educated experiences the so called "waiting period" situation. The waiting period and also the growth of educated unemployed depend on the inverse relationship between the supply of educated persons and the organised job availability. At present the base of the educated people is visibly wide as a result the steep competition among them for the limited opportunities in which the employers attempted to accommodate the more educated for a given job. As a result an overqualified people are in demand leading to the growth of unemployment and increase demand for higher education. The employer's preference for experienced workers remains the problem for the new entrants into the workforce.

The Government of India is expanding, all over the country including Sikkim, all levels of educational institutions amidst the high prevalence of educated unemployment, which would accommodate some of the unemployed in higher studies acting as a mechanism to control unemployment problem in short-run. The rapid expansion of schooling facilities induces to the rise of educated unemployment because "the absorption of the 'educated' in productive employment has proven difficult" (Shingi, *et al.*, 1988). Hence, for long-run, the need of the hour is to introduced and speed up various means to reduce, if not remove, educated unemployment problem for lasting economic and social prosperity.

Concluding Remarks

Education has expanded in terms of attainment of qualifications both for private benefit for earnings through a formal job and for social benefit. However, educational system and institutions need to be more focused and restructured depending on the emerging structure of employment for employability in all levels and types of education. Education needs to be restructured towards work-oriented scheme. Population has been rapidly growing which necessitate an expansion of educational base. Concerning the consumption expenditure on education Sikkim expended relatively higher money than the national average due to the larger access of private educational institutions which normally incurred higher cost compared to government institutions. The expenditure on education has increased for the State following the national trend. Amidst the above mentioned situation educated unemployment problem has escalated in Sikkim against the general decline at the national level for rural males in the recent years from the early nineties. For females in both the areas and urban males the problem has become milder as the rate falls over the years in Sikkim and at national level. Interestingly, educated unemployment level has dropped to a negligible level only in Sikkim among the Indian States in urban areas. The major challenge is to ensure the employability of these unemployed by providing proper education, appropriate training and marketable skills in order to participate adequately for productive work with flexibility in choosing job with their innovative ideas, skill and knowledge.

NOTES

1. Figure for 2004 for Sikkim is generalized by NSS for hilly North-Eastern States excluding Arunachal Pradesh, Assam, Manipur and Tripura for rural areas and Assam, Manipur and Mizoram for urban areas.
2. Government provision of free or subsidies educational facilities determine by the level of income tax. These facilities are provided by the government only when the social benefit or social rate of return is greater than the private benefit or private rate of return. Social benefits are "more rapid economic growth; promoting social tolerance and cohesion; enabling

participatory democracy; facilitating social mobility; and greater tax revenues from better educated higher earners" (Smith, 2003:133).

REFERENCES

Azad, J.L. (1991). *Graduate Unemployment in India: An Analytical Study of its Incidence, Nature and Causation.* New Delhi: Association of Indian University.

Blaug, Mark *et al.* (1969). *The Causes of Graduate Unemployment in India.* London: Penguin Press.

Borjas, George J. (2005). *Labor Economics.* New York: McGraw-Hill.

Callaway, Archibald and Klaus Bettenhausen (1973). *Approaches to Employment Problems in Africa and Asia.* London: Youth and Development in the Commonwealth.

Census of India. (1981, 1991, 2001, 2011). New Delhi: Government of India.

Government of Sikkim. (2008). Human Resource Development Department: *Annual Reports.*

Gumber, Anil. (2000). Correlates of Unemployment among the Rural Youth in India: An Inter-State Analysis. *The Indian Journal of Labour Economics,* 43(4):657-671

Marga (1974). *Youth, Land and Employment.* Colombo: Marga Publication.

Nair, P.S. *et al.*, (ed.) (1989). *Indian Youth: A Profile.* Delhi: Mittal Publications.

NSSO. (1997). *Employment and Unemployment in India 1993-94.* Report No. 409. GOI: Department of Statistics.

NSSO. (2000). *Household Consumer Expenditure in India 1999-2000.*Report No. 454 GOI: MOSPI.

NSSO. (2001). *Employment and Unemployment Situation in India 1999-2000* (Part-I). Report No. 458. GOI: MOSPI.

NSSO. (2005). *Household Consumer Expenditure in India.* Report No. 505. GOI: MOSPI.

NSSO. (2006). *Employment and Unemployment Situation in India 2004-05* (Part-I), Report No. 515. GOI: MOSPI.

NSSO. (2011). *Employment and Unemployment Situation in India 2009-10.* Report No. 537. GOI: MOSPI.

Parthasarathy, G. and K. A. Nirmala. (2000). Employment and Unemployment of Youth. *The Indian Journal of Labour Economics.* 43 (4):683-701.

Puttaswamaiah, K. (1977). *Unemployment in India: Policy for Manpower.* New Delhi, Bombay and Calcutta: Oxford and IBH Publishing Co.

Roberts, Kenneth. (1985). *Youth and Leisure.* London: George Allen and Unwin Ltd.

Shingi, Prakash M. and Pravin M., Visaria. (1988). *Youth in Asia: Viewpoints for the Future.* New Delhi: New Statesman Publishing Company.

Smith, Stephen. (2003). *Labour Economics.* London: Routledge.

Todaro, Michael P. (1991). *Economic Development in the Third World*. Delhi: Orient Longman.

Watson, Keith (ed.) (1983). *Youth, Education and Employment – International Perspectives*. London: Croom Helm.

6

Human Rights in Armed Conflict: The Role of Civil Society

M. Amarjeet Singh

Introduction

North-East India (hereafter the North-East or region), consisting of eight federal States, occupies about eight per cent of country's land area. It has about four per cent of country's population. It is connected to the rest of the country through a 22 km long land corridor passing through Siliguri sub-division of West Bengal, and hence almost bordered by Bangladesh, Bhutan, China, Myanmar and Nepal. The region is inhabited by different ethnic groups which are relatively little known, both within and outside the country.

The region began increasing contact with the rest of India just few centuries ago, primarily after its incorporation into British ruled India in early nineteenth century. This brought far reaching transformations of its society, economy and polity. Since then it has become one of the great destinations of migrants. The English-educated middle class people from erstwhile Bengal were recruited to assist the British officers in running the new administration followed by labour recruitment from other parts of British ruled India to work in tea plantation, coal mining and oil exploration in the region. In addition, the administrative boundary of Assam, then constituted major area of North-East region, was also reorganised. First, it was administratively integrated into Bengal from 1826 to 1873; and secondly, became a separate province of British ruled

The armed group UNLF came into existence in 1964, followed by People's Revolutionary Party of Kangleipak (PREPAK) in 1977, and People's Liberation Army (PLA) in 1978. Security forces operated extensively against the PLA in the 1980s in which apart from killing top leaders, the arrest of its chief, Nameirakpam Bisheswar. It was huge setback for them. Bisheswar and three others decided to contest in the Manipur Legislative Assembly elections held in 1984. Bisheswar won from Thongju but never was vocal inside the assembly. He was later killed by his former colleagues. In the seventies and eighties, the UNLF concentrated mainly on mobilisation and recruitment. By 1990, it started an armed campaign and formed an armed wing called Manipur People's Army (MPA). Rajkumar Meghen (also popularly known as Sanayaima) is its Chairman, who is currently lodged in a jail in Guwahati. A large number of armed groups were formed in the 1990s in Manipur.

One of the most destructive effects of prolonged conflict has been the damage which it inflicted on the social, economic, legal and political organisation of the society, i.e., its institutions. Institution, according to Jack Knight (1992), is a set of rules that structure social interaction in particular ways. And for a set of rules to be an institution, knowledge of these rules must be shared by the members of the relevant community or society. In this chapter, an institution is taken to be a public system of rules which defines offices and positions with their rights and duties, powers and immunities, and the like. These rules specify certain forms of action as permissible, others as forbidden; and they provide for certain penalties and defences, and so on, when violation occurs. Thus, an institution may be thought of in two ways: first as an abstract object, that is, as a possible form of conduct expressed by a system of rules; and second, as the realisation in the thought and conduct of certain persons at a certain time and place of the actions specified by these rules (Rawls, 1999). The picture of the conflict has a place for institutions in both the senses that John Rawls has suggested. The present crisis can be seen as a result of the inability to enforce a set of abstract rules leading to the emergence of new institutional practices. These could include the government and its agencies, armed groups and others. All have come to be associated in different capacities in the course of the conflict. Therefore, an overview of the institutions that cause conflicts, ease conflicts, and institutions that emerge from conflicts are important.

The armed groups have established parastatal organisations in the areas they controlled and lay down a set of rules and have the means and resources to enforce them. Thus, they not only monitored the state institutions but also administered their own social welfare services to gain public support. In this way, many of the functions which are ordinarily within the domain of the state institutions have been encroached upon by the non-state institutions. The overall impact has been the dilution of the legitimacy of state institutions. Many of them claimed to have established their own government, such as Federal Government of Nagaland and Government of the People's Republic of Nagaland. They also claimed to have constituted parliamentary institutions, such as Tatar Hoho, and standing armies such as Naga Home Guards and Naga Army (Singh, 2012). They have set up an efficient mechanism to raise funds locally to run their programmes. The taxes are collected from government and its officials, traders, contractors, politicians and common people.

Human Rights and Civil Society Movement

One aspect of protracted conflict has been the proliferation of different kinds of civil society groups. Many of them are of recent origin, and the direct consequences of conflict. They have been playing diverse role in the course of these conflicts. Some focus on human rights issues and advocacy, and while others focus on upholding the interests of the community which they represent. Some have been also at the forefront of promoting localised peace-building efforts and initiating reconciliation processes.

The concept of civil society is diverse and can carry different meanings. As a result there is no commonly agreed upon definition. However, it has been recognised as one of the basic pillars of democracy. It can be defined as (Spurk, 2011: 8-9): "a sphere of voluntary action that is distinct from the State, political, private and economic spheres, keeping in mind that in practice the boundaries between these sectors are often complex and blurred. It consists of a large and diverse set of voluntary organisations—competing with each other and oriented to specific interest—that are not purely driven by private or economic interests, are autonomously organised and interact in the public sphere. Thus civil society is independent from the State and the political sphere, but it is oriented towards and interacts closely with them". Civil society broadly performs the following functions:

(1) *Protection:* Protect the lives, freedom and property against attack and despotism by the state and other authorities.
(2) *Monitoring for Accountability:* Monitoring the activities of state

apparatus and government. Monitoring can refer to human rights, public spending, corruption and so forth.

(3) *Advocacy and Public Communication*: To articulate interests—especially of the marginalised groups—and to create channels of communication in order to bring them to the public agenda, thereby raising public awareness and facilitating debate.

(4) *Socialization:* With its associational life civil society contributes to the formation and practice of democratic attitudes among citizens. People learn to develop tolerance, mutual trust, and the ability to compromise through democratic procedures.

(5) *Building Community*: Engagement and participation in voluntary associations also has the potential to strengthen bonds among citizens.

(6) *Intermediation and Facilitation between Citizens and State*: Civil society fulfils the role of balancing the power of, and negotiating with, the state at different levels (local, regional and national). It establishes diverse relations (communication, negotiation, control) among various interest groups or between independent institutions and the state.

(7) *Service Delivery*: The direct provision of services to citizens is an important activity of civil society associations, such as self-help groups. Especially in cases where the state is weak, it becomes essential to provide shelter, health and education (Spurk, 2011: 24-25).

Several human rights organisations were established in Manipur in the 1980s and worked fearlessly to monitor rights-violating government. I define human rights organizations as those non-governmental organizations that are concerned with the promotion and the protection of human rights. Human rights here refer to civil, political, economic, social and cultural rights of human beings.

The government has attempted to address the problem of armed conflict through military, political and economic measures. Firstly, since the governments viewed the problem as a law and order problem and the militants as criminals, misguided youths or terrorists has legitimised the use of force under special laws. Thus the Indian State has diverted vast resources into its security bureaucracy.[1] This gives more power to security forces which has been controversial because of the alleged human rights violations. Extra-judicial killings by State forces are common in conflict-affected areas of India. These killings were projected as self-defence by

State forces. This is an acknowledged strategy of the State for eliminating certain kinds of opposition to the State and the established order (Ramanathan, 2001: 12).

Secondly, when the military means failed to produce the desired results, the political means were deployed. This included the creation of new States and autonomous regions. Finally, the economic development measures included rolling out populist measures in the name of promoting economic development and more so to win the hearts and minds of people. North-East is the only territory of India whose development is the mandate of a separate ministry of Central government known as Ministry of Development of North-Eastern Region (DoNER).

When there was gradual deterioration of law and order situation in Naga Hills district in the 1950s the armed forces were deployed, and the Naga National Council was banned. In 1953, the Assam Maintenance of Public Order (Autonomous Districts) Act 1953 was promulgated in the district followed by the declaration of the district as a "disturbed area" by promulgating the Assam Disturbed Areas Act, 1955 in 1956. It was followed by the promulgation of Armed Forces (Special Powers) Regulation 1958. This regulation was converted into Armed Forces (Special Powers) Act 1958. This Act was subsequently extended beyond Naga Hills district to the "disturbed areas" of Manipur.

Under the Armed Forces (Special Powers) Act 1958 the armed forces such as Assam Rifles, Rashtriya Rifles and Army enjoy "special powers" in a locality declared as "disturbed area". It was to be remained in force for one year. It has its origin in the colonial legislation known as Armed Forces (Special Powers) Ordinance 1942, enforced by the British immediately after the Quit India Movement started, with intent to desist Indian from participating in the movement. It was strengthened after Independence and given more power to arrest, torture and use of force (even kill) against civilians on mere suspicion (Hashmi, Undated). After Independence it was amended as Armed Forces (Assam and Manipur) Special Powers Ordinance 1958 which subsequently was replaced by Armed Forces (Special Powers) Act 1958 (AFSPA) in September 1958. It is in force in seven States of North-East India, i.e., Assam, Manipur, Mizoram, Arunachal Pradesh, Meghalaya, Nagaland and Tripura. It was amended in 1972 to confer the power to declare an area "disturbed" to the Central government. This power was previously vested to the State government. A version of the same law was introduced in Jammu and Kashmir in 1990. Under this Act:

> "Any commissioned officer, warrant officer, non-commissioned officer or any other person of equivalent rank in the armed forces may, in a disturbed area, (a) if he is of opinion that it is necessary so to do for the maintenance of public order, after giving such due warning as he may consider necessary, fire upon or otherwise use force, even to the causing of death, against any person who is acting in contravention of any law or order for the time being in force in the disturbed area prohibiting the assembly of five or more persons or the carrying of weapons or of things capable of being used as weapons or of firearms, ammunition or explosive substances."

The allegations of the misuse of "special powers" by armed forces have been rampant, and hence the local residents of North-East and Kashmir have been demanding its withdrawal. Judicial review of the Act used to be terribly slow. It is difficult to punish soldiers who have violated the "special powers" because the State governments cannot act against them. The local residents and human rights groups alleged that the Act is counterproductive and only accentuated a vicious cycle of violence. They called it a "draconian law" which created a vicious cycle of violence. Instead of addressing the problem of insurgency it has become the major cause behind its perpetuation and growth (Navlakha, 2004: 4235). Recently, the Supreme Court had issued notices to Central and Manipur governments on a petition filed by Extrajudicial Execution Victim Families Association Manipur. It sought a probe into cases of extra-judicial killings in the State. The petitioner placed before the Court details of 62 cases from 2007 to 2012 and also a list of 1,528 cases of extra-judicial executions carried out by the security forces since 1979. It said the large majority of the victims were killed in custody and in cold blood.[2] The petition stated, "this is a frightening situation that should shock the conscience of the entire nation ... During the last decade, the torture and killings in Manipur of innocent civilians with no criminal records whatsoever, who are later on conveniently labelled as militants, has been widely covered in the print media and television. In this way, it would appear to the people of Manipur that the Constitution and the Criminal Procedure Code have ceased to operate within the boundaries of this State."

In the words of Chasie and Hazarika (2009: 60) "AFSPA was the barest, the most controversial, and also the most powerful legislation drawn up by lawmakers in Delhi to crush the first armed and political challenge to independent India's territorial and political integrity. It also authorised the first use of the Army in India against a major political uprising". Vashum (2005: 96) also stated that "In the past decades, especially, beginning from about the mid-1950s, India was charged for having committed many human rights violations on the Nagas. But all this happened without being known to the outside world, either because it was deliberate on the part of the Government of India or because of the inaccessibility of the region and backwardness in many respects, specifically, in the media world. Except for few cases of human rights violations being given some justice under the judicial system of India, many cases were unattended to."

Interestingly in 1997, the Supreme Court of India also upheld the constitutional validity of this Act. The Court ruled that the powers given to the Army were not arbitrary or unreasonable and concluded that "the Central Act does not displace the civil power of the State by the armed forces of the Union and it only provides for deployment of armed forces of the Union in aid of the civil power. The Central Act cannot be regarded as a colourable legislation or a fraud on the Constitution. It is not a measure intended to achieve the same result as contemplated by a Proclamation of Emergency under Article 352 or a proclamation under Article 356 of the Constitution."[3] State and Army officials alleged that this Act is necessary to protect the State against what are known as internal disturbances, uphold the integrity of the nation, fight terrorism and insurgency and protect sensitive border areas. Army officials also cited the need to protect the morale and integrity of the Army as reason not to scrutinise allegations against army personnel. Also, State and army officials were of the view that it cannot be withdrawn since the situation is disturbing in North-East. One senior security official predicted a grim scenario if it is repealed from Manipur. He felt that the withdrawal of the Act from Manipur would cause a chain reaction in other States where the Act has been in force. The security forces would be reluctant to carry out counter-insurgency operations without proper legal protection and hence the repeal would demoralise the soldiers. Whenever any offensive action was taken by armed forces, the armed groups would instigate the people and local authorities to initiate legal cases against armed forces. Justice would then be biased under the influence of militants. The militants would get an upper hand and may be difficult to contain. The civil administration would be overrun by the militants and there would be chaos all around (Kamboj, 2004: 616-620). Likewise, the then Indian Army Chief, General V. K. Singh stated that the demand for the removal of AFSPA in Jammu and Kashmir was made for narrow political gains and emphasised that soldiers operating in a hostile environment need legal protection to ensure that they perform their tasks efficiently (*Indian Express, June* 26, 2010). The then Indian Air Chief P. V. Naik also advocated that a soldier fighting anywhere at the request of government must have legal protection otherwise he would be left inefficient to complete the job in which either the Central or the State government has interest in" (*Daily Excelsior, October* 5, 2010).

On the other hand, in order to protect themselves from excesses of armed forces the local residents of North-East and Kashmir have come forward to defend their basic human rights. Their efforts led to the emergence of different civil society groups. Some of them such as Meira Paibis, Naga Mothers' Association and NPMHR (Naga People's Movement for Human Rights) came into existence in the 1970s. Others such as Apunba Lup of Manipur came into existence in response to specific incident.

The Meira Paibis came into existence to defend the men-folk from harassment by security forces (Devi, 2008: 105) and pleaded for human rights (Parratt and Parratt, 2001: 905-919). They also extensively campaign against alcoholism and substance of abuse. The Meira Paibi has their presence felt in villages and towns of the State. The tussle between volunteers of Meira Paibi and security forces has become a routine matter in the State. Other notable women's groups are Naga Mothers' Association[4] and Naga Women's Union, Manipur. The former with the slogan "Shed No More Blood" has been actively involved in peace-building activities, eradication of social evil and exploitation in Manipur and Nagaland, respectively.

Among the Human Rights groups the NPMHR is notable. It was formed "in response to the Naga peoples long felt need for an organized movement to further their human rights which had been systematically abused by the Indian State." It has served as a platform to work towards achieving respect for, protection of and promotion of the rights of the Naga people and others. It has consistently highlighted and exposed violation of rights perpetrated by the Indian State against the ordinary citizens.

The campaign initiated by Meira Paibi, NPMHR and the like was taken up at another level by Apunba Lup, a conglomeration of groups campaigning against Armed Forces (Special Powers) Act. It was formed following the alleged rape and murder of Thangjam Manorama Devi, a young lady, by Assam Rifles soldiers in July 2004 in Manipur. She was allegedly first taken into their custody, raped and her bullet-ridden body was found near her home the next day. The incident triggered a protest in the State. On 11th July, 2004, a dozen of women demonstrated naked in front of the Kangla Fort, located in Imphal, which was at that time the base camp of Assam Rifles, to protest the death of Manorama. They shouted "Indian Army, rape us too".

Earlier Irom Sharmila Devi, another young lady, had began her fast unto death on 2nd November, 2000 following the killing of ten innocent civilians at Malom, near Imphal International airport, by security forces following an explosion. Since then, she has been demanding the repeal of Armed Forces (Special Powers) Act. She is now kept alive by forced feeding. Arrested for attempting to commit suicide, she was confined inside a room in a government hospital in Imphal, closely guarded by armed security forces, and force-fed through a tube attached to her nose. Every year she was officially freed and immediately rearrested on the same charge.

After months of strikes following the killing of Thangjam Manorama Devi, the Prime Minister Dr. Manmohan Singh had visited Imphal in November 2004 to persuade the people for calm. Prior to the visit, his government had appointed a five-man Committee to review the Armed Forces (Special Powers) Act under the chairmanship of B.P. Jeevan Reddy, a retired Judge of Supreme Court. The leaders of Apunba Lup also met Dr. Singh in Imphal in which he promised to consider replacing the Act with "a more humane law that will address both the concerns of national security and the rights of citizens." The Prime Minister also announced the shifting of Assam Rifles from the historic Kangla Fort in Imphal to a new location. In order to pacify the agitators, the State government also withdrew the "disturbed area" status from Imphal Municipal limit, to render Armed Forces (Special Powers) Act ineffective there. This action failed to assuage the public anger, but succeeded in appeasing the leaders of Apunba Lup.

About a year later, the five-man Committee submitted a report to the Union Ministry of Home Affairs in which it sought to balance the views of security forces and different sections of the society. Unfortunately, the Jeevan Reddy Committee report has also not been made public, the contents were leaked, and it is now known that the committee recommended repeal of the AFSPA. The report, however, remains with the cabinet in New Delhi for consideration, and no action has been taken (Human Rights Watch 2008). The Committee felt that it is a "symbol of oppression (and) instrument of high-handedness" and suggested the strengthening of Unlawful Activities Prevention Act 1967 that applies to the rest of the country. The Committee rejected the Army's arguments on why the Act should be continued and even said that while the Supreme Court may have upheld the constitutional validity of this law, it "is not an endorsement of the desirability or advisability of the Act." It also called for greater accountability for acts committed by Army where it is deployed to fight terrorism. The report of the Committee stated thus:

> "Keeping in view the material placed before us and the impressions gathered by the Committee during the course of its visits and hearings held within and outside the North-Eastern States, the Committee is of the firm view that: (a) The Armed Forces (Special Powers) Act 1958 should be repealed. Therefore, recommending the continuation of the present Act, with or without amendments, does not arise. The Act is too sketchy, too bald and quite inadequate in several particulars. It is true that the Hon'ble Supreme Court has upheld its constitutional validity but that circumstance is not an endorsement of the desirability or advisability of the Act ... The Committee is also of the firm view that it would be more appropriate to recommend insertion of appropriate provisions in the Unlawful Activities (Prevention) Act 1967 (as amended in the year 2004) ..."

These recommendations were considered to have the potential to undermine the security of the country and hence the Central government had decided to remain silent amidst raising human rights concerns. Differences have also reportedly cropped up within the government. For instance, at one point of time the Union Home Ministry was ready to recommend the lifting of this Act from Jammu and Kashmir. The move was, however, strongly opposed by the Union Ministry of Defence.

Unlike the Central forces, the local police do not fall under Armed Forces (Special Powers) Act, but they are highly notorious. There are reports of extra-judicial killings by them. To the local residents both Central forces and local police are involved in human rights violations. For instance, on 23 July, 2009, a young man named, Chongkham Sanjit, was shot dead by the police in the heart of Imphal city. A pregnant woman was also killed in the cross-fire. The police claimed that – "Sanjit, an alleged former insurgent, was cornered near a shop and was asked to surrender. Instead, he fired at the police. As a result, the police retaliated.

The police also claimed that a pistol was recovered from him." The police version was soon proved wrong by a photographer who clandestinely filmed the incident. The photographs, first published by *Tehelka*, an investigative newsmagazine, clearly indicated that Sanjit was standing calmly as the police frisked him. He was escorted inside a shop and shot him at point-blank. The dead body was brought out.

The killing led to a wave of protests. People defied curfew. The movement spearheaded by Apunba Lup included public meeting; *bandhs* (strikes), burning of effigies of politicians, poster campaign and boycott of elected representatives. The agitators also demanded the resignation of Manipur Chief Minister, life imprisonment of the culprits, action against police officers who tried to protect the culprits and release of Apunba Lup volunteers. The movement paralysed normal life for many days. The government also imposed curfew in Imphal from time to time and the agitating leaders were taken into their custody to prevent the situation from going out of hand. In an attempt to appease the agitators the State government had even ordered a magisterial enquiry and suspended the policemen involved in the fake encounter. These actions failed to pacify the agitators. The agitation intensified, on September 9, 2009, the All Manipur Students Union called for the boycott of classes. As a result most educational institutions were virtually shut down for about four months till January 8, 2010. The classes were resumed after the State government assured to hand over the case to the Central Bureau of Investigation. Like any other inquiries in the past the people of the State are clueless about the progress of this inquiry.

The divide between the State and the people in Manipur has been so wide that the local residents have started protesting against the government's decision to deploy its police force or Central forces in their localities. This is because the local residents never trust the security forces and hence they are not welcome. Recently, several local organisations protested against the deployment of police commandos at Moreh, the border town. They shouted "Commando, No Thanks", "We Prefer Peace", "We Do not Need Commando in Moreh", "Mr Ibobi, Do not disturb peace in Moreh", "Go Back Commando", "We have sufficient security in Moreh" and so on. Senior police officials were rushed to the town to pacify the agitators. The local residents must have thought that peace in the border town would be disturbed once police commandos were deployed. They were also worried of the likely misuse of powers by the police commandos.

Community's Stand and Support

By and large, the human rights movement in North-East India in general and Manipur in particular, have been democratic, although State and its officials often labelled them as instigated by armed groups. This movement is of fairly recent origin. It has gradually transformed from an unorganized into an organised one. Few incidents had played key role in influencing the direction of this movement. These included: (1) The killing of ten civilians near Imphal International airport in 2000 by security forces and subsequent fast unto death by Irom Sharmila Devi; (2) Student leader Mr. Pebam Chitaranjan's self immolation against the Centre's attempt to divide Manipur in 2001; (3) The alleged rape and murder of Thangjam Manorama Devi by Assam Rifles soldiers in 2004; and (4) The killing of Chongkham Sanjit in 2009 by the police in Imphal in a fake encounter.

One of the issues that united the local residents of North-East India is their movement for upholding human rights. This is happening despite the existing political divisions among the people. In States like Manipur the human rights movement is supported by all sections of the people despite their political differences.

This movement is no more confined to North-East India alone. Several civil society groups and individuals in different parts of India and abroad have expressed their solidarity to the suffering of the people of this region. Protest rallies against Armed Forces (Special Powers) Act were regularly held in various cities and towns of the country. Several noted individuals including Aruna Roy, Medha Patekar and Niketu Iralu have extended their support to the movement. The "Save Sharmila Solidarity Campaign" led by Medha Patekar has been actively campaigning against human rights violations in the region. In one of its programmes about twenty volunteers undertook a 4500 km long march covering 11 States from Srinagar to Imphal in 2011 to express solidarity with Irom Sharmila Devi. They covered cities like Jammu, Ludhiana, New Delhi, Kanpur, Lucknow, Varanasi, Ranchi, Patna, Kolkata and Guwahati, with the final destination being Imphal. In course of this long march, public meetings, distribution of pamphlets, candle light vigils, street plays and school and college meetings were held in association with various local organisations. It is, therefore, appropriate to say that the struggle for the repeal of such a repressive Act is not the battle of the Manipuris alone; it is a struggle that every Indian must actively support (*Economic and Political Weekly*, October 21, 2006).

Beyond India, organisations such as United Nations Human Rights

Commission and Amnesty International have come down heavily on the Government of India for the brutality let loose under such controversial law. Several others also speak of arbitrary powers aiding the repression of the people trapped by this law. The Amnesty International has urged the government to recognise the need to repeal the law as it did for the Prevention of Terrorism Act.[5] The seventh national conference of autonomous women's movements in Kolkata in September 2006 endorsed the demand for repeal of Armed Forces (Special Powers) Act, signed by 120 women's organisations. Recently, an official of United Nations stated that such law had no role to play in a democracy. "The AFSPA in effect allows the State to override rights in the disturbed areas in a much [more] intrusive way than would be the case under a State of emergency, since the right to life is in effect suspended, and this is done without the safeguards applicable to states of emergency," Christof Heyns, the UN Special Rapporteur on Extrajudicial, Summary or Arbitrary Executions told reporters in New Delhi on 31 March, 2012. Heyns further stated that "The repeal of this law will not only bring domestic law more in line with international standards, but also send out a powerful message that instead of a military approach the government is committed to respect for the right to life of all people of the country." While Heyns visited Jammu and Kashmir, he was not allowed to visit Manipur but met some people from there in Assam.[6]

Conclusion

North-East India has a strong civil society base, active in diverse fields. Most of them have worked at the grass root level with little external interference. When the armed conflict escalated in the region civil society came forward to mitigate some of the consequences of violence by supporting individuals under threat, settlement of disputes and by monitoring the excesses of the State as well as the non-State actors. Since then the relationship between civil society and State has been tense, and successive governments were suspicious of civil society viewing them as potential agents of armed groups.

Nonetheless, despite the political divide, some of civil society groups have generated the support of cross-community on human rights and mobilised public opinion against violence by the State. But they were not able to sustain interest among the general population for long. They were motivated primarily by need to do something rather than by a clear political objective. It is often said that the civil society protection functions has been one sided—guarding against the abuses from the State and not militants. Further, their protective function has limited because most residents of remote areas are almost untouched.

The complex composition of North-East society has produced many social and interest-based groups, with differentiation along ethnic lines. And hence cooperation among them has been limited. However, there are some initiatives for bringing all people together. In fact, the civil society is part of society and hence reflects its characteristics. In conflict areas, high emotional salience is attached to group identity. In most cases, in-group socialization reinforces members' shared identity at the expense of developing cross-ethnic ties. Membership in single-identity groups exacerbates differences between groups' insiders and outsiders while intensifying intergroup competition and conflict (Paffenholz, *et al.*, 2011: 414). The civil society groups have started drawing on a variety of existing domestic and international networks. Yet, they are mostly funded locally. The movement is fragmented and attempts to build coalitions or to form umbrella organisations have not been sustained.

In summary, decades of armed conflict resulted in the brutalization of society as violence, emergency legislation and limits on freedom of association and expression became part of everyday life. This clearly impinged on the development of civil society. The main impediment to civil society activity has been repression by the State and the armed groups. The movement against Armed Forces (Special Powers) Act has not been fully organised but spontaneous following a chain of events that rocked Manipur. However, the armed forces remain the main hurdle to the withdrawal of the controversial law despite the political leadership's willingness to address the genuine concern of the suffering people. The region's location, surrounded by not so friendly nations, has further strengthened the arguments of those who are in favour of its continuation. Even if the situation improves in Manipur or elsewhere in the region this law may not get out easily in view of the region's strategic location far away from the mainland of the country. As a result the peaceful States like Mizoram and Meghalaya continued to have this law. If centre really respects the international *Border States* including Manipur and develop economically and infrastructural condition as China has done at the Arunachal border, the present sense insecurity that has been felt by the Centre may not arise.

NOTES

1. Media reports stated that about 45,000 personnel of central forces such as Army, Assam Rifles, CRPF and BSF were deployed in Manipur. The number will be more if the local police, Manipur Rifles, etc., were included. (See 'One central security personnel for every 60 citizens in the State', *Imphal Free Press*, 20 January 2005, p. 1).
2. Notice to Centre, Manipur on extra-judicial killings, *The Hindu*, 3 October 2012.
3. Supreme Court of India on Armed Forces (Special Powers) Act 1958, (available at http://www.upr-info.org/IMG/pdf/COHR_IND_UPR_S1_2008anx_Annex_XXIII_Supreme_Court_ruling_on_AFSPA.pdf (accessed on 22 July 2012).
4. The Naga Mothers Association came into being in 1984 at Kohima. Its objectives include upholding womanhood, human values and rights; serving as a channel of communication for Naga women's mutual interest and welfare; encouraging human development by educating the masses for responsible and wholesome living; and recreating interest in the traditional socio-cultural values of the Nagas and maintaining their self-identity and sense of self-reliance.
5. The United Progressive Alliance which came to power in May 2004 repealed POTA after recognizing "concerns with the manner in which POTA had been grossly misused." Similar concerns exist with regard to the AFSPA.
6. Aarti Dhar, U.N. asks India to repeal AFSPA, *The Hindu*, New Delhi, 31 March, 2012.

REFERENCES

Chasie, Charles and Sanjoy Hazarika (2009): *The State Strikes Back: India and the Naga Insurgency*, (Policy Studies 52), New York: East-West Centre.

Devi, Ksh. Bimola (2008): *Society and Politics in Manipur*, In A. K. Ray and S. Chakravorty (eds.), *Society, Politics and Development in North-East India*, pp. 99-107, New Delhi: Concept Publishing Company.

Economic and Political Weekly (2006): Mockery of Law, *Economic and Political Weekly*, 41(42) (Oct. 21-27), p. 4392.

Government of India (2005): *Report of the Committee to Review the Armed Forces (Special Powers) Act* 1958, New Delhi: Ministry of Home Affairs.

Human Rights Watch (2008). *These Fellows Must Be Eliminated: Relentless Violence and Impunity in Manipur*. Human Rights Watch, New York.

Knight, Jack (1992): *Institutions and Social Conflict*, New York: Cambridge University Press.

Kamboj, Anil (2004): *Manipur and Armed Forces (Special Powers) Act 1958*, Strategic Analysis, 28(4): 616-620.

Navlakha, Gautam (2004): *Securing India: Treating Unlikely as Likely*, Economic and Political Weekly, 39(38) (Sep. 18-24), pp. 4235-4239.

Paffenholz, Thania *et al.*, (2011): *Enabling and Disenabling Factors for Civil Society Peacebuilding*. In Thania Paffenholz (ed.) *Civil Society and Peacebuilding: A Critical Assessment*, Colorado: Lynne Rienner Publishers, Inc., pp. 405-424.

Parratt, Saroj N. Arambam and John Parratt (2001): *The Second 'Women's War' and the Emergence of Democratic Government in Manipur*. Modern Asian Studies, 35(4), pp. 905-919.

Ramanathan, Usha (2001): *Human Rights in India: A Mapping*. Nairobi: International Environmental Law Research Centre.

Rammohan, E. N. (2002): *Blue Print for Counterinsurgency in Manipur*. In KPS Gill (ed.), *Faultlines – Writing on Conflict and Resolution*, Volume 12, May, pp. 1–22.

Rawls, John (1999): *A Theory of Justice*. Oxford: Oxford University Press.

Singh, M. Amarjeet (2012): *The Naga Conflict*. NIAS Backgrounder, Bangalore: National Institute of Advanced Studies.

Singh, M. Amarjeet (2011): *Armed Conflict in Manipur: The Case of UNLF*. In Anant, Arpita (ed.) *Non-State Armed Groups in South Asia: A Preliminary Structured Focused Comparison*, New Delhi: Pentagon Security International, pp. 65-75.

Spurk, Christoph (2011): *Understanding Civil Society*. In Thania Paffenholz (ed.) *Civil Society and Peacebuilding: A Critical Assessment*, Colorado: Lynne Rienner Publishers, Inc.

Vashum, R. (2005): *Nagas' Right to Self-Determination*, New Delhi: Mittal Publications.

7

Educational Development in the Midst of Conflict in Manipur: A Theoretical Perspective

Komol Singha and *Achintya Mahapatra*

Introduction

Education is the cornerstone of socio-economic and cultural development of a society/country, and its importance on human development, economic growth, etc., is analysed extensively in the seminal works of T.W. Schultz since early 1960s (Singha, *et al.*, 2012). Education has emerged as the most important single input in promoting human resource development, achieving rapid economic development and technological progress, creating a social order, based on the virtues of freedom, social justice and equal opportunities (Singha, 2010; Reddy, 2008; Gill, *et al.*, 2005). Also, it plays a vital role in the present world, for not only raising the standard of living but also as a mechanism to prevent conflict situation.

On the other side, conflicts and violence have concurrently rife with an increase in educational attainment in all levels and also affects lives on economic (such as hunger or poverty or joblessness), social (like deprived or homeless or widow) political and psychological aspects (Singha, *et al.*, 2012). However, detail study on the relationship between conflict and education is a very recent phenomenon and limited research has been done on the issue (Gates and Strand, 2012). In 2007, Brendan O'Malley's work, '*Education under Attack*' published by *United Nations Educational Scientific and Cultural Organization* (UNESCO) is considered as the first ever detail study of its kind (UNESCO, 2010a), and till today, the role of education on conflict resolution is highly debated upon, among the academia. Also the analysis of "conflict in fragile states" has gained significant attention within the community of academia and policy makers in the recent past.

With the notions portrayed above, the present study tries to assess educational development status in the midst of conflict and violence in Manipur, one of the most north-eastern States of India. An assessment is also made if the growth of education curtails conflict or conflict restrains educational development. The type of conflict that affects educational growth on the one hand and the type of education that curtails conflict on the other hand, if any, are also discussed in this chapter.

To achieve the above mentioned objectives, both primary and secondary data were employed. The primary data were randomly collected in the month of June-July 2012, from fifty-two *Manipuri students* of Manipur studying in Bangalore (India). The secondary data were collected from published sources like Directorate of Economics and Statistics, Registrar General and Census Commissioner, National Sample Survey Organisation, etc. The collected data have been processed and presented by employing simple statistical methods like correlation, frequency distribution and percentage change over time, etc. Due to some constraints and nature of data available with us, the present study could not apply advanced econometric models like causal analysis, panel data analysis, etc. Therefore, some approximation was bound to be made and the study was confined on to simple growth and structure of education and conflict in the State.

Conceptual Framework

Conflicts are regarded as key catalysts for social change (Dupuy, 2008). Their productive transformation towards social progress can, as a rule, only succeed when the particular ability of individuals and collectives to manage and resolve conflicts peacefully and constructively, in addition to the reliability of the corresponding societal, institutional and legal framework conditions (Seitz, 2004). Resolving conflict and sustainable dialogue in a society can be achieved after certain level of educational development, when the society is well convinced, aware of the consequences of war and conflict (UNESCO, 2011; 2010a; 2010b; Amamio, 2004).

Smith (2010) pointed that education may be a driver of conflict by fuelling grievances, stereotypes, xenophobia and other antagonisms but can also be a way of contributing to conflict transformation and peace building. Education can play the role of preventive measure during peaceful situations, protective during violent conflict situation and social transformative in a situation where peace processes are underway. Violent conflict free situation requires teaching children peaceful approaches to conflict resolution, reducing poverty level, lowering economic inequality and good governance.

According to Mitchell (2006), conflict is a necessary and inevitable dynamic in all human relationships. However, education gives awareness and opens mind and expands our horizon. Education spreads not only awareness but also informs us about our rights and the services that we can access. It also enables us to understand our duties as a citizen and encourages us to follow them. Though education creates some sort of conflicts and misunderstandings in the initial stage, it controls and resolves conflicts at the end as the educational level increases and reaches a certain level in the society (Dupuy, 2008; Brahm, 2003). In the process, it looks like an inverted U shaped, as provided in Fig. 7.1.

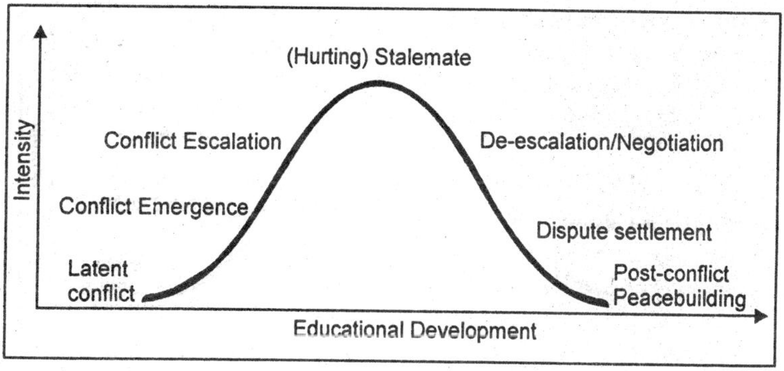

Fig. 7.1: Conflict Pyramid with the Growth of Education

Source: Modified from Brahm (2003).

When and how fast the peak point of conflict (Stalemate, as given by Figure 7.1) will reach and how long it will remain in the state of stalemate, is determined by the institutional effort, level of education and enlightenment (Singha, *et al.*, 2012; Brahm, 2003). In this context, the study reports of UNESCO have recommended for peace and quality education of children for peaceful world (UNESCO, 2011; 2010a; 2010b). Similar recommendation was also given by many scholars, viz., Kotite (2012); Burde, *et al.*, (2011); Agbor (2011); Collier (2004); Smith and

Vaux (2003); Bush and Saltarelli (2000); Tyack and Hansot (1981) and others. Therefore, conflict and violence that we are confronting at present will definitely come down after a certain level of education and development.

Brief Literature of the Study

Conflict, violence and social upheaval have been one of the greatest threats to mankind since the down of civilization (Amamio, 2004). Poorest communities, children and the educational sector are among the most severely affected by conflicts, especially in the developing countries (UNESCO, 2010b; Boyden, *et al.*, 2002). Despite a number of affirmative actions, conflict resolution programmes, rehabilitation works done by *UNESCO*, the United Nations Children's Fund (UNICEF) and other agencies to resolve conflict in the world and their anticipation for a peaceful world after the Cold War or at least halving the conflict incidence by 2015 (Collier, 2004), has been shattered by ever increasing conflicts in the world, especially the Muslim nations (Dupuy, 2008; Amamio, 2004). Several new threats in varied forms have emerged in the world in the recent past. According to Yilmaz (2008), most of these conflicts (almost 90%) are intra-national conflicts, occurring within the borders of States primarily ethnically-driven over self-determination, succession or political dominance.

As for the study of nexus between education and conflict, many scholars like Amamio (2004); Seitz (2004); Boyden, *et al.* (2002); Bush and Saltarelli (2000); and others have opined that initially education often leads to highly complex conflict situations in the world, and it is proved by ever growing spurt of conflicts across the globe. According to Bush and Saltarelli (2000), education can be a part of the problem not the solution, because it serves to divide and antagonize groups both intentionally and unintentionally. The study by Seitz (2004) explored that the formal education system contributes to exacerbating and escalating societal conflicts in particular when it produces and reproduces socio-economic disparities and brings about social marginalization or deprivation or promotes the teaching of identity and citizenship concepts which deny the cultural plurality of society and which then lead to intolerance towards others. Also, the study of Boyden, *et al.* (2002), found that *Jihadi Terrorism* all over the world is an outcome of the greater effort made by the *Madrassa* system of education. For instance, the very system of education in the North-West Frontier Province of Pakistan provides an example of education used for the very particular, ideological ends that may have strong implications for the reinforcement of conflict (*ibid.*, p. 54).

In a slightly different manner, analysis made by Smith and Vaux (2003) found that education can be a part of the problem as well as part of the solution. Therefore, it is a factor to be considered in the strategic assessment of conflict. However, in the findings of Bird (2006), the access to formal schooling may often be jeopardised by the conflicts. On the other hand, Patricia (2010) found that a relatively minor shock to educational access can lead to significant and long-lasting detrimental effects on individual human capital formation in terms of educational attainment, health outcomes and labour market opportunities. He further established that general civil wars have a negative impact on educational attainment. It affects education, particularly the children and girls. They are more vulnerable in violent conflict and the tendency to drop out from school is relatively higher than the boys.

Many studies have pointed out that children are used as civilian shields to protect military forces or as army pack animals. They are forced to become soldiers, army slaves or prostitutes under the threat of violence (Levy and Parker, 2000). In the study by Mann (1987), it was found that there is an increasing use of children in armed conflicts, particularly in Indo-China during the 1960s. The wars in Indo-China and elsewhere have seen a growing number of children used in a variety of capacities. Therefore, parents all over the world live in web of fear that their children will be recruited by the forces—state or rebel group. For instance, many children have been recruited by the *Liberation Tigers of Tamil Eelam* (LTTE) in Sri Lanka (Boyden, *et al.*, 2002); on their way to or at school, in Somali (Richards and Bekele, 2011). Moreover, the examination of the situation of children affected by armed conflicts, to date, has been little reported on (Boyden, *et al.*, 2002).. Theorics of causality that fail to account for this complexity obscure understanding of the many ways in which young people and conflict may be linked (Boyden, 2006).

On the other side, the study by Agbor (2011) with the help of panel data, using thirty-one African countries, found that education *per se* has no significant influence on the frequency of intra-State conflicts happening in the continent; but potentially reduces the frequency of conflicts in Africa. Similarly, the panel data study result by Gates and Strand (2012) could not find any effect of conflict on education levels, none of their estimate was found to be statistically significant. Although some papers have tried to estimate a linkage between educational outcomes and violence through regression analysis, no clear causal direction of the two could be established (Lindquist, 2012) and no formal model has been developed yet (Boyden, 2006; Barrera and Ibenez, 2004). Based on the fieldwork conducted in three countries of Guatemala, Nepal and Liberia, Dupuy (2008) highlighted that education is only a part of the peace-building process, and it cannot by itself resolve the root causes of a conflict. However, there are number of ways in which education is contributing to building the conditions for long-term, positive peace in those countries.

On the flip side, Agbor (2011) using an aggregated measure of all intra-State major episodes of political violence obtained from the Political Instability Task Force (PITF) as proxy for conflict, and controlling some other variables; explored that education effectively reduces the likelihood of intra-State conflicts in Africa. Also, using a cross-sectional survey in Colombia, Brrera and Ibenez (2004) found that the school enrolment decreases homicide rates rise in Colombian municipalities. Similarly, one of the seminal works on the issue by UNESCO explored that education can help in banishing prejudices and tensions that exist, especially between communities, and possibly even prevent any such conflict in the future (Sinclair, 2002). Collier and Hoeffler (2002) also recommended that a high enrolment rate of male in secondary school can reduce conflict risk to a great extent.

Further, at the end, almost all the scholars who explored education as a creator of conflict have come to a common consensus that if education is nurtured properly, it will empower people to have the ability, to form opinions and act on issues concerning societal development (Amamio, 2004). In reality, education goes beyond the provision of a mere programme for peace; rather it reflects the cumulative benefits of the provision of good quality education. These include the conflict-dampening impact of educational opportunity, the promotion of linguistic tolerance, the nurturing of ethnic tolerance, etc. (Bush and Saltarelli, 2000).

Conflict and Education in Manipur

Manipur is one of the most North-Eastern States of India, bordering Myanmar (Burma) in the east, and three Indian States – Nagaland in the north, Assam in the west and Mizoram in the south. Manipur is endowed with rich natural resources and has a long history of geo-political development in the South-East Asia (Tensuba, 1993). Unfortunately, at present, the State is passing through different social turmoil, ethnic violence and social upheavals, etc., ranging from insurgency for secession to the movement for greater autonomy, from terrorism to ethnic clashes and the fight over resources (Sharma, 2011; Bohlken and Sergenti, 2010; Mentschel, 2007). Often, frequent eruption of violence and conflict that arises from the different ethnic communities in search of and to assert their identities, disturb educational environment in the State. For instance, most educational institutions in Manipur, especially Imphal city, were virtually shut down for about four months from September 9 to January 8, 2010 due to the agitation initiated by All Manipur Students Union, against the custodial killing of Mr. Sanjit.

Conflict in Manipur

This chapter looks into the relationship between education and conflict in Manipur, causes of conflict is not studied, but a brief note on the type and structure of conflict in the State is analysed. Broadly, the type of conflict that have been haunting the State can be divided into two – (1) *Internal conflict* which includes inter-community and intra community conflict for resource dominance, power and identity reconciliation, (2) Conflict between *state and society*, which implies conflict between insurgent groups and state for secession or sovereignty of Manipur. Both the types of conflict affect greatly normal life and educational environment in the State.

Internal Conflict: Internal conflict in this chapter refers to the conflicts that arise within and among the ethnic groups in the State. The State of Manipur is a home to thirty-three recognised (33 tribes) and many other non-recognised tribes, besides *Meitei* (commonly known as Manipuri), the dominant community living in the valley districts of the State. As a consequence of dominance over economic and political power by the Meiteis for long, in Manipur, after statehood in 1972, the processes of polarisation of different tribes into two broader groups – as Naga and Kuki, have been intensified in the State, for economic and political interests of the groups (Singha, 2012). A number of internal conflicts among the ethnic communities have increased significantly in the recent past, especially since 1980s in search of identity, economic and political power. In a seminal work by Collier and Hoeffler (2002) have also warned that the ethnic polarization of community (dominance of one group makes up 45 per cent and more population) is likely to experience more conflict. Without going into the causes of conflict, some impact of internal conflicts in Manipur since 1990s is given in Table 7.1.

Table 7.1: Internal Conflict and Population Displacement in Manipur

Year of Conflict (Inter- and Intra-Community)	*Conflict between the Communities*	*Approx. Population Displaced*	*% of the total Population Displaced**
1992	Kuki–Naga ethnic	11,000	2.6
1993-1997	Kuki–Zomi conflict	15,000	5.8
-do-	Thadou–Paite conflict	7500	3.5
-do-	Meitei–Pangal (Meitei Muslim)	1000	1.0
2001	Naga Ceasefire Extension	7000	2.4
Total	—	**41,500**	**3.1**

Note: * Share of total population of the respective ethnic community displaced by Conflict

Source: Kumar, *et al.* (2011) and Author's Estimation based on 1991 population Census.

From Table 7.1 we can find that almost 42 thousand people (against 1800 thousand population in 1991) have been displaced by different ethnic conflicts in Manipur in 1990s. It is estimated that almost 2.3 per cent of the State's total population was displaced by ethnic violence in 1990s. However, if we estimate communities who actually were involved in the conflict, the share of population displaced by internal or ethnic conflicts turns out to be 3.1 per cent. Of which, first three incidents (Kuki-Naga, Kuki-Zomi, Thadou-Paite conflicts) were purely in the thinly populated tribal/hill districts. According to Hussain and Phanjoubam (2007), altogether 800 people were killed, 480 wounded and 5,713 families displaced during the bloody Kuki-Naga conflict in the 1990s. In 1997, in the Kuki-Paite clash, altogether 162 people were killed, 93 injured, 71 were kidnapped and 3,521 houses were burnt. There are a number of other indirect effects of internal conflict as well, that leads to displacement of the many people in the State. In the study by Srikanth and Ngaihte (2011), education contributed to the birth of educated elite that played an important role in giving shape to ethnic identity of the respective communities, and in turn it led to ethnic movement.

Conflict between State and Society: Here, the conflict is directed against the State by the armed groups. The Indian army, including the Assam Rifles, the Border Security Force, the Central Reserve Police Force and the Manipur Police, are currently engaged in fighting against armed rebels in Manipur. With the growth of separatist movement, Manipur was declared as a 'disturbed area' in 1980 and subsequently the Armed

Forces (Special Powers) Act 1958 was imposed (Harriss, 2002). There are allegations of the very Act (AFSPA) being misused by the members of the State forces, as the Act allows them to kill anybody in mere suspicion of anti-national. Also, the Act permits/allows even the lowest rank of security force (e.g., Sepoy) to kill anybody on a mere suspect of anti-national, and no complaint can be made against them. Besides killing, there have been number of cases of enforced disappearances of young children by the State forces (Manoharan, 2012). As mentioned above, some of the consequences of the conflict between State and society is given in Table 7.2.

Table 7.2: Number of Insurgency related to Fatalities in Manipur

Year	*Civilian*	*Security*	*Terrorist*	*Total*	*% to NER#*	*Total NER*	*% to India#*
2000	93	51	102	246	18	1367	5
2001	70	25	161	256	24	1067	4
2002	36	53	101	190	26	731	5
2003	27	23	148	198	22	900	5
2004	40	41	127	208	34	612	8
2005	138	50	143	331	46	720	10
2006	107	37	141	285	45	633	10
2007	150	40	218	408	39	1046	16
2008	131	13	341	485	46	1054	19
2009	77	18	321	416	49	849	19
2010	26	8	104	138	43	321	7
2011	25	10	30	65	26	250	6

Note: #Authors' Estimation from SATP (2012); NER = North-Eastern Region.

Source: South Asia Terrorism Portal (2012).

Table 7.2 shows that the volume of violence related fatalities and the share of State's fatalities to total eight North-Eastern Region[1] and national level. About 34 per cent of the region's total fatalities have been from by Manipur in the last ten years. As a result of which, at present in Manipur, a large section of people are living in a web of insecurities which are not induced by them. Common people of the State are being caught in the cross-fire between the forces – State and insurgency groups, and ethnic groups; insurgency groups, etc.

Whether it is positive or negative, *Meitei* revivalist movement, especially the *Meetei Erol Eyek Loinasillon Apunba Lup* (MEELAL) has also created a number of conflicts and violences in the valley districts.

Its impact has been felt directly or indirectly in the hill communities as well, and reacted in many forms especially by the Naga community. For instance, the dictate of MEELAL to introduce *Meitei-Mayek* (Manipuri script) as a compulsory subject, at least in the school level in 1980s and 1990s was felt as an autocratic rule of *Meitei* (dominant community) to the hill communities in Manipur (Shimray, 2007). Consequently more than 2000 (two thousand) Nagas students from Manipur were directed by the *Naga Civil Organisations* to appear matriculation examination in the neighbouring Nagaland in 2007 (*ibid.*, p. 2).

Whatsoever the reason, the major displaced victims are the women and children, and definitely the educational environment was greatly affected. In the processes of movement and counter movements of the ethnic communities in the State, for different agendas, the common populace are being grappled between the warring groups. Table 7.3 depicts the nature and degree of *bandh* and economic blockades in Manipur. Economic blockades are called by different organisation of tribes along the National Highways (NH) passing through hill regions and the *bandhs*

Table 7.3: Bandh/Forceful Closure, Blockade and Economic Loss in Manipur

(*Rs in Crore*)

Year	Days of Bandh	Economic Loss of Bandh	Days of Economic Blockade	Economic Loss of Economic Blockade	Total Loss (3+5)	NSDP*
1	2	3	4	5	6	7
2004-05	20	111.4 (2.43)	60	130.2 (2.85)	241.6 (5.28)	4575 (100.00)
2005-06	48	306.24 (5.98)	97	236.68 (4.62)	542.92 (10.60)	5120 (100.00)
2006-07	94	642.96 (11.71)	77	201.74 (3.67)	844.7 (15.38)	5493 (100.00)
2007-08	52	382.2 (6.28)	43	122.12 (2.01)	504.32 (8.29)	6087 (100.00)
2008-09	56	442.4 (6.46)	63	178.91 (2.61)	621.31 (9.07)	6851 (100.00)
2010-11	27	229.5 (2.58)	135	415.8 (4.67)	645.3 (7.25)	8896 (100.00)

Note: * Net State Domestic Product at current 2004-05 prices; Figures in the parenthesis are the per cent of NSDP.

Source: Author's estimation from different Local Dailies.

are called by the valley organisations. On an average, 9 to 10 per cent of the State's NSDP was lost due to *bandh* and blockades in the last six years. The year 2011 recorded the highest number of days ever, to have called for economic blockades in the State (135 days of economic blockades in Mao-Imphal section of the National Highway No 39). The blockade has caused violation of human rights as this has resulted in immense suffering of the majority of the State's people mainly valley people who had to go without basic essentials for over four months in a stretch in 2011.

According to the Directorate of Statistics and Economics, Government of Manipur, in 2004-05, the State experienced 20 days State-wide blockades, and it led to a loss of Rs. 22 per head per day, totalling to a loss of Rs. 5.34 crores per day. In the same year, the State faced 60 days National Highways (NH), led to a loss of Rs. 9 per head per day totalling to a loss of Rs. 2.32 crores per day (DES, 2010). In 2005-06, the State-wide *bandh* led to a loss of Rs. 24 per head per day totalling to a loss of Rs. 6.13 crores per day and loss of Rs. 11 per head per day totalling to Rs. 2.67 crores per day for National Highway blockade. In the case of 2006-07, State-wide *bandh* led to a loss of Rs. 6.44 crores per day in the State (Singha, 2009). If not estimated accurately, the losses caused on education environment by the *bandh* and blockades in the State were not less than the economic losses mentioned above, during the same period.

Education in Manipur

In Manipur, irrespective of the persistent stirring of violence and conflict, the rate of literacy has increased substantially for both males and females across the districts or regions over the last two decades. When compared to the national trend, growth trend of literacy rate in the last two decades, particularly for the rural area is highly appreciable. Despite poor road and communication infrastructure, people of Manipur have shown great enthusiasm in acquiring education and knowledge. Also, the performance of women especially in the rural area is very significant, and is much higher than the national level (refer to Table 7.6).

Table 7.4 shows that the literacy rate in Manipur on the eve of country's independence was much lower than the national level and thereafter it has constantly increased from 13 per cent (13 literates per 100 persons) in 1951 to 80 per cent in 2011. The growth of literacy rate in the State was also much higher than that of national level. Within the

State, educational growth in rural and tribal districts has improved significantly in recent years.

Table 7.4: Literacy Rate in Manipur and India

Year	*Manipur*	*India*
1951	12.57	18.33
1961	36.04	28.30
1971	38.47	34.45
1981	49.66	43.57
1991	59.89	52.21
2001	70.53	64.84
2011	79.85	74.04

Source: GoI (2012).

In Table 7.5, despite recent conflicts in 1990s and 2000s, the hill districts, namely, Senapati, Chandel, Ukhrul, Churachandpur and Tamenglong have made better improvement than the valley districts in terms of literacy rate. However, from 1991 to 2001, the change in the literacy rate has been in the favour of valley districts like Bishnupur and Thoubal. Overall decadal change in the literacy rate was also found to be higher in the hill areas than the valley. The growth of literacy rate in hill areas is credited to the Christian Missionaries (Singha, 2010), not to the government. Compound Annual Growth Rate (CAGR) of literacy rate in 20 years from 1991-2011 in the State has turned out to be 1.45 per cent.

Table 7.5: Literacy Rates in the Districts of Manipur and its Change Rate (1981-2011)

State/district	*1981*	*1991*	*2001*	*2011*	*Change 81 to 91*	*Change 91 to 01*	*Change 01 to 11*	*CAGR 1991-11*
Senapati	36.05	46.04	50.47	75.00	9.99	4.43	24.53	2.47
Tamenglong	44.22	50.16	58.56	70.40	5.94	8.40	11.84	1.71
CC pur	54.34	58.17	74.67	84.29	3.83	16.50	9.62	1.87
Bishnupur	39.23	54.94	71.59	76.35	15.71	16.65	4.76	1.66
Thoubal	41.13	52.47	67.90	76.66	11.34	15.43	8.76	1.91
Imphal West	*	73.01	80.61	86.70	*	7.60	6.09	0.86
Imphal East	*	68.05	76.38	82.81	*	8.33	6.43	0.99
Ukhrul	49.94	62.54	68.96	81.87	12.60	6.42	12.91	1.36
Chandel	39.51	46.68	57.38	70.85	7.17	10.70	13.47	2.11
Manipur	**49.66**	**59.89**	**68.87**	**79.85**	**10.23**	**8.98**	**10.98**	**1.45**

Source: Kumar, *et al.* (2011); RGCC (2012).

Table 7.6 makes a comparison of literacy rate between males and females in the State, with all India in the last two decades. The literacy rate in rural area of Manipur went up from 64 per cent in 1993-94 to 79.1 per cent in 2009-10. While, in all India level, it was 43.5 per cent in 1993-94 and went up to 62.1 per cent in 2009-10 which is still lower than Manipur's level in 1993-94. Similarly, in urban area of Manipur, the literacy rate was 76 per cent of 1993-94 and went up marginally to 82.1 per cent in 2009-10. While for national level, it was 69 per cent in 1993-94 and went up to 78.6 per cent in 2009-10.

Table 7.6: Literacy Rate in Manipur

State/ India	*Year*	*Rural*			*Urban*		
		Male	*Female*	*Person*	*Male*	*Female*	*Person*
Manipur	2009-10	83.5	74.4	79.1	86.3	77.5	82.1
	2004-05	80.0	66.5	73.3	85.4	75.1	80.3
	1999-00	68.5	56.6	62.8	84.7	74.1	79.4
	1993-94	71.9	56.1	64.0	83.8	68.2	76.0
India	2009-10	70.5	53.2	62.1	83.5	73.4	78.6
	2004-05	63.5	44.9	54.5	80.5	69.3	75.1
	1999-00	58.5	38.5	48.6	78.2	65.6	72.0
	1993-94	54.4	32.0	43.5	75.8	61.5	69.0

Source: Different NSS Rounds

In the early nineties, about 75 per cent of the literate population of the State has studied up to middle level and the rest acquired secondary and higher education in rural areas in Manipur. However, in the national level, about 85 per cent of total literate populations have studied up to middle level and the rest about 15 per cent attained more than secondary during the same period in rural areas.

Over the years, with the increase in government expenditure on education and increase in the aspiration of formal employment, eventually the number of educated people, (secondary and above), has grown significantly touching about 38 per cent in Manipur, against the 24 per cent at the national level, in rural areas during 2009-10. Larger proportion of literate people from Manipur has attained secondary and above, against the national level. It indicates a relatively more number of educated individuals in Manipur than at the national level, especially in rural areas.

Further, from Table 7.7 we can clearly see that a larger proportion of males than females have attained secondary and above level of education in Manipur when compared to the national level. For example, during

Table 7.7: Percentage Distribution of Literate Persons by Ceneral Educational Level

State/ India	Area	Year	Male			Female			Person		
			upto primary	upto middle	secondary & above	upto primary	upto middle	secondary & above	upto primary	upto middle	secondary & above
Manipur	Rural	2009-10	30.8	26.3	42.9	39.1	29.3	31.6	34.6	27.7	37.7
		2004-05	45.1	26.8	28.1	54.1	24.8	21.1	49.1	25.9	25.0
		1999-00	39.9	28.5	31.7	50.9	26.7	22.4	44.6	27.7	27.7
		1993-94	46.5	24.8	28.8	59.7	19.8	20.5	52.2	22.7	25.2
	Urban	2009-10	26.9	17.7	55.4	28.5	24.0	47.5	27.6	20.6	51.8
		2004-05	33.8	17.6	48.6	38.9	21.3	39.8	36.2	19.3	44.5
		1999-00	31.3	18.4	50.3	36.4	23.9	39.7	33.5	20.9	45.6
		1993-94	38.4	18.4	43.2	44.6	23.2	32.3	41.2	20.5	38.3
India	Rural	2009-10	50.6	22.7	26.7	59.8	20.9	19.4	54.4	21.9	23.7
		2004-05	56.9	22.0	21.1	65.3	19.8	14.9	60.2	21.1	18.7
		1999-00	58.5	21.5	20.0	67.5	19.5	13.0	62.1	20.8	17.1
		1993-94	61.9	20.0	18.0	71.9	17.5	10.6	65.5	19.1	15.4
	Urban	2009-10	32.8	18.0	49.2	36.8	18.5	44.7	34.6	18.2	47.2
		2004-05	37.3	19.9	42.9	42.4	20.8	36.8	39.5	20.2	40.2
		1999-00	39.5	19.9	40.5	45.6	20.1	34.3	41.9	20.1	37.9
		1993-94	43.8	19.1	37.1	50.4	19.2	30.4	46.7	19.1	34.2

Note: Literates given per 1000 distribution of persons by general educational level is summed up; then each level of education is divided by the total literate in percentage term.

Source: Authors calculation different NSS rounds.

1993-94, about 32 per cent of the female against about 43 per cent of males completed secondary and above level of education in urban Manipur.

Further, the percentage of literate people of Manipur received higher education (secondary and above level of education) were far greater than the national level for both males and females particularly in rural areas. For example, about 43 per cent and 32 per cent for the males and females respectively attained secondary and above education level in Manipur, against about 27 per cent and 19 per cent for male and female respectively at the national level in rural areas during 2009-10. From Table 7.8 we can see decadal growth rate of school enrolment at different levels in different districts. To reflect a glimpse of State level average annual growth rate of enrolment in three decades from 1991 to 2006, it was 8.2 per cent at the primary level (not shown in Table). It increased to 40 per cent in the Middle School level (VI to VIII) and further jumped to 107 per cent in the High School level. In totality, the annual average growth rate of school enrolment (including Class XI to XII) in Manipur from 1991 to 2006 turned out to be 20 per cent.

When we compared to the national level for Gross Enrolment Ratio (GER) of 2009-10, Table 7.9 shows that the State is much ahead of the national level. In the category of Class I to V (6-10 years of age), the GER of Manipur was 186 compared to 115.5 of the national level. It was slightly lower in the second stage of class VI to VIII (11 to 13 years of age group) with the GER of Manipur being 103.3 and 151.6 for Class I to VIII level together. While, it was 81.5 and 102.3 for the level of Class VI to VIII and Class I to VIII level respectively for the national in 2009-10.

As on September 30, 2007, as for the total enrolment of UG courses and its percentage to total population, Table 7.10 shows that the State of Manipur was found to be below the national level of the courses like general Arts and Sciences, Engineering, Management and Law. The enrolment per cent of Medicine to total population of the State is very close to national level. However, the percentage of enrolment in Commerce and Teacher's training to total population in Manipur is much higher than the national level.

As for the total enrolment of PG courses and its percentage to total population, Table 7.11 shows that Manipur was found to be much higher than the national level. Especially, the enrolment percentage of M.Phil./ Ph.D., General Arts and Sciences, Agriculture and Management courses was found to be much higher than the national level. This shows that overall higher education level of the state is much higher than the national

Table 7.8: District-wise Decadal School Enrolment in Manipur

Stage	*Year*	*S'pati*	*T'long*	*CC Pur*	*Chandel*	*Imphal#*	*B'pur*	*Thoubal*	*Ukhrul*	*Manipur*
Primary	1991	26845	13714	25220	12456	102300	24916	44230	14338	264019
	2001	29057	18130	25610	17714	102932	27056	44736	20345	285580
	2006*	–	–	–	–	–	–	–	–	–
Middle (VI-VIII)	1991	6413	2560	6093	2589	35353	7720	13674	3256	77658
	2001	10230	3263	8918	3107	54590	12817	23440	4835	121200
	2006*	15155	9005	13112	8807	39302	14166	19093	13412	149933
High (IX-X)	1991	3164	1103	3325	1144	22003	5332	9023	1606	46700
	2001	4513	1694	4897	1895	30604	6990	11435	2652	64680
	2006*	14013	7279	22492	8476	50360	15341	28533	10635	178196
Total School**	1991	36495	17524	34638	16189	162641	38908	67243	19213	392851
	2001	44516	23764	40316	22716	197327	48659	81348	28434	487080
	2006*	63311	39724	50984	28960	137912	50244	79626	43243	565868

Note: # Data for both Imphal East and West; * data for Imphal West only; ** Total school enrolment is including class XI to XII in the State.

Source: Author's Compilation from GoI (2011); DES (2010).

Table 7.9: Gross Enrolment Ratio of Primary and Middle School in 2009-10

Category	*Sex/Total*	*Manipur*	*India*
Classes I-V (6-10 years)	Boys Girls	189.7 182.3	115.6 115.4
	Total	**186.0**	**115.5**
Classes VI-VIII (11-13 yrs)	Boys Girls	107.2 99.2	84.5 78.3
	Total	**103.3**	**81.5**
Classes I-VIII (6-13 yrs)	Boys Girls	155.4 147.7	103.8 101.1
	Total	**151.6**	**102.5**

Source: GoI (2011).

level, especially for the conventional courses available to the people of the state.

Interfacing Education with Conflict in Manipur

If not plunge into the detail causes of conflict, it is clear that the State of Manipur is passing through social turmoil in various regards, ranging from insurgency for secession to greater autonomy, from terrorism to ethnic clashes and the fight over resources (Sharma, 2011; Bohlken and Sergenti, 2010; Mentschel, 2007). In the past, the violence was confined mainly with the revolutionary groups and the State or security forces. But, in the recent years, especially after 1990s, the situation has turned into a different picture, affected the masses (CICS, 2005), education, children and women (Singha, *et al.*, 2012). In the midst of conflict, education in Manipur has been developing at a faster rate, compared to national level. What is the driving force of this paradox?

Expenditure on Education

According to Singh (2011), there is a bilateral relationship between the expenditure on education and development of economy. In Manipur, despite an increasing conflict in the last two to three decades, the development pace of education has been quite appreciable as depicted by the Table 7.4 to 7.11. Also, the growth rate of women's education in rural areas of Manipur is relatively higher than the national as well as

Table 7.10: Total Enrolment and Percentage to Total Population under UG Courses

(As on 30th September, 2007)

	Arts			*Commerce*			*Science*		
	Boys	**Girls**	**Total**	**Boys**	**Girls**	**Total**	**Boys**	**Girls**	**Total**
Manipur	4863 (3.12)	951 (0.62)	5814 (1.88)	477 (12.29)	243 (6.14)	720 (9.19)	5018 (8.85)	3909 (6.90)	8927 (7.87)
India	2679564 (3.85)	2092171 (3.36)	4771735 (3.62)	1003820 (9.10)	621670 (6.29)	1625490 (7.77)	1062430 (21.42)	743490 (14.77)	1805920 (18.07)
	Engineering/Tech/Arch/Design			**Medicine**			**Agriculture and Allied Courses**		
Manipur	495 (0.32)	155 (0.10)	650 (0.21)	71 (1.83)	47 (1.19)	118 (1.51)	368 (0.65)	237 (0.42)	605 (0.53)
India	1028896 (1.48)	404043 (0.65)	1432939 (1.09)	180679 (1.64)	147384 (1.49)	328063 (1.57)	74877 (1.51)	16495 (0.33)	91372 (0.91)
	Mgt/Hotel/Tourism/Travel			**Education/Teacher Training**			**Law**		
Manipur	22 (0.01)	19 (0.01)	41 (0.01)	315 (8.11)	549 (13.88)	864 (11.02)	421 (0.74)	210 (0.37)	631 (0.56)
India	112537 (0.16)	70195 (0.11)	182732 (0.14)	244052 (2.21)	222237 (2.25)	466289 (2.23)	146139 (2.95)	61827 (1.23)	207966 (2.08)

Note: (i) Excluding Open Universities; UG implies Under Graduates.

(ii) Figures in the Parentheses are Percentage of State/Country Population.

Source: GoI (2011).

Table 7.11: Total Enrolment and Percentage of Total Population under PG Courses

(As on 30th September, 2007)

	MPhil/PhD			*Arts*			*Commerce*		
	Boys	*Girls*	*Total*	*Boys*	*Girls*	*Total*	*Boys*	*Girls*	*Total*
Manipur	1304 (0.84)	940 (0.61)	2244 (0.72)	823 (21.20)	845 (21.36)	1668 (21.28)	61 (0.11)	75 (0.13)	136 (0.12)
India	45740 (0.07)	30487 (0.05)	76227 (0.06)	339798 (3.08)	311833 (3.15)	651631 (3.11)	104341 (2.10)	82383 (1.64)	186724 (1.87)
	Science			**Engineering/Tech/Architect/Design**			**Medicine**		
Manipur	424 (0.27)	656 (0.43)	1080 (0.35)	0 (0.00)	0 (0.00)	0 (0.00)	52 (0.09)	32 (0.06)	84 (0.07)
India	220553 (0.32)	167989 (0.27)	388542 (0.29)	53046 (0.48)	21441 (0.22)	74487 (0.36)	14336 (0.29)	7970 (0.16)	22306 (0.22)
	Agriculture & Allied			**Mgt/ Hotel/Travel/Tourism Mgt**			**Educational/Teacher Training**		
Manipur	45 (0.03)	29 (0.02)	74 (0.02)	104 (2.68)	22 (0.56)	126 (1.61)	18 (0.03)	66 (0.12)	84 (0.07)
India	9330 (0.01)	2514 (0.01)	11844 (0.01)	71678 (0.65)	33040 (0.33)	104718 (0.50)	9681 (0.20)	9573 (0.19)	19254 (0.19)
	Law			**Others**					
Manipur	25 (0.02)	0 (0.00)	25 (0.01)	35 (0.90)	69 (1.74)	104 (1.33)			
India	7364 (0.01)	3679 (0.01)	11043 (0.01)	26221 (0.24)	17345 (0.18)	43566 (0.21)			

Note: (i) Excluding Open Universities; PG implies Post Graduate.
(ii) Figures in the Parentheses are Percentage of State/Country Population.

Source: GoI (2011).

State level. Its credit goes to the enthusiasm for better and higher education of the people of Manipur and further grounded by English education, especially in the hill districts, with the help of Christian Missionaries (Singha, 2010). This aspiration of the people for education is reflected by the level of per capita expenditure spent on education.

Table 7.12: Average Annual Expenditure (Rs.) per Student (Age 5-29) in 2007-08

(Rural + Urban)

Stage	General Education					Tech-nical	Voca-tional	All
	Primary	Middle	Secondary/ Hr. Sec.	Above Hr. Sec.	All			
Manipur	3285	4087	6171	6915	4242	29287	—	4372
India	1413	2088	4351	7360	2461	32112	14881	3058

Source: NSS 64th Round (July 2007–June 2008).

From Table 7.12, we can see that the annual expenditure spent per student in Manipur as in 2007-08 was much higher than the national level and stood at Rs. 4,372 as compared to Rs. 3,058 of national level. Though the expenditure spent per student at the national level for technical education was slightly higher than Manipur, the per capita expenditure spent on the rest of the courses/levels of education was found to be above the national level, almost double of the national level. This implies that the parents in Manipur give more emphasis on education and the statement is supported by Table 7.13.

Table 7.13: Monthly Per Capita Expenditure (in %) on Education (MPCE)

Year	NSS Round	Manipur		India	
		Rural	Urban	Rural	Urban
1999-00	55th	3.76	6.49	1.93	4.33
2004-05	60th	6.39	8.93	2.86	6.52
2007-08	64th	7.24	9.04	3.70	7.11

Source: NSS Rounds: 55th, 60th and 64th.

Also, from the Table 7.13, it is seen that the MPCE on education in the 55th NSS round (1999-00) in Manipur in rural area was 3.76 per cent of the total expenditure spent by an individual compared to 1.93 per cent of all India level. While, in urban areas of the state, the MPCE on education during the same period (same NSS round) was 6.49 per cent compared to 4.33 per cent of national level.

With the passage of time, in 2007-08 (64th NSS round), the MPCE on education in rural areas of Manipur was 7.24 per cent against 3.7 per cent in all India level. In the case of urban area during the same period, the MPCE on education in Manipur was 9.04 per cent compared to 7.11 per cent of all India level. This clearly shows that the emphasis on education in the tiny State of Manipur is at the highest level. Only expenditure indicator is not sufficient to measure the outcome level of the sector, performance parameter is also needed to be looked into. For the purpose, as the development of rural areas is more important, using different parameters, quality of rural school children was evaluated in Table 7.14.

From the Table 7.14 we can observe that the quality of education and the performance of children in the school level of Manipur are much higher than the national level where 51 per cent of Manipuri students (rural) of Class V standard can do basic arithmetic of division compared to the 38 per cent of all India level. In terms of "subtraction" arithmetic for standard III and IV in rural areas of Manipur, 70 per cent and 84.4 per cent respectively can work it out. While, at the all India level, at the most 39 per cent and 59 per cent of standard III and IV children respectively can do the same.

Table 7.14: Performance of Rural School Children in 2009-10

Parameter		*Standard*	*Manipur*	*India*
% of Children who can read English	Capital Letters or More	I	94.0	43.8
	Capital Letters or More	II	98.4	66.2
	Words or More	III	82.4	28.6
	Words or More	IV	90.2	44.1
	Sentences	V	66.6	25.7
% of Children who can read...	Letters or more	I	96.4	68.8
	Words or more	II	84.4	55.2
	Std. I level Text or More	III	64.1	46.6
	Std. I Level Text or More	IV	80.2	67.4
	Std. II Level Text or More	V	53.9	52.8
% of Children who can.....	Recognize Nos. 1-9 or do more	I	96.8	69.3
	Recognize Nos. 11-99 or do more	II	87.9	54.6
	Subtract or do more	III	69.8	39.0
	Subtract or do more	IV	84.4	58.8
	Do Division	V	51.0	38.0

Source: GoI (2012).

Similarly, the efficiency of identification of English letters at the primary level and knowledge of English subject for upper primary level are also found to be much higher for the Manipuri students as compared to the national level. Despite prolonged conflicts, the above evidences clearly reiterate the superiority of Manipur over the national level in terms of educational standard and educational development in the recent past.

Impact of Conflict on Education in Manipur

Literatures and evidences show that there is a negative effect of violent conflict on the human capital of individuals particularly among the children and women, due to their vulnerability (Patricia, 2010). Violent conflict, that is destructive, may affect the level and distribution of returns to education considerably. It results in deaths, injuries, disability and psychological trauma to a physical body; and have an adverse effect to economic and social well-being apart from political instability.

Nevertheless, in Manipur, as depicted above, the growth of education was not affected by the conflicts in the State. How is that possible when the State was plagued with blockades and strikes for month and month at a stretch? A preliminary result says that the students moved out of the State for study, either due to the frequent conflicts or blockades in the State or lack of educational infrastructures. For this purpose, a total of fifty-two Manipuri students (who are studying in Bangalore) were interviewed and the results are given below.

Table 7.15: Reasons for Studying Outside Manipur

Main Reason	*No. of Students*	*Percent*
Law and Order Condition	30	57.7
Limited Educational Infrastructure	8	15.4
Status Sake	2	3.8
Low Quality of Education in Manipur	7	13.5
Others	5	9.6
Total	**52**	**100.00**

Source: Primary Field Survey.

From the Table 7.15 we can ascertain the fact that the law and order condition is the most important factor that pushes students outside Manipur for study. Though there are many factors which influence the Manipuri people for coming out of the State for their studies, thirty students out of the fifty-two students (57.7%) revealed that the frequent violence and blockades disrupted their studies in Manipur, and compelled them to come out. When we look at the variables like, *limited educational infrastructure* and *low quality of teaching* in the State, they have least influence on the student's decision to come out of the State. Next to the unfavourable law and order condition for study in the state, 15.4 per cent of respondents revealed that lack of educational infrastructure compelled them to come out of the State for their study. In the third position, 13.5 per cent of respondents revealed that low quality of higher education in the State is also a factor for their departure from Manipur.

People are increasingly aiming to acquire greater education for which the people from Manipur are not restricting to study only within their State, but are also migrating towards other States in search of better quality higher education. The State is persistently disturbed with violence, conflict, strike or lockout throughout the academic year which hampers the academic progress. As a result, most of the affluent as well as those who want to pursue sincere and quality education for future livelihood do migrate to other relatively developed and peaceful States. Therefore, Bangalore, being a relatively peaceful city, has become one of the preferred destinations of the majority of Manipuri students.

Table 7.16: Courses pursued by the Sample Manipuri Students in Bangalore

Course/Class	*No. of Students*	*Percent*
Schooling (Up to XII Standard)	15	28.8
UG (General—Arts, Science, Commerce)	15	28.8
UG (Tech—Mgt, Medical, Engineering)	10	19.2
PG (General—Arts, Science, Commerce)	7	13.5
PG (Tech—Mgt, Medical, Engineering)	5	9.6
Total	**52**	**100.0**

Source: Primary Field Survey

From Table 7.16, out of the total fifty-two sample students interviewed collected altogether fifteen students each (28.8% each) are studying in the school and the undergraduate level. There are some limitations with regard to the infrastructure and quality of PG courses in Manipur. However, schooling and undergraduate (General) level courses do not have such constraints in the State. This further proves that the conflict and violence in Manipur is as an important reason for students' migration outside the State.

Brief Analysis and Findings

Despite prolonged conflict in Manipur it does not appear to have had a strict relationship with the literacy or enrolment rates. With the help of twenty-one years projected data on population, enrolment, and literacy rate and conflict fatalities (as the survey of these variables is not done yearly), a statistical correlation "Pearson correlation" is worked out and it is found that there exists a positive correlation between public expenditure on education, enrolment rate and literacy rate in the State. However, the correlation between insurgency related fatalities and other educational variables (e.g., public expenditure on education, enrolment rate and literacy rate) are found to be insignificant (refer to Table 7.17). It implies that the conflict within the State does not affect educational development in the State.

As we have seen in Table 7.1, approximately 41,500 people have been displaced by ethnic conflicts in the 1990s in Manipur. Around 2.3 per cent of the total State's population was displaced by the ethnic conflict in the State (18.3 lakhs population in 1991 in Manipur). Mention may be made that the major ethnic conflict that has changed demographic equation greatly in Manipur was the Naga-Kuki conflict. In this very ethnic conflict, altogether 800 people were killed, 480 injured and 5,713 families displaced between 1992 and 1999 (Hussain and Phanjoubam, 2007).

Besides, in 1997, in the Kuki-Paite clash, altogether 162 people killed, 93 injured, 71 kidnapped and 3,521 houses were burnt and many children's education was disturbed. As also mentioned, as a part of Naga integration movement, more than 2000 (two thousand) Nagas students of Manipur were directed by the Naga Civil Organisations to delink from Manipur Board of Matriculation Examination and affiliate to Nagaland board in Nagaland in 2007 (Shimray, 2007). It disturbed many of the students' educational careers. It is only a physically known figure; there were many students, especially the school goers who were living in a great fear and felt insecurity though no incidence of attacking to student community was made by any of the organisation at that time.

Despite these uncertainties, the growth rate of educational development of the State has been increasing at a faster rate than the national level. However, within the State, the trend of higher education level is slightly lower than the school education. Higher expenditure of private higher education and limited higher educational infrastructure within the State may probably be the reasons for relatively slower growth of higher education than the school education within the State. From the analysis, it is clear that

Table 7.17: Correlations between Insurgency related Fatalities and Education

	Pearson Correlation	*Public Expenditure on Education*	*Projected Literacy Rate*	*Projected Population*	*Insurgency Related Fatalities*	*Projected School Enrolment*
Public Expenditure on Education	Pearson Correlation	1				
	Sig. (2-tailed)					
	N	21				
Projected Literacy Rate	Pearson Correlation	.959(**)	1			
	Sig. (2-tailed)	.000	.			
	N	21	21			
Projected Population	Pearson Correlation	.941(**)	.992(**)	1		
	Sig. (2-tailed)	.000	.000	.		
	N	21	21	21		
Insurgency Related Fatalities	Pearson Correlation	.138	.151	.144	1	
	Sig. (2-tailed)	.552	.513	.532	.	
	N	21	21	21	21	
Projected School Enrolment	Pearson Correlation	.950(**)	.981(**)	.990(**)	.155	1
	Sig. (2-tailed)	.000	.000	.000	.503	.
	N	21	21	21	21	21

** Correlation is significant at the 0.01 level (2-tailed).

Source: Estimated from RGCC (2006), (2012); SATP (2012); Indiastat.com

conflict and violence do not affect educational growth in the State, but conflict makes children to go out of the State for their study. It means, conflicts and violence disturb educational environment within the State and it might lead to higher expenditure on education for the Manipuris. But, whether the educated children or education creates conflict in the State or not, requires more research. Because, we have understood that the employment opportunities within the State is relatively smaller than other bigger States of the country, and educated unemployment problem is one of the major problems in the State now.

Some Policy Measures and Conclusion

Controlling conflict has become the need of the hour. Seeing the trend of global damages created by conflict and wars, it is warned that if we do not control on time, a substantial group of the youths and communities are likely to be stuck in a '*conflict trap*'—a cycle of war and economic decline. Definitely, a fruitful dialogue or negotiation can bring peace. A fruitful dialogue or negotiation can again be arrived at only when people are well educated with ethics and morality. Dialogue does not mean that one's grievance or demand is tabled for negotiation and get stuck onto it. One should have an understanding of the other's need and constraints. In this context, Kotite (2012) has emphasised that the root cause of the conflict should be understood. Education can contribute to mitigating conflict along the three primary aspects—structural, behavioural and attitudinal. Education can alter societal contradictions (structural), improve relations and interactions (behavioural) and encourage in changes (attitudinal) in ways that can reduce the risk of conflict and help in building sustainable peace (*ibid.*, p. 13).

Dupuy (2008) identified six interconnected areas of *key findings* on how education can contribute to building peace:

1. Educational inclusion lowers motivation and raises opportunity costs for those participating in armed conflict.
2. Government investment in formal education systems is critical for building peace.
3. Quality education delivered in violence-free, cooperative learning environments teaches children critical lessons about non-violent conflict resolution.
4. The curriculum is a critical element in efforts to heighten constraints against the use of violence and promote human rights.

5. Participatory education systems can raise the social costs of and constraints against engaging in armed conflict.
6. Education that fosters positive socio-economic development can help prevent armed conflict.

Finding stability and peace is certainly the greatest collective challenge that mankind has ever faced. In many cases, the energy stemming from conflict can be directed towards achieving positive change. People need to be taught of alternatives in resolving conflict, that violence is not a necessary means to achieve their goals. For the goal mentioned, education should be further strengthened. Of the whole education system, the primary education system is to be given more emphasis, to achieve better higher education and employability with morality (Singha, 2010). In the research findings of Shah (2006) it was revealed that the working of the whole education system gets crippled when one level, especially elementary education which is the basis/foundation of the whole system, is kept weak. The cycle of low access, equity and quality starts from here affecting in turn the other two higher levels and *vice versa.* Secondary education cannot be strengthened without strengthening primary education from where the students enter the secondary education system (Gill *et al.* 2005; Mukherjee 2005). As Manipur has been looming with conflict for long and education has not been disturbed, definitely within no time the State will return to a peaceful society. Conflict in the State has only boosted the need to study and work outside the State among the varied communities with competitive notion. This will result in a significant contribution to avoiding violent conflicts in the State. Also, Dupuy (2008) found that with improved quality and safer, protective learning environments, individuals may have fewer grievances, and thus less motivation—as well as fewer opportunities—to engage in armed conflict. In this manner, if the educated Manipuris, especially those who have returned home from outside get engaged themselves in productive activities they will not have time to engage in unlawful activities. As the conflict in the State has reached its peak point (stalemate) and at the same time the growth of education has also increased at the faster rate (as shown in Fig. 7.1), definitely, conflict can be brought down easily if the supply side of employment is raised slightly. Therefore, education should not be compromised and it can be used as a preventive measure to control and avoid conflict.

As policy measures, for bringing peaceful educational environment and further development of the State by curtailing conflict, the following three principles have been recommended.

1. Government should be very deterministic about the development projects in the State. Government should first treat the communities equally (Ravi, 2012) and give more emphasis on infrastructure, especially the road and communications (Singha, 2012). Central fund should not be pumped for political interest and making the State a captive market (Sharma, 2012). The State should be prepared fully for exploitation of the resources. Also, government should ensure inclusive education, developing trust among the communities through appropriate modification of syllabi and by including socio-cultural elements of the major communities, if not all. For which, necessary security and political arrangement should be made.
2. Higher educational institutions of the State should be monitored and quality should not be compromised. Besides, employment opportunities should be created to absorb educated youths, especially, those who have returned home from outside the State, after their UG level of education and could not reach beyond that. Otherwise, this age group gets frustrated easily and looks for easy alternatives for their survival.
3. Government should proportionately invest in all levels of education with world class infrastructures to retain out-migration of Manipuri students to some extent. Besides, no compromise should be made in making the teaching and learning process in the elementary level innovative. Education for the sake of raising literacy rate should be avoided. Education should establish a strong foundation for quality education which includes ethics, employability and adaptability. English may be envisaged as a medium of instruction from the elementary level without forgetting the regional language or mother tongue. Also, teachers' absenteeism should be avoided or strictly monitored. Social organisations or communities should also encourage the initiative of educational development in the State.

NOTE

1. NER consists of eight States – Arunachal Pradesh, Assam, Manipur, Mizoram, Meghalaya, Nagaland, Sikkim and Tripura.

REFERENCES

Agbor, Julius A. (2011). *Does School Education Reduce the Likelihood of Societal Conflict in Africa*? Working Paper 218, Cape Town: Department of Economics, University of the Western Cape.

Amamio, May Christine (2004). *The Role of Peace Education in Preventing Conflict*. UNESCO First Committee, Session VI. United Nations Educational, Scientific and Cultural Organization.

Barrera, F. and A.M. Ibañez (2004). *Does Violence Reduce Investment in Education? A Theoretical and Empirical Approach*. Working Paper, Colombia: CEDE-Universidad de Los Andes.

Bird, Lyndsay (2006). *Education and Conflict: An NGO Perspective in Marion Couldrey and Dr Tim Morris* (eds.), Forced Migration Review, Refugees Studies Centre, UK.

Bohlken, Anjali Thomas and Ernest John Sergenti (2010). Economic Growth and Ethnic Violence: An Empirical Investigation of Hindu-Muslim Riots in India. *Journal of Peace Research*, 47(5): 589–600.

Boyden, J. (2006). *Children, War and World Disorder in the 21st Century: A Review of the Theories and the Literature on Children's Contributions to Armed Violence*. QEH Working Paper Series No. 138, Department of International Development, Queen Elizabeth House: University of Oxford

Boyden, Jo; Jo de Berry; Thomas Feeny; and Jason Hart (2002). *Children Affected by Armed Conflict in South Asia.* A discussion paper prepared for UNICEF Regional Office, South Asia. Refugee Studies Centre: University of Oxford.

Brahm, Eric (2003). *Conflict Stages*. In Guy Burgess and Heidi Burgess (eds.): Beyond Intractability. Conflict Information Consortium, University of Colorado, Boulder. [Retrieved: http://www.beyondintractability.org/bi-essay/conflict-stages]

Burde, Dana; Amy Kapit-Spitalny; Rachel Wahl and Ozen Guven (2011). *Education and Conflict Mitigation: What the Aid Workers Say.* Washington, DC: US Agency for International Development, Education Quality Improvement Program 1.

Bush, Kenneth D. and Diana Saltarelli (2000). *The Two Faces of Education in Ethnic Conflict: Towards a Peace-building Education for Children.* Florence, Italy: The UNICEF Innocenti Research Centre.

CICS (2005). *The Impact of Armed Violence on Poverty and Development*, West Yorkshire, Centre for International Cooperation and Security, UK: Department of Peace Studies, University of Bradford.

Collier, Paul and A. Hoeffler (2002). *Greed and Grievance in Civil War.* Working Paper Series, CSAE WPS/2002-01, Centre for the Study of African Economics, Oxford (UK): Oxford University.

Collier, Paul (2004). *Development and Conflict.* Centre for the Study of African Economies, Department of Economics, Oxford: Oxford University.

Dupuy, Kendra (2008). *Education for Peace.* Oslo: International Peace Research Institute (PRIO) and Save the Children Norway.

DES (2010). *Statistical Handbook of Manipur*, Directorate of Economics and Statistics, Imphal: Government of Manipur.

Gates, Scott and Havard Strand (2012). *Development Consequences of Armed Conflict.* World Development, 40(9): 1713-22.

Gill, Sucha Singh; Sukhwinder Sigh; and Jaswinder Singh Brar (2005). Educational Development, Public Expenditure and Financing of Secondary Education in Punjab. *Journal of Educational Planning and Administration*, XIX (3): 335-74.

Kotite, Phyllis (2012). *Education for Conflict Prevention and Peace-building: Meeting the Global Challenges of the 21st Century.* IIEP Occasional Paper, Paris: United Nations Educational, Scientific and Cultural Organization.

NSS 55th Round (1999-00). *National Sample Survey Organisation*, Department of Statistics: Government of India, NSSO Report No.409.

NSS 60th Round (2004). *National Sample Survey Organisation*, Department of Statistics: Government of India.

NSS 64th Round (2007-08). *National Sample Survey Organisation*, Department of Statistics: Government of India.

NSS 66th Round (2007-08). *National Sample Survey Organisation*, Department of Statistics: Government of India.

GoI (2012). *Data for use of Deputy Chairman*, Planning Commission, 10th April, 2012. New Delhi: Government of India.

GoI (2011). *Statistics of Higher and Technical Education 2007-08.* Ministry of Human Resources, New Delhi: Government of India.

Harriss, John (2002). *The State, Tradition and Conflict in the North-Eastern States of India.* Working Paper No. 13 (August), London: Crisis States Programme, Development Research Centre, London School of Economics.

Hussain, Monirul and Pradip Phanjoubam (2007). *A Status Report on Displacement in Assam and Manipur*, Kolkata (India): Mahanirban Calcutta Research Group.

Kumar, Anand; Kamei Aphun; Khuraijam Bijoykumar Singh and Homen Thangjam (2011). *Situating Conflict and Poverty in Manipur.* CPRC-IIPA Working Paper No. 37, Chronic Poverty Research Centre, New Delhi: Indian Institute of Public Administration.

Levy, Barry S. and David Parker (2000). *Children and War, Public Health Reports*-1974, Volume 115, No. 4, Washington DC.

Lindquist, Katharine M. (2012). *Horizontal Educational Inequalities and Civil Conflict: The Nexus of Ethnicity, Inequality, and Violent Conflict.* Undergraduate Economic Review, Vol. 8, Issue 1, Article. 10 [Accessed on November 30, 2012: http://digitalcommons.iwu.edu/uer/vol8/iss1/10]

Mann, Howard (1987). *International Law and the Child Soldier.* The International and Comparative Law Quarterly, 36(1): 32-57.

Manoharan, Arlene (2012). *Impact of Armed Conflict on Children of Manipur.* Occasional Paper (Draft), Bangalore: Juvenile Justice Center for Child and the Law. National Law School of India University [accessed on September 6, 2012 http://www.nls.ac.in/ccl/Occasional%20Paper %20for%20univ.pdf]

Mentschel, B. Nepram (2007). *Arm Conflict, Small Arms Proliferation and Women's Responses to Armed Violence in India's North-East*. Working Paper No. 33 (December), South Asia Institute, Department of Political Science, University of Heidelberg.

Mitchell, Christopher R. (2006). *Conflict, Social Change and Conflict Resolution: An Enquiry*. In David Bloomfield, Martina Fischer and Beatrix Schmelzle (Eds.): Social Change and Conflict Transformation, Berghof Handbook Dialogue Series, No. 5 [accessed on 28th Nov. 2012 and available at : http://www.berghof-handbook.net/documents/publications/dialogue5_sochange_complete.pdf]

Mukherjee, Dipa (2005). Educational Attainment in India: Trends, Patterns and Policy Issues. *Journal of Educational Planning and Administration*, XIX (4): 523-41.

Patricia, Justino (2010). *How Does Violent Conflict Impact on Individual Educational Outcomes? The Evidence So Far*. Background paper prepared for the Education for All Global Monitoring Report 2011 UNESCO "*The Hidden Crisis: Armed Conflict and Education*". Institute of Development Studies, Brighton, UK: University of Sussex.

Reddy, C. Y. (2008). Privatization of Higher Education. *Southern Economist*, 46 (23 & 24): 31-32.

RGCC (2012). *Population Projections for India and States 2001-2026*. Registrar General and Census Commissioner, Report of the Technical Group on Population Projections Constituted by the National Commission on Population: New Delhi.

Ravi, R.N. (2012). Chasing A Chimeric Peace. New Delhi: *The Hindu* November 15, 2012. [Accessed on 15th November 2012 http://www.thehindu.com/opinion/op-ed/chasing-a-chimeric-peace/article4095592.ece]

Richards, Simon and Gezu Bekele (2011). *Conflict in the Somali Region of Ethiopia: Can Education Promote Peace-Building?* Feinstein International Center, USA: Tufts University.

Seitz, Klaus (2004). *Education and Conflict: The role of education in the creation, prevention and resolution of societal crises – Consequences for development cooperation*, Eschborn: German Technical Cooperation.

Shah, K. R. (2006). State Inaction in Education in India. *Journal Educational Planning and Administration*, XX (4): 465-72.

Sharma, H.S. (2011). Conflict and Development in India's North-Eastern State of Manipur. *The Indian Journal of Social Work*, 72(1): 5-22.

Shimray, U.A. (2007). Meetei-Mayek: Uneasy Script, October 3, 2007, *The Sangai Express*, Imphal, Manipur [access on 18th August 2012: http://e-pao.net/epSubPageExtractor.asp?src=news_section.opinions.Opinion_on_Manipur_Integrity_Issue.Meitei-Mayek_Uneasy_script]

Sinclair, Margaret (2002). *Planning Education in and after Emergencies*. Paris:

United Nations Educational, Scientific and Cultural Organisation (International Institute for Educational Planning).

Singha, Komol (2009). Bandh Syndrome and its Impact on Trade and Commerce in North-East India. *Journal of Global Economy*, 5(2): 91-101.

Singha, Komol (2010). *English Education and Rural Development: A North East Perspective.* In Singha, Komol (ed.), 'Rural Development in India: Retrospect and Prospects', New Delhi: Concept Publishing Company.

Singha, Komol; Marchang Reimangam and Saju Mathew (2012): *Educational Development in Manipur: Interface with Conflict.* Presented at the National Seminar at St. Joseph's College, Kohima (Nagaland) on 21-22 September.

Singha, Komol (2012). Identity, Contestation and Development in North-East India: A Study of Manipur, Mizoram and Nagaland. *Journal of Community Positive Practices*, XII (3):403-424.

Singh, Surat (2011). Causality between total Expenditure on Education and Economic Growth: A Case Study of Haryana. *The Indian Journal of Economics*, XIIC (I): 1-8.

Smith, Alan (2010). The Influence of Education on Conflict and Peace Building. Background paper prepared for the Education for All Global Monitoring Report 2011 UNESCO—*The Hidden Crisis: Armed Conflict and Education.* 2011/ED/EFA/MRT/PI/48, University of Ulster.

Smith, Alan and T. Vaux (2003). *Education, Conflict and International Development*. London: Department for International Development.

Srikanth, H. and Th. Ngaihte (2011). Ethnicity and Ethnic Identities in North East India. *Man and Society*, Vol. VIII (summer), Pages 125-133.

South Asia Terrorism Portal (2012). *Insurgency Related Killings,* [accessed March 2012: http://www.satp.org/satporgtp/countries/india/database/index.html]

Tensuba, K.C. (1993). *Genesis of Indian Tribes: An Approach to the History of Meiteis and Thais*, New Delhi: Inter-India Publications.

Tyack, David and Elisabeth Hansot (1981). *Conflict and Consensus in American Public Education*. Dadelus, 110 (3): 1-25.

UNESCO (2011). *The Hidden Crisis: Armed Conflict and Education.* EFA Global Monitoring Report 2011, Paris: United Nations Educational, Scientific and Cultural Organization.

UNESCO (2010a). *Protecting Education from Attack.* Paris: United Nations Educational, Scientific and Cultural Organization.

UNESCO (2010b). *The Hidden Crisis: Armed Conflict and Education.* The Quantitative Impact of Conflict on Education 2011/ED/EFA/MRT/PI/50, UNESCO Institute for Statistics. Paris: United Nations Educational, Scientific and Cultural Organization.

Yilmaz, M.E. (2008). The New World Order: An Outline of the Post-Cold War Era. Alternatives: Turkish *Journal of International Relations*, 7(4): 44-58 (Winter).

8

Entrepreneurship and Unemployment in Manipur: An Empirical Analysis

Md. Samsur Jaman

Introduction

Entrepreneurship has been considered as the backbone of economic development. It has also been well established that the level of economic growth of a region to a large extent, depends on the level of entrepreneurial activities in the region. The myth that entrepreneurs are born, no more holds good, rather it is well recognised now that the entrepreneurs can be created and nurtured through appropriate interventions in the form of entrepreneurship development programmes. In the era of liberalisation, privatisation and globalisation along with ongoing information technology (IT) revolution, capable entrepreneurs are making use of the opportunities emerging from the evolving scenario. However, a large segment of the population, particularly in the industrially backward regions/rural areas generally lags behind in taking advantage of these opportunities. Therefore, there is a need to provide skill development and entrepreneurship development training to such people in order to mainstream them in the ongoing process of economic growth.

Entrepreneurship development and training is, thus, one of the key elements for development of micro and small enterprises (MSEs), particularly, the first generation entrepreneurs. To undertake this task on regular basis, the Ministry of Micro, Small and Medium Enterprises

(MMSME), Government of India has set up three national-level Entrepreneurship Development Institutes (EDIs). They are: The National Institute for Micro, Small and Medium Enterprises (NI-MSME), Hyderabad; The Indian Institute of Entrepreneurship (IIE), Guwahati and The National Institute for Entrepreneurship and Small Business Development (NIESBUD), Noida. Further, the Ministry has implement (in addition to the schemes of MSME-Do) an important scheme, namely, Scheme for Assistance for Strengthening of Training Infrastructure of Existing and New Entrepreneurship Development Institutes (EDIs). The main objectives of the schemes are (i) promoting entrepreneurship for creating self-employment; (ii) facilitating creation of training infrastructure; and (iii) supporting research on entrepreneurship related issues.

However, the relationship between unemployment and entrepreneurship has been covered with ambiguity. On the one hand, the simple theory of income choice, which has been the basis for numerous studies focusing on the decision confronted by individuals to start a firm and become an entrepreneur (Evans and Leighton, 1990), suggests that increased unemployment will lead to an increase in start-up activity on the grounds that the opportunity cost of not starting a firm has decreased. On the other hand, the unemployed tend to possess lower endowments of human capital and entrepreneurial talent required to start and sustain a new firm (Lucas, 1978), suggesting that high unemployment is associated with a low degree of entrepreneurial activities. A low rate of entrepreneurship may also be a consequence of the low economic growth levels, which also reflect higher levels of unemployment (Audretsch, *et al.*, 2001). Entrepreneurial opportunities are not just the result of the push effect of (the threat of) unemployment but also of the pull effect of produced by a thriving economy as well as by entrepreneurial activities in the past. In addition to unemployment leading to more or less entrepreneurial activity, the reverse has also been claimed to hold. On the one hand, new firm start-ups hire employees which resulting in subsequent decreases in unemployment (Pfeiffer and Reize, 2000a). On the other hand, the low rates of survival combined with the limited growth of the majority of small firms imply that the employment contribution of start-ups is limited at best, which would argue against entrepreneurial activities reducing unemployment.

The ambiguities found in the empirical evidence reflect these two conflicting forces. Some studies have found that unemployment is associated with greater entrepreneurial activities, but others have come to the opposite conclusion, that entrepreneurship and unemployment are inversely related. For example, Evans and Leighton (1990) found that unemployment is positively associated with a greater propensity to start a new firm, but Garofoli (1994) found that unemployment is negatively related to new-firm start-ups. In the study of Carree (2001), it is found that no statistically significant relationship exists between the two. Audretsch and Thurik (2000) explored that an increase in the number of business owners reduces the level of unemployment. They identify a "Schumpeter" effect in terms of the positive impact on employment resulting from the entry of new firms. In reviewing the empirical evidence relating unemployment rates to new-firm start-up activity, Storey (1991: 177) concludes that, "The broad consensus is that time series analyses point to unemployment being, *ceteris paribus*, positively associated with indices of new-firm formation, whereas cross-sectional, or pooled cross sectional studies appear to indicate the reverse. Attempts to reconcile these differences have not been wholly successful". The study results of Audretsch, *et al.* (2008); Stel, *et al.* (2008) and Audretsch, *et al.* (2001), etc., based on the empirical evidence from OECD countries suggests that the relationship between unemployment and entrepreneurship is, in fact, both negative and positive. Changes in unemployment clearly have positive impact on subsequent changes in self-employment rates. At the same time, changes in self-employment rates have negative impact on subsequent employment rates.

Thus, while there are not just theoretical reasons, but also empirical support as well, that while unemployment leads to increased entrepreneurial activity, entrepreneurship leads to reduced unemployment. Unravelling the relationship between entrepreneurship and unemployment is crucial, because policy is frequently on assumptions that do not reflect this ambiguity (Audretsch, *et al.*, 2001). In order to advocate a greater role for public policy to promote entrepreneurship in Europe, the President of the European Commission, Romano Prodi (Audretsch, *et al.*, 2001), recently asserted that "increases in entrepreneurial activity tend to result in higher subsequent growth rates and a reduction of unemployment." The purpose of this chapter is to explore the relationship between unemployment and entrepreneurship. We do this by introducing a equation model where changes in unemployment and self-employment are linked to subsequent changes in those variables for the State of Manipur.

In the following section, we introduce a framework, based on the Gibrat's Law literature, for analyzing the employment impact of shifting employment from large to small firms. In the second section the relationship between self-employment and unemployment is established. In the third section measurement issues are discussed. Two empirical models are presented in the fourth section and in the fifth section the empirical estimation results are reported. Finally, in the last section a summary and conclusion are given.

Linking Entrepreneurship to Unemployment

According to Audretsch, *et al.* (2001), unemployment is linked to entrepreneurship dates back at least to Oxenfeldt (1943), who pointed out that individuals confronted with unemployment and low prospects for wage employment turn to self-employment as a viable alternative. This was an extension of Knight's view that individuals make a decision among three states—unemployment, self-employment and employment. The actual decision is shaped by the relative prices of these three activities but there was a clear prediction that entrepreneurship would be positively related to unemployment. However, according to Storey (1991), the empirical evidence linking unemployment to entrepreneurship is fraught with ambiguities. While some studies find that greater unemployment serves as a catalyst for start-up activity (Hamilton, 1989; Evans and Leighton, 1990), still others have found that unemployment reduces the amount of entrepreneurial activity (Audretsch, *et al.*, 2001).

On the other hand, why should an increased amount of entrepreneurial activity impact unemployment? One approach to address this question can be inferred from the literature on Gibrat's Law. Gibrat's Law asserts that firm growth is independent of size. Sutton (1997: 43) interprets "Gibrat's Legacy", as "The probability that the next opportunity taken up by any particular active firm is proportional to the current size of the firm." An important implication of Gibrat's Law is that shifting employment from large to small enterprises should have no impact on total employment, since the expected growth rates of both types of firms are identical. Thus, a restructuring of the economy away from large enterprises and towards small ones should have no impact on the unemployment rate.

However, there is strong and systematic empirical evidence suggesting that, in fact, Gibrat's Law does not hold across a broad spectrum of firm sizes. Two comprehensive and exhaustive compilations of studies relating firm size to growth have produced what is termed as a stylized fact that smaller firms have higher growth rates than their larger counterparts (Audretsch, *et al.*, 2001). Beginning with the pioneering studies by Evans (1987a and 1987b) and Hall (1987), along with Dunne, *et al.* (1988 and 1989); a central finding of this literature is that firm growth is negatively related to firm size and age. These findings have been confirmed in virtually every subsequent study undertaken, despite differences in country, time period, industry, and methodology used.

Thus, if the growth rates of smaller firms systematically exceed those of their larger counterparts, restructuring economic activity away from large firms and towards new and small firms should not result in a neutral impact on employment. Rather, the higher growth rates of small firms should result in lower unemployment rates. Formally, following Audretsch, *et al.* (2001), this can be shown by starting with the basic structure used to test Gibrat's Law, which relates the employment size E, of firm i at time t–1, to growth in period t,

$$\ln (E_t) - \ln (E_{i-1}) = a - b \ln (E_{i-1}), \qquad \text{...(1)}$$

where $b > 0$, which implies

$$E_t = e^a E_{t-1}^{1-b} \qquad \text{...(2)}$$

Firms do not change size only in the case $E_{t-1} = e^{a/b}$. Assume that the labour force equals L, that there are M large firms and that these variables do not change over time. Workers can either be employed by a small firm (i.e. managed by an entrepreneur), by a large firm, or be unemployed:

$$L = N_t s_t + M r_t + U_t \qquad \text{...(3)}$$

where N_t is the number of entrepreneurs, s_t is the average number of employees employed by them, r_t is the average number of employees at large firms and U_t is the number of unemployed. We assume that in the first period the number of employees at small firms is below the size at which firms do not change size while the number of employees at large firms is above this level, or $s_1 < e^{a/b} < r_1$.

To analyze the impact of restructuring we consider two regimes. In the first we assume the *Routinised Regime*, which is assumed that there is no exit or start-up of new firms, so that the composition of firms remains constant over time. In the second, or *the Entrepreneurial Regime*, is assumed that a certain percentage of large-firm employees spins off from their employers and starts new firms (Audretsch, *et al.*, 2001). The *Routinised Regime*, which precludes the possibility of start-ups *via* large-firm spin-offs, the levels of unemployment in the subsequent two periods can be computed as:

$$U_2 = L - N_1 s_2 - M r_2 = L - N_1 e^a s_1{}^{1-b} - M e^a r_1{}^{1-b} \text{ and} \quad \ldots(4)$$
$$U_3 = L - N_1 s_3 - M r_3 = L - N_1 e^a e^{a(1-b)} s_1{}^{(1-b)^2} - M e^a e^{a(1-b)} r_1{}^{(1-b)^2} \quad \ldots(5)$$

In the second, or *Entrepreneurial Regime*, a fraction of workers leave the incumbent large firms to start a new firm. That is, the total numbers of entrepreneurs increase from N_1 to N_2. These new start-ups attain the same size as the incumbent small firms (s_1). The unemployment levels in the *Entrepreneurial Regime* are therefore:

$$U_2' = L - N_2 s_2 - M r_2 = L - N_2 e^a s_1^{1-b} - M e^a \left[r_1 - (N_2 - N_1) s_1 / M\right]^{1-b} \text{ and } (4')$$
$$U_3' = L - N_2 s_3 - M r_3 = L - N_2 e^a e^{a(1-b)} s_1^{(1-b)^2} - M e^a e^{a(1-b)} (r_1 - (N_2 - N_1) s_1 / M)^{(1-b)^2} \quad \ldots(5')$$

The difference in the *change* in unemployment between the *Entrepreneurial Regime* and the *Routinised Regime* is given below:

$$U_3' - U_2' - (U_3 - U_2) = (N_2 - N_1) e^a (s_1^{1-b} - e^{a(1-b)} s_1^{(1-b)^2}) + Me^a \{(r_1 - (N_2 - N_1) s_1 / M)^{1-b} - r_1^{1-b} + e^{a(1-b)} (r_1^{(1-b)^2} - [r_1 - (N_2 - N_1) s_1 / M)^{(1-b)^2}]\} \quad (6)$$

This difference is negative in case of $b > 0$, which suggests that restructuring economic activity away from large enterprises towards smaller firms should result in lower unemployment. In general, the extent to which unemployment increases or decreases depends upon the shift towards smaller enterprises, $N_2 - N_1$, whenever $b \neq 0$. We test this relationship using model in equation (7).

The model based upon the violation of Gibrat's Law is one approach to derive the hypothesis that an increased degree of entrepreneurial activity leads to subsequent decreases in unemployment. Another approach is to argue that new entrants increase the number of participants in markets, and hence decrease market power of monopolists or oligopolists. As a consequence total market output is increased, for which additional labour input is required to achieve this output. In the following sections we perform an analysis based on time series data set to investigate the relationship between unemployment and entrepreneurship empirically.

Measurement Issues

The concept of entrepreneurship clearly is a heterogeneous phenomenon that has been broadly interpreted in many different contexts. In this chapter we follow the concept of entrepreneurship, in operationalising it, as the number of self-employed. There are a number of important qualifications that should be emphasized when using and interpreting this measure. First, it lumps all types of a very heterogeneous activity across a broad spectrum of sectors and contexts into a solitary measure. This measure treats all businesses as the same, both high-tech and low-tech. Second, it is not weighted for magnitude or impact. Again, all self-employed businesses are measured identically, even though some clearly have a greater impact than others. Third, this variable measures the stock of self-employed businesses and not the start-up of new ones. Still, this measure has two significant advantages. The first is that, while not being a direct measure of entrepreneurship, it is a useful proxy for entrepreneurial activity. Second, it is measured and can be compared across countries and over time.

The relationship between entrepreneurship and unemployment is concerned, as we have seen above there are many consequences of the shift from a managed economy to the entrepreneurial one. On the one hand there is the important question whether, at the end of the day, the entrepreneurial economy leads to less unemployment than the managed one. On the other, the change in the level of unemployment will probably affect the propensity of people to start firms. Moreover, we have seen above there are two types of entrepreneur, the "refugee" or "shopkeeper" type and the "Schumpeterian" type. These two types have different economic roles in their relation with unemployment. The number of "shopkeepers" is likely to go up if the level of unemployed rises and that same level are expected to go down if the number of "Schumpetarians" increases (Audretsch, *et al.*, 2001).

We present some calculations as to whether these relations exist. We will do so in the framework of Granger causality tests (Granger, 1969). In other words, we will regress both current changes in the level of unemployment (i.e., the "Schumpeter" effect) and current changes in the number of self-employed per labour force (i.e., the "refugee" or "shopkeeper" effect) on the lagged changes in the level of unemployment and the lagged number of self-employed per labour force. If the change in the number of unemployed is high (low) the lagged change in this number may also be high (low) due to autocorrelation. If this lagged change is left out of a regression equation testing the "Schumpeter" case, the influence of the change of the number of entrepreneurs might become positive because of the cyclical "shopkeeper" effect (Audretsch *et al.*, 2001). This has nothing to do with the "Schumpeter" effect of the rate of entrepreneurship shift influencing unemployment growth. That is why lagged unemployment growth is used in the "Schumpeter" equation. An analogous reasoning justifies the use of lagged changes in the level of entrepreneurship in the "shopkeeper" equation. We use data material of Manipur. The following equations are used for testing:

$$U_t - U_{t-L} = \alpha + \beta(E_{t-L} - E_{t-2L}) + \gamma(U_{t-L} - U_{t-2L}) + \varepsilon_{1t} \qquad \ldots(7)$$

Where, L is the time span in number of years and the expected sign of the coefficient β is negative. To test the second hypothesis, that the propensity to start a new firm is positively related to increases in unemployment, we estimate

$$E_t - E_{t-L} = \kappa + \lambda(U_{t-L} - U_{t-2L}) + \mu(E_{t-L} - E_{t-2L}) + \varepsilon_{2t} \qquad \ldots(8)$$

Where, the expected sign of the coefficient λ is positive.

In both equations (7) and (8) are lagged endogenous variable, used on the right hand side to "correct" for reversed causality.

Empirical Results

Using the time series data set having the period 1985-2007, Equations (7) and (8) are estimated using ordinary least squares and the results shown in Table 8.1 and 8.2. The weighting variable is the number of self-employed. The equations are estimated for two different time spans, four years and eight years (L is 4 or 8), in order to gain insight in the lag structures between unemployment and entrepreneurship. A longer lag structure of at least eight years is more compelling because the employment impact of entrepreneurship is not instantaneous but rather requires a number of years for the firm to grow. In this respect Geroski, (1995: 148) states that "Even successful entrants may take more than a decade to achieve a size comparable to the average incumbent." Beesley and Hamilton (1984) pointed out that at the seedbed role of new and small firms challenge incumbent firms. The essentially innovative seedbed activities with the inevitable trial and error (birth and death) mechanism may take more than just a few years to result in creatively destroy incumbent enterprise, the emergence of new enterprise and subsequent growth. Audretsch (1995) shows that share of total employment accounted for by a cohort of new-firm starts in U.S. manufacturing more than double as the firms age from two to six years old (no evidence was provided beyond six years).

Table 8.1 shows when a four-year time span is used in Equation (7), the explanatory power of the model is 14 per cent and it is increased to 76 per cent when the longer time span of 8 years is used in the estimation. In the shorter lag of four years span changes in shelf employment leads to a positive effects on unemployment rate whereas increase in self employment leads to subsequent increase in unemployment in the short period. However, when the longer time spans of eight years, changes in self-employment are found to reduce subsequent unemployment. This is in line with our expectations. There exists a clear "Schumpeter" effect of entrepreneurship reducing unemployment. The magnitudes of these coefficients are 0.15 and –0.05, respectively but these are statistically insignificant.

Table 8.1: Determining the Changes in Rate of Unemployment, $U_t - U_{t-L}$ using Equation (7)

		Lag structure	
	L	4 years	8 years
Constant	α	–2.35	–6.69
		(1.51)	(5.61)
$E_{t-L} - E_{t-2L}$	β	0.15	–0.05
		(0.99)	(0.30)
$U_{t-L} - U_{t-2L}$	γ	0.24	0.53
		(1.02)	(2.89)
R-squared		0.14	0.76
Durbin-Watson		1.70	2.50

Note: Absolute *t*-values are between brackets. The results are from a weighted least squares regression with the weighting variable as the number of self-employed.

The negative effect of self-employment on subsequent unemployment is in conformity with the stylized fact that Gibrat's Law does not hold.

The results from estimating Equation (7) suggest that growth rates are enhanced when there is a greater presence of entrepreneurial firms and are lower when there is a greater presence of large enterprises. The implicit 'failure' of Gibrat's Law may be due to the occurrence of competing products while the newer products are generated by new and small firms following a trial and error process with the consequence that older products are replaced. This Schumpeterian process is driven by a sequence of independent and isolated opportunities (Sutton, 1997: 48). In the Kirznerian perspective (Kirzner, 1973) entrepreneurship is the response to previously unnoticed profit opportunities. This may lead to more consumer satisfaction at lower cost, hence to economic growth and lower levels of unemployment.

Table 8.2 shows that changes in unemployment have a negative impact on subsequent self-employment for all two time periods. This is the "refugee" or "shopkeeper" effect of unemployment stimulating entrepreneurship. The results here indicate that this positive impact is larger when longer time lags are incorporated.

Table 8.2: Determining the Change in Rate of Self-Employment, $E_t - E_{t-L}$ using Equation (8)

		Lag structure	
	L	4 years	8 years
Constant	κ	4.00 (2.05)	7.83 (2.63)
$U_{t-L} - U_{t-2L}$	λ	–0.40 (1.27)	–1.42 (2.26)
$E_{t-L} - E_{t-2L}$	μ	–0.42 (1.27)	–1.39 (4.58)
R-squared		0.40	0.77
Durbin-Watson		2.31	1.90

Note: Absolute *t*-values are between brackets. The results are from a weighted least squares regression with the weighting variable as the number of self-employed.

Thus, empirical results confirm that the Schumpeter's hypothesis that higher levels of entrepreneurship reduce unemployment is accepted on the other hand the refugee's hypothesis or shopkeeper's hypothesis that unemployment stimulates entrepreneurial activity is rejected.

Conclusion

A large number of literatures are trying to ascertain the relationship between unemployment and entrepreneurship but they have produced ambiguous results at best. Some studies find a positive link between unemployment and entrepreneurship (the "refugee" effect), while some others find evidence supporting a negative relationship (the "Schumpeter" effect). This study has attempted to test the complex relationship between unemployment and entrepreneurship. The study based on the data of Manipur from 1985 to 2007 suggests that the relationship between unemployment and entrepreneurship is, in fact, positive in the short period and negative in the longer period. Changes in unemployment clearly have a negative impact on subsequent entrepreneurship. At the same time, changes in entrepreneurship have a positive impact on subsequent unemployment. Because these are essentially dynamic inter-temporal relationships, previous studies estimating contemporaneous relationships have confounded what essentially two relationships each are working in the opposite (dynamic) direction.

The OLS regression results of weighting the self employment, equation (7) by taking 4 years and 8 years lag span are presented in Table 8.1. Our main conclusion is that a change of the number of entrepreneurs Granger causes a change of the rate of unemployment. Interpreting this as causality, one could say that a growth of the number of entrepreneurs leads to an increase of rates of unemployment in the short span whereas it again leads to a reduction of the rate of unemployment in the longer span. Equation (7) also includes lagged unemployment growth in order to correct for the autocorrelation of unemployment growth over time. This autocorrelation of the rate of unemployment appears to be relevant, since γ is in excess of zero. The negative value of the intercept is a representation of the general decline in the rate of unemployment in the period 1985 through 2007 of Manipur. Again the results of OLS regression weighting with the number of entrepreneurs applied in equation (8) are reported in Table 8.2. Our main conclusion is that growth of the number of entrepreneurs Granger causes a reduction of the rate of unemployment. Interpreting this as causality, one could say that a growth of the rate of unemployment leads to a fall of the number of entrepreneurs. Equation (8) also includes lagged growth of the number of entrepreneurs in order to correct for the autocorrelation of the number of entrepreneurs over time. The positive value of the intercept is a representation of a small autonomous rise in entrepreneurship. By and large, support is found for the "Schumpeter effect" of higher level of entrepreneurship reduce unemployment but against the "refugee" or "shopkeeper" effects of unemployment stimulating entrepreneurship. An important qualifier to the present exercises is that entrepreneurship and self employment are synonymous. Self-employment certainly is a vehicle in which entrepreneurship thrives. We have to conclude that, based on the findings of this exercise, there is at least some evidence suggesting that entrepreneurship contributes fighting unemployment.

REFERENCES

Acs, Zoltan J.; Pia Arenius; *Michael Hay and Maria Minniti (2005). Global Entrepreneurship Monitor 2004: Executive Report.* London, UK: London Business School and Wellesley, MA: Babson College.

Audretsch, David B. and Michael Fritsch (1994). The Geography of Firm Births in Germany, *Regional Studies*, 28 (4), 359-365.

Audretsch, David B. and A. Roy Thurik (2000). Capitalism and Democracy in the 21st Century: from the Managed to the Entrepreneurial Economy. *Journal of Evolutionary Economics*, 10, 17-34.

Audretsch, D.B.; M. Carree; A. Stel; and A. Roy Thurik (2001). Does Self-employment reduce Unemployment,? Manuscript.

Audretsch, D. B.; Carree, M.; Stel., A. and A. Roy Thurik (2007). Does Self-employment reduce Unemployment,? Jena Economic Research Papers.

Audretsch, David B. and A. Roy Thurik (2001). What is New about the New Economy: Sources of Growth in the Managed and Entrepreneurial Economies? *Industrial and Corporate Change*, 19, 795-821.

Blau, D. (1987). A time series analysis of self employment in the United States, *Journal of Political Economy*, 95, 445-467.

Blanchflower, D.G. (2000). Self-employment in OECD countries, *Labour Economics*, 7, 471-505.

Bosma, N.; Acs, Z. J.; Autio, E., Coduras, A., Levie, J., (2008). Global Entrepreneurship Monitor Executive Report. *Kauffman Centre for Entrepreneurial Leadership*, the Ewing Marion Kauffman Foundation.

Carree, Martin, Andre van Stel, Roy Thurik and Sander Wennekers (2001). "Economic Development and Business Ownership: An Analysis Using Data of 23 OECD Countries in the Period 1976-1996," *Small Business Economics*.

Carree, Martin (2002). Does Unemployment Affect the Number of Establishments? A Regional Analysis for U.S. States, *Regional Studies*, 36, 389-398.

Chiang and Wainwright (2005). *Fundamental Methods of Mathematical Economics*, 4th Ed., McGraw-Hill, New York.

Evans, D. and L. Leighton (1990). Small business formation by unemployed and employed workers, *Small Business Economics*, 2, 319-330.

Evans, David S. (1987a). The Relationship between Firm Growth, Size and Age: Estimates for 100 Manufacturing Industries, *Journal of Industrial Economics*, 35 (2), 567-581.

Evans, David S. (1987b). Tests of Alternative Theories of Firm Growth, *Journal of Political Economy*, 95 (4), 657-674.

Dickey, D.A. and W.A. Fuller (1979). Distribution of the Estimators for Autoregressive Time Series with a Unit Root, *Journal of the American Statistical Association*, 74, 427-431.

Dunne, Timothy, Mark J. Roberts and Larry Samuelson (1988). Patterns of Firm Entry and Exit in U.S. Manufacturing Industries, *RAND Journal of Economics*, 19, 495-515.

Dunne, Timothy, Mark J. Roberts and Larry Samuelson (1989). The Growth and Failure of US Manufacturing Plants, *Quarterly Journal of Economics*, 104, 671-698.

Garofoli, Gioacchino (1994). New Firm Formation and Regional Development: The Italian Case, *Regional Studies*, 28 (4), 381-394.

Geroski, Paul A. (1989). Entry, Innovation, and Productivity Growth, *Review of Economics and Statistics*, 71, 572-578.

Geroski, Paul A. (1995). What Do We Know About Entry? *International Journal of Industrial Organization*, 13, 421- 440.

Granger, C.W.J. (1969). Investigating Causal Relations by Econometric Models and Cross-Spectral Methods, *Econometrica*, 37, 424-438.

Hall, Bronwyn H. (1987). The Relationship between Firm Size and Firm Growth in the U.S. Manufacturing Sector, *Journal of Industrial Economics*, 35, June, 583-605.

Hamilton, Robert T. (1989). Unemployment and Business Formation Rates: Reconciling Time Series and Cross Section Evidence, *Environment and Planning*, 21, 249-255.

Holcombe, Randall G. (1998). Entrepreneurship and Economic Growth, *Quarterly Journal of Austrian Economics*, 1(2), summer, 45-62.

Kirzner, Israel M. (1973). *Competition and Entrepreneurship*, Chicago: University of Chicago Press.

Knight, Frank H. (1921). *Risk, Uncertainty and Profit*, New York: Houghton Mifflin.

Lucas, R. E. (1978). On the Size Distribution of Business Firms, *Bell Journal of Economics*, 9, 508-523.

Madsen, Jakob B. (2002). The Causality between Investment and Economic Growth, *Economics Letters*, 74, 157-163.

Oxenfeldt, A. (1943). New Firms and Free Enterprise, Washington, D. C., American Council on Public Affairs.

Pfeiffer, F. and Reize, F. (2000a). Business Start-ups by the Unemployed—An Econometric Analysis Based on Firm Data. *Labour Economics*, 7(5), 629-663.

Pfeiffer, F. and Reize, F. (2000b). From Unemployment to Self-Employment—Public Promotion and Selectivity, *International Journal of Sociology*, 30(3), 71-99.

Reynolds, Paul D.; Michael Hay; William D. Bygrave; S. Michael Camp and Erkko Autio (2000). Global Entrepreneurship Monitor: 2000 Executive Report, Kauffman Centre for Entrepreneurial Leadership at the Ewing Marion Kauffman Foundation.

Schumpeter, Joseph A. (1934). *The Theory of Economic Development*, Cambridge, MA: Harvard University Press.

Sims, Christopher A. (1980). Macroeconomics and Reality, *Econometrica*, 48, 1-48.

Storey, David J. (1991). The Birth of New Firms– Does Unemployment Matter? A Review of the Evidence. *Small Business Economics*, 3 (3), 167-178.

Sutton, John (1997). Gibrat's Legacy, *Journal of Economic Literature*, 35, 40-59.

Wennekers, A. and A.R. Thurik (1999). Linking Entrepreneurship and Economic Growth, *Small Business Economics*, 13(1), 27-55.

Part - III
Micro Finance and Rural Development

village artisans and craftsmen, etc. (Ibrahim, 2010), who failed to get credit from cooperative institutions.

The credit is a function of deposit. The higher the amount of deposit, the higher can be the fund for credit to a financial institution to deploy in the economy. The deposit mobilisation of a bank like RRB depends on the income of the surrounding environment where the bank exists and the number of branches spread by it. To make successful deposit accumulation, the RRBs need to bring the rural masses. Similarly, the deployment of credit depends upon the availability of funds, business condition in the economy and the recovery rate. Deposit mobilisation is a significant indicator of bank's performance. The main idea is to tap deposit and culminate savings habit of the community. Further, tapping of potential savings and marshalling them especially for rural uses through small credit and to increase the village level income was the concern area for the RRBs of the country.

The RRBs follow usually the same methods of operation and procedures as followed by commercial banks which have not found favourable for the rural masses. In many cases, banks have not been located at the right place. For instance, the sponsoring banks are also running their branches in the same areas where RRBs are operating. The issue whether location matters for the performance has been addressed in detail by Malhotra (2002). The Narasimham Committee (GoI, 1998) emphasised that while discharging their functions as purveyors of rural credit and as mobilisers of rural savings, RRBs should not ignore the importance of financial viability and operational efficiency. The productivity, profitability and solvency of the RRBs must be maintained and sustained to enable them to function as an effective and efficient institution of rural credit. Hadi and Bagchi (2006) assessed the performance of RRBs in India in general and in West Bengal in particular. The study reviewed the progress of the RRBs in West Bengal in terms of expansion of branches, credit expansion and deposit mobilisation since inception till the end of June 2001. Shivappa (2007) in a study examined the growth in advances, deposits and financial performance of the RRBs. The study covered the RRBs as a whole and discussed mostly theoretical issues rather than any analytical depth. Kumar (2008) opined that amalgamation became a death blow to the credit starved rural poor, most of them are small and marginal farmers, agricultural and landless labourers, and artisans. The study recommended for an immediate de-amalgamation of RRBs in the interest of the vast majority of the rural poor.

However, in the context of present day competition with other banking and non-banking institutions, improvement of performance level is essential for the survival of RRBs. Keeping in view the above facts in mind, the following paragraphs attempt to analyse the performance of RRBs in terms of deposit, credit and credit deposit (CD) ratio, etc. In order to examine the performance of RRBs at all India level, the data have been collected for the period 2000-01 to 2010-11 and interpreted the same with statistical method.

Meghalaya Rural Bank

Meghalaya Rural Bank (MRB) is the only RRB (sponsored by State Bank of India) operating in 6 districts out of 7 districts of Meghalaya as on March 2010. The bank was established on 29th December, 1981 under the RRBs Act of 1976 as a joint undertaking of Government of India, the Government of Meghalaya and State Bank of India with the share capital at the ratio of 50 : 15 : 35. Prior to 1st May, 2007, the name of this RRB was 'Ka Bank Nonkyndong Ri Khasi Jaintia' and replaced the name by 'Meghalaya Rural Bank'. The MRB is operating in 6 districts with 58 branches as on March 2011. It is the 2nd largest bank in the State in terms of branches. The network of MRB is presented in Table 9.1 and Table 9.2.

Table 9.1: Network of Meghalaya Rural Bank as on March 2011

Sl. No	*Districts*	*No. of Branches*
1.	East Khasi Hills District	25
2.	West Khasi Hills District	14
3.	Jaintia Hills District	13
4.	Ri Bhoi District	4
5.	East Garo Hills District	1
6.	West Garo Hills District	1
7.	South Garo Hills District	0
Total		**58**

Source: Annual Report of Meghalaya Rural Bank, Various Issues.

Table 9.1 depicts that as on 2010-11, the East Khasi Hills constituted 25 branches, West Khasi Hills 14 branches, Jaintia Hills 13, Ri Bhoi district 4, West Garo Hills and East Garo Hills districts are having 1 branch each. The branch expansion in Garo Hills district is very negligible because the bank has started functioning in West Garo Hills from

31.03.2008 and East Garo Hills district from 09.01.2009 with only one branch in each district.

Table 9.2: Region-wise Branches of Meghalaya Rural Bank

Year	Rural	Semi-urban	Urban	Total
2000-01	43	3	5	51
2001-02	42	7	2	51
2002-03	42	7	2	51
2003-04	42	7	2	51
2004-05	42	7	2	51
2005-06	42	7	2	51
2006-07	42	7	2	51
2007-08	42	8	2	52
2008-09	42	9	3	54
2009-10	42	10	3	55
2010-11	43	12	3	58

Source: Annual Report of Meghalaya Rural Bank, Various Issues.

It is also observed that more number of branches is expanded in rural areas than the semi-urban or urban areas except in East and West Garo Hills districts as revealed from Table 9.2. The growth of branches was stagnant at the number of 51 till 2006-07 and slightly rose thereafter and reached to 58 branches till 2010-11.

Performance of Meghalaya Rural Bank

In order to measure the general performance of the MRB in Meghalaya various operational indicators like expansion of branches, employee per office, deposits and advances, population served per branch, occupation-wise distribution of credit, priority sector lending, etc., are taken into consideration during the period 2000-2001 to 2010-11.

Branch Network of MRB

The bank has the distinction of accounting for over 50 per cent of the total number of rural bank branches in its area of operation. However, it has not set up any satellite branch or extension counter. The initiatives have taken in the area of renovation of branches with a view to improve the public image of the banks. It is revealed from Table 9.3 that in 2000-01, there were only 51 branches functioning in 4 districts out of seven districts of the State. In 2010-11, the total number of branches has increased to 58 in 6 districts of Meghalaya.

Table 9.3: Branch Network of MRBs

Year	No. of Branches	No. of employees per office	No. of Districts covered	Population Per Branch*
2000-01	51	3.6	4	58,118
2001-02	51	3.5	4	58,118
2002-03	51	3.6	4	58,118
2003-04	51	3.6	4	58,118
2004-05	51	3.6	4	58,118
2005-06	51	3.5	4	58,118
2006-07	51	3.5	4	58,118
2007-08	52	4.1	5	57,000
2008-09	54	3.8	6	54,889
2009-10	55	3.9	6	53,891
2010-11	58	4.4	6	51,104

* Population per branch of MRB is calculated with the total population of Meghalaya as per 2011 Census divided by the number of branches

Source: Annual Report of Meghalaya Rural Bank, Various issues.

It may be observed that during the period of 11 years, the MRB has been able to expand seven more additional branches in the State. The population served per branch is 58.1 thousand in 2000-01 which slightly improved and figured at 51.1 thousand populations served per branch in 2010-11. The scenario is relatively better while compared with the population per branch as a whole which covered 77.3 thousand populations by each branch during 2010-11. The number of employee per branch found to be very low, i.e., around 3 to 4 persons throughout the period. This may be due to the abolition of clerical cadre over a period of time by converting the staff into multipurpose workers. The staff norms, i.e., 4.2 numbers of staff per branch as recommended by Agarwal Committee (2000), has not achieved by MRB till 2009-10. In 2000-01, the average number of employee per office was 3.6 which have risen to 3.9 in 2009-10 and a further increase of 4.4 during the year 2010-11.

The district-wise expansion of bank branches indicates that the East Khasi Hills district is having the highest number of branches. As on 2010-11, the East Khasi Hills constituted 25 numbers of branches, West Khasi Hills 14 branches, Jaintia Hills 13, Ri Bhoi district 4, West Garo Hills and East Garo Hills districts are having 1 branch in each district. The branch expansion in Garo Hills district of Meghalaya is very negligible because the bank has started functioning in West Garo Hills w.e.f. 31.03.2008 and East Garo Hills district w.e.f. 09.01.2009, with only one branch in each district. It is also observed that more number of branches are expanded in rural areas than the semi-urban or urban areas except in East and West Garo Hills districts. The Table 9.4 presents the district-wise and rural-urban area-wise expansion.

Deposit Mobilisation of MRB

The total amount of deposit mobilised by the MRB in 2000-01 was Rs.12,26,293 thousands and the amount has increased to Rs. 67,74,188 thousands in 2010-11. It indicates that the increase in total deposit mobilisation is 5.52 fold during 2000-01 to 2010-11. The amount of deposit per branch was Rs. 2.4 crores in 2000-2001 which has increased to Rs.11.6 crores in 2010-11. The average deposit per branch of RRBs was Rs. 2.59 crores in 2000-01 which has gone up to Rs. 10.47 crores per office during the year 2010-11. The MRB have been doing at par with the RRBs in terms of mobilisation of deposits. However, scenario of per capita deposits indicates that MRB is performing much better than the RRBs as a whole. The per capita deposit of MRB increased from Rs. 0.41 thousands in 2000-01 to Rs. 2.28 thousands in 2010-11; the corresponding figure for RRBs increased from Rs. 0.31 thousands to Rs. 1.35 thousands. The data relating to deposit mobilisation of MRB may be had from Table 9.7.

Credit Allocation of MRB

Similarly, the total loans and advances outstanding of the MRB in 2000-01 was Rs. 3,03,392 thousands. In 2010-11 the quantum of total loans and advances outstanding has increased to Rs. 21,61,545 thousands. The loans and advances per branch of the MRB was Rs. 0.59 crore in 2000-01 which increased to Rs. 3.72 crores in 2010-11; the corresponding figures for RRBs was Rs. 1.1 crores in 2000-01, increased to Rs. 6.27 crores in 2010-11. The information relating to loans and advances per branch indicate that MRB is lagging behind the RRB's loan performance. It is also observed that in terms of per capita loans and advances, the MRB has been maintaining the same rate at which RRBs of the country are deploying loans and advances. Table 9.5 presents the data relating to credit channelization of MRB.

Table 9.4: District-wise Branch Expansion of Meghalaya Rural Bank

(Figures in number)

Year	East Khasi Hills			West Khasi Hills			Jaintia Hills			Ri-Bhoi			West Garo-Hills			East Garo Hills			Grand Total
	Rur-al	Semi urban & Urban	Total	Rural	Semi urban & Urban	Total	Rural	Semi urban & Urban	Total	Rural	Semi urban & Urban	Total	Rural	Semi urban & Urban	Total	Rural	Semi urban & Urban	Total	
2000-01	16	5	21	14	1	15	12	1	13	1	1	2	—	—	—	—	—	—	51
2001-02	15	6	21	14	1	15	12	1	13	1	1	2	—	—	—	—	—	—	51
2002-03	15	6	21	14	1	15	12	1	13	1	1	2	—	—	—	—	—	—	51
2003-04	15	6	21	14	1	15	12	1	13	1	1	2	—	—	—	—	—	—	51
2004-05	15	6	21	14	1	15	12	1	13	1	1	2	—	—	—	—	—	—	51
2005-06	15	6	21	14	1	15	12	1	13	1	1	2	—	—	—	—	—	—	51
2006-07	15	6	21	14	1	15	12	1	13	1	1	2	—	—	—	—	—	—	51
2007-08	15	6	21	13	1	14	12	1	13	2	1	3	—	1	1	—	—	—	52
2008-09	15	7	22	13	1	14	12	1	13	2	1	3	—	1	1	—	1	1	54
2009-10	15	8	23	13	1	14	12	1	13	2	1	3	—	1	1	—	1	1	55
2010-11	15	10	25	13	1	14	12	1	13	3	1	4	—	1	1	—	1	1	58

Source: *Annual Report of Meghalaya Rural Bank, Various Issues.*

Table 9.5: Performance of MRB: Deposit, Advances and CD Ratio

(Amount in Rs. thousands)

Year	Total Deposits	Deposit per branch	Per Capita Deposit	Total Loans & advances	Loans and advances per branch	Per Capita Loans and Advances	CD Ratio
2000-01	12,26,293	24,044.91	0.414	3,03,392	5,948.86	0.102	30.00
2001-02	14,32,184	28,082.02	0.483	3,52,205	6,905.98	0.119	25.00
2002-03	15,53,924	30,470.00	0.524	4,06,167	7,964.06	0.137	26.00
2003-04	17,58,127	34,473.08	0.593	4,62,522	9,069.06	0.156	26.31
2004-05	21,99,196	43,121.49	0.742	5,42,438	10,636.04	0.183	24.67
2005-06	25,04,085	49,099.71	0.845	6,66,700	13,072.55	0.225	26.63
2006-07	28,01,385	54,929.12	0.945	8,25,357	16,183.47	0.279	29.36
2007-08	31,59,848	61,957.80	1.066	9,73,316	19,084.63	0.328	30.80
2008-09	40,39,445	74,804.54	1.363	11,86,477	23,264.26	0.400	29.37
2009-10	53,23,070	96,783.09	1.796	16,04,869	29,179.44	0.542	30.15
2010-11	67,74,188	1,16,796.34	2.286	21,61,545	37,268.02	0.729	31.91

Source: *Annual Reports of Meghalaya Rural Bank, various issues.*

Credit Deposit Ratio of MRB

The credit deposit ratio of the Meghalaya Rural Bank was 30 per cent in 2000-01 which increased to 31.91 per cent in 2010-11 as displayed in Table 9.7. The CD ratio of MRB is not up to the mark while compared with RRB as a whole. The same for RRBs was 41.0 per cent in 2000-01 which augmented to 59.6 per cent in 2010-11. The reason of significant low ratio of MRB may be attributed to non-recovery of loans, intentional defaulters, lack of supervision of end use of bank credit, lack of implementation of bankable schemes. This exhibited poor credit absorption capacity of the entire area along with lack of entrepreneurial zeal to undertake viable projects.

Relationship between Growth of Deposit and Growth of Advances

In order to examine the degree of relationship between growth of deposits and growth of advances of MRB, coefficient of correlation analysis has been employed. For this purpose, deposit per office and advance per office have been considered for the period of 11 years from 2000-2001 to 2010-11. The result obtained as under:

$r = 0.997$; $t = 21.06$ (cal.); $t_{0.05}$ (9 df.)=1.833 (tab); $t_{0.01}$ (9 df.)=2.821 (tab)

The high correlation (r =0.997) value between deposit per office and advances per office are statistically significant at 1 per cent and 5 per cent level of significance. The calculated value of 't' is significantly higher than the table value at (5% and 1% level). It confirms that over the years deposit per office and advance per office of the MRB are increasing in the same proportion. The high correlation coefficient will undoubtedly indicate more savings habit of the people as well as higher volume of credit deployment of MRB in the area. Hence, the hypothesis *"There is no difference in the growth of deposit as well as the growth of credit of MRB"* is found correct. It is also found that the relationship between deposits and advances per branch of MRB is exactly same as RRB as a whole.

Further, an attempt has been made to assess the relationship between growth of deposits both RRB as a whole and MRB. We employ in this respect the analysis of correlation co-efficient between incremental deposits per branch of RRB and incremental deposits per branch of MRB during 2000-01 to 2010-11. The result of correlations is as follows:

$r = 0.83$; $t = 4.19$ (cal.); $t_{0.05}$ (8 df.) = 1.860; $t_{0.01}$ (8 df.) = 2.896

The result shows high correlation ($r = 0.83$) between the incremental deposit per office of RRBs and the MRB is statistically significant. This indicates that the MRB is mobilizing the deposits at the same rate what the RRB at the national level does. Hence, the hypothesis, "*The MRB is mobilizing the deposits at par with RRB over the years*" found valid.

In order to assess the extent of credit channelization by the MRB in the context of RRBs at the national level, we have calculated correlation coefficient between incremental advances per branch of MRB and RRB. The result obtained as under:

$r = 0.93$; $t = 7.11$ (cal.); $t_{0.05}$ (8 df.) = 1.860; $t_{0.01}$ (8 df.) = 2.896

The highly positive correlation (r =0.93) between the incremental loans and advances per branch in the RRBs of India and per branch loans and advances of MRB is significant both at 1 per cent and 5 per cent level of significance. It indicates that along with the increase in incremental credit in the national level RRBs, the incremental credit in the MRB is also increasing at the same pace. Hence, our hypothesis, "*There exists a close relationship between the extent of credit channelization of MRB as well as RRBs*" found to be correct. This implies that MRB maintained the national tempo of credit channelization rural banks. In other words, MRB are deploying credit for the economic growth of the area from which they have mobilised funds.

Priority and Non-Priority Sector Lending of MRB

The lending practices of MRB may be divided into priority sector lending and non-priority sector lending. Table 9.6 presents the facts relating to priority and non-priority sector lending of MRB.

From Table 9.6, the total amount of priority sector lending wa Rs. 60,800 thousands in 2000; the amount, however, has increased to Rs. 5,39,552 thousands in 2010. The share of priority sector lending declined from 61.97 per cent to 58.79 per cent. In case of non-prioity sector lending the aggregate amount in 2000 was Rs. 37,311 thousands. In 2010, the amount has increased to the quantum of Rs. 3,78,90 thousands. The percentage share of priority sector lending to total lending is declining over the years but the percentage share of non-priority sector has increased over the years. In the year 2000, the share of non-priority

Table 9.6: Priority and Non-Priority Sector Lending of Meghalaya Rural Bank (As on March)

(Amount Rs. in Thousand)

Year	Sector-wise Advances			Percentage Share of Priority Sector Advances	Percentage Share of Non-Priority Sector Advances	Priority Sector Advances Per Branch	Non-Priority Sector Advances Per Branch	Advances Per Branch
	Priority Sector	Non-Priority Sector	Total					
2000	60,800	37,311	98,111	61.97	38.03	1,192.16	731.59	5,948.86
2001	71,450	52,166	1,23,616	57.80	42.20	1,400.98	1,022.86	6,905.98
2002	78,646	73,515	1,52,161	51.69	48.31	1,542.08	1,441.47	7,964.06
2003	77,281	94,367	1,71,648	45.02	54.98	1,515.31	1,850.33	9,069.06
2004	97,531	92,580	1,90,111	51.30	48.70	1,912.37	1,815.29	10,636.04
2005	1,20,051	1,28,543	2,48,594	48.29	51.71	2,353.94	2,520.45	13,072.55
2006	2,01,848	1,34,775	3,36,623	40.04	40.04	3,957.80	2,642.65	16,183.47
2007	2,58,688	1,54,011	4,12,699	62.68	37.32	4,974.77	2,961.75	18,717.62
2008	2,73,253	1,94,927	4,68,180	58.36	41.64	5,060.24	3,609.76	21,971.80
2009	3,92,945	3,30,195	7,23,140	54.34	45.66	7,144.46	6,003.55	29,179.44
2010	5,39,552	3,78,190	9,17,742	58.79	41.21	9,302.62	6,520.52	37,268.02

Source: Calculated based on Annual Reports of MRB, Various Issues.

sector lending was 38.03 per cent, increased to 41.2 per cent in 2010. This indicates that a positive attitude of MRB in lending the non-priority sector. Similarly, the priority sector advances per branch was Rs. 1,192.16 thousands in 2000 and it increased to Rs. 9,302.62 thousands in 2010. In the same manner, the non-priority sector advances per branch was Rs. 731.59 thousands in 2000 which increased to Rs. 6,520.52 thousands in 2010. However, the declining share of priority sector lending of MRB over the years has a direct contradiction with the RRBs. The share of priority sector lending of RRBs as a whole has been improved from 67.6 per cent to 83.1 per cent. This necessitates a further enquiry on the relationship of total advances with priority and non-priority sector advances.

An attempt has been made in the following paragraph to ascertain the relationship among priority sector advances, non-priority sector advances and the total advances. For this purpose, correlation coefficient analysis is employed among the variables, i.e., incremental priority sector advances per branch, incremental non-priority sector advances per branch and incremental advances per branch for the period of 2001 to 2010.

It reveals that the coefficient of correlation between priority sector and non-priority sector advances ($r = 0.46$) is neither significant at 5 per cent level nor at 1 per cent level of significance. This indicates that the increase in non-priority sector lending is not followed the growth of priority sector lending of MRB. In other words, there exists a difference in lending practices of MRB for priority and non-priority sector. The MRB shows a reverse trend in lending to priority and non-priority sector while compared with RRBs as a whole. In case of RRB, there is no difference in lending practices in priority and non-priority sector. Similarly, the coefficient of correlation between advances and priority sector lending ($r = 0.88$) is statistically significant both at 5 per cent level and at 1 per cent level of significance. It indicates that along with the increase in advances, the priority sector lending is also increasing at the same pace.

From Table 9.7, the coefficient of correlation between the advances and non-priority sector lending ($r = 0.61$) is statistically significant at 5 per cent but not at 1 per cent level of significance. It also suggests that along with the increase in advances of the MRB, the non-priority sector lending is also increasing but not in the same rate. By and large, it inferred that the MRB is giving more weightage to the priority sector than the non-priority sector by providing proportionately more advances to fulfil the motto of rural economic development of the region.

Table 9.7: Correlation Matrix

Variables	*PSAPB*	*NPSAPB*	*APB*
PSAPB	1		
NPSAPB	0.46NS (1.46)	1	
APB	0.88* (5.19)	0.61** (2.19)	1

$t_{0.05}$(8 df.) = 1.860 and $t_{0.01}$(8df.) = 2.896.
*significant at both 5 per cent and 1 per cent level.
**significant at 5 per cent level only.
NS—not significant.
PSAB = Priority Sector Advances Per Branch.
NPSAB = Non-Priority Sector Advances Per Branch.
APB = Advances Per Branch.

Source: Calculated based on Table 9.6.

Deployment of Priority Sector Lending by MRB

The RRBs were established to serve the rural poor and backward areas. The MRB as a regional bank has an enormous role to strengthen the backward economy of the State by way of lending to the priority sector like agricultural loan, SHGs loan, retail trade, small industries and business loan, etc. Table 9.8 presents the position of priority sector lending by MRB. It provides crop loans to the farmers. The crop loan is required to farmers for buying seeds, manure and in harvesting time, etc. Under priority sector lending, the total amount of crop loans provided was Rs. 8,357 thousands in March 2000 increased to Rs. 1,48,237 thousands in March 2010. During the period under consideration, there has been increased in percentage share of crop loan from 22.40 per cent to 27.47 per cent. For long term purposes like land development, irrigation, etc., the bank gives loan as agricultural term loans. The agricultural term loans increased from Rs. 2,341 thousands to Rs. 22,771 thousands but its percentage share declined from 6.27 per cent to 4.22 per cent over the years. Similarly for other agro allied activities the aggregate amount of credit increased from Rs. 8, 371 thousands to Rs. 20,589 thousands but its share to total priority sector lending declined sharply. In similar manner, the MRB's loans for self-help groups swelled from Rs. 15 thousands to

Table 9.8: Priority Sector Lending of the MRB (As on March)

(Amount Rs. in Thousand)

Category/ Year	2000	2001	2002	2003	2004	2005	2006	2007	2008	2009	2010
Crop Loans	8,357	11,572	13,133	16,531	18,023	30,744	45,336	64,707	85,951	1,17,005	1,48,237
	(22.40)	(16.20)	(16.70)	(21.39)	(18.48)	(25.61)	(22.46)	(25.01)	(31.45)	(29.78)	(27.47)
Agricultural Term Loans	2,341	794	798	857	603	3,441	26,905	19,182	19,425	20,336	22,771
	(6.27)	(1.11)	(1.01)	(1.11)	(0.62)	(2.87)	(13.33)	(7.42)	(7.11)	(5.18)	(4.22)
Allied Agriculture Term Loans	8,371	3,391	2,326	3,582	3,357	3,624	10,565	5,579	4,996	7,556	20,589
	(22.44)	(4.75)	(2.96)	(4.64)	(3.44)	(3.02)	(5.23)	(2.16)	(1.83)	(1.92)	(3.82)
Self Help Groups	15	627	1,047	2,493	3,762	3,351	4,866	15,388	9,149	9,749	14,505
	(0.04)	(0.88)	(1.33)	(3.23)	(3.86)	(2.79)	(2.41)	(5.95)	(3.35)	(2.48)	(2.69)
Retail Trade/Small Business	12,052	15,024	18,437	14,499	22,429	22,169	37,508	49,492	46,334	82,727	1,08,254
	(32.30)	(21.03)	(23.44)	(18.76)	(23.00)	(18.47)	(18.58)	(19.13)	(16.96)	(21.05)	(20.06)
Transport Operators	17,627	21,699	21,823	23,463	31,560	34,387	31,433	25,751	22,264	44,015	1,11,406
	(47.24)	(30.37)	(27.75))	(30.36)	(32.36)	(28.64)	(15.57)	(9.95)	(8.15)	(11.20)	(20.65)
Small Scale Industries	9,259	13,765	15,753	7,336	10,608	12,587	14,440	17,786	33,134	34,303	37,788
	(24.82)	(19.27)	(20.03)	(9.49)	(10.88)	(10.48)	(7.15)	(6.88)	(12.13)	(8.73)	(7.00)
Housing	2,772	4,578	108	8,329	6,770	5,911	21,021	48,971	43,250	37,820	55,777
	(7.43)	(6.41)	(0.14)	(10.78)	(6.94)	(4.92)	(10.41)	(18.93)	(15.83)	(9.62)	(10.33)
Education Loan	0	0	5,221	191	191	150	314	1,663	1,871	2,194	3,534
			(6.64)	(0.25)	(0.20)	(0.12)	(0.16)	(0.64)	(0.68)	(0.56)	(0.65)
Others	0	0	0	0	228	3,687	9,460	10,169	6,879	7,236	16,691
					(0.23)	(3.07)	(4.69)	(3.93)	(2.52)	(1.84)	(3.09)
Total of Priority Sector Lending	37,311	71,450	78,646	77,281	97,531	1,20,051	2,01,848	2,58,688	2,73,253	3,92,945	5,39,552
	(100)	(100)	(100)	(100)	(100)	(100)	(100)	(100)	(100)	(100)	(100)

Note: Figures in parentheses indicate percentage to total priority sector advances.

Source: *Annual Reports of Meghalaya Rural Bank, various Issues*

Table 9.9: Correlation Matrix on Priority Sector Lending

	Row I	Row 2	Row 3	Row 4	Row 5	Row 6	Row 7	Row 8	Row 9	Row 10	Row 11
Row 1	1										
Row 2	0.990628	1									
Row 3	0.608236	0.632382	1								
Row 4	0.795227	0.742752	0.603515	1							
Row 5	0.712384	0.737492	0.565085	0.507539	1						
Row 6	0.993307	0.973855	0.60443	0.815673	0.737826	1					
Row 7	0.791582	0.726703	0.269158	0.91066	0.456736	0.810029	1				
Row 8	0.911033	0.952691	0.566726	0.577503	0.627597	0.868936	0.571081	1			
Row 9	0.799779	0.845179	0.72227	0.578188	0.946754	0.800069	0.465604	0.795193	1		
Row 10	0.950635	0.968269	0.561644	0.708525	0.847577	0.94449	0.719372	0.916651	0.911012	1	
Row 11	0.794224	0.782858	0.794955	0.878736	0.771125	0.806373	0.711961	0.621311	0.820234	0.7863	1

Source: Calculated by the Researcher based on Table 9.9.

Variables Indicated from Row 1 to Row 11 are as follows:

Row 1 = Crop Loans, Row 2 = Agricultural Term Loans, Row 3 = Allied Agricultural Term Loans, Row 4 = Self-Help Groups, Row 5 = Retail Trade/Small Business, Row 6 = Transport Operators, Row 7 = Small Scale Industries, Row 8 = Housing, Row 9 = Education Loan, Row 10 = Others, Row 11 = Total Credit.

10

Financial Institutions in Financing Small and Medium Enterprises : A Study of Garo Hills in Meghalaya

J.U. Ahmed and *Md. Abdul Rashid*

Introduction

The financial institutions play a very significant role in the economic development of any country. The commercial banks emerged as the purveyor of credit requirement of the small borrowers and played a positive role in institutionalising the community savings. An excessive focus has been laid on quantitative achievement and social obligations. Apart from this, the reason of expansion of bank branches may be attributed to develop a strong banking base to serve the economy efficiently and meet the banking needs of various segments of the economy by developing specialized banks. However, with the development of alternative sources of funds, the dependence of industry on commercial banks for meeting their credit requirements has been declined although the share of credit to industry in India was significantly highest among all countries (Ahmed, 2010a). The corporate sector of India is heavily dependent on the banking sector in comparison with other countries (Chavan and Lamba, 2007).

The diversification of a large fraction of bank credit from the traditional sector to the priority sector like small sector is a remarkable feature of credit deployment in the post-nationalization era. The concept of priority sector lending is mainly intended to ensure assistance from the banking system in an increasing manner to those sectors of the economy which has not received adequate support of institutional finance in the past. Since seventies, Reserve Bank of India (RBI) and Government of India have stipulated some guidelines, viz., financing in the priority sector on an increasing scale, more deployment of credit backward regions, preparation and implementation of district credit plan (DCP) and measures for enhancing productivity, employment and economic growth with social justice (Narasimham, 1994).

The commercial banks have of late emerged as the major supplier of industrial credit for Small and Medium Enterprises (SME) in the national and State levels as well as in the districts under study. A large variety of financial institutions including banks have emerged basically after independence to satisfy the financial requirements of both small and large scale industries at national, regional and State levels. There have been several confusing features of credit flow to the small sector in recent years as is evident from the various studies reviewed earlier. The overall availability of credit to micro and small enterprises (MSEs) as percentage of net bank credit (NBC) of the scheduled commercial banks (SCBs) has declined from 13.9 per cent in March 1997 to 6.2 per cent in March 2006 and thereafter it experienced a swelling trend and reached to 10 per cent of bank credit in March 2009 (RBI, 2010). In the light of the above, an attempt has been made in this chapter to analyze the bank financing of SME sector in Garo Hills of Meghalaya.

The Background

The economic history of the developed nations shows that economic growth and growth of financial infrastructure moves together. The role of banks is a very crucial in the industrial development of any country or region. A sound and progressive banking system is prerequisite for industrial development. The loan/credit is the pillar to industrial development in any region. In India, commercial banks are granting short term and medium term loans to industries. Banks are the major apparatus of rapid industrializations of an economy. Basu (1977) observed that the commercial banking system can play to help in the process of economic development by lending money in short and medium term. Since the lion's share of deposits is repayable on demand, they cannot lock up funds for longer periods. Usually, loans are guaranteed against collateral securities. The commercial banks are a major source of financing SMEs. The industrial houses require credit for short period for working capital and for long periods for their fixed capital requirements. The commercial banks continue to be the major institutions, meeting over 90 per cent of the institutional credit need of SME sector (SIDBI, 2010). Also, Gomez (2008) observed that the commercial banks have maintained an attitude of superiority as regards the provision of long-term capital to industry. As the deposits in commercial banks are for short periods and repayable on demand, they cannot lock up their funds for long periods by providing fixed capital to industries. So, they provide only short-term capital to meet the working capital requirements of industries. Banks extended/ granted loans and advances to industries in the form of hypothecation and often in clean advances. The role played by the commercial banks in financing industries is not adequate especially, their share in the sphere of long term finance for industries in undoubtedly negligible. Shekher and Shekhar (2005) opined that even in the case of providing short term finance, banks granted loans only on the security of easily realizable assets and not on fixed assets and they insist a large margin even in the case of easily realizable assets, thereby making the system expensive. Further, most of the banks do not maintain adequate technical staff required for the proper valuation of assets and naturally, to be on the safer side, they undervalue the assets. In the opinion of Sharma (1974) the role of commercial banks lies in accelerating investment and growth in a developing economy. The report of the task force chaired by V.S. Vyas (1974)[1] stated that about 80 per cent of the commercial banks credit are available to the SSI sector is in the form of working capital and the balance is as term loans. The study group (1969) headed by D.R Gadgil recommended for the adoption of an "area approach" for development of credit and banking in the country on the basis of local conditions. All India Rural Credit Review Committee in 1969 endorsed the view that commercial banks should come forward to finance activities in rural areas. The committee of bankers appointed by RBI under Sr. F.K.F. Nariman also endorsed this area approach. RBI accepted the recommendations and formulated the Lead Bank Scheme (LBS) in 1969. Under the scheme, each district had been assigned to different banks (public and private) to act as a consortium leader to co-ordinate an effort of the banks in the district, particularly in the matters of branch expansion and credit planning. The most important development in the history of LBS was the constitution of district consultative committees (DCCs) in all the districts, to facilitate co-ordination of activities of all the banks and financial institutions on the one hand and government department on the other. Under the LBS the designated banks were made key instruments for local development and entrusted with the responsibility of indentifying growth centres, assessing deposit potential and credit gaps and evolving a coordinated approach for credit deployment in each district, in association with other banks and other agencies. The LBS underwent significant transformation in 1989 when "service area approach" was merged into the scheme. The service area restrictive provisions were removed in 2004, except for the government sponsored programme. As in March 2009, there were 26 numbers of banks mostly in the public sector, which have been assigned lead responsibility in 622 districts of the country (RBI, 2009). The prime objective of LBS is to bring about overall improvement in branch expansion, mobilization of deposits and lending to the priority sectors, especially in rural/semi-urban areas.

The State Bank of India (SBI) is to act as consortium leader of the districts under study. The lead bank prepares the district credit plan (DCP) and annual action plan (AAP) with the help of bank officials, developmental agencies, district industries centres, etc. The LBS was evolved as a framework to be more responsive to the need of rural and semi-urban economy. The objectives of the scheme cannot be achieved unless rural lending is properly tied to well designed programmes of development. This requires an effective co-ordination and co-operations not only between lead banks and other banks but also between banks on one side and the concerned government machineries and other development agencies on the other side.

Garo Hills Districts of Meghalaya

Garo Hills is the westernmost part of Meghalaya and lies south western corner of Assam, covers an area of 8167 sq km comprising 16 towns and 19 Community Rural Development Blocks in 6 sub-divisions of three districts (East Garo Hills, West Garo Hills, South Garo Hills) of Meghalaya (GoM: 2006). It is bounded on the north by the district of Goalpara district and west by Dhubri district of Assam, on the east by West Khasi Hills of Meghalaya and on the south by the Rangpur and Mymunsing districts of Bangladesh. The region presents an attractive topography with a vast forested area grown from the foothills and containing rich biological resources (Gassah, 1984). This land is traversed from north -west to south-east by a central hill range known as Tura range, dividing the valleys of Brahmaputra and Surma. The average height of these hills is two thousand feet, and the highest peak, Nokrek (4652 feet), is a little to the east of Tura town. As per 2001 Census, the literacy rate in the districts under study was 57.4 per cent which is lower than State's average (63.31%) and national average (65.4%) (GoI, 2005-06). Nearly 55 per cent of the geographical area is under forest and 23 per cent are under agriculture. High lands within the district are generally planted with tea, coffee, betelnut, cotton, rubber and cashewnut while plain areas of districts are covered with jute, rice, muster seed, etc. The sugarcane, oil seeds, potatoes, pulses, etc. are also produced. The district of Garo Hills is identified as one of the industrially backward district. As per official records of the district, total number of registered small enterprises 1,388 in 2007-08 (GoM, 2008-09). The district industries centres (DICs) are imparting training to the rural artisans in trade, leatherwork, knitting, weaving, tailoring, bamboo work, carpentry, etc. There is only one Industrial Training Institute (ITI) at Tura of West Garo Hills district catering specialized training to the entrepreneurs of the districts under study. Regional Vocational Training Institute (RVTI) at Tura is also offered the courses to the women in tailoring, computer training, beautician, etc.

Transportation is one of the important infrastructural needs of the people in order to help productive activities and the well-being of the society. Unfortunately the road transportation is not up to the mark. The districts have a road density of 33 km per 100 sq km area during 2001-02. However, regular helicopter services and taxis and buses are available from Tura, the headquarters of West Garo Hills district to Shillong, the capital city of Meghalaya. There is no railways. Guwahati, the capital city of Assam is connected with rail transportation with rest of the country. 52 per cent of the total villages are electrified in the districts while 60 per cent in Meghalaya. The number of registered unemployed in the districts has increased over the years.

The adequacy of finance is essential for development of a dynamic industrial sector. The rate of growth of flow of institutional finance in the districts has not shown significant rise. For accelerating the pace of industrialization the Meghalaya Industrial Development Corporation (MIDC) which was incorporated in 1971 extended a branch office at Tura in 1980 which is catering the requirements of the study area. The districts of Garo Hills have 25 per cent of bank offices of the State (SLBC, 2010). At present, there are 48 number of branches of commercial banks, 2 number of branches of Meghalaya Rural Bank and 16 numbers of branches of Meghalaya Co-Operative Apex Bank are operating in the districts. The Table 10.1 shows the banking network of the area under study.

Table 10.1: Banking Network in Garo Hills Districts as on December 2010

Types of Bank	*Number of Bank Branches*			
	East Garo Hills	*West Garo Hills*	*South Garo Hills*	*Total*
1. Commercial Banks	15	29	4	48
2. Meghalaya Rural Banks	1	1	0	2
3. Meghalaya Co-operative Apex Banks	4	10	2	16
Total	**20**	**40**	**6**	**66**

Source: State Level Bankers Committee, Meghalaya.

It may be observed that the existing bank branches are inadequate to serve the population in those districts. Therefore, major areas are still remaining unserved by the banks and the rural masses are yet to access the banking services. The area under study is economically backward and that could be observed from the presence of few numbers of registered industries, untapped and under-utilization of resources, geographical isolation, poor communication network, etc. In order to improve the economic condition of the people, attention for the development of industries particularly SMEs with appropriate developmental strategy may have to be taken.

Objectives and Hypotheses of the Study

After having observed the issues relating to institutional financing of small and medium enterprises the present work is ventured with an intensive study in Garo Hills, the western part of Meghalaya over the years. The proposed study sets the following objectives:

1. To study the pattern of institutional financing of SMEs over the years.
2. To study the interrelationship between institutional finance and performance of small and medium enterprises.

The following hypotheses have been framed to meet the objectives of the proposed study:

1. Consequent upon change in structure of industrial finance, the financial intermediaries have enlarged their assistance.
2. There exists a close relationship between institutional finance and performance of SMEs in the area under study.

Banks Performance in the Districts

Network of Banks and Financial Institutions in Garo Hills

Banks and financial institutions are the nerve system of an economy. The institutional finance plays a decisive role in industrial financing both developed and underdeveloped area of any country. So, a well developed banking and financial institutions are *sin qua non* for industrial development. There is a dearth of banks and financial institutions in Garo Hills. There is no any branch of development financial institutions in Garo Hills except a branch of MIDC. But SIDBI branch in Shillong and NEDFI in Guwahati expected to look after the financial requirements of industrial houses of Garo Hills. The MIDC, the only institution is processing, sanctioning and disbursing loan, etc., from its headoffice in Shillong through the branch office at Tura. A detailed discussion of MIDC has been done in the later pages of this chapter.

Apart from these, the commercial banks like State Bank of India (Lead Bank in entire Garo Hills), United Bank of India (UBI) and Central Bank of India (CBI) are the nationalized banks; ICICI bank, AXIS bank and HDFC bank are the newly opened private sector banks; the only Regional Rural Banks—the Meghalaya Rural Bank (MRB); the only State Co-operative Bank—Meghalaya Co-operative Apex Bank (MCAB) operating in Garo Hills. The Table 10.2 shows the picture of banking network in the three districts of Garo Hills.

The rural areas of the districts are holding the lion's share of bank branches as on March 2010. The number of urban branches are only 6 out of 66. The West Garo hills districts are ventured with maximum number of bank branches, the figure being 40 in number. Out of the total bank branches, the commercial banks hold the majority share, i.e., 48 number of branches. It is clear from the above that the three districts of Garo hills are underbanked and there is a dearth of financial institutions in the districts under study.

Expansion of Bank Branches

There has been a rapid expansion of bank branches in the country since the introduction of lead bank scheme, especially in the rural and backward areas. At the national level, the number of bank branches of all scheduled commercial banks grew from 65,543 on March 1997 to 92,534 at the end of March 2009 and to 98,694 at the end of March 2010. In Meghalaya, total number of bank branches was 180 in March 1997; the figure increased to 213 in March 2012 showing an increase of 33 bank branches within 14 years. While assessing branch expansion in Garo Hills, it is observed that only 7 scheduled commercial banks with 48 number of branches were operating in the three districts of Garo Hills as on March 1997. During 1997-2010, only 1 branch in West Garo Hills, 1 in East Garo Hills district and no branches in South Garo Hills district were opened. The poor progress towards the opening of the branches may be due to lack of proper infrastructural facilities in the districts. The branch expansion of the scheduled commercial banks is presented in Table 10.3.

Population Per Branch of the Commercial Banks in the Districts

The nationalization of commercial banks evidenced rapid expansion of bank branches in the country, especially in the rural and backward areas. But there has been an uneven growth of banking in different States of the country. Table 10.4 reveals that the all India average population per branch office was 13,721 persons in 2010 as compared to 20,027 persons in Meghalaya. But the average population per branch in Garo Hills were much higher than the national as well as State average. The same for Garo Hills were much higher than the national and State's average. The East Garo Hills district is having 21,175 persons, West Garo Hills 22,170 persons and South Garo Hills 35,644 persons. The average population of Garo Hills in per bank branch is 22,982. The three districts of Garo Hills carrying about 37.22 per cent of population of the State but in case of share of commercial bank branches, it possesses only 30.38 per cent. It is clear from the above figures that financial exclusion is most acute in Garo Hills in general and the South Garo Hills in particular.

Deposit Mobilization by Commercial Banks

The resource mobilization is a fundamental part of banking activity. The basic principle of branch expansion is to tap deposits and culminate

Table 10.2: Networks of Banks and Financial Institutions in Garo Hills as on 31st March, 2010

Number of Branches

Districts	*Rural*	*Semi-Urban*	*Urban*	*Total*	*Commercial Banks*	*RRB*	*MCAB*	*Total*
	1	*2*	*3*	*4 (1+2+3)*	*5*	*6*	*7*	*8 (5+6+7)*
East Garo Hills	16	2	2	20	15	1	4	20
West Garo Hills	26	11	3	40	29	1	10	40
South Garo Hills	5	0	1	6	4	0	2	6
Total of Garo Hills	47	13	6	66	48	2	16	66
Meghalaya	142	45	71	258	158	56	44	258

Source: SLBC, Meghalaya.

savings habit of the community. Further, tapping of potential saving and marshalling them for strategic uses for productive purposes in particular is the main objective. As a result, various schemes were launched over the years. Under 20-point programme (1975) the government directed the banks to make all possible efforts to access to new deposits that can only expedite the pace of lending activities. The most important functions of the commercial banks are to mobilize savings in the form of deposits from public. Bank nationalization and expansion of bank branches have contributed greatly to the development of banking habit among the people, thereby boost up mobilization of savings in the form of deposits in the economy. In this context, Bhattacharya (1985) studied implications of bank deposit mobilization and opined that the ability of banks to play developmental role depends on mobilization of deposits. It is observed that there has been a substantial rise of bank deposits during the period under consideration. The trend of increase in deposits of the scheduled commercial banks in the study area is presented in the Table 10.5.

The Table 10.5 clearly shows that deposits have grown up from Rs.10,019 lakhs in March 1997 to Rs. 73,520 lakhs in March 2010 recording a growth of 7.34 times during the period of 14 years. During the same period, deposits have grown 8.43 times in the State level and 8.89 times at the national level. The growth of deposit in the study area is lower (CAGR = 16.6) than the State's average growth (CAGR = 17.8)

Table 10.3: Branch Expansion of Scheduled Commercial Banks

Number of branches

District/ (31st March)	*1997*	*1998*	*1999*	*2000*	*2001*	*2002*	*2003*	*2004*	*2005*	*2006*	*2007*	*2008*	*2009*	*2010*
East Garo Hills	15	15	15	15	15	15	15	15	15	15	15	15	16	16
South Garo Hills	3	3	3	3	3	3	3	3	3	3	3	3	3	3
West Garo Hills	30	30	30	31	31	31	31	31	31	31	29	29	30	31
Total of Garo Hills	48	48	48	49	49	49	49	49	49	49	47	47	49	50
Meghalaya	180	180	180	181	181	181	181	182	185	189	192	192	205	213

Source: Reserve Bank of India, Banking Statistics.

Table 10.4: Average Population per Commercial Bank Branch as on 31st March, 2010

Population in Persons

District	Population as per 2011 census	Number SCBs Branches	Average Population per Branch
East Garo Hills	3,17,618	15	21,175
West Garo Hills	6,42,923	29	22,170
South Garo Hills	1,42,574	4	35,644
Total of Garo Hills	11,03,115	48	22,982
Meghalaya	29,64,007	158	20,027
India	121,01,93,422	88,203	13,721

Source: Statistical Tables relating to Banks in India, RBI.

Table 10.5: Deposit Mobilizations by Bank in Garo Hills Districts

Year End March	Garo Hills (Amount Rs. lakhs)	Meghalaya (Amount Rs. lakhs)	India (Amount Rs.crores)
1997	10019	90680	505599
1998	10732 (7.12)	103999 (14.69)	605410 (19.74)
1999	12632 (17.70)	114758 (10.35)	722203 (19.29)
2000	14668 (16.12)	140283 (22.24)	851593 (17.92)
2001	17332 (18.16)	164624 (17.35)	989141 (16.15)
2002	20204 (16.57)	195233 (18.59)	1131187 (14.36)
2003	21718 (7.49)	214320 (9.78)	1311761 (15.96)
2004	23923 (10.15)	275800 (28.69)	1542284 (17.57)
2005	29718 (24.22)	306465 (11.12)	1732858 (12.36)
2006	33730 (13.50)	324621 ((5.92)	2109049 (21.71)
2007	41263 (22.33)	389446 (19.97)	2611933 (23.84)
2008	43059 (4.35)	451162 (15.85)	3196939 (22.40)
2009	59969 (39.27)	620465 (37.52)	3834110 (19.93)
2010	73520 (22.60)	764267 (23.18)	4492826 (17.18)
CAGR	**16.57%**	**17.82%**	**18.3%**

Note: Figures in parentheses indicate percent change over previous year.
Source: *Basic Statistical Return of SCBs, RBI.*

and in India as a whole (CAGR = 18.3). It could thus be inferred from the above analysis that the banking reform measures introduced following Narasimham Committee (GoI, 1991) and (GoI, 1998), have played a little role in mobilizing deposits in the area under study. At this juncture, it is essential to analyze the compositions and directions of advances channelized in the study area.

Advances Channelized by Banks

The commercial banks have been playing an important responsibility of channelizing the funds with most important sectors to fulfil the pre-determined objectives. There is a rapid expansion in banking network, deposit mobilization and credit development due to which there is change in the scope of banking operations. The banks were especially concerned with financing the priority sector of agriculture, small scale enterprises and small transport operators. In course of time, other priority sectors were also added, such as retail trade, professional and self-employed persons, education, housing, loans for weaker sections and consumption loans (Ahmed, 2010b). The commercial bank credit is an important input variable in the production functions of agriculture, industry, commerce and allied productive activities for the socio-economic development of the country. Apart from the quantum of bank credit, its development, composition and direction is equally important in the realization of the country's various macro-economic goals. Pandey (1968) suggested for the channelization of bank credit in proper direction, as otherwise, there will be adverse effect on the economy of the country. Raj Committee (1977) recommended 40 per cent of lending to the priority sector. The bank had earlier adopted a purely traditional approach in lending based on 'self liquidating theory'. Under this approach the banks followed the 'commercial loan theory', *i.e.*, the banks granted loans only against negotiable and tangible securities offered as well as on the basis of business reputation of borrowers. According to Mithani (1999) after nationalization, banks have attempted to steer the direction of change and strive towards achieving fundamental objectives of mitigation of regional disparities, dispersal of industries and reduction of concentration of economic wealth (Raul, 1997). As a result, implicit weightage was given to the socially desirable sectors in the credit policy with sizable increase in the sector-wise advances. Ramala and Nagi (1994) suggested proper end-use of loans to the entrepreneurs which could ensure economic development of the area and the country as a whole. Hartough (1994) studied the implications of bankers' action plan for profitable small business portfolio and suggested that customer's payment track record and market condition, etc. Bank should make advances to most attractive and growth potential units. Kohli (1997) found the significant linkages between bank credit and investment in both agriculture and industries in India. He suggested that although directed credit programme is effective and in that respect affirmative support of small scale sector is required. In this respect, to improve credit delivery, RBI has taken various initiatives which include: (i) augmentation of credit flow to priority sector; (ii) simplification of systems and procedures; (iii) permitting use of banking correspondents, etc. In order to review the efficacy of existing framework of money lending, a technical group, was constituted under the chairmanship of S.C. Gupta, who submitted its report on July 2007 and recommended alternative avenues of credit dispensation such as micro finance institutions (RBI, 2007). The following paragraphs attempted to study the growth, composition and direction of bank credit during the period under consideration. During the past four decades, some noticeable positive changes have been taking place in the credit advances by the SCBs. Table 10.6 presents the bank advances channelled in the area under study.

From Table 10.5a, the total advances (bank credit) by all SCBs in Garo Hills stood at Rs. 2,502 lakhs as on 31st March, 1997, increased to Rs. 29,327 lakhs as on March 2010 which shows 11.72 times increase in advances over the period. The rate of growth of advances is higher in

Table 10.5a: Bank Advances Channelized in Garo Hills

March End	*Garo Hills (Rs.lakhs)*	*Meghalaya (Rs. lakhs)*	*India (Rs. crores)*
1997	2502	13735	278401
1998	2985	15996	324079
1999	3298	20774	368837
2000	3796	22862	454069
2001	3749	28084	529272
2002	4462	35817	609053
2003	5705	62177	746432
2004	6873	95304	865594
2005	16036	133712	1124300
2006	19084	156204	1507077
2007	22325	139037	1931189
2008	25089	149732	2361914
2009	24843	175331	2775549
2010	29327	195779	3244788
CAGR	**20.85**	**22.68**	**20.79**

Source: Basic Statistical Return of SCBs, RBI.

Meghalaya (CAGR = 22.68) than that of the study area (CAGR = 20.85). The scenario of advances growth is better than the deposit growth in the study area. This may be due to the reduction of priority sector lending norms from 40 per cent to 10 per cent on the basis of recommendations of the committee on financial system (GOI, 1991) as the repayment in non-priority sector is better than priority sector.

In order to assess the extent of credit channelization by the banks in the districts under study, we have calculated the correlation coefficients among the bank advances during 1997-2010.

Table 10.5b: Matrix of Correlation Coefficient of Bank Advances

	Garo Hills	*Meghalaya*	*India*
Garo Hills	1		
Meghalaya	0.963 (12.378)**	1	—
India	0.969 (13.587)**	0.929 (9.0702)**	1

Source: Self-calculated on the basis of Table 10.5a:
$t_{0.05}$(12 df) =2.179, $t_{0.01}$(12 df) =3.055.
** indicates significant both at 0.05 and 0.01 level of significance.

As shown by Table 10.5b, it manifests that correlation coefficients (*r*) in respect of advances of the districts under study in the context of national scenario is positive. The *r* values are, however, statistically significant at 1 per cent and 5 per cent level of significance at their respective degree of freedom. This implies that the districts under study are maintaining the national tempo of credit channelization. In other words, banks are deploying credit for the economic growth of the area from which they have mobilized funds.

Credit Plans (District Credit Plan and Annual Action Plan)

District Credit Plans (DCP) are prepared under Lead Bank Scheme to increase production, productivity and job opportunity in different sectors of the economy especially in rural and semi-urban areas of the country, to reduce regional disparities in the country. DCPs are simply aggregation of the Block Credit Plans operating in the concerned district. To make credit plan successful, Block, district, State, regional and national level forums are created. Annual Credit Plan (ACP) or Annual Action Plan

individuals, the absorbing capacity of the economy to utilize the credit for various productive purposes, the attitude of people in availing bank credit, recovery rate and entered non-performing assets, financial climate in an economy and quantum of funds mobilized by banks. Mehrotra (1992) stated that the CD ratio of the SCBs of India varies substantially across the country with the industrially advanced or traditionally well banked states enjoying higher ratios as compared with the relatively backward States having lower ratios. Raul (1997) opined that CD ratio is not an unbiased indicator, since it depends on two variables, viz., total deposit and total advances. It has been observed that the banks may have to grant advances to the beneficiaries through several government sponsored schemes. The Table 10.8 delineates the CD ratios in the area under study.

Table 10.8: CD Ratio in Garo Hills *vis-à-vis* in Meghalaya (in %)

Year End March	*Credit Deposit Ratio*		
	Garo Hills	*Meghalaya*	*India*
1997	24.97	15.15	55.1
1998	27.81	15.38	53.5
1999	26.11	18.10	51.1
2000	25.88	16.30	53.3
2001	21.63	17.06	53.5
2002	22.08	18.35	53.8
2003	26.27	29.01	56.9
2004	28.73	34.56	56.1
2005	53.96	43.63	64.9
2006	56.58	48.12	71.5
2007	54.10	35.70	73.9
2008	58.27	33.19	73.9
2009	41.43	28.26	72.4
2010	39.89	25.62	72.2

Source: Basic Statistical Return of SCBs, RBI.

From the Table 10.8, it is observed that the CD ratio of all SCBs in India by arch 2010 was 72.2 per cent, which was 55.1 per cent in March 1997. In Meghalaya, CD ratio was 15.15 per cent in 1997 which increased to 48.12 per cent in 2006. This has further declined to 25.62 per cent in 2010. The CD ratio for Garo Hills over the 13 years (1997-2010) is far behind than the national average.

Bank-wise CD Ratio

The bank-wise CD ratio for each of commercial banks, Meghalaya Rural Bank and Meghalaya Co-operative Apex Bank can be observed from Table 10.9. The table manifests that Meghalaya Rural Bank and Meghalaya Co-operative Apex Bank in the East Garo Hills district and West Garo Hills district, and Meghalaya Co-operative Apex Bank in South Garo Hills district have above the national target (60%) of CD ratio. The CD ratio of the newly opened private sector banks, viz., ICICI, AXIS and HDFC is very poor.

Table 10.9: Bank-wise CD Ratio of Garo Hills (As on 31.3.10)

Amount Rs. *in Lakhs and ratios in percentage*

Districts	*Name of banks*	*Deposit*	*Advance*	*CD Ratio*
West Garo Hills	SBI	46260.00	18679.00	40.38
	CBI	891.45	150.23	16.85
	UNI	5196.94	1047.47	20.16
	ICICI	314.00	3	0.96
	AXIS	2012.00	63.20	3.14
	HDFC	123.15	9.80	7.96
	MRB	449.51	492,93	109.66
	MCAB	9006.37	5774.73	64.12
	MIDC	118.94	–	–
	Total	**64130.27**	**263229.50**	**40.99**
East Garo Hills	SBI	20156.00	7364.00	36.54
	UBI	397.00	203.00	51.13
	UNI	0.17	0.00	0.00
	MRB	119.65	145.45	121.56
	MCAB	3408.69	2601.77	76.33
	MIDC	–	25.63	–
	Total	**24081.51**	**10339.85**	**42.94**
South Garo Hills	SBI	11713.00	2195.00	18.74
	MCAB	1896.70	1502.55	79.22
	Total	**13609.70**	**3697.55**	**27.25**
Total of Garo Hills		**101820.98**	**40366.90**	**39.64**

Source: SLBC, Meghalaya, www.slbcne.nic.in

Credit Deployment of Commercial Banks

Bank credit is an important factor for the development of agriculture, industry, commerce and allied economic activities for the socio-economic development of the nation. Ahmed (2009) observed that apart from the quantum of bank credit, its development, composition and direction is equally important in the realization of the country's various macro-economic goals. During the past four decades, some noticeable changes have been taken place in the credit portfolio of the scheduled commercial banks. To improve the productive use of bank credit the RBI from time to time adopted various measures including augmentation of credit flow to priority sector, simplification of systems and procedures of bank credit, permitting use of banking correspondents, etc. The sectoral flow of advances out of the net bank credit in Garo Hills from 1997 to 2010 is given in Table 10.10.

As per Table 10.10, the flow had been increasing steadily in absolute term (except in 2004-2005 and 2005-2006). The total credit deployment of SCBs in Garo Hills has increased from Rs. 3,11,265 thousands in March 1997 to Rs. 46,01,920 thousands in March 2010 which shows 14.78 fold increase in outstanding credit during 13 years. The credit flow towards agriculture sector was very much volatile. During 1997 to 2001, share of agriculture sector was high; the percentage flow was in the range of 20.28 per cent to 28.69 per cent. Since 2002, the decline had started and had come down and reached to a low level of 2.56 per cent in 2004 and further deteriorated to 1.01 per cent in 2005. Again in 2006 onwards, flow towards this sector had picked up. In case of industrial sector from 1997 to 2002, the percentage flow was in the range of mere 9.07 per cent to 15.99 per cent only. In 2003, the flow has gone up and reached a maximum of 62.11 per cent in 2005. Since 2006, the decline had started and had come to a low level of 17.56 per cent in March 2009. Personal loans grew faster than any other segment. The percentage of credit to SSI was 5.07 per cent in 1997 and increased to a maximum of 7.49 per cent in 1999. Since 2000, the decline had started and had come to a lower level of 0.16 per cent in March 2004 and again it increased to 2.42 per cent in 2005, 4.70 per cent in 2006. During 2007 the flow was 3.63 per cent only.

Bank Finance to the SME Units

The Table 10.11 shows comparative position of total credit, credit to

Table 10.10: Distribution of Outstanding Credit of Scheduled Commercial Banks according to Occupation in Garo Hills

Amount Rs. in Thousands

Occupation	*1997*	*1998*	*1999*	*2000*	*2001*	*2002*	*2003*
Agriculture	75689	90353	74726	98620	81494	156982	108134
	(24.32)	(28.69)	(22.87)	(26.30)	(20.28)	(15.51)	(9.47)
Industry	28318	41480	52260	43847	36453	116205	424981
	(9.10)	(13.17)	(15.99)	(11.69)	(9.07)	(11.48)	(37.21)
Transport operators	12709	37298	27974	45177	33968	57249	63181
	(4.08)	(11.84)	(8.56)	(12.05)	(8.45)	(5.65)	(5.53)
Professional and other services	3749	6154	11444	3910	7245	25963	32715
	(1.20)	(1.95)	(3.50)	(1.05)	(1.80)	(2.56)	(2.86)
Personal Loans	72155	80699	78320	97224	111458	160535	205048
	(23.18)	(25.62)	(23.97)	(25.93)	(27.73)	(15.86)	(17.95)
Trade	49757	53393	55990	67536	86263	159215	111664
	(15.99)	(16.95)	(17.13)	(18.01)	(21.46)	(15.73)	(9.78)
Finance	-----	122	318	920	------	181	175
	(----)	(0.04)	(0.10)	(0.25)	(----)	(0.02)	(0.02)
All Other	68888	5395	25761	20749	45019	336082	196309
	(22.13)	(1.71)	(7.88)	(5.53)	(11.20)	(33.20)	(17.19)
Total Bank Credit	311265	314983	326793	374983	401900	1012412	1142207
	(100)	(100)	(100)	(100)	(100)	(100)	(100)
Artisans & Village Industries	7163	14378	21048	21010	13463	33834	42107
	(2.30)	(4.56)	(6.44)	(5.60)	(3.35)	(3.34)	(3.69)
Other Small Scale Industries	15787	18439	24490	19427	21279	44569	20899
	(5.07)	(5.85)	(7.49)	(5.18)	(5.29)	(4.40)	(1.83)
	53867	125492	1363638	736948	461806	293285	609849
Agriculture	(2.56)	(1.01)	(6.34)	(21.71)	(9.99)	(8.31)	(13.25)
Industry	567138	7737849	8653826	827165	1051649	619638	829260
	(26.89)	(62.11)	(40.23)	(24.37)	(22.45)	(17.56)	(18.02)
Transport operators	45209	70770	476704	45512	48251	72268	136436
	(2.14)	(0.57)	(2.22)	(1.34)	(1.03)	(2.05)	(2.96)
Professional and other services	17489	264436	1420702	69008	130247	118343	141752
	(0.83)	(2.12)	(6.60)	(2.03)	(2.97)	(3.35)	(3.08)
Personal Loans	1153538	3434872	7865800	1411971	1818630	1831422	1887037
	(54.69)	(27.57)	(36.57)	(41.59)	(38.83)	(51.90)	(41.01)
Trade	78824	575666	1158981	226124	980318	552910	849097
	(3.74)	(4.62)	(5.39)	(6.66)	(20.93)	(15.67)	(18.45)
Finance	449	10097	21879	-----	7	62	7513
	(0.02)	(0.08)	(0.10)	(----)	(neg)	(neg)	(0.16)
All Other	192880	239637	549586	48143	183793	41156	31617
	(0.91)	(1.92)	(2.55)	(1.42)	(3.92)	(1.17)	(0.69)
Total Bank Credit	2109394	12458819	21511116	3394871	4683701	3529084	4601920
	(100)	(100)	(100)	(100)	(100)	(100)	(100)
Artisans & Village Industries	50373	464427	308705	94421	NA	NA	NA
	(2.39)	(3.73)	(1.44)	(2.78)			
Other Small Scale Industries	3316	301211	1012014	123365	NA	NA	NA
	(0.16)	(2.42)	(4.70)	(3.63)			

Note: Figures in parentheses indicate percentage to total bank credit.
Source: Basic Statistical Return of SCBs, RBI.

Table 10.11: Bank Financing to Industries in Garo Hills *vis-à-vis* in India

Year 31st March	Garo Hills (Rs. in thousands)				All India (Rs. in lakhs)			
	Total Bank credit	Credit to Industries	Credit to SSIs	Artisans & Village Indust-ries	Total Bank Credit	Credit to Industries	Credit to SSIs	Artisans & Village Industries
1997	311265 (100)	28318 (9.10)	15787 (5.07)	7163 (2.30)	28437330 (100)	14031360 (49.3)	2679332 (9.4)	182465 (0.6)
1998	314983 (100)	41480 (13.17)	18439 (5.85)	14378 (4.56)	32994444 (100)	16109594 (48.8)	2862829 (8.7)	194214 (0.6)
1999	326793 (100)	52260 (15.99)	24490 (7.49)	21048 (6.44)	38242503 (100)	18794688 (49.2)	3142843 (8.2)	251874 (0.7)
2000	374983 (100)	43847 (11.69)	24490 (7.49)	21010 (5.60)	46008068 (100)	21377882 (46.5)	3506987 (7.62)	267688 (0.58)
2001	401900 (100)	36453 (9.07)	21279 (5.29)	13463 (3.35)	53843379 (100)	23643041 (43.9)	3690487 (6.85)	207205 (0.38)
2002	1012412 (100)	116205 (11.48)	44569 (4.40)	33834 (3.34)	65599308 (100)	27162550 (41.4)	3197030 (4.87)	560042 (0.85)
2003	1142207 (100)	424981 (37.21)	20899 (1.83)	42107 (3.69)	75596882 (100)	30982757 (41.0)	3794034 (5.02)	522556 (0.69)
2004	2109394 (100)	567138 (26.89)	3316 (0.16)	50373 (2.39)	88031203 (100)	33480348 (38.0)	3843255 (4.37)	491212 (4.9)
2005	12458819 (100)	7737849 (62.11)	301211 (2.42)	464427 (3.73)	115246793 (100)	44682498 (38.8)	4707642 (4.08)	614894 (4.6)
2006	21511116 (100)	8653826 (40.23)	1012014 (4.70)	308705 (1.44)	151384213 (100)	56621595 (37.4)	5516398 (2.83)	729012 (4.1)
2007	3394871 (100)	827165 (24.37)	123365 (3.63)	94421 (2.78)	194709962 (100)	74189713 (38.1)	6831207 (3.51)	853120 (3.9)
2008	4683701 (100)	1051649 (22.45)	NA	NA	241700652 (100)	92853578 (38.4)	NA	NA
2009	3529084 (100)	619638 (17.56)	NA	NA	284771312 (100)	113444298 (39.8)	NA	NA
2010	4601920 (100)	829260 (18.02)	NA	NA	334516932 (100)	135523235 (40.51)	NA	NA

Source: Basic Statistical Return of SCBs, RBI.

industries, credit to SSIs and credit to artisan and village industries advanced by the SCBs in Garo Hills and India during 1996-97 to 2009-10. It is clear from the table that the share of industrial credit to total bank credit in Garo Hills is far below than all India level. The average share of industrial credit to total credit for Garo Hills is 37.44 per cent as against all India shares of 40.14 per cent. The average share of SSIs credit to total bank credit in Garo Hills is only 2.87 per cent as against all

Table 10.12: Performance of Small Scale Industries in Garo Hills

Year Ended 31st March	*Number of Registered SSI Units*	*Investments in Plant and Machinery (Rs. in lakhs)*	*Employment (numbers)*	*Credit to SSI (thousand)*
1998	624	228.59	3255	18439
1999	703	288.54	3778	24490
2000	761	385.29	4157	24490
2001	776	394.70	4206	21279
2002	840	445.52	4897	44569
2003	918	526.78	5120	20899
2004	972	579.63	5874	3316
2005	1072	629.14	6124	301211
2006	1237	742.82	6913	1012014
2007	1316	820.73	7256	123365
2008	1388	902.08	7750	NA

Source: 1. Statistical Hand Book of Meghalaya Various Issues; 2. District Statistical Hand Book Various Issues (West Garo Hills, East Garo Hills and South Garo Hills); 3. DICs of the West Garo Hills, East Garo Hills and South Garo Hills.

India shares of 4.92 per cent during 1997-2007. The share of cottage and village industries to total bank credit in Garo Hills is 2.47 per cent as against all India share of 0.55 per cent during 1997-2007. Thus, it is clear that the SSI sector of the study area is getting a lesser amount of credit while compared with the all India level.

Relationship between Institutional Finance and Growth of Small Enterprises

The Table 10.12 reveals the number of registered SSI units, investment in plant and machinery, employment and deployment of credit to SSI sector in three districts of Garo Hills. The Garo Hills has witnessed a phenomenal growth of registered SSI units since 1998. In the year 1998, there were only 624 registered SSI units in Garo Hills. The number of registered SSI units increased to 1388 in 2008. The cumulative investment for registered SSI units was Rs. 228.59 lakhs in plant and machinery in the year 1998. It increased to Rs. 902.08 lakhs in 2008. Thus, there was almost 3.95 fold increase in investment in plant and machinery in registered SSI units over the period. In the year 1998, 3,255 persons were employed in registered SSI units in the study area. The cumulative number of persons employed in such units had gone up to 7,750 in 2008.

An attempt has been made to analyze the impact of institutional finance on the growth of SSI units in the area under study. For this we have calculated correlation coefficient between institutional finance to SSI and the growth of number of units during 1998-2007. The result in presented in Table 10.12a:

Table 10.12a: Correlation between Institutional Finance and SMEs

r	*t (cal)*	*t (tab) at 8 df*
0.608	2.166	2.306 at 5% level 3.355 at 1 % level

The positive *r* value (0.608) is statistically not significant at both 5 per cent and at 1 per cent levels of significance which indicates that the hypothesis "*there exists a close relationship between institutional finance and growth of small enterprises*" is not true. The growth of institutional finance does not have much impact on the growth of industries in the study area. Further, in order to examine whether the growth of investment in plant and machinery of small sector resulted in the growth of institutional finance, we have employed correlation analysis between investment in plant and machinery of the units operating in the study area and credit deployed to SSI sector during 1998-2007. The result of correlation and *t* value are presented in Table 10.12 b:

Table 10.12b: Correlation between Investment and SSI Machinery sector

r	*t (cal)*	*t (tab) at 8 df*
0.557	1.898	2.306 at 5% level 3.355 at 1 % level

The positive *r* value (0.557) is not statistically significant at 5 per cent and 1 per cent level of significance. This indicates that with the increase in investment in plant and machinery of SSI sector, the institutional finance to SSI units are not increasing in the study area. Hence, the hypothesis "*With the change of investment structure of small sector, financial intermediaries have enlarged their assistance*" found to be incorrect.

This has again confirmed with the district-wise analysis of correlations between bank finance available for manufacturing industries and growth of SSI units during 1998-2009. For this purpose, we have used the data presented in Table 10.13.

Table 10.13: District-wise Data relating to Small Scale Industries

Year 31st March	Bank Finance to Manufacturing and Processing Industries (Rs. in thousands)			Number of Small Scale Industries		
	East Garo Hills	West Garo Hills	South Garo Hills	East Garo Hills	West Garo Hills	South Garo Hills
1998	1,43,56	1,91,19	60,46	260	317	47
1999	1,40,04	2,90,87	84,77	292	350	61
2000	1,32,99	2,38,53	59,30	314	375	72
2001	1,13,13	2,06,91	34,05	320	382	74
2002	1,13,82	7,56,01	1,36,18	370	391	79
2003	1,18,98	7,08,25	3,53,73	405	414	99
2004	51,75,20	3,66,17	90,45	437	428	107
2005	2,46,94	271,87,53	79,16	501	456	115
2006	3,40,31	520,83,61	2,25,18	617	490	130
2007	2,64,46	17,44,47	4,30,39	645	525	146
2008	2,45,53	10,63,44	49,28,67	676	549	163
2009	2,64,51	12,80,81	24,24,77	683	563	164

Source: Statistical Hand Book, Meghalaya, Various issues and Basic Statistical Returns of Scheduled Commercial Banks, Various issues, RBI.

From the correlations result presented in Table 10.13a, it is observed that *r* values between bank finance and growth of units in both East Garo Hills and West Garo Hills are insignificant but correlation in South Garo Hills is significant at 5 per cent level but not at 1 per cent level. This indicates an inter-district disparity in extending the financial assistance by banks and thereby growth of SME units.

Table 10.13a: Correlation between Financial Assistance and Growth of SMEs

Districts	Correlations	t value at 10 df		
		Calculated	Tabulated	
			1 per cent level	5 per cent level
East Garo Hills	0.038	0.12024	3.169	2.228
West Garo Hills	0.254	0.83045	3.169	2.228
South Garo Hills	0.682	2.94886	3.169	2.228

Table 10.14: Sector-wise Classification of Term Loans Sanctions by MIDC in Garo Hills Districts

Year	Small and Medium Enterprises		Small Road Transport Operators		Total	
	No. of units	Amount (Rs.)	No. of units	Amount (Rs.)	No. of units	Amount (Rs.)
1997-98	2	78,000	6	4,32,078	8	5,10,078
1998-99	Nil	0	14	21,40,000	14	21,40,000
1999-00	2	6,00,000	36	51,33,500	38	57,33,500
2000-01	1	50,000	19	48,02,000	20	48,52,000
2001-02	1	75,000	1	2,60,000	2	3,35,000
2002-03	2	8,60,000	3	5,97,000	5	14,57,000
2003-04	4	23,43,000	4	3,85,000	8	27,28,000
2004-05	3	1,65,000	4	11,55,000	7	13,20,000
2005-06	6	57,99,000	3	9,33,000	9	67,32,000
2006-07	1	4,50,000	Nil	Nil	1	4,50,000
2007-08	1	3,80,000	Nil	Nil	1	3,80,000
2008-09	4	24,00,000	2	8,34,000	6	32,34,000
2009-10	2	10,25,000	8	36,79,387	10	47,04,387
2010-11	1	3,50,000	6	38,95,000	7	42,45,000
Total	**30**	**1,45,75,000**	**106**	**2,42,45,965**	**136**	**3,88,20,965**

Source: Loan Sanction and Disbursement Registered MIDC Ltd, Tura Branch.

Performance of Meghalaya Industrial Development Corporation (MIDC)

The MIDC was incorporated under the Companies Act 1956 on 6th April, 1971 to promote and develop industries in the State performing the dual task as:

(1) Industrial Development Corporation (IDC) – Involved in the creation and maintenance of industrial infrastructure.
(2) State Finance Corporation (SFC) – Involved in setting up of assisted companies and performs agency functions for Government schemes.
(3) The MIDC is operating financial assistance schemes under the refinance assistance schemes of SIDBI. The limit of finance assistance provided to entrepreneurs by way of term loan is to the tune of Rs. 90 lakhs. The corporation can collaborate with other financial institutions for consortium finance to finance a

large project. The MIDC can participate in share capital in the following manner:

- For subsidiary undertakings 100 per cent equity participation;
- Private sector SSI units, participation should be 10 per cent to 20 per cent subject to a maximum of Rs. 20 lakhs;
- For private sector medium scale units participation should be 10 per cent subject to a maximum of Rs. 20 lakhs;
- For joint and public sector units participation should not be more than 26 per cent; and
- If a sick industrial unit is to be rehabilitated, the capital participation would be determined as per the merits of the cases but no case investment should exceed 49 per cent.

There is no any branch of DFI in Garo Hills except MIDC. The branch of SIDBI is located in Shillong and NEDFI in Guwahati expected to meet the financial requirement of SME sector of Garo Hills. The MIDC has only one branch at Tura to provide finance to industries in the three districts of Garo Hills. An attempt is made to analyze the performance of MIDC for financing of SMEs in the three districts of Garo Hills. Table 10.14 presents amount sanctioned by MIDC.

The MIDC usually provides financial assistance to SMEs and small road transport operators (SRTOs). It is evident from the Table 10.15 that the SRTO is dominated in terms of number of units and amount of financial assistance during the period from 1997-98 to 2010-11. During this period 62.46 per cent of total sanctioned amount of financial assistance of the MIDC has gone in favour of SRTO and only 37.54 per cent in favour of SMEs. The MIDC sanctioned the highest amount of Rs. 57,99,000 for 6 number of SME units in 2005-06 while the SRTO received the highest amount of Rs. 51,33,500 in respect of 36 number of units in 1999-00. However, sanctioned to both the sectors has witnessed a fluctuating trend. On an average, the MIDC sanctioned about 2 units only per annum in the three districts and average sanctioned in each units during the period was only Rs. 4,85,833. During the period it advanced term loans only to new projects. No financial assistance has been sanctioned to existing units for rehabilitation, expansion, and/or modernization.

The sanctioned amount of financial assistance to SMEs as ratio of total sanction varies between the lowest 0 per cent in 1998-99 and the highest of 100 per cent in 2006-07 and 2007-08. But in terms of amount and units, SMEs received highest financial assistance of Rs. 57,99,000 for 6 number of SMEs units in 2005-06. The overall financial assistance sanctioned by the MIDC in Garo Hills District is not satisfactory at all. The Table 10.15 reveals the total sanction and disbursement of loans made by the MIDC from 1997-98 to 2010-11.

Table 10.15: Term Loan Sanctioned and Disbursement by MIDC Ltd. in Garo Hills Districts to SMEs

Year	Sanctioned			Disbursed		
	No. of Units	Amount (Rs.)	Cumulative Total (Rs.)	No. of Units	Amount (Rs.)	Cumulative Total (Rs.)
1997-98	2	78,000	78,000	2	75,073	75,073
1998-99	Nil	Nil	78,000	Nil	Nil	75,073
1999-00	2	6,00,000	6,78,000	2	5,89,240	6,64,313
2000-01	1	50,000	7,28,000	1	47,600	7,11,913
2001-02	1	75,000	8,03,000	1	71,083	7,82,996
2002-03	2	8,60,000	16,63,000	2	8,11,914	15,94,910
2003-04	4	23,43,000	40,06,000	4	23,29,028	39,23,938
2004-05	3	1,65,000	41,71,000	3	1,61,300	40,85,238
2005-06	6	57,99,000	99,70,000	6	45,16,984	86,02,222
2006-07	1	4,50,000	1,04,20,000	1	4,65,500	90,67,722
2007-08	1	3,80,000	108,00,000	1	3,64,000	94,31,722
2008-09	4	24,00,000	1,32,00,000	4	21,16,000	1,15,47,722
2009-10	2	10,25,000	1,42,25,000	2	9,85,000	1,25,32,722
2010-11	1	3,50,000	1,45,75,000	1	2,96,000	1,28,28,722

Source: Loan sanction and disbursement Register, MIDC Ltd., Tura Branch.

Table 10.15 shows that the corporation has sanctioned Rs. 1,45,75,000 in aggregate to 30 units, thus giving an average amount of Rs. 4,85,833 per unit during the period. The MIDC has assisted more number of units during 2005-06, the average amount sanctioned per unit has Rs. 9,66,500 which has been appreciably higher than the overall average of the period. So far as the disbursement of loan is concerned, the aggregate amount stood at Rs. 1,28,28,722 in respect of 30 units giving Rs. 4,27,624 per unit during the period.

The correlation coefficient (r) is calculated between loan sanctioned and disbursement. The r value found (0.994) positive. The high positive correlation signifies that MIDC has disbursed the sanctioned loan as early as possible. In this context, the hypothesis, "*There exists a close association between loan sanctioned and loan disbursement of MIDC*" found to be correct. It indicates that MIDC disbursed the loan whatever they sanctioned meant for the purpose. Another positive aspect of disbursement is that the MIDC disbursed loan to all the units every year whatever they sanctioned. Such attitude of institution definitely helps the entrepreneurs to implement their ventures as early as possible.

Conclusion

The availability of credit is one of the critical weaknesses in the industrial development of Garo Hills. The various financing indicators showed that despite banking facilities, the level of financial outreach is low in Garo Hills. The main constraints for banking and financial development are hilly trait of the districts, sparse population settlements, poor infrastructure, small size of market, lack of entrepreneurship, law and order conditions, peculiar land tenure system, low banking network, lack of simple, customize and flexible financial products to suit the needs of the local population, poor loan recovery experience, lack of awareness of banking services and inadequate payment system.

The penetration of banking in Garo Hills particularly in rural areas has been very low. Though the annual growth rate of deposit was more or less aligned with the national average, there is a wide variation among the districts of Garo Hills. The credit deposit ratio of Garo Hills as well as the State is far below than the national average which is a matter of concern. The sectoral share of total credit indicates that significant discrepancy from the national level. The trend clearly shows the low level of commercialization of agriculture and low level of industrialization which leads to less absorption capacity of credit in the districts. Poor recovery of loans acts as a disincentive for granting fresh loans. The land tenure system prevalent in the Garo Hills restricting transfer of land together with absence of individual ownership rights makes it difficult for the banks to lend in the districts under study. There is need for conscious effort in financial sector development to ensure free credit flow for enhancing the development efforts of the government.

NOTES

1. Report of 1974 Task Force on Access to Finance, Raw Materials and Marketing, National Commissions for Enterprises in Unorganized Sector, Financing of Enterprises in Unorganized Sector.

2. http://www.articlesbase.com/business-articles/priority-sector-lending-by-commercialbanks110615 1.html#ix zz 19 Pmxg wvk (visited on 10th Sept, 2010)

REFERENCES

Ahmed, J. U. (2010a). The Growth Performance of Micro and Small Enterprises in the Global Era: Evidence from Indian Industrial Sector. *International Journal of Economics*, December, 2010, Vol. 4, No. 2, pp. 295-310.

Ahmed, J. U. (2010b). Priority Sector Lending by Commercial Banks in India: A Case of Barak Valley. *Asian Journal of Finance & Accounting*, December, 2010, Vol. 2, No.1:E5, pp. 92-110

Ahmed, J.U. (2009). *Efficiency of Commercial Banks in Backward Region*. The ICFAI University Press, Hyderabad, pp. 77-78.

Basu, C.R. (1977). *The Role of the Commercial Banking in the Planned Economy of India*. Ph.D. Thesis, Burdwan University, Burdwan.

Bhattacharya, B.N. (1985). *Regional Behaviour of Bank Deposits and Its Implications to Deposit Mobilizations*. National Institute of Bank Management, Pune.

Chavan, M. and A. S. Lamba (2007). *An International Perspective on Internal Controls in Small and Medium Enterprises*. The Business Review, 8(1).

Gomez, Clifford, (2008). *Financial Markets, Institutions and Financing Services*, Prentice Hall of India, New Delhi, p.357.

Government of Meghalaya (2006). "*Statistical Hand Book*," Directorate of Economics and Statistics, Meghalaya.

Gassah, L.S. (1984). "*Garo Hills and Land and the People*," Western Book Depot, Guwahati, Assam..

Government of India, (2005-06). *Economic Survey*.

Government of Meghalaya (2008-09). *Statistical Hand Book*, Directorate of Economics and Statistics.

Government of India, (1991). *Report of the Committee on Financial System (Narasimham Committee-1)*, Ministry of Finance.

Govt. of India, (1998). *Report of the Committee on Financial System (Narasimham Committee-11)*, Ministry of Finance.

Government of India, (1991). *Report of the Committee on the Financial System*.

Hartough, K.J. (1994). *Entrepreneurial Bankers; The Banker's Personal Action Plan for Building a Profitable Small Business Portfolio*," Probus Publishing, Chicago.

Kohli, R. (1997). "Directed Credit and Financial Reforms," *Economic and Political Weekly*.

Mithani. D. M. (1991). "*Money, Banking, International Trade and Finance*," Himalaya Publishing House, New Delhi.

Mehrotra, R. (1992). "Credit Deposit Ratio, Current Status and Future

Corrections," RBI staff studies, Department of Economic Analysis and Policy, Reserve Bank of India, (June).

Narasimham, M. (1994). *Financial Sector Reform: The Unfinished Agenda*, Platinum Jubilee Conference Volume, Indian Economic Association, Indira Gandhi Institute of Development Research, Bombay.

Narasimham, M. (1994). *Financial Sector Reform: The Unfinished Agenda*, Platinum Jubilee Conference Volume, Indian Economic Association, Indira Gandhi Institute of Development Research, Bombay.

Pandey, K. L, (1968). *Development of Banking in India Since 1949*, Calcutta Scientific Book Agency, pp. 80.

Rual, R. K., (1997). *Industrial Finance in India*, Anmol Publication Pvt Ltd, New Delhi

Raul, R.K. (1997). *Industrial Finance in India,* Anmol Publications Pvt. Ltd., New Delhi, p. 119.

Ramala, K.S and Nagi, K.S., (1994). "Sickness in Small Scale Industries; Problems and Prospects," *New Trends in Indian Industries*, Chugh Publications, Allahabad, Vol. 2.

Report of 1974 Task Force on Access to Finance, Raw Materials and Marketing, National Commissions for Enterprises in Unorganized Sector, Financing of Enterprises in Unorganized Sector.

Report of the High Level Committee to Review Lead Bank Scheme, RBI, August, 2009.

RBI (2007). Report of the Technical Group to Review Efficacy of Existing Legislative Framework Governing Money Lending and its Enforcement Machinery.

Reserve Bank of India, Report on Currency and Finance, 1998 and 2010.

Reserve Bank of India (1977). *Committee's Report on financing of Public Sector Banks*, RBI (Raj, J. as Chairman).

SIDBI Report on MSME Sector, 2010, p xiv.

Shekhar, K. C. and Shekhar, L., (2005). *Banking Theory and Practice,* Vikash Publishing House Pvt. Ltd., New Delhi 14, p. 86.

Sharma, B.P. (1974). *The Role of Commercial Banks in India's Developing Economy,* S. Chand & Co., New Delhi.

State Level Bankers Committee, Meghalaya, 2010.

11

Microfinance in Nagaland: A Study

Gautam Patikar

Introduction

One of the major programmes which made a big difference to the lives of millions of rural poor in the country is the Self-Help Group (SHG)-Bank linkage programme initiated by National Bank for Agriculture and Rural Development (NABARD) in 1992. The SHG-Bank Linkage Programme of NABARD is a proven tool of extending the unbanked rural clientele access to formal financial services. The programme has covered more than 5.8 crores poor household across the country, making it the largest microfinance programme in the world. Encouraged by the success of the programme, NABARD promoted the linkage of Micro Finance Institutions (MFIs) with the banking sector, which, too, is gaining importance with the increasing trend of banks financing the MFIs. SHGs are voluntary associations of persons from homogeneous background comprising of usually 10 to 20 people to undertake certain economic activities such as thrift, credit, use of a common asset or a tool on the basis of equality and mutual trust. In such a group, the poorest people generally come together at the time of emergency, disaster, social reasons, and economic support to each other; have ease of conversation, social and economic interactions. The SHG-bank linkage programme suits rural conditions and has found a favourable response from people across the country. Besides making financial services accessible to the rural poor, it has also proved to be a cost effective delivery mechanism for all developmental programmes. In also be used for a variety of non-crop activities such as: dairy cow rearing, cattle fattening, poultry farming, weaving, basket making, leasing farm and other capital machinery and woodworking. Of course, funds may be used for a number of other activities, such as crop and animal trading, cloth trading and pottery manufacture. Credit is also issued to groups consisting of a number of borrowers for collective enterprises, such as: irrigation pumps, building sanitary latrines, power looms, leasing markets or leasing land for cooperative farming. The potential of loan usages are virtually endless, and differ between villages and districts. Loans provide a source of income for diverse activities chosen specifically by the borrower, to create their own life.

Credit Requirements of Tribal People

Despite opening bank branches even in rural areas, the commercial banks could not fully meet the credit requirement of tribal people in the State. The following reasons can be attributed to the unsatisfactory level of credit flow to the tribal people:

- The banks are meant to provide traditional credit support for farmers while in tribal areas, the people follow unirrigated and unscientific farming practices, viz., *jhum* and terrace cultivation making traditional business unviable.
- The poor harvest due to unscientific cultivation reduces loan recovery. In view of minimum loan collection stipulations for eligibility of fresh finance, sale proceeds of marketing of consumer business is siphoned away for loans repayment due to pressure from banks, resulting in non-availability of funds for procurement/marketing of consumer operations in tribal areas.
- The absence of proper market and due to inaccessibility and poor monitoring, the marketable produce fails to yield good return.

The security oriented-lending approach of banks is a hindrance in the flow of adequate credit to the tribal people. The banks insist on security—two to three times of the loan assistance provided. While the present security norms merit further relaxation by the Reserve Bank of India, a system is required to be developed by the State government to provide guarantee for payment of interest and repayment of principal by tribal people.

It is, therefore, necessary that SHGs having linkages with the financing banks may be encouraged among the tribal. This innovative credit dispensation system not only will reduce the transaction costs of the banks and borrowers, but will also enable leadership development. This can meet the emergent credit requirements and ensures recovery of loan. The 100 per cent refinance facility available from NABARD for financing of SHGs can also be availed by the banks.

The Sri Lanka experiment known as Community Credit Facilitators (CCFs) Schemes can be adopted in tribal areas like Nagaland, where formal bank credit cannot be extended to individuals due to non-availability of collateral securities because of the customary laws and tribal landholding pattern. The land of tribal people cannot be mortgaged as collateral security. The existing microfinance through Village Development Board (VDB) in the State is a blessing for the tribal people. The beneficiaries of this programme are the loanees, who receive credit support for carrying economic activities.

Credit for the Rural Non-Farm Sector

The rural non-farm sector provides employment to a large number of people and is estimated to generate a quarter of all rural employment. This includes employment for small/marginal farmers during the non-crop seasons. Income from non-farm activities contributes about 30 per cent of the total income of rural households. With limited quality arable land with irrigation facilities and with increasing population every year, the rural non-farm sector has to employ a vast number of unskilled labourers (Karmakar, 2008: 161). The rural non-farm sector serves as an important safety net for many rural households in times of natural calamities. It also provides an opportunity for rural women to take up remunerative work beyond casual labour and household labour. The growth of rural non-farm sector has had a positive impact on poverty alleviation and benefited most sections of rural society. However, wealthier rural households benefit most by way of increased non-farm incomes. This has enhanced rural income disparities to some extent. The rural non-farm activities are not confined to traditional villages industries but cover a vast range across the primary, secondary and tertiary sectors.

As employment and incomes in the rural non-farm sector are increasing, this sector has become economically dominant and an important part of the structural changes in the State's rural economy. In Nagaland, there is vast potential for the growth of non-farm sector. The local handloom and handcrafts is rich in quality having market demand. Micro credit can help in furthering this sector.

The time taken for getting a loan sanctioned by the banks for the rural non-farm sector varies from two months to 18 months. NABARD and Small Industries Development Bank of India (SIDBI) were created to cater the need of non-farm sector, they have number of promotional and development programme including primary marketing support, upgrading technology and adopting areas for special development inputs. However, rural industries have not benefited much from these institutions. Again, the money-lenders rarely provide credit for capital assets acquisition. They concentrate on lending for consumption needs and social/medical contingencies while trader-lenders provide working capital. Thus, venture capital for the rural non-farm sector is generally financed from own resources and supplemented by loans from friends and relatives.

In a State like Nagaland, with great divergence in social and economic levels, a single strategy or approach may not be feasible. Multi-pronged strategies for promotion of micro-enterprises, including stable policy institutions, providing different types of financial products and adoption of promotional approaches (credit and non-credit) are needed. The most viable strategies that can be adopted in Nagaland are:

- Target group specific approaches;
- Area or region specific approaches; and
- Sector or issue specific approaches.

Policies will have to address the need for strengthening the credit delivery system and for developing entrepreneurs/enterprises.

Credit for Rural Women

Given our male-dominated rural society, it is not surprising to note that prior to the 1990s, there were hardly any credit schemes designed for rural women. It is only after women-oriented studies highlighted the deprivation and struggle for survival that the concept of women's credit was born. There is growing realization that rural women have been underestimated and discriminated against in all walks of life, despite their substantial contribution to the household economy and in turn, the national economy. The UN Commission on Status of Women observed "women, who contributed half of the world's population by virtue of an accident of birth, perform two-thirds of the world's work, receive one–tenth of its income and own less than one-hundredth of its property." In India, women produce 30 per cent of all food commodities consumed but get only 10 per cent of the income, and own 10 per cent of the property or wealth of the country (Karmakar, 2008: 168).

Women have been deprived of their economic status, especially in rural areas. Thus, the empowerment of women and improvement of their status and economic role needs to be integrated into economic development programmes. Rural women, especially those belonging to the weaker sections of society have limited access to resources or employment opportunities that would make them financially independent. They live in conditions that do not permit them to meet bare minimum consumption needs. Institutional credit is difficult to access as women rarely have any property rights to mortgage or collateral to offer, and they have to depend on rural money-lenders for their production-cum-consumption needs. This entraps them into a vicious cycle of perpetual poverty and indebtedness. The only way to lift them up is by encouraging and helping them to achieve economic independents and self reliance through the NGOs/SHGs.

So far, rural credit packages had been exclusively male-oriented and women were largely ignored. However, with various supervisory credit programmes for rural women and the number of SHGs exclusively for women, the neglect of earlier years is being slowly erased. But the economic empowerment of women can only be marginally improved upon by microfinance programme. Various studies on women SHGs reveals that the formation of SHGs has led to a growing awareness, education and availability of information has led to confidence-building and the ability to handle complex issues. It also shows that there is a positive correlation between credit availability and women's empowerment.

Credit for women which was adopted in the late 1980s suffers from the problems of screening, monitoring, enforcement and bias. One novel solution has been group lending with joint liability. Group credit schemes involve borrowers to form homogeneous groups which reduce transaction costs both for the lender and the borrower. Group credit also reduces monitoring costs by involving group members to monitor loan usage and repayment. In contrast, the SHGs set up by NGOs, with the assistance of bank linkage, ensure individual loans for women beneficiaries and individual/joint liability for repayment. The stress is less on asset creation and more on production-cum-consumption loans, ensuring quicker repayment and less borrower fatigue in loan repayment. The repayment rate is much higher in SHGs as there is no subsidy involved.

Thus, banks need to reorient themselves to handle the needs of women entrepreneurs with a focus on the micro-credit needs of poor rural women.

Credit for Micro-enterprise Development

In developing countries with vast sections of the population caught up in the web of poverty, the challenge is to generate enough employment and income opportunities for the rural and urban poor, but in a sustainable manner. Micro-enterprises can play an important role in improving the quality of life and poverty alleviation. Ensuring their success is cost-effective and enables the vulnerable sections, such as women and weaker sections of society, to smooth over seasonal fluctuations in household income.

Globalization and economic liberalization with the doctrine of free market have opened up tremendous opportunities. But without a 'safety net' these economic changes are making the marginalized and poor sections of the society more vulnerable. After many years of centralized planning, it is clear that employment cannot be ensured by the government. The industrial and agricultural sectors are unable to absorb the growing labour force. Micro-enterprises, whether in the informal or organized sectors, provide opportunities for gainful employment while preserving the social structure.

The area of concern for the micro-enterprises is the non-availability of adequate and timely credit. Banks need to develop new financial products and adopt innovative approaches to meet the growing financial requirements of micro-enterprises. Self-employment has now become a necessity rather than an option. Microfinance in rural areas is meaningful only if the poor are empowered with crucial skills to run micro-enterprises successfully. Long-term entrepreneurial education, access to cheap loans and the formation of SHGs will enable the poor to fight poverty with dignity and built up various skills.

Implications of Microfinance in Nagaland

In Nagaland, 21 out of the 52 Blocks are unbanked, covering 421 villages. This indicates that more than 40 per cent of the rural areas do not have adequate banking infrastructure. The latest innovative venture to include the excluded in the development process through financial inclusion has been a revolutionary step. The microfinance initiative in the State has been made to declare the VDBs as "Financial Intermediaries" or

Non-Banking Financial Intermediaries to integrate the ever important credit mechanism in the rural areas for faster economic development. The ramification to this approach, if successful, would ensure that grass root level organizations of Nagaland would control the credit/loan mechanism. Thus, the base of the economic progress of rural India will be determined by the poorest of the poor.

Microfinance through SHGs has been recognized as a powerful instrument for poverty alleviation and rural development. Besides, the social role of SHGs is highly impressive, as has been indicated in the subsequent paragraphs.

There are apparent synergies between SHGs and local politics since through membership of SHGs, or SHG clusters and federations, village women can gain experience of relevant processes (regular meetings, taking decisions, allocating money). They also become more 'visible' in the village, which is important for campaigning. Woman SHG members also ran for local political office, i.e., in the Village Development Board.

The population of Nagaland is basically tribal. The society here is split by tribalism that has traditionally discriminated one tribe from the other. The fact that the majority of SHGs are single tribe groups is based on the principle of 'affinity groups' and neighbourhoods proximity. It is observed that members living nearby are able to get together more easily and village neighbourhoods are usually tribe based. The government's benefits for Scheduled Tribes and Swarna Jayanti Gram Swarojgar Yojana (SGSY) subsidies have been easier to channel to the target population, since all members of a group belong to the same tribe category.

SHGs seem uniquely placed to support their members on issues of social justice affecting women. Nevertheless, it is not found that SHGs are dealing regularly with issues of social justice. Nor did many groups report such actions. However, it is observed that some groups whose members already enjoy some 'socio-economic' status are able to assist their own members or extent support to other vulnerable women in the village, while more disadvantaged ST groups and poorest groups provided correspondingly fewer instances of such action.

Women in SHGs are working together to address issues that affect not only their own members, but others in the larger community. But very few SHGs have been involved in community actions. These community services included improving education, health care, veterinary care and village road. Some SHGs are found to contribute finance and labour for new infrastructure and trying to stop sale and consumption of alcohol.

Economic Impact of SHGs

Impact of SHGs in terms of economic indicators is both direct and indirect. The direct impact includes the impact on expenditure, annual income of beneficiaries and improvement in economic position, while indirect impacts include the impact on working days of beneficiaries.

Table 11.1: Impact of SHGs in terms of Economics Indicators

Economic Indicators	*Response*		*Total*
	Constant	*Increase*	*Total Respondents*
Working days of beneficiaries	80 (14 %)	480 (86%)	560 (100%)
Annual Income	63 (11%)	497 (89%)	560 (100%)
Consumption Expenditure	240 (43%)	320 (57%)	560 (100%)

The Table 11.1 shows that the economic impact on SHGs in terms of the working days of beneficiaries, annual income and consumption expenditure. Out of 560 samples of SHG members, 480 members representing 86 per cent reported that the number of working days increased after joining SHG and only 80 members representing 14 per cent expressed that there was no change in the number of working days after joining SHG. Regarding annual income, 497 SHG members representing 89 per cent reported that there has been increased after joining SHG while 63 members representing 11 per cent expressed that their annual income did not increase, rather remained constant after joining SHG. With regard to consumption expenditure, 320 members representing 57 per cent expressed that their consumption expenditure increased after joining SHG, while 240 members (i.e., 43%) of the sampled SHG members reported that their consumption expenditure remain constant even after joining SHG. Thus, it can be inferred that in Nagaland, the economic impact of SHG is positive as the economic condition of majority of the SHG members improved after joining SHG.

Other Benefits of SHGs

Joining SHG helps its members economically as well as in enhancing knowledge about group behaviour, shouldering responsibility, social justices, health care, saving habits, etc. The impact of SHG is considered favourable, if it benefits the members to develop saving habits, provides access to promotional assistance and increases the awareness about the healthcare and knowledge.

Table 11.2 indicates that out of 560 samples SHG members, 425 members representing 76 per cent were of the opinion that they had developed saving habit, while 20 per cent of the members were undecided and mere 4 per cent of the members did not subscribe to the opinion that SHG could benefit its members in developing saving habits. There were 336 members (i.e., 60%) who were in the opinion that SHGs has given its members access to various promotional assistance. While 140 members representing 25 per cent of the SHG members, were undecided and only 84 members disagreed about having any access to promotional schemes. Regarding the 'awareness in healthcare education', members numbering 271 i.e., 48 per cent expressed that their awareness about healthcare education improved significantly after becoming SHG member. About 38 per cent of the members disagreed that SHG could increase awareness in healthcare education and 14 per cent of the members were undecided. Similarly, 424 members representing 76 per cent reported that their overall knowledge increased after joining SHG. Only 14 per cent of the members did not agree and about 10 per cent of the members were undecided on the issues of 'increase in knowledge'.

Table 11.2: Benefits of SHGs

Benefits of SHGs	*Response*			*Total Respondents*
	Agreed	*No Opinion*	*Disagreed*	
Development of savings habits	425 (76%)	112 (20%)	23 (4%)	560 (100%)
Access to various promotional assistances	336 (60%)	140 (25%)	84 (15%)	560 (100%)
Awareness in Healthcare education	271 (48%)	79 (14%)	210 (38%)	560 (100%)
Increase in Knowledge	424 (76%)	58 (10%)	78 (14%)	560 (100%)

Source: Field Survey.

Thus, it can be concluded that in Nagaland, SHGs contributes significantly in benefiting the SHG members as being opined by the sample members.

Women Empowerment Through SHGs

The SHGs generally focus attention on empowerment of rural women and making them financially and socially capable. The Table 11.3 analyses the empowerment of women in Nagaland during the period under study.

Table 11.3: Women Empowerment through SHGs

Indicators of Empowerment	*Response*			*Total Respondents*
	Agreed	*No Opinion*	*Disagreed*	
Able to contribute towards family income	432 (90%)	38 (8%)	10 (2%)	480 (100%)
Skill Up-gradation	216 (45%)	72 (15%)	192 (40%)	480 (100%)
Ability to understand banking operations	384 (80%)	72 (15%)	24 (5%)	480 (100%)
Standard of living has improved	182 (38%)	154 (32%)	144 (30%)	480 (100%)
Better leadership and communication skill	288 (60%)	72 (15%)	120 (25%)	480 (100%)

Source: Field Survey.

It is observed from the Table 11.3 that about 90 per cent of the women SHG members numbering 432 reported that they were able to contribute to the family income after joining SHG. Skill upgradation possibility is mainly because of SHG membership for 216 members representing 45 per cent. These women who had develop skill prior to being the SHG members and have upgraded their skill. About 80 per cent numbering 384 women members expressed their happiness in ability to understand the banking operation. 182 women members representing 38 per cent reported that their standard of living improved mainly because of SHG membership. As many as 288 women members representing 60 per cent were of the opinion that because of SHG membership there has been improvement in communication and leadership skill. Thus, it is inferred that evolution of SHGs in Nagaland will help in attending self reliance for women.

Conclusion

Thus to sum up, it can be said that despite of making significant headway, microfinance in Nagaland is still in its nascent stage. Microfinance yet remains a powerful tool for development. It may not be a panacea, but it has brought a sea of change in the lives of many. By reaching the unreached poor in the rural areas microfinance innovations are yielding results and giving hope to the large number of poor through providing credit. The real change will come when women are treated at par with men and given equal opportunities. When that happens, Nagaland will be able to harness its women power. In this regard, microfinance through SHGs in Nagaland is taking the lead and playing a pivotal role in social transformation.

REFERENCES

Karmakar, K. G. (2008). *Rural Credit and Self- Help Groups.* New Delhi: Sage Publications.

NABARD (2009). *Status of Microfinance in India, 2008-09*, Mumbai: NABARD

12

Rural Credit and Debt in Nagaland : A Survey Result

Subhendu Dutta

Introduction

Rural transformation and the attainment of a sustainable development has been one of the main objectives in India. It was conceived in the minds of visionary leaders, politicians, and economists from the pre-independence period in the country. Rural India is beset with many problems, the prominent being debt ridden society living under acute misery. One of the ways out for rural poverty is the injection of sufficient credit, its proper use and timely repayment of the same. Credit plays an important role in rural development and poverty alleviation (Pitt and Khandker, 1998). Credit promotes capital investment and adoption of new technology, leading ultimately to better standards of life due to increased production and incomes (Vatta, 2003). J.M. Keynes' multiplier effect of investment can be vividly demonstrated in a credit programme for the rural poor through the continuous expansion of their economic base. Incomes also rise with additional investment through borrowing. The vicious cycle of low income/low savings/low investment/can be broken by injecting credit in the cycle. Credit/more investment/more income/more savings/more investment/more income is the result that is sought through credit intervention (Karmakar, 1999). However, there is still crunch of adequate inflow of credit in rural areas of the country despite major developmental projects undertaken, posing the major constraint in the economic upliftment of rural households. Until recently conventional wisdom held that imposing low ceilings on interest rates and allocating massive amounts of credit to rural financial markets would speed rural development and improve income distribution. But, by and large, policies directed along these lines have failed. Low interest rate ceilings provide income transfers to loan recipients, distorting the real price ratio of investment opportunities by undervaluing the real cost of capital in different sectors. To standard cost of distorted resource allocation, add the specific costs and consequences of implementing credit programmes in rural financial markets for the full measure of impact. The record overwhelmingly shows credit programmes' objectives have not been met (Meier and Rauch, 2000).

There has been a significant drop in the agricultural credit flow from government and other institutional sources over the 1990s. Government sources of credit did register a significant increase from around 3 per cent to more than 8 per cent between 1983 and 1993. But it almost halved to 4 per cent in 1999-2000 (GoI, 2007). Despite all high claims of microfinance and so-called SHG revolution, the share of commercial banks in total credit supply has declined from 21 per cent to 16.6 per cent between the Sixth (1993-94) and Seventh (1999-2000) (GoI, *ibid.*). This is the overall scenario of the country. Here, we have tried to examine whether credit has sufficiently been infused in the rural sector in Nagaland and what impact has it made on the life of rural people. Further, an effort is made to assess rural credit flow and its utilization in this chapter.

Review of Literature

French proverb is quite appropriate in the present context "credit supports the farmer as the hangman's rope supports the hanged". That agriculturalists cannot carry on his business without outside finance is a fact proved by history and evidenced by the poverty and indebtedness of the persons engaged in the business of agriculture (Mamoria, 1983). Several studies have been carried out to reflect the importance of rural credit in rural transformation and rural development in general. Adequate credit flow in the rural areas is, therefore, very essential for overall development of a rural area. For instance, the study by Mishra (2005) in Orissa which examined the impact of institutional finance on farm income and productivity revealed that the increase in yield of borrowing farms was due to use of credit financed inputs. A similar study by Kareemulla (2005) in Uttar Pradesh analyzed the credit flow to agriculture and identified the reasons for farmers' indebtedness. This study observed that measures to widen the crop insurance coverage and post-finance guidance would probably help to ensure proper use of credit and prompt repayment, which will pave way for smooth credit flow to agriculture. Another study on the spatial and temporal variations in the growth of Scheduled Commercial Banks' (SCB) credit to agriculture sector in the North-Eastern Region of India examined the relative shares of different states in scheduled commercial banks' credit to agriculture sector (Borah and Chakraborty, 2005). Their study showed that the growth rate of SCBs credit to rural sector was lowest in Mizoram and highest in Assam. There was significant evidence of structural difference or temporal variation in the percentage share of agriculture in total SCBs credit (outstanding) for NER between the time periods from 1990-91 to 1994-95 and from 1995-96 to 2000-01. The study expressed concern over the low percentage share of agriculture to State-wise SCBs credit and emphasis on particular focus to priority sector advances to strengthen the credit portfolio of the States in the NER. Their study mainly focused on the role of SCBs in rural credit flow and did not include other financial institutions to capture a more comprehensive picture.

The extent of debt a household is burdened is determined by the source of credit, besides the purpose for which the debt has been used. Though institutional sources have gained the ground, adequate inflow in rural areas is still not satisfactory. This is also experienced outside India. One study by Cooperative Statistics and Research Organization (1965) in East Pakistan estimated agricultural credit need and found that the credit in rural areas were mainly obtained from well to do rural people as well as friends (52%) and relatives (26%). Among the institutional source, the Cooperative Society stands first as a loan giving agency. When we say that credit in rural areas is not adequate we do not mean that government has not done anything on this front. In fact in our country, the drastic effort taken by the government since independence has reduced the activities of informal agencies. But the main question concerning us is whether poor farmers with low resource base are getting their legitimate share or not. Since, indebtedness would arise only when debt is not serviced in time and for that generation of income is required which in turn depends on the availability of finance to run the farm operation smoothly. Several studies reveal that well to do households living in rural areas have grabbed not only their share of credit but even the share of rural poor. A study in Punjab which assessed loans and advances made by State Bank of Patiala found that large farmers enjoyed larger share in loans advanced than the medium and small farmers (Singh and Kahlon, 1971). Another study in Bihar examined the flow of rural credit to different categories of farmers and found that the loan advanced by the institutional and non-institutional agencies accounted for about 77 per cent and 23 per cent of the total loan respectively (Sinha, *et al.*, 2005). Commercial banks provided the highest loan (50.68%) followed by RRBs and cooperative banks, when all the farms were considered together. Similarly, a study undertaken on farmers in Punjab highlighting the different sources of agricultural finance available and the extent of agricultural loans obtained by different categories of farmers. A higher percentage of small farmers obtained loans from non-institutional agencies like commission agents as compared to medium and large farmers. It was also seen that with the increase in farm size, the percentage of farmers getting credit also increased. The flow of agricultural credit with special reference to inter-farm size class bias of formal credit agencies was examined in west Godavari district in Andhra Pradesh and it was revealed that about 86 per cent of the total credit supply is provided by the institutional agencies consisting of cooperatives and commercial banks (Sai, 1988). Cooperatives were the main source of finance to the marginal and small farmers followed by private sources and commercial banks in that order. Again, in a study in Coimbatore district which assessed the supply of farm credit, the extent of overdues and causes thereof, impact of credit and identified the strategies for the expansion of supply of institutional credit to farm sector found that 79 per cent of the sample households borrowed from different sources and the expansion of institutional credit substituting non-institutional credit resulted in more efficient use of credit by farmers (Mohideen, 1991).

An Overview of Credit Flow in Nagaland

In general, the banking outreach in the NER, particularly in the rural districts, is significantly low. This is also true in case of Nagaland. The low level of financial inclusion, which is generally considered to be the outcome of poverty, ignorance and environmental factors, is mostly related to supply related issues, i.e., lack of appropriate financial services for those that are excluded by the traditional instruments. There is lack of adequate branch network in the region. Moreover, owing to difficult terrain, sparsely distributed population in hill regions, poor infrastructure, difficulties in obtaining land as collateral, insurgency/law and order problems, complicated systems/procedures of banks, shortage of suitably skilled staff, lack of awareness amongst large segments of the population about formal banking transactions and the general preference for grants rather than loans (RBI, 2006), formal banking penetration in the region has been very low. The data shown in Table 12.1 is the reflection of poor performance of banking outreach in North-East.

Table 12.1: Indicators of Banking Development in North-East India

States	*APPBO**	*CD Ratio#*	*Current and Savings Accounts per 100 adult population*	*Credit Accounts per 100 adult population*	*Per Capita Deposit (in Rs.)*	*Per Capita Credit (in Rs.)*	*Credit to NSDP$ Ratio (%)*
Arunachal	16211	22	37.8	6.2	10869	2287	17
Assam	20960	35	39.1	5.9	6669	2261	26
Manipur	29791	42	19.5	4.0	4289	1713	11
Meghalaya	12658	44	40.9	8.3	13087	5281	41
Mizoram	11278	48	29.0	7.7	8741	4028	NA
Nagaland	27990	23	19.7	3.6	6425	1356	9
Tripura	17429	29	36.7	13.6	8200	2240	18
NER	19885	35	37.3	6.7	7199	2407	NA
All India	14949	66	59.3	13.3	16700	10474	62

Source: Compiled from the Report of the Committee on Financial Sector Plan for North-Eastern Region, 2006, RBI, July 2006.

*APPBO: Average Population covered per Bank Branch.

#CD ratio: Credit- Deposit Ratio.

$NSDP: Net State Domestic Product.

The important indicators of financial outreach like average population covered per bank branch (APPBO), deposit and credit growth, etc., are generally lower than the national average in the region. Though the region has been registering branch expansion in the recent decades, the result is not pleasing. Rapid branch expansion of scheduled commercial banks in the region in the eighties have resulted in reduction of the average population covered per branch (APPBO) from over 32,000 in 1981 as against the national average of 18,000 to less than 17,000 in 1991 (national average 13,700). This is a quite significant outcome, but even now APPBO is very high in all the North-Eastern States. The Average Population per Branch Office (APPBO) of 19885 in NER (2005) is strikingly higher than the all-India figure (14,949) and is also very high in the rural areas of Nagaland. The APPBO (total) in Nagaland is 27,990, which is more than twice the national average. In rural areas, it is 49,272 in the State, whereas the rural regional and national averages are 27,796 and 24,856 respectively. Two non-functional bank branches in Nagaland have raised the APPBO in Nagaland. These are Chetheba branch in Phek district and V.K. Station branch in Zunehobhoto district; both branches belong to Nagaland Rural Bank. We know that the lower the APPBO ratio, higher the outreach and *vice versa.* The very high APPBO coupled with larger area per bank branch (227 to 286 sq km) indicates the extremely low level of banking penetration, particularly in the rural areas. The annual growth rate of deposit in the State was 10.0 per cent, while the figure for the NER and All India were 15.9 and 16.5 per cent respectively.

If we take a look at the CD ratio in the State and in the region, it shows a dismal picture as compared to the national average, which is indeed a matter of concern. While the CD ratio for all India was 66 per cent and that for NER as a whole was 35 per cent, the figure for Nagaland was lower at 23 per cent. One of the indicators that currently are being used for measuring the extent of financial inclusion is the number of current and savings deposits per 100 adult populations. The ratio of current and savings accounts of scheduled commercial banks per 100 adult populations as on March 31, 2005, is only 19.7 in Nagaland, with a regional average of 37.3, distinctly lower than the national average of 59.3. In rural Nagaland, it is only 5.1 per cent which is lowest among the NER States and much below the regional average of 21.3 per cent and national average of 25.7 per cent. The low ratios both for total and rural in Nagaland indicate that majority of the rural adult population are financially excluded. As far as credit accounts per 100 adult populations in the State are concerned, it is also significantly below the national and regional average. The percentage of adult population availing credit facility is merely 3.6 per cent in Nagaland, whereas in NER it is 6.7 per cent as against the national average of 13.3 per cent. There is a wide variation in the per capita deposit in the State, region and the national average. Per capita deposit in Nagaland is just Rs. 6,425 as against NER average of Rs. 7,199 and the national average of Rs. 16,700. The per capita credit in 2005 is Rs. 1356 for Nagaland and the regional average was Rs. 2407, which continues to remain lower than the national average of Rs.10,474. Credit to Net State Domestic Product (NSDP) ratio is 9 per cent in Nagaland which is much lower than the national average of 62 per cent and the lowest among all NER States.

As far as bank coverage is concerned, it is insufficient in Nagaland.

There are at present only 14 banks operating in the State having 93 branches. Dimapur has the largest number of branches (24), followed by Kohima (18) and the rest are spread over nine districts covering a population of about 14.62 lakh. Thus, 75 per cent of the banks in the State cater to only 23 per cent of the population. In some districts like Mon (4 branches), Longleng (1 branch), Kiphire (2 branches) and Peren (3 branches), the banking network is not considered adequate. About 421 villages in the State are yet to have banking access. District-wise percentage of total deposit accounts to 100 of Population and APPBO in Nagaland during 2001-2005 is shown in Table 12.2.

Table 12.2: District-wise Percentage of Total Deposit Accounts to 100 of Population

State/District	*2001*	*2002*	*2003*	*2004*	*2005*	*APPBO*
Nagaland	14.7	13.5	13.2	12.5	12.5	30360
Dimapur	0.0	39.8	36.8	36.1	36.6	20772
Kohima	63.3	17.3	18.9	18.3	16.8	19999
Mokokchung	13.0	12.6	11.1	8.6	7.8	28911
Mon	5.0	4.8	5.2	4.1	4.5	99089
Phek	5.3	4.9	6.1	5.9	6.9	28292
Tuensang	3.5	3.3	2.9	3.3	3.4	67854
Wokha	8.8	8.2	8.9	8.1	8.3	26353
Zunheboto	9.9	9.8	9.3	9.0	6.1	29564

Source: Compiled from the Report of the Committee on Financial Sector Plan for North-Eastern Region, 2006. Reserve Bank of India, July 2006.

Within this low level of banking penetration, there was also wide inter-district divergence. The total deposit accounts (including term deposits) per 100 population reveal that in 2005, the range in the State is 3.4 in Tuensang to 37 in Dimapur. Looking at APPBO, the number is highest in Mon district with 99,089, followed by Tuensang (67,854). These are the most backward districts of the State and banking system has yet to penetrate there. APPBOs in Dimapur and Kohima indicate that these two districts are relatively better in terms of banking outreach. Districts that had the highest ratio were almost always the district with respective State capital or commercial town/cities having better banking facility. This inter-district disparity is partly explained by APPBO, i.e., the districts with higher bank penetration (lower than the APPBO); in general also has higher deposit accounts per 100 population. Sector-wise, average share of agriculture in credit in the State during 2001-2005 is 11.5 per cent which is, however, higher than the national average of 10.7 per cent. Three banks in the State have been running at loss for considerable time. One is the Nagaland State Cooperative Bank Ltd., the SCB, which is running at loss of Rs 398.00 lakh. NSCB Ltd. is also unable to comply with the provisions of Section 11(1) of the Banking Regulation Act 1949 with regard to minimum capital requirement. The other bank, i.e., the Urban Cooperative Bank Ltd., located in Dimapur is also running at heavy loss and on the verge of closure. Further, Nagaland Rural Bank, the RRB of the State has incurred accumulated loss of Rs. 3.1 crores in 2005. As per the RBI circular dated September 8, 2005 all eleven districts in Nagaland are considered as underbanked (RBI, 2005). What we find is that banking culture in the State is almost non-existent with only about 5 per cent of the population having bank accounts. The banks have not reached out to the people. Penetration of bank credit is hindered by non-establishment of transferable property rights on land. The land tenure system in the hill areas, inhabited mostly by tribal population, is markedly different from the system found in the plain areas. As in most other parts of the country, in the plains of the NER individual rights over landholding are transferable, and buying and selling of such rights are ordinarily unrestricted. However, in the hill areas, transfer of these rights is subject to restrictions, if not impossible.

The genesis of the cleavage in the land tenure systems in the hills and the plains of the region is the difference in the nature of traditional agricultural activity. Agriculture in the plains has been settled. In contrast, agriculture in the hills has been shifting in nature. Land used to be communally held and the indivisible right to land used to be distributed to families according to customary norms by the village council or the village chief as the case may be. Nevertheless, incursion of market forces, the practice of settled cultivation and also rapid urbanization have induced settling down of hill tribal population in fixed locations. The process has been instrumental in emergence of individual holding in hill areas. For instance, in Nagaland, as far back as 1976-77, altogether 86 per cent of the holdings covering 89 per cent of the area was under terrace cultivation, and wholly owned and self-operated. There are broadly two systems of land tenure in hill areas existing side by side: (a) community ownership of land in areas where shifting cultivation is still in vogue (households enjoy user rights to land allocated to them by traditional authority); and (b) individual ownership of land which is transferable only within members of local tribal community. As indicated earlier, where the household enjoys the usufruct and there is a document to establish this, such as possession certificate, the provision of crop loans is not a problem as banks can accept such document. As stated there is no system of *patta*, which legalizes ownership of land in the hilly States of the regions, banks are reluctant to provide loans beyond certain limit without land collateral. The land tenure system prevalent restricts separation of land from a tribal to a non-tribal. However, as per the present instructions of Reserve Bank of India, banks are required to provide agricultural loans up to Rs. 50,000 and loans to agri-clinics and agri-businesses up to Rs. 5 lakh without insisting on collateral. Even then, banks may require some documentary evidence of the farmer's right to cultivate the land so that need based credit can be provided and appropriate scales of finance can be applied. Though the banks are not required to ask for any documentation in case they are satisfied about the borrower's ownership of land, the community ownership of land prevents them in the hilly parts of the region. There are many NGOs but nearly all of them are involved in social activities and not oriented towards rendering financial services in the State. This is another bottleneck in bringing more and more people in the banking net. Poor recovery of loans, especially those under government sponsored schemes and default by borrowers act as a deterrent for granting fresh loans (RBI, 2005).

Source of Credit

The extent of exploitation of a borrower is largely determined by the source of debt from where he has raised the loan together with the nature, extent and purpose of debt. A household with huge debt of hereditary nature raised for unproductive purposes from non-institutional sources represents a case of absolute misery. These non-institutional sources charge exorbitant rates of interest which a poor borrower cannot afford to pay. Moreover, the unproductive loans fail to generate additional income by which the loans can be paid off. Such loans only multiply the poor borrowers' problem and increase intensity of their indebtedness. On the contrary, institutional and government credit agencies discourage the non-productive loans. Besides, rates of interest are regulated by the government, concessional rates are charged from weaker sections of the society with regard to their productive loan investment. Therefore, it becomes essential to study the various sources of debt together with nature and purposes of debt in order to have a clear picture of the pattern of rural indebtedness (NSSO, 1999) in the State.

The amount of debt taken from various credit agencies is broadly

Table 12.3: Source of Credit among rural households in Nagaland

Districts/ State/ Categories	*Non-Institutional*					*Institutional*				
	Agri. & Prof. moneylenders	*Traders*	*Relatives & friends*	*Doctors, lawyers & other prof.*	*Sub-total*	*Government*	*Co-operative Societies*	*Commercial & other banks*	*Sub-total*	*Total*
Dimapur Agri. Lab.	–	–	10000.00 (100.00)	–	10000.00 (100.00)	–	–	–	–	10000.00 (100.00)
Marginal Farmers	5544.62 (27.42)	403.70 (1.99)	4924.99 (24.35)	–	10873.31 (53.77)	1824.07 (9.02)	4859.62 (24.03)	2662.03 (13.16)	9345.72 (46.22)	20219.07 (100.00)
Small Farmers	2327.08 (8.81)	1161.45 (4.39)	3349.99 (12.68)	–	6838.52 (25.90)	14854.16 (56.26)	3686.66 (13.96)	1020.83 (3.86)	19561.65 (74.09)	26400.20 (100.00)
Large Farmers	18425.00 (64.32)	–	–	–	18425.00 (64.32)	10220.00 (35.67)	–	–	10220.00 (35.67)	28645.00 (100.00)
Others	–	–	20000.00 (100.00)	–	20000.00 (100.00)	–	–	–	–	20000.00 (100.00)
All/Total	5175.66 (23.32)	551.94 (2.48)	4959.44 (22.34)	–	10687.04 (48.15)	5736.88 (25.85)	3898.88 (17.56)	1869.44 (8.42)	11505.20 (51.84)	22192.27 (100.00)
Kohima Agri. Lab.	500.00 (4.28)	333.33 (2.85)	10833.33 (92.85)	–	11666.66 (100.00)	–	–	–	–	11666.66 (100.00)
Marginal Farmers	3300.00 (10.49)	4320.00 (13.74)	10640.00 (33.84)	11000.00 (34.98)	29260.00 (93.06)	–	–	2180.00 (6.93)	2180.00 (6.93)	31440.00 (100.00)
Small Farmers	–	1968.75 (3.75)	687.50 (1.30)	–	2656.25 (5.06)	3975.00 (7.57)	9012.50 (17.17)	36840.00 (70.19)	49827.50 (94.93)	52483.75 (100.00)
Large Farmers	–	9340.00 (20.95)	17000.00 (38.13)	–	26340.00 (59.09)	15984.00 (35.85)	–	2250.00 (5.04)	18234.50 (40.90)	44574.00 (100.00)
Others	–	–	3071.42 (6.88)	–	3071.42 (6.88)	10599.57 (23.77)	–	30911.17 (69.33)	41510.74 (93.11)	44582.17 (100.00)

(Contd....)

Table 12.3: *(Contd.)*

Districts/ State/ Categories	*Non-Institutional*					*Institutional*				
	Agri. & Prof. moneylenders	*Traders*	*Relatives & friends*	*Doctors, lawyers & other prof.*	*Sub-total*	*Government*	*Co-operative Societies*	*Commercial & other banks*	*Sub-total*	*Total*
All/Total	513.15 (1.30)	2264.47 (5.75)	6623.68 (16.84)	1447.36 (3.68)	10848.66 (27.59)	6845.10 (17.40)	1897.36 (4.82)	19727.01 (50.17)	28469.47 (72.40)	39318.17 (100.00)
Mon										
Agri. Lab.	3940.83 (18.42)	3416.66 (15.97)	9533.33 (44.56)	–	16890.82 (78.96)	–	4000.00 (18.69)	500.00 (2.33)	4500.00 (21.03)	21390.83 (100.00)
Marginal Farmers	7704.00 (18.42)	–	14160.00 (33.85)	2360.00 (5.64)	24224.00 (57.91)	–	800.00 (1.91)	16800.00 (40.16)	17600.00 (42.08)	41824.00 (100.00)
Small Farmers	5933.33 (6.99)	3333.00 (3.92)	4933.33 (5.81)	–	14199.99 (16.73)	3000.00 (3.53)	6666.66 (7.85)	60977.77 (71.87)	70644.43 (83.26)	84844.44 (100.00)
Large Farmers	–	–	25000.00 (19.05)	–	25000.00 (19.05)	28640.00 (21.82)	18600.00 (14.17)	58965.00 (44.94)	106205.00 (80.94)	131205.00 (100.00)
Others	6883.33 (13.06)	7666.66 (14.55)	–	–	14549.99 (27.61)	9000.00 (17.08)	–	29141.66 (55.30)	38141.66 (72.38)	52691.66 (100.00)
All/Total	5479.78 (9.83)	2489.36 (4.46)	10557.44 (18.94)	753.19 (1.35)	19279.77 (34.58)	4770.21 (8.55)	4531.91 (8.13)	27159.04 (48.72)	36461.16 (65.41)	55740.95 (100.00)
Nagaland										
Agri. Lab.	2646.84 (14.93)	2263.15 (12.77)	9968.41 (56.25)	–	14878.40 (83.96)	–	2526.31 (14.25)	315.78 (1.78)	2842.09 (16.03)	17720.51 (100.00)
Marginal Farmers	5994.99 (21.17)	691.48 (2.44)	8480.31 (29.95)	1923.40 (6.79)	17090.18 (60.37)	1047.87 (3.70)	3047.01 (10.76)	7122.86 (25.16)	11217.74 (39.62)	28307.96 (100.00)
Small Farmers	2804.30 (5.42)	2058.08 (3.97)	3106.89 (6.00)	–	7969.27 (15.40)	8174.13 (15.80)	6080.68 (11.75)	29509.30 (57.04)	43764.11 (84.59)	51733.52 (100.00)
Large Farmers	4251.92 (5.72)	3592.30 (4.84)	16153.34 (21.76)	–	23998.06 (32.33)	19521.53 (26.30)	7153.84 (9.63)	23544.23 (31.72)	50219.60 (67.66)	74217.67 (100.00)
Others	1877.27 (4.21)	2090.90 (4.69)	3772.72 (8.46)	–	7740.89 (17.37)	9199.72 (20.64)	–	27618.47 (61.98)	36818.19 (82.62)	44559.10 (100.00)
All/Total	3922.72 (9.97)	1752.97 (4.45)	7469.80 (18.99)	695.38 (1.76)	13840.87 (35.19)	5711.33 (14.52)	3542.68 (9.00)	16232.50 (41.27)	25486.51 (64.80)	39327.43 (100.00)

categorized into (i) institutional and (ii) non-institutionals, in the State which is evident from Table 12.3. It is revealed that an average rural household in Nagaland has taken loan of about Rs. 13,840.87 from non-institutional agencies while the debt is Rs. 25,486.51 from institutional sources. This is rather a reverse picture as against common experience in rural India, where most of the loans are taken from non-institutional sources, particularly from village moneylenders. A study in the Ballia district of Uttar Pradesh showed the similar trend where it was found that the marginal and small farmers obtained about 80 per cent of their total borrowing from the institutional sources like the government and the cooperatives (Singh and Mehrotra, 1973). Again in Palanpur district of Uttar Pradesh, it was observed that nearly 80 per cent of total debt was provided by public lending institutions and private credit played a relatively minor role in the village economy (Lanjouw and Stern, 1984). Another study in Himachal Pradesh showed that institutional sources of credit were very popular among the farmers (Sharma and Gupta, 2005). Evidence suggests that as farm size increases, private credit sources, village moneylenders and pawnbrokers, chit funds with an array of implicit interest rates, and friends or relatives grow less important than banks. With the implementation of development plans, official lending complements but clearly does not supersede informal sources (Meier and Rauch, 2000).

In case of Nagaland, we cannot say that due to increase in farm size (though size of holding is higher as compared to other States in the region) the importance of informal sources has declined. Flow of formal credit has increased in the rural sector due to efforts taken by the State government and this, though not totally, have influenced life of rural families quite significantly. Again, except relatives and friends, professional moneylenders have insignificant role in Naga society.

As per the NSSO Report on indebtedness of 1999-2000, it was found that the non-institutional sources of credit dominate the rural credit scene accounting for the largest share of the debt. Among these sources, in majority of the States, the money lenders and relatives and friends continued to be the most important sources of debt. The studies made by Singh (1990) in Punjab, Singh and Mehrotra (1973) in Uttar Pradesh, NSSO Survey (2003), Mandal (1977) in Kalipur village in West Bengal, Ramachandran and Swaminathan (1977; 1985; 1999) in Gokilapuram village in Tamil Nadu, Dunn (1996) from reviews of selected studies in Africa, Asia, and Latin America, Vijaya Kumari (2002) in Northern Telangana region of Andhra Pradesh, Jagannath Lenka (2005), Atteri and

Alka (2005), revealed that rural households mainly depend upon non-institutional sources and particularly, moneylenders and friends and relatives for their loan requirements. However, the banking institutions provided the highest proportion of debt in some of the NER States like Mizoram (98%) and Tripura (42%) (55th Round of NSSO, 1999-2000), which is also apparent from the study in Nagaland where these institutions provided 41.27 per cent of debt to the rural households. Like in other parts of the country and from various studies, it was revealed that friends and relatives constituted one of the important sources of debt in Nagaland. The share of money lenders in rural debt is, however, insignificant. In fact, in Naga society the system of professional money lending is nearly absent. Nonetheless, in the present time, some moneylenders have gradually been emerging in the scene, though most of these are non-Naga people who live near suburban areas and sometimes provide loans to known persons who come from nearby villages. They are not professional moneylenders. Though penetration of banking in rural parts of the State is poor as in other States of NER and one of the reasons is non-establishment of transferable property rights on land; rural people in Nagaland are now becoming relatively aware of credit availability by formal institutions than their counterparts in other States of the region due to various efforts being taken by the Government of Nagaland, and agency like Nagaland Empowerment of People through Economic Development (NEPED). However, a significant part of the rural population still remains ignorant about credit availability from banks, etc. They are mostly residing in far-flung areas of the State. NGOs, Village Development Boards (VDBs), Village Councils (VCs) and SHGs are significantly contributing towards creation of mass awareness in rural areas about micro-credit facilities available to them. The role of VDBs/Village Councils and *Gaon Buras* (village elders) in this respect is quite prominent in the villages. Both VDBs and VCs enjoy a very respectable status in the society. While the former has core competence in building infrastructure in villages, the latter has it in the social aspects. The VCs/VDBs function as a grassroots level credit institution. They operate the credit mechanism at village level, assess the credit need of the farmers, and ensure and monitor the repayment of loans. NEPED has developed the rural micro credit mechanism known as Revolving Fund, which was started in April 2001 in 105 villages across Nagaland. It is very strongly linked to traditional organizations like Village Councils and VDBs. The main aim was to enable farmers to cultivate cash crops and uplift the income level of poor farmers in the State. For this, Corpus Funds were made available and created in each village that is managed by Village Councils. Farmers were asked to take loans from VCs, the interest rate of which range between 5-10 per cent per year as opposed to local informal loans that charge 5-10 per cent per month. The programme has been a grand success and set the ground for micro-credit development in the region. About Rs. 82.6 million has already been disbursed to 105 villagers for establishing a revolving credit mechanism (NEPED, 2007). Such effort is helping farmers in transition from the traditional subsistence economy to the modern market economy.

In fact, banks find it comfortable to provide finance to individuals through VDBs and Village Councils as Community guarantee (in line with group guarantee in case of SHG based micro-credit) in lieu of land collateral. This has been tried in the State and seen that while credits to individuals against the guarantee of VDBs/VCs have been of limited success, financing of VDBs/VCs for their lending operations to individuals have been relatively more successful (RBI, 2006). Moreover, people in the State are fairly literates than their counterparts in the rest of India. It has also been the outcome of the survey that Naga people help each other at the time of financial crisis, so they hardly need to go moneylenders.

The total debt taken by an average rural household is Rs. 39,327.43, which includes both debts from non-institutional and institutional sources of credit. Debt is skewed towards institutional sources. This is due to much dependence of credit on institutional agencies in the State by small and large farmers and particularly, the households belonging to 'Others', i.e., non-cultivators category. These categories are aware of advantages of credit supplied by institutional agencies, where rate of interest is relatively less and repayment modes are quite comfortable. Moreover, most of the households belonging to these categories are literates and do not hesitate to approach a bank or any government agency for their credit needs. Large farmers are able to get loans quickly owing to their better financial standing. They are mostly absentee farmers, who are engaged in some or other non-farm businesses. It was observed that rich borrowers are able to secure consumption loans from formal sources by offering suitable collateral and claiming that the loan would be used for some productive purpose, an observation that reinforces the importance of fungibles (Dunn, 1996).

Among the different categories, agricultural labourers who are under debt of Rs. 17,720.51 have acquired credit of Rs. 14,878.40 from non-institutional agencies and the remaining Rs. 2842.09 from institutional agencies. Marginal farmers are indebted to the extent of Rs. 17,090.18 to the non-institutional and Rs. 11,217.74 to the institutional sources. Contrary to this, small and large farmers and household belonging to 'Others' category relied more on institutional sources than on non-institutional ones. Of Rs. 51,733.52 as debt for an average small farmer household, only Rs. 7969.27 has been taken from non-institutional sources and the major amount of credit, i.e., Rs. 43,764.11 has been taken from institutional sources. Large farmers also depended on institutional agencies such as government, commercial banks and co-operative societies for their credit of Rs. 50,219.60 out of the total debt of Rs. 74,217.67 for an average indebted household. Similar is the case for the household belonging to 'Others' category that mostly depends on institutional sources for their credit requirements. About Rs. 36,818.19 is taken from institutional sources and only Rs. 7740.89 from non-institutional sources out of total debt of Rs. 44,559.10 under this category. The institutional source from where most of the loans have been taken by rural households is 'Commercial and other banks'. A study in Uttar Pradesh also revealed that the share of commercial banks in the total availability of credit per ha was the highest followed by the RRBs, Primary Agricultural Credit Societies and Land Development Banks for all the categories of farmers (Singh *et al.*, 2005).

In Nagaland, the key players are the State Bank of India and Nagaland State Cooperative Bank Ltd., who provide loans to the farmers for development of agricultural farms and for the rearing of livestock and poultry birds through on-lending facility provided by NABARD. The Nagaland State Cooperative Bank Ltd. is the bank which has deep penetration into the rural sector of the State and as such is the sole player in advancing much needed credit to the agro and farming sectors in the State. The State Bank of India with a Zonal Office at Dimapur is the lead bank of the State. SBI has various special schemes for agricultural finance such as Kisan Credit Card, General Credit Card, Agriculture Cash Credit, Agriculture Term Loans, etc., for meeting credit needs of local people. It is also providing housing loans known as 'Tribal Plus' which is a tailor made for NER where mortgage of land is not permitted. SHG financing also has been one of the thrust area for the SBI in the State. For financing of activities like Contract Farming, it has tied up with the National Horticulture Board; Exotic Juice Limited, Mao of Manipur and Noah-Grandpa (an NGO), for passion fruit cultivation and production and with DIMUL for milk production. Subsidy is another attraction for availing loans from various commercial banks in the State.

Among the non-institutional agencies, 'relatives and friends' have been found to be the most preferred source of credit in the State, followed by 'agricultural and professional moneylenders'. The borrowing from 'relatives and friends' is similar to that for all India as evident from the 55th NSSO Report, 1999-2000. Most of the studies undertaken confirm the fact that rural households prefer availing loans from friends and relatives and moneylenders (Singh and Mehrotra, 1973; Mandal, 1977; Dunn, 1996; Hanumappa and Ninan, 1971; Singh, 1990). In a study conducted by the Institute of Development and Communication in Punjab, of the 91 per cent farmers who had never gone to the commercial banks, 26 per cent did not know of their existence, while 40 per cent feared the paperwork and other formalities at these Banks (Singh, 1997).

Interest-free loans can reflect a variety of motives on the part of the lender. In a majority of cases, the reported purpose are to 'help a friend or relative', but this response is not very informative. In some cases, as interest free loan is simply unrequired favour made by the lender to the borrower, possibly due to genuine concern or a sense of social obligation. In other cases, the loan is embedded in a broader relationship of 'balanced reciprocity' between the borrower and the lender, involving careful mental accounting of what the partners do for each other and a strong expectation that every gift or favour will be returned at some stage. A third possibility is that the lender sees the loan as a way of gaining the sympathy or loyalty of the borrower (Dreze, *et al.*, 1998). As far as borrowers are concerned, an interest-free loan is likely to be more readily obtainable if the borrower's need for cash is seen as compelling, urgent, and legitimate; this suggests that the 'purpose' of interest-free borrowing would often be related to some kind of unforeseen distress. As seen in a study in Palanpur village in Uttar Pradesh, that nearly half of outstanding interest free debts are accounted for by medical expenses and other crisis related needs, not including expenditure on social functions such as marriage ceremonies and death rites. The importance of unforeseen distress as a motive for interest-free borrowing contrasts with the predominance of productive investment as a motive for borrowing from institutional sources (Dreze, *et al.*, 1998).

Evidence showed that interest-free lending within the village has low overall incidence. One possible explanation for the limited reach of interest-free credit within the village is that short-term income fluctuations are highly correlated across households. Covariate risks (arising, for instance, from common exposure to agro-climatic uncertainties) reduce the scope for reciprocal interest-free lending, since periods of economic hardships for one household are also likely to be the periods of hardship for other households (Dreze, *et al.*, 1998).

It would be worthwhile to point out here that, in Naga society, a culture of caring among fellow villagers was assiduously nurtured and the bonds of kinship were usually very strong in the village. The community shares the responsibility of taking care of the basic needs of the disadvantaged, for instance the landless are provided opportunity to cultivate the community-owned land. This ensures that there is no destitute, shelterless and famished in the society (NSHD Report, 2004). Thus people help each other in times of crisis. There is absence of beggary in the society.

Pattern of Debt according to Source of Credit

From the Table 12.3 we can infer that an average household in rural Nagaland takes only 35.19 per cent of the loan from non-institutional agencies while about 64.80 per cent of the debt is availed from institutional sources. This is because an average household in the State takes most of the loan requirement from commercial and other banks (41.27%). The NSSO 59th Report, 2005 also reveals almost similar picture. Out of every Rs.1000, distribution of outstanding loans by source of loan for all sizes of class of land possessed by farmer households in Nagaland shows that about Rs. 311 have been borrowed from non-institutional sources and Rs. 688 from institutional sources. It is to be mentioned here that in our estimation share by 'Others' category is included, which is not included in the said report.

However, high share of institutional credit in Nagaland does not mean that there is good presence of banking facilities even in remote parts of the State. Banks are normally reluctant to open branches in rural areas of the NER States. For instance, out of 52 Rural Development (RD) Blocks in Nagaland, as many as 21 RD Blocks are yet to have any banking facilities (Rio, 2005) covering 421 villages. The presence of only 14 banks with 93 branches in the State is not at all adequate. Of these 42 branches are concentrated in Kohima and Dimapur alone. About, 75 per cent of the banks in the State cater to only 23 per cent of the population. In some districts like Mon, Longleng, Kiphire and Peren, the banking network is not considered adequate (RBI, 2006).

To improve this situation, the government is taking initiatives to provide financial grants to the Village Development Boards to enable them to function as financial intermediaries to give cheap credit to local farmers and artisans. These VDBs are constituted in every village and they already have substantial corpus of fixed deposits worth about Rs. 9.82 crore, which requires to be supplemented by grants from the government. Because of the well knit village society, and the sound village administration, the VDBs/Village Councils are in advantageous position to ensure timely recovery of such loans. This measure will also save the farmers and artisans from the clutches of unscrupulous moneylenders, who normally charge exorbitant rates of interest (Rio, 2005). The success of the rural micro credit mechanism of NEPED in the State, with almost 100 per cent repayment rates, has impressed financial and banking institutions. It is also evident that only 1.76 per cent of total debt is availed from doctors, lawyers and other professionals. However, these professionals give loans only to their kith and kin without charging any interest and sometimes such loans are fully waived depending on the amount of loan and relation to the borrower.

Agricultural labourers take the highest proportion from non-institutional source, i.e., 83.96 per cent, out of which 56.25 per cent is taken from relatives and friends. They are the households who have least access to formal credit lending agencies. When they require loan, they easily take advance from *Marwari* traders and pay back after harvest. This is particularly seen in Dimapur. In other parts of the State also they prefer to go to informal sources. Agricultural labourers do not dream of formal loans as they think these are out of their scope. Most of them have no knowledge about the availability of credit from institutional sources. This is because of their illiteracy. Only few parents send their children to schools and colleges. About 42 per cent of agricultural labour households are illiterates and nearly 52 per cent have completed schooling up to primary and middle levels. None of the agricultural labourers whom we contacted were found to be graduate or above. However, one belonging to *Bihari* community is found to be continuing his graduation.

Next to agricultural labourers are marginal farmers and large farmers, who have taken about 29.95 per cent and 21.76 per cent respectively from relatives and friends. Out of every Rs.1000, distribution of outstanding loans by source of loan for farmer households having size of land below 1 hectare shows that they take most of the loans from relatives and friends (Rs. 454) in Nagaland. Institutional sources constituted only Rs. 251. The contribution of moneylenders in providing credit to the rural households in the State is significant only in the lives of agricultural labourers and marginal farmers. About 14.93 and 21.17 per cent of non-institutional loans are taken from moneylenders by agricultural labourers and marginal farmers respectively. Small farmers mostly take loans from institutional sources, particularly from commercial banks. The NSSO 59th Report also shows the similar trend. Out of every Rs.1000, distribution of outstanding loans by source of loan for farmer households in Nagaland having size of land between 1 to 5 hectares is Rs. 763 from banks. Relatives and friends constituted only Rs. 47. Similarly, the households belonging to 'Others' category in rural Nagaland depends more on institutional sources for their credit needs. This category includes households who are engaged in non-farm business and are in government or private services, who bring cash income to the family. They have better contacts in government offices and banks and are also partly cultivators. They are better educated than other categories and are not hesitant to undergo various lengthy procedures of the formal lending agencies. All of the households in this category were found to be literate. They have better knowledge of credit availability sources in the State.

Conclusion

Though over 70 per cent of the population is dependent on agriculture for livelihood and sustenance in the State, the productivity of most of the agricultural crops has remained too low as compared to its full harvesting potential. Consequently, returns from agriculture are low and, therefore, a major part of the rural population is forced to live in the conditions of poverty and deprivation. The government is, however, taking initiatives to provide financial grants to the Village Development Boards (VDBs) to enable them to function as financial intermediaries to give cheap credit to local farmers and artisans. VDBs already have substantial corpus of fixed deposits worth about Rs.9.82 crore. The VDBs/Village Councils (VCs) are in advantageous position to ensure timely recovery of such loans. This measure will also save the farmers and artisans from the clutches of unscrupulous moneylenders, who normally charge exorbitant rates of interest (Rio, 2005). The initiative taken by NEPED in 2001 in regard to rural micro credit mechanism known as Revolving Fund has confirmed the significance of micro credit in the lives of rural households. Farmers are now cultivating cash crops like cardamom, turmeric, ginger, passion fruit and pineapple along with traditional crops. Cropping systems are now changing and more farmers are going in for settled cultivation and in this way uplifting their income level. Farmers are now in transition process from the traditional subsistence economy to the modern market economy. The success of the rural micro credit mechanism of NEPED in

Kareemulla, K. (2005). Institutional Credit Flow to Agriculture and Farm Indebtedness in Uttar Pradesh. *Indian Journal of Agricultural Economics*, July-Sept., Vol. 60, No. 3.

Karmakar, K.G. (1999). *Rural Credit and Self-Help Groups: Micro Finance Concepts in India*. Sage Publication, 1st Edition, pp. 208-211.

Kikhi, Chozhule and Temsuinla Jamir (2007). Recognizing the Role of Women in Agriculture in Adding Value to Shifting Cultivation in Nagaland, India. New Delhi: *Nagaland Empowerment of People through Economic Development*, February, pp. 16.

Kumari, R.Vijaya (2005). An Economic Analysis of Rural Indebtedness in Northern Telengana Zone of Andhra Pradesh. *Indian Journal of Agricultural Economics* 60 (3): 307-308 July-Sept.

Lenka, Jagannath (2005). Indebtedness of Rural Farmer Households: A Profile of Major States in India. *Indian Journal of Agricultural Economics*, July-Sept., Vol. 60, No. 3.

Mandal, P.K. (1977). *Nature of Rural Indebtedness*. cited In Sukhpal Singh's Dynamics of Rural Poverty, Anmol Publications, New Delhi.

Mamoria, C.B. (1953). *Agricultural Problems in India*. Allahabad: Kitab Mahal, pp. 522.

Meier, Gerald M. and James E. Rauch (2000). *Leading Issues in Economic Development*. (7th Edition). New York: Oxford University Press, pp. 360-361.

Mishra, S.K. (1999). *Rural Development in the North-Eastern Region of India: Constraints and Prospects*. MPRA Paper 1833, Germany: University Library of Munich.

Mitra, M. K; D.C. Roy and S.K. Mishra (1986). Rural Indebtedness: Concept, Correlates and Consequences: A Study of Four Tribal Villages in the North Lakhimpur Subdivision, Assam. NEHU, *Journal of Social Sciences and Humanities*, IV (4): 37-43.

Mohideen, K.S.S. Uduman (1991). *Institutional Credit and Agricultural Development—A Study of Annur Block of Coimbatore District*. Mittal Publications, New Delhi.

Nagaland State Human Development Report (2004). Department of Planning & Coordination Government of Nagaland.

Pitt, M. M and S.R Khandker (1998). The Impact of Group-based Credit Programmes on Poor Households in Bangladesh: Does the Gender of Participants Matter? *Journal of Political Economy*, 106(5): 958-96.

Press Release (2007). *Ministry of Labour and Employment*. Government of India, 25 June.

Ramachandran, V.K. and Swaminathan, Madhura (2001). *Does Informal Credit Provide Security*? International Labour Office, Geneva, October.

RBI Circular (2005). DBOD No, BL.BC.36/22.01.001/2005 dated September 8, 2005, RBI.

Report of the Committee on Financial Sector Plan for North Eastern Region (2006), Reserve Bank of India, July.

Rio, Neiphiu (2005). Chief Minister, Nagaland, New Delhi: *Excerpts from 51st Meeting of the National Development Council* on 27th June.

Rural Labour Enquiry Report on Indebtedness among Rural Labour Household (1999-2000), 55th Round of N.S.S.O.

Sai, K. J. S. Satya (1988). Flow of Institutional Credit to Agriculture in Deltaic Regions-A Case West Godavari District, Andhra Pradesh. *Indian Journal of Agricultural Economics*, July-Sept., Vol. 43, No. 3.

Selected Socioeconomic Statistics India (2006). Central Statistical Organisation, Ministry of Statistics and Programme, Implementation Government of India.

Sema, Akali (2006). *Economic Development in Nagaland: Prospects and Constraints*. NUTA, Nagaland University: 3-15.

Singh, Surjit and Vidya Sagar (2004). *State of Indian Farmers—A Millennium Study: Agricultural Credit in India*. Ministry of Agriculture, Government of India, pp.45 -49.

Singh, Harwant and Kahlon, A.S. (1971). A Study of Credit Requirements and Advances to Farmers in Patiala District. *Indian Journal of Agricultural Economics*, Oct-Dec., Vol. XXVI, No. 4.

Singh, Sukhpal (1996). *Dynamics of Rural Poverty*. Anmol Publications, New Delhi, First Edition.

Sinha, R.P.; Gupta, S.P. and Singh, U.K. (2005). Analysis of flow of credit to different categories of farmers- A study in Nalanda district of Bihar. *Indian Journal of Agricultural Economics*, July-Sept., Vol-60, No-3.

Some Aspects of Farming Situation Assessment Survey of Farmers (2005). NSS 59th Round (January–December 2003) NSSO, July.

Some Aspects of Operational Land Holdings in India (2002-03). NSS 59th Round (January–December 2003), NSSO, August 2006, NSS Report No. 492(59/ 18.1/3).

Vatta, Kamal (2003). Microfinance and Poverty Alleviation. *Economic and Political Weekly*, 38(05 :) 432-433.

13

Credit Deployment and Non-Performing Assets under Priority Sector in Nagaland

Samir K. Mahajan

Introduction

Priority sector in credit lending includes those activities or segments of the economy which are presumed to have national importance and thus, are assigned priority for development. It is emphasised that supply of credit to these sectors impact large sections of the population, the weaker sections and the sectors which are employment-intensive such as agriculture, and tiny and small enterprises (RBI, 2008). As these sectors remained neglected in domain of credit deployment by banks, the strategy of priority sector lending has been adopted in which supply of credit by commercial banks was prioritized through RBI intervention. As a policy of social control over banks, RBI issues directives to banks to advance loans to priority sector at differential rates of interest fixed by RBI. The Apex bank also fixes certain predetermined targets and sub-targets to be achieved by the banks while deploying to priority sector. Thus, banks have assigned to play a greater developmental role for socio-economic upliftment of certain disadvantaged areas that remain neglected in the domain of credit deployment. At present, the priority sector broadly comprises agriculture, small scale industries and other activities/borrowers such as small business, retail trade, small transport operators, professional and self-employed persons, housing, education, micro credit etc (RBI, 2005; Uppal, 2009). In July 2005, a target of 40 per cent of net bank credit has been stipulated for lending to the priority sector by domestic commercial banks. Within this, sub-targets of 18 per cent and 10 per cent of net bank credit have been stipulated for lending to agriculture and weaker sections respectively (RBI, 2005).

Form the bankers' point of view; priority sector lending imposes obligations on commercial banks to increase credit deployment on priority basis. Banks have to fulfil the targets set by the apex bank, supply loans at concessional rates. Such mandatory credit deployment assisted in achieving some quantitative targets. At the same time, it is also associated with certain unwanted qualitative aspects such as: loan defaults/non-performing assets and erosion of repayment ethics under priority sector. The end result is the burdens of overdue, non-performing loans and poor recovery falling on the banking activities. When recovery rate are poor and non-performing assets are alarmingly high, it not only hampers the recycling of scarce resources of banks, but also affects profitability and viability of banks (Thorat, 2006). The present study is confined to these two broad aspects of priority sector lending such as: quantum of loan advances and the extent of Non-performing Assets[1] (NPAs) by banks in Nagaland during the year 2011-12.

Objectives and Methodology

Specific objectives of the study are:

- To examine priority sector lending by different bank groups;
- To examine priority sector lending under its different components;
- To examine NPAs under priority sector lending; and
- To examine the extent NPAs in different components under priority sector.

As for the methodology, the universe of the present study is commercial banks in Nagaland. The banks have been classified into four major groups such as: scheduled public sector commercial banks/ nationalised banks, scheduled private sector commercial banks, one regional rural bank such as: Nagaland Rural Bank, and one cooperative bank such as: Nagaland State Co-operative Bank. The study attempts to accomplish its objectives by analyzing four parameters such as: priority sector loan advances, segregation of loan advances under priority sector, NPAs under priority sector lending, and its segregation in Nagaland. All the parameters have been analyzed for the period 2011-12.

Observation and Discussion

Fourteen public sectors scheduled commercial banks, four private sectors scheduled commercial banks, Nagaland Rural Bank and Nagaland State Co-operative Bank are operative in Nagaland. Out of these, Bank of India did not have any share in priority sector lending in Nagaland as on December 12, 2011.

Outstanding Advances made by Banks under Priority Sector

As on 31st December, 2011, the loan outstanding advanced by all banks to priority sector in Nagaland is Rs. 63715.75 lakhs which is 38.58 per cent of total (Priority Sector plus Non-priority Sector) advances. Nationalized banks play a dominant role in the activities of public sector lending in the State. Priority sector advances extended by public sector banks, is Rs. 56241.58 lakhs in 2011 which is 38.71 per cent of total loan advances. The accumulated share of private sector commercial banks, Nagaland Rural Bank and Nagaland State Co-operative Bank are Rs. 2253.51 lakhs, Rs. 1099.8 lakhs and Rs. 4120.86 lakhs respectively which accounts for 39.23 per cent, 78.79 per cent, and 32.33 per cent of total loan advances respectively. Among the list of banks, State Bank of India is the largest lender allocating loan outstanding of Rs. 35,367 lakhs (refer Table 13.1).

The proportion of priority sector lending to total advances has been the highest (92.76%) by the Syndicate Bank which is followed by UCO Bank (90.96%). For State Bank of India, it is 31.71 per cent (refer Table 13.1). A major portion of priority sector advances has gone to the weaker sections. Proportion of weaker sector advances to priority sector advances by all banks is 62.45 per cent. The proportion is 66.92 per cent of public sector commercial banks, 25.29 per cent for private sector commercial banks, 39.79 per cent for Nagaland Rural Banks, and 27.93 per cent Nagaland State Co-operative Bank respectively as on December 31, 2011 (refer Table 13.1).

Segregation of Priority Sector Lending

A very high proportion of priority sector lending goes to service and other priority sector. Of the total loan outstanding under priority sector by the banks, service and others account for 57.52 per cent with a volume of Rs. 36650.7 lakhs as on December 31, 2011. Bank group-wise, 93.32

Table 13.1: Share of Priority Sector in Total Advances in Nagaland as on 31.12.2011

Banks/Bank Groups	*Advances (Rs. in Lakhs)*			*Proportion of Advances (in %)*		
	Total (Priority Sector plus Non-priority Sector)	*Priority Sector*	*Weaker Section*	*Priority Sector to Total*	*Weaker Section to Total*	*Weaker Section to Priority Sector*
(Scheduled Public Sector Commercial Banks)						
Allahabad Bank	4062.25	3159.27	3050.61	77.77	75.1	96.56
Bank of Baroda	7618	2641.65	1695.76	34.68	22.26	64.19
Central Bank of India	1800	1008.61	825.65	56.03	45.87	81.86
IDIBI Limited	1920.15	1644.15	0	85.63	0	0
Indian Bank	357.26	287.47	0	80.47	0	0
Punjab and Sind Bank	705	510.93	409.51	72.47	58.09	80.15
Punjab National Bank	2286.79	677.63	251.34	29.63	10.99	37.09
Syndicate Bank	1292	1198.47	667	92.76	51.63	55.65
State Bank of India	111545	35367	24125	31.71	21.63	68.21
United Bank of India	5234	3045.68	2146.79	58.19	41.02	70.49
UCO Bank	2357	2144	251	90.96	10.65	11.71
Union Bank of India	204.34	36.37	4	17.8	1.96	11
Vijaya Bank	5887.84	4520.35	4207.54	76.77	71.46	93.08
(Scheduled Private Sector Commercial Banks)						
Axis Bank	2947	828.47	16.55	28.11	0.56	2
Federal Bank	2188	1278	551	58.41	25.18	43.11
HDFC Bank	580.47	140.04	2.31	24.13	0.4	1.65
ICICI Bank	29	7	0	24.14	0	0
(Regional Rural Banks)						
Nagaland Rural Bank	1395.9	1099.8	437.6	78.79	31.35	39.79
(State Co-operative Banks)						
Nagaland State Co-operative Bank	12745.83	4120.86	1151.15	32.33	9.03	27.93
All Scheduled Public Sector Commercial Banks	145272.8	56241.58	37634.2	38.71	25.91	66.92
All Scheduled Private Sector Commercial Banks	5744.47	2253.51	569.86	39.23	9.92	25.29
All Scheduled Commercial Banks	151017.27	58495.09	38200.00	38.73	25.3	65.3
All Banks	165159*	63715.75	39788.81	38.58	24.09	62.45

Source: SBI Regional Office (2012).

* Total advances by all banks include the share of Bank of India.

per cent of priority sector lending (outstanding) by private banks is meant for service sector. Proportion of service and other to total priority sector loan outstanding is 54.3 per cent for nationalized banks, 73.19 for Nagaland Rural Bank, 77.78 per cent for Nagaland State Co-operative Bank respectively as on 31st December, 2011. Hence most of the loan advances goes to service and other priority sectors (refer Table 13.2).

The agriculture component shares 26.66 per cent of priority sector loan outstanding of all banks taken together. Bank-wise, Union Bank of India has advanced the highest proportion of its priority loans to agriculture which is 68.66 per cent. The bank was followed by Allahabad Bank which supplies 51.11 per cent of its priority sector lending to agriculture. Share of small scale industries in priority sector lending by all banks is the lowest with 15.82 per cent. Among the banks, Syndicate Bank, Union Bank of India, HDFC Bank, Nagaland State Co-operative Bank have loaned no credit to small scale industries as on December 31, 2011 (refer Table 13.2).

Loan Target of Banks under Priority Sector

Under annual credit plan of 2011-12, target of priority sector lending by all banks is Rs 362.24 crores. Targeted loan advances of public sector commercial banks, private sector commercial banks, Nagaland Rural Bank and Nagaland State Co-operative Bank amounts to Rs. 269.31, Rs. 26.21, Rs. 20.1, and Rs. 46.62 respectively. Among the list of banks, State Bank of India has fixed the highest target which amounts to Rs. 171.36 lakhs. State Bank of India is followed by Vijaya Bank which targets a loan amount of Rs. 21.21. Clearly loan target of Vijaya Bank is much below the target of State Bank of India. This only speaks voluminous role played by State Bank of India in priority sector lending in the State of Nagaland (refer Table 13.3).

Share of agriculture to priority sector loan target by all banks is the highest with 57.7 per cent, followed by service and others with 30.75 per cent and small scale industries 11.55 per cent during 2011-12. Similar impression can be drawn in bank group-wise targets. Share of agriculture is 54.4 per cent, 59.14 per cent, 79.6 per cent, and 66.5 per cent in the priority sector loan target of Scheduled Public Sector Commercial Banks, Scheduled Private Sector Commercial Banks, Nagaland Rural Bank, Nagaland State Co-operative Bank respectively.

Table 13.2: Segregation of Priority Sector Lending in Nagaland as on 31.12.2011

Banks/Bank Groups	*Outstanding (in Rs. in Lakhs)*				*Share in Priority Sector Lending (in %)**		
	Priority Sector	*Agri-culture*	*Small Scale Industries*	*Service and Other Priority Sector*	*Agri-culture*	*Small Scale Industries*	*Service and Other Priority Sector*
(Scheduled Public Sector Commercial Banks)							
Allahabad Bank	3159.27	1614.78	724.67	819.82	51.11	22.94	25.95
Bank of Baroda	2641.65	260.65	1865	516	9.87	70.6	19.53
Central Bank of India	1008.61	144.21	624.96	239.44	14.3	61.96	23.74
IDIBI Limited	1644.15	0	73.15	1571	0	4.45	95.55
Indian Bank	287.47	87.2	110.15	90.12	30.33	38.32	31.35
Punjab and Sind Bank	510.93	5.73	175.51	329.69	1.12	34.35	64.53
Punjab National Bank	677.63	157.72	65.52	454.39	23.28	9.67	67.06
Syndicate Bank	1198.47	397.78	0	800.69	33.19	0	66.81
State Bank of India	35367	11599	4643	19125	32.8	13.13	54.08
United Bank of India	3045.68	752.37	1033.7	1259.61	24.7	33.94	41.36
UCO Bank	2143.52	242.5	313.06	1587.96	11.31	14.6	74.08
Union Bank of India	36.37	24.97	0	11.4	68.66	0	31.34
Vijaya Bank	4520.35	413.01	374.87	3732.47	9.14	8.29	82.57
(Scheduled Private Sector Commercial Banks)							
Axis Bank	828.47	1	38.19	789.28	0.12	4.61	95.27
Federal Bank	1278	71	19	1188	5.56	1.49	92.96
HDFC Bank	140.04	18.4	0	121.64	13.14	0	86.86
ICICI Bank	7	1	2	4	14.29	28.57	57.14
(Regional Rural Banks)							
Nagaland Rural Bank	1099.8	278.32	16.56	804.92	25.31	1.51	73.19
(State Co-operative Banks)							
Nagaland State Co-operative Bank	4120.86	915.59	0	3205.27	22.22	0	77.78
All Scheduled Public Sector Commercial Banks	56241.1	15699.92	10003.59	30537.59	27.92	17.79	54.3
All Scheduled Private Sector Commercial Banks	2253.51	91.4	59.19	2102.92	4.06	2.63	93.32
All Scheduled Commercial Banks	58494.61	15791.32	10062.78	32640.51	27	17.2	55.8
All Banks	63715.27	16985.23	10079.34	36650.7	26.66	15.82	57.52

Source: Same as Table 13.1.

*Share in Priority Sector Lending (%) is calculated

Table 13.3: Targeted Priority Sector Lending of the Banks in Nagaland during 2011-2012

Banks/Bank Groups	*Target (Rs. in Crores)*				*Share in Priority Sector Target (in %)**		
	Priority Sector	*Agri-culture*	*Small Scale Indus-tries*	*Service and Other Priority Sector*	*Agri-culture*	*Small Scale Indus-tries*	*Service and Other Priority Sector*
(Scheduled Public Sector Commercial Banks)							
Allahabad Bank	12.16	7.5	0.98	7.5	61.68	8.06	30.26
Bank of Baroda	14.63	7.5	2.27	7.5	51.26	15.52	33.22
Central Bank of India	8.14	4	1.12	4	49.14	13.76	37.1
IDIBI Limited	4.24	2	1.07	2	47.17	25.24	27.59
Indian Bank	3.84	2	0.32	2	52.08	8.33	39.58
Punjab and Sind Bank	3.73	2	0.21	2	53.62	5.63	40.75
Punjab National Bank	3.96	2	0.21	2	50.51	5.3	44.19
Syndicate Bank	5.45	2	0.53	2	36.7	9.72	53.58
State Bank of India	171.36	100	2.15	100	58.36	1.25	29.3
United Bank of India	10.05	4	1.43	4	39.8	14.23	45.97
UCO Bank	8.3	4	2.33	4	48.19	28.07	23.73
Union Bank of India	2.24	0	1.07	0	0	47.77	52.23
Vijaya Bank	21.21	9.5	2.36	9.5	44.79	11.13	44.08
(Scheduled Private Sector Commercial Banks)							
Axis Bank	12.15	7.5	1.11	7.5	61.73	9.14	29.14
Federal Bank	4.87	2	0.53	2	41.07	10.88	48.05
HDFC Bank	2.34	2	0.11	2	85.47	4.7	9.83
ICICI Bank	6.85	4	1.03	4	58.39	15.04	26.57
(Regional Rural Banks)							
Nagaland Rural Bank	20.1	16	0.5	16	79.6	2.49	17.91
(State Co-operative Banks)							
Nagaland State Co-operative Bank	46.62	31	3.51	31	66.5	7.53	25.98
All Scheduled Public Sector Commercial Banks	269.31	146.5	16.05	146.5	54.4	5.96	32.59
All Scheduled Private Sector Commercial Banks	26.21	15.5	2.78	15.5	59.14	10.61	30.26
All Scheduled Commercial Banks	295.52	162	37.83	162	54.82	12.8	32.38
All Banks	362.24	209	41.84	209	57.7	11.55	30.75

Source: Same as Table 13.1.

* Share in Priority Sector Target (in %) is calculated.

Non-Performing Assets under Priority Sector

The total size of NPAs under priority sector lending in Nagaland is Rs. 12248.79 lakhs as on 31st December, 2011. Bank group wise, a lion's share of this bad loan burden is shared by nationalized banks for whose NPAs is Rs. 11108.49 lakhs. The remaining residual burden is shared as Rs. 24.63 lakhs by Nagaland Rural Bank, Rs. 940.79 by Nagaland Co-operative Bank and Rs. 174.88 lakhs by private banks. Proportion of NPAs as percentage of loan outstanding under priority sector lending by all banks is 19.22 per cent. Bank group wise, the NPAs under priority sector are 2.24 per cent for Nagaland Rural Bank, 22.83 per cent for Nagaland State Co-operative Bank, 19.75 per cent for scheduled public sector commercial banks, 7.76 per cent for private sector banks. Among the banks, 50.64 per cent of loan outstanding of Indian Bank has turned out to be bad loans. The bank was followed by Syndicate bank with 30.66 per cent NPAs (refer Table 13.4).

Of the total NPAs, share of Agriculture, small scale industries, and services and other priority sectors are Rs. 2766.25 lakhs, Rs. 2554.25 lakhs, and Rs. 6985.14 lakhs respectively. NPAs as proportion of loan outstanding of all banks are 19.22 per cent under agriculture, 25.34 per cent under small scale industries and 19.06 per cent under service and priority sectors. Bank-group wise, 67.83 per cent (largest) of loan outstanding of private banks under agriculture sector has turned out to be NPAs. Bank-wise, Axis Bank has the largest proportion of NPAs (85.92%) under this sector. The other banks with high NPAs are Bank of Baroda (46.04%) and Vijaya Bank (40.47%) under agriculture sector (refer Table 13.4).

Under small scale industries, 84.54 per cent of loan outstanding of Nagaland Rural Bank has turned out to be bad loans. The other banks with similarly high NPAs under small scale industries are Axis Banks (78.95%) and Indian Banks (73.74%). Under service sector and others, 47.88 per cent of loan outstanding of Indian Bank has turned out to NPAs. The other bank with similar result is Syndicate Bank NPAs of which is 43.64 per cent under service and other priority sectors (refer Table 13.4).

Conclusion

Expansion of credit through the priority sector strategy is a worthy step in a backward economy like Nagaland. Credit needs of farmers, small entrepreneurs, small business, etc., can be met through such institutional

Table 13.4: NPAs under Priority Sector in Nagaland as on 31-12-2011

Banks/Bank Groups	*NPAs Amount (in Rs. in Lakhs)*				*NPAs as portion of Loan Outstanding (in%)**			
	Priority Sector	*Agri-culture*	*Small Scale Indus-tries*	*Service and Other Priority Sector*	*Priori-ty Sector*	*Agri-culture*	*Small Scale Indus-tries*	*Ser-vice and Other Priority Sector*
(Scheduled Public Sector Commercial Banks)								
Allahabad Bank	339.56	34.91	166.21	138.44	10.75	2.16	22.94	16.89
Bank of Baroda	734.13	120	579.13	35	27.79	46.04	31.05	6.78
Central Bank of India	272.4	36.5	199.75	93	27.01	25.31	31.96	38.84
IDIBI Limited	4.15	0	4.15	0	0.25	0	5.67	0
Indian Bank	145.57	21.2	81.22	43.15	50.64	24.31	73.74	47.88
Punjab and Sind Bank	0	0	0	0	0	0	0	0
Punjab National Bank	10.95	0.5	3.15	7.3	1.62	0.32	4.81	1.61
Syndicate Bank	367.47	18.06	0	349.41	30.66	4.54	0	43.64
State Bank of India	7602	2050	1141	4411	21.49	17.67	24.57	23.06
United Bank of India	664.68	43.86	268.82	352	21.82	5.83	26.01	27.95
UCO Bank	0	0	0	0	0	0	0	0
Union Bank of India	0	0	0	0	0	0	0	0
Vijaya Bank	967.58	167.16	65.26	735.16	21.4	40.47	17.41	19.7
						0	0	0
(Scheduled Private Sector Commercial Banks)					0	0	0	0
Axis Bank	35.88	1	16.56	18.32	4.33	100	43.36	2.32
Federal Bank	139	61	15	63	10.88	85.92	78.95	5.3
HDFC Bank	0	0	0	0	0	0	0	0
ICICI Bank	0	0	0	0	0	0	0	0
(Regional Rural Banks)								
Nagaland Rural Bank	24.63	3.03	14	7.6	2.24	1.09	84.54	0.94
(State Co-operative Banks)								
Nagaland State Co-operative Bank	940.79	209.03	0	731.76	22.83	0	0	22.83
All Scheduled Public Sector Commercial Banks	11108.49	2492.19	2508.69	6164.46	19.75	15.87	25.08	20.19
All Scheduled Private Sector Commercial Banks	174.88	62	31.56	81.32	7.76	67.83	53.32	3.87
All Scheduled Commercial Banks	11283.37	2554.19	2540.25	6245.78	19.29	16.17	25.24	19.14
All Banks	12248.79	2766.25	2554.25	6985.14	19.22	16.29	25.34	19.06

Source: Same as Table 13.1.

*NPAs as portion of Loan Outstanding (in %) is calculated.

credit deployment. Priority sector lending thus can play a significant role in the development and diversification of agriculture sector, expansion of small scale industries and business, and generation of employment. However, high NPAs can come as an obstacle to the priority sector lending. Banks offers loan with motive of earning profit and through the process of lending meets the financial requirements of agriculture, trade, business, industries and the economy as a whole. High NPAs adversely affect the profitability and lending capacity of banks may result in losses. When financial institutions or banks advance loans and credit, repayment of principal along with interest by borrowers in due course of time is crucial for recycling of funds deployed in priority sector. Expansion of credit delivery is seriously affected and delivery system gets chocked limiting the supply of credit if repayment by borrowers is not timely and becomes overdue and the loans become NPAs. Good recovery increases the chance of profitability of banks and results in increased financial capacity to deliver further credits (Sharma *et al.*, 2001, 3-5).

NOTE

1. Non-Performing Assets (NPA) or a bad debt is a loan/advance/lease which ceases to yield/generate any income to the lender/bank. To be more precise, NPA is defined as a credit facility in respect of which the interest and /or instalments of principals has remained 'past due' or 'overdue' on the part of borrower beyond a specified period of time.

REFERENCES

Reserve Bank of India (2005). *Draft Technical Paper by the Internal Working Group on Priority Sector Lending*. Rural Planning and Credit Department Central Office, Mumbai.

Reserve Bank of India (2008). *Master Circular on Priority Sector Lending*. Urban Banks Department, Central Office, Mumbai.

SBI Regional Office (2012). State *Level Bankers' Committee Nagaland: Quarterly Report as on December 2011*. Dimapur.

Sharma, K.C.; P. Josh; J.C. Mishra; Sanjay Kumar; R. Malorpavanathan; R. Bhaskaran (2001). 'Recovery Management in Rural Credit'. Occasional Paper -21: National Bank for Agriculture and Rural Development. Mumbai.

Thorat, Y.S.P. (2006). 'Rural Credit in India; Issues and Concerns'. *Indian Journal of Agricultural Economics,* Vol. 61, January-March 2006, No. 1.

Uppal, R. K. (2009). 'Priority sector advances: Trends, Issues and Strategies', *Journal of Accounting and Taxation*, Vol.1 (5), pp. 079-089.

Part - IV

Social Organisations and Community Development

Inidia. There are four ways in which the links between the SHGs and financial institutions are organised in India (Ghadoliya, 2004):

1. Provision of micro-finance by banks to NGOs for lending to SHGs and through them to the micro entrepreneur;
2. Direct financing by banks to SHGs for lending to the micro entrepreneur;
3. Direct financing by banks to SHGs for lending to the micro entrepreneur with NGOs acting as financial intermediaries; and
4. Banks providing loans directly to individual SHG members on the basis of the recommendations of SHGs and NGOs with the latter helps the former in supervision and loan recovery.

SHGs are self-governed, with decisions about production and marketing taken collectively, although the group leader is responsible for identifying potential marketing centres and consumers. These groups represent a new culture in rural development, in contrast to the traditional bureaucratic structure. Informal groups empower rural women to manage rural industries and make decisions collectively for their common economic interests. The functioning of SHGs is concerned, as many as two-thirds of the SHGs in the country falls under the second kind of linkage.

One of the salient features of the SHGs is that they are predominantly involved by womenfolk. Historically, this has been emerged out of the fact that while devising a solution as an alternative to conventional banking which failed in providing financial support to the poor. It was also realised that women as a group were much more disadvantaged compared to men. Consequently the involvement of women emerged as an essential aspect of SHGs, and on the other hand, the role of women in development has been well recognised universally. In Indian context celebrated instances of success in cooperative ventures like *Amul*, *Lijjat Papad*, etc., have demonstrated the efficacy of the involvement of women at the grass root level. Again, renowned management expert C.K. Prahlad has pointed out that entrepreneurial efforts by women have been greeted with remarkable success in different parts of the world (Sriraman, 2006). While participation of women in SHGs is thus justified, a natural corollary that arises is the issue of women empowerment. Empowerment has been described as "the ability to make strategic life choices" involving three aspects, namely, resources, agencies and achievements (Kabeer, 1999). One of the opinions on empowerment is that it needs to occur across multiple dimensions, namely, economic, socio-cultural, familial or interpersonal, legal, political and psychological (Malhotra, *et al.*, 2002).

Women's empowerment has been described as a process through which women are able to achieve greater control over resources thus gaining greater participation in leadership activities with the ability to take their own decisions so that they can become active participants in the process of social change (Dhavamani, 2010). The goal of the empowerment process is to introduce transformative structures and institutions in order to tackle perpetual problems like gender discrimination and social inequality (Batliwala, 1994). In patriarchal societies, special efforts are needed to ensure women's development and participation in the decision making process at home, in the community and in governance (Sriraman, 2006). There is a need for conducive environment so as to help them to maximise their potentials. This should include basic amenities such as better health and nutrition, education and sensitization to their rights and protection under the law and employment opportunities, etc. One of the methods that have often been referred to in this connection is to encourage entrepreneurial activities for empowering rural women. In order to be successful entrepreneurs, women need access to capital, technical and managerial know-how.

The formation of SHGs among women is regarded as one of the most effective approaches to women empowerment and rural entrepreneurship. It has provided results in various parts of the world including India. Credit and its delivery through self-help groups have also been taken as a means for empowerment of rural women. A self-help group can be regarded as a sustainable people's institution that provides the poor rural women with space and support necessary for them to take effective steps towards achieving greater control of their lives. The SHG approach has proved successful not only in improving the economic conditions through income generation but in creating awareness about health and hygiene, sanitation and cleanliness, environmental protection, importance of education and better response for development schemes. SHGs are enabling rural women in India to provide credit and extension support for various production-oriented income generating activities including garment making, embroidery, food processing, bee keeping, basketry, gem cutting, weaving, and knitting.

As for the North Eastern Region (NER) of the country, some kind of informal groupings have been commonly found in certain areas. However, the fact remains that SHG linkage with banks through the intermediation of NABARD has been insignificant compared to the larger national picture. Further, these linkages are also not uniformly distributed across the region. Approximately, as 90 per cent of the linkages are found in Assam alone in the entire region. In contrast linkages are very poor in States like Mizoram and Nagaland. And coming to the State of Sikkim, the SHG movement is not well organised as there is a dearth of responsible NGOs who can really help the movement to grow at the grass root level. Besides, the banks are also not demonstrated a pro-active attitude in assisting the economically deprived sections of society. The combination of these two factors has seemingly crippled the growth of SHGs in the State.

Brief Literature and Rationale of the Study

Kay (2002) has addressed the same issue by looking at self-help microcredit programmes in India and other countries in South and South East Asia. She concluded that SHGs need to be developed in a phased manner moving through economic strengthening, empowerment and finally collective action at the community level. Further, she illustrated that government can play a very important role in this process and only true empowerment of the poor can lead to successful poverty alleviation.

Sinha, *et al.* (2003) have done an impact assessment of microfinance in India as a part of the Micro Finance Support Project (MFSP) supported by the Department for International Development, UK (DFID) and the International Fund for Agricultural Development (IFAD). The project was implemented by the Small Industries Development Bank of India (SIDBI) through its Foundation for Micro-Credit. The study followed a longitudinal design coinciding with the seven-year period of the MFSP. On the basis of their interim findings the authors conclude that on an overall basis microfinance contributes to women's empowerment. They go on to list some indicators of the empowerment of women through microfinance.

Umashankar (2006) in her dissertation also addressed this issue in Mewat district of Haryana, India. In order to do so she has employed the personal narrative method. The unique feature of this study is that it has tried to look at empowerment through a number of different dimensions, viz., material, cognitive, perceptual and relational. The author found that involvement in SHGs was instrumental in helping women to overcome established social norms like *purdah*. It has led to greater say for women in community affairs so that they have been able to contribute actively to the solution of basic day-to-day problems. It has even led to political empowerment of women. The author also notes that bringing about material changes may be easier than the more desirable changes in power structures, ideologies and attitudes. Among her recommendations the author suggests, converging the inputs so that women can be involved more proactively with the programme, bringing about changes in social norms and perceptions and linking up with larger movements of social change.

Anjugam and Ramasamy (2007) have dealt with a different aspect, i.e., the factors that determine the participation of women in SHGs in Tamil Nadu, India. He observed that people from more deprived backgrounds were more likely to participate in SHGs. The application of the probit model for analysing the women's participation showed that age and value of productive assets other than land have a significant negative effect, while social backwardness, indebtedness and presence of other microcredit programmes in the same or nearby villages had a significant positive influence.

Sahu and Das (2007) have dealt with the role and performance of SHGs in promoting women's empowerment in Gajapati district of Orissa. At a broader level the study tries to analyse the operating system of SHGs with regard to mobilisation of savings, delivery of credit to the needy, management of group funds, repayment of loans, building up leadership and establishment of linkages with banks. It also examines the social benefits derived by the members. The authors have found that participants in SHGs in this region derived benefits like the development of savings habit, economic independence, self confidence, social cohesion, asset ownership, freedom from debt, and additional employment. Hence, the authors are of the view that SHGs promote women empowerment, social solidarity and socio-economic betterment of the poor.

Nirmala (2008) has considered the role of SHG micro-credit as a tool of capability development and women's empowerment in rural areas of Pondicherry region in union territory of Puducherry. Her findings confirmed that SHG micro-credit has led to better employment opportunities and higher annual family income in the post-credit period. While analysing the determinants of rate of return to SHG credit, the author found that among the significant factors experience and education had a positive impact while current education, skill and experience were negative, thus suggesting that further education, relevant training and experience were important to improve the rate of return to SHG credit. On the one hand involvement of SHGs leads to socio-economic development and on the other hand, problems are being encountered limited credit or timely availability, low profits, competition from mechanized products, marketing and work place problems, etc.

Sudha and Selvam (2009) have attempted to evaluate the role of NGOs in formation and promotion of SHGs in Vellore district, Tamil Nadu. In doing so, they have utilised statistical tools like the chi square test along with multiple and panel regression. The authors suggested that NGOs should follow a more persistent strategy for both formulation and development of strategies.

Dhavamani (2010) has examined the role of SHGs in empowerment of rural women in Sattur taluk of Virudhnagar district. For this purpose he employed both primary and secondary data. Using the proportionate random sampling technique, the primary data was collected from a total of 398 groups functioning in the area. Statistical tools like the *Z* test and Garret's ranking have been utilised for this study. On the basis of the study the author has found that SHGs provide a viable alternative for bringing about rural development and women empowerment. According to him the micro credit distributed through this system encourages entrepreneurial efforts by the members.

Amutha (2011) has conducted a study in three villages in Tuticorin district of Tamil Nadu. Based on her study she has concluded that the performances of SHGs have varied with some being able to function effectively, while others have encountered problems. Her study findings say that there is potential for empowering women and bringing about their economic upliftment using the SHG mechanism.

On the basis of the above review of literature, it is clear that there is limited literature relating to SHGs and women empowerment in North Eastern India in general and Sikkim in particular. This was the main motivation behind the present effort. As has been discussed, the SHG movements in the State are still in its infant stages. Hence, this effort is intended to get to know how far empowerment of women is actually taking place in Sikkim, even when the SHG movement itself was in a very nascent state.

Objectives and Methodology of the Study

The basic objectives of this chapter include the following:

1. To get an idea about the borrowing and repayment behaviour among the sample respondents in Sikkim;
2. To analyse the empowerment of the women through SHGs in Sikkim;

3. To identify the factors that contribute to the economic behaviour of the respondents; and
4. To understand the relationship between human capability and the rate of return on SHG credit.

The study was carried out in and around the Gangtok, the capital city of Sikkim. The data utilised for this study is primary in nature, collected through structured questionnaires. The sample size considered for the study is thirty. A total of ten SHGs were chosen for the study, with three women being randomly selected from each SHG. In other words, 10 per cent of the participants were selected for the study.

In order to test the hypotheses regarding condition of the respondents before and after using SHG micro credit, we have employed the *Z* test. Again the ordinary least squares (OLS) method has been employed for investigating the relationship between human capability and the rate of return on SHG credit.

Results and Discussions

The collection of data as well as the analysis of results has been carried out under the following heads:

(i) Family Income,
(ii) Mode of saving, and
(iii) Loan particulars

For analysing the collected data under the above heads, the statistical tools used were mean, *Z*-test and OLS regression technique in Log-form.

Family Income of the Respondents

People earn for satisfying their basic needs. Depending upon the educational qualification, they settle in a particular occupation and accordingly earn their income. For analysing the family income of the respondents, before and after joining the group, the data have been collected and presented in the Table 14.1.

Let us take the null hypothesis that there is no significant difference in the average family income of the respondents before and after joining the group, against alternative hypothesis that the mean family income of the respondents before joining the group is less than that of the mean

Table 14.1: Family Income of the Respondents (Pre- and Post-SHG)

Sl. No.	*Monthly Income (In Rupees)*	*Before joining (No. of Respondents)*	*After joining (No. of Respondents)*
1	0-5000	3	1
2	5000-10000	8	5
3	10000-15000	9	6
4	15000-20000	3	9
5	20000-25000	7	9
Total		**30**	**30**

Source: Primary Data.

family income of the respondents after joining the group. That is symbolically we can write

H_0: $\mu_1 = \mu_2$, against alternative, i.e., H_1: $\mu_1 < \mu_2$

Particulars	*Before joining*	*After joining*
Mean Monthly Income (in Rs.)	13000	15833
Standard Deviation (in Rs.)	6500	5850
Sample size	30	30

$$Z = \frac{\bar{X}_1 - \bar{X}_2}{\sqrt{\frac{S_1^2}{n_1} + \frac{S_2^2}{n_2}}} = -1.77$$

Since, the calculated value of $|Z| = 1.77$ is greater than the critical value of 1.64 at 5 per cent level of significance, the null hypothesis is rejected. Hence, it is inferred that there is a significant difference in the family income. In other words, it also implies that the mean income of the respondents has increased after joining the group.

Mode of Savings

Bank Savings: Savings is the key factor of each self-help group. Savings in the bank is safe and secure. Thus banks offer the best mode of savings.

For analysing the saving details of the respondents before and after joining SHG, let us consider the Table 14.2.

Table 14.2: Bank Savings

Sl. No.	*Amount of savings (In Rupees)*	*Before Joining (No. of Respondents)*	*After Joining (No. of Respondents)*
1.	0-1000	8	5
2.	1000-2000	10	8
3.	2000-3000	6	4
4.	3000-4000	3	5
5.	4000-5000	3	8
Total		**30**	**30**

Source: Primary Data.

Let us take the null hypothesis that there is no significant difference in bank savings of the respondents before and after joining the group, against the alternative hypothesis that the mean savings of the respondents before joining the group is less than that of the mean savings of the respondents after joining the group. That is symbolically we can write

H_0: $\mu_3 = \mu_4$, against alternative, i.e., H_1: $\mu_3 < \mu_4$

Particulars	*Before joining*	*After joining*
Mean (in Rs.)	1933	2600
Standard Deviation (in Rs.)	1260	1468
Sample size	30	30

$$Z = \frac{\overline{X}_1 - \overline{X}_2}{\sqrt{\frac{S_1^2}{n_1} + \frac{S_2^2}{n_2}}} = 1.89$$

Since the calculated value of $|Z| = 1.89$ is greater than the critical value of 1.64 at 5 per cent level of significance, the null hypothesis is rejected in this case also. Therefore, it can be said that the mean savings of the respondents has increased after joining the group.

Loan Particulars

Internal loan received by respondents: In Sikkim, each self-help group consists of 10 to 12 members. These members make monthly or weekly investments in bank regularly. The money saved in banks is provided as loan to the needy members in the form of internal loan. 2 per cent of interest is being charged on internal loan. Table 14.3 depicts the internal loan received by the respondents before and after joining the group.

Table 14.3: Internal Loan Details

Sl. No.	*Amount of savings (In Rupees)*	*Before Joining (No. of Respondents)*	*After Joining (No. of Respondents)*
1.	0-1000	8	2
2.	1000-2000	5	1
3.	2000-3000	7	2
4.	3000-4000	5	4
5.	4000-5000	3	6
6.	5000-6000	2	15
Total		**30**	**30**

Source: Primary Data.

Let us take the null hypothesis that there is no significant difference in internal loan received by the respondents before and after joining the group, against alternative hypothesis that the mean internal loan received by the respondents before joining the group is less than that received after joining the same. Symbolically we can write

H0: μ5= μ6, against alternative, i.e., H_1: μ5 < μ6.

Particulars	*Before joining*	*After joining*
Mean (in Rs.)	2367	3000
Standard Deviation (in Rs.)	1543	2390
Sample size	30	30

$$Z = \frac{\bar{X}_1 - \bar{X}_2}{\sqrt{\frac{S_1^2}{n_1} + \frac{S_2^2}{n_2}}} = -1.22$$

Since, in this case the calculated value of $|Z| = 1.22$ is less than the critical value of 1.64 at 5 per cent level of significance, the null hypothesis is accepted which implies that there is no such significant difference in internal loan received by the respondents before and after joining the group.

Bank Loan Received by Respondents

Members of the group make the savings in a particular bank and that bank provides loan to the group amounted to three times greater than the savings after six months. The interest rate charged by bank for the loan is 2.5 per cent. In order to compare the loan received by the respondents before and after joining the group. Let us now consider Table 14.4 containing the bank loan details.

Table 14.4: Bank Loan Details

Sl. No.	*Loan Amount (In Rupees)*	*Before Joining (No. of Respondents)*	*After Joining (No. of Respondents)*
1.	0-10000	10	6
2.	10000-15000	3	1
3.	15000-20000	4	5
4.	20000-25000	7	7
5.	25000-30000	4	7
6.	30000-35000	2	4
Total	.	**30**	**30**

Source: Primary Data.

Let us take the null hypothesis that there is no significant difference in bank loan received by the respondents before and after joining the group, against alternative hypothesis that the mean bank loan received by the respondents before joining the group is less than that of the mean bank loan received by the respondents after joining the same. That is symbolically we can write

H_0: $\mu_7 = \mu_8$, against alternative, i.e., H_1: $\mu_7 < \mu_8$

Particulars	*Before joining*	*After joining*
Mean (in Rs.)	17166.67	20833.33
Standard Deviation (in Rs.)	8359.95	7958.27
Sample size	30	30

$$Z = \frac{X_1 - \bar{X}_2}{\sqrt{\frac{S_1^2}{n_1} + \frac{S_2^2}{n_2}}} = -1.74$$

Since, the calculated value of $|Z| = 1.74$ is greater than the critical value of 1.64 at 5 per cent level of significance, the null hypothesis is rejected in this case which implies that there is a significant difference with regard to the bank loan received by the respondents before and after joining the group. In other words, it can also be inferred that after joining the group the mean bank loan received by the respondents has been increased than before.

So far we have tried to get an idea about the change in economic conditions, if any, of the participants in the SHGs. It would also be relevant to find out how far the individual capabilities in the form of education and experience are affecting the rate of return on SHG credit. Accordingly, the influence of human capability on rate of return to SHG credit has been analysed using alternative forms of the following ordinary least square (OLS) regression equation in log form:

$$\text{Log YGNR} = \log a_0 + a_1 \log \text{EDCN} + a_2 \log \text{EDCN}^2 + a_3 \log \text{EXPN} + a_4 \log \text{EXPN}^2 + \text{U}$$

where, YGNR = Income generation rate,

where $\dfrac{Y_t - Y_{t-1}}{Y_{t-1}} \times 100$

where, Y = income per annum;

t = post-SHG credit period;

and t–1 = pre-SHG credit period.

EDCN = education of respondent in years,

EDCN^2 = education square,

EXPN = work experience of respondent in years,

EXPN^2 = work experience square, and

U = error term.

The theoretically expected associations between economic returns from SHG credit and human capabilities of the respondents may be discussed here. Education and experience of the respondent are expected to fetch higher rate of returns to the credit, provided the experience is in the same line of current production activity. A further increase in education and experience, as reflected by their respective squared values, is also hypothesised to raise the rate of return to SHG credit. Let us now consider the least square results which are depicted in Table 14.5.

Table 14.5: Regression Results for the Respondents: Method: Least Square

Variable	*Coefficient*	*Std. Error*	*t-Statistic*	*Prob.*
log EDCN	–0.154908	0.071493	–2.166761	0.0346
log $EDCN^2$	0.147727	0.200538	0.736654	0.4645
log EXP	–0.091084	0.049451	–1.841883	0.0709
log EXP^2	–0.242710	0.253987	–0.955600	0.3435
C	0.409610	0.394689	1.037804	0.3039
R-squared	0.224251	Mean dependent var		0.136760
Adjusted R-squared	0.167833	S.D. dependent var		0.828517
S.E. of regression	0.755799	Akaike info criterion		2.357574
Sum squared resid	31.41780	Schwarz criterion		2.532103
Log likelihood	–65.72722	Hannan-Quinn criterion		2.425842
F-statistic	3.974813	Durbin-Watson stat		0.439973
Prob (F-statistic)	0.006648			

From the above Table 14.5 it is revealed that education and experience have a negative and significant impact on credit productivity. The negative impact of education on credit productivity is attributable to the fact that the mean education of the respondents is only around lower middle school. Due to lower levels of education credit productivity has an inverse relationship with education. On the other hand, as the experience of the participants in this field is relatively low, it is not able to positively impact the amount of credit productivity. Moreover, it is observed from the Table 14.5 that in case of log $EDCN^2$, the value of the coefficient is positive but the probability value is more than 0.05. This suggests that higher level of education will have greater effect on the rate of return from SHG credit, though the variable itself is relatively insignificant. Again, the value of R^2 indicates quite moderate fit of the model that is also prominent from the F-value which is highly significant.

In the preceding analysis we have seen that family income, savings and the utilisation of loans has improved due to involvement in SHGs. With the betterment of the economic status of women their involvement in decision-making has increased. At the same time there has been an upliftment in social status along with generation of greater social awareness.

Thus empowerment does not arise from one or two isolated factors, but rather a conglomeration of factors that impact one another. The principal determinants for empowerment of women can be taken as employment, increased family income, enhanced social stature, ability to take one's decision without having to depend on others, leadership qualities and social awareness. The following figure illustrates the

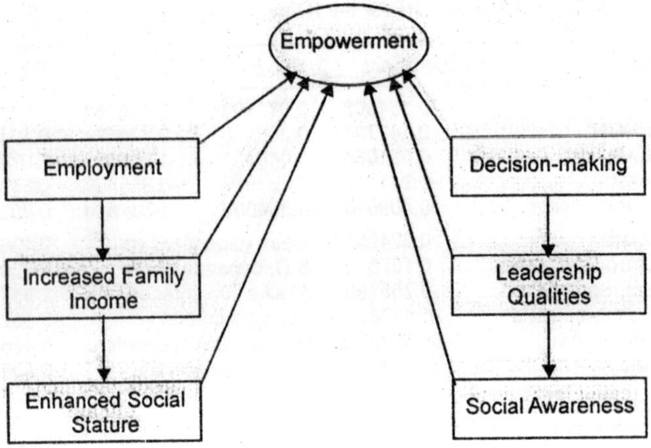

Fig. 14.1: Women Empowerment Elements

inter-relationship among these factors along with their contribution to the overall process of empowerment.

Thus the process of empowerment encompasses the following related aspects:

1. *Employment*: The immediate result of involvement in SHGs is employment generation, leading to the improvement in economic profile.
2. *Increased Family Income*: Obvious fallout of SHG participation is higher family income, which contributes to economic independence.
3. *Enhanced Social Staturc*: Economic independence and greater control over their lives results in improved social stature for the participants.
4. *Decision making*: Decision making capability is largely the consequence of the economic independence. Hence, it is not surprising that the majority of SHG participants have gained the confidence to take their own decisions without depending on others.
5. *Leadership qualities*: Leadership entails initiative and risk-taking. As participants take more and more of their own decisions, they develop leadership qualities that help them in both their personal and professional lives.

6. *Social Awareness*: Combined effect of better economic stature and more decision making experiences lead to higher social participation and thus generate increased social awareness.

Major Findings of the Study

As per the preceding discussions we have tried to examine the changes in economic conditions of the women as a result of joining the SHGs. We have found that family income, household savings and loans received from the banks have increased after joining the SHGs. However, no significant differences could be found in case of the internal loans taken from the SHG. This implies that the utilisation of loans provided by the SHGs is very low.

Another area of investigation related to the effect of human capability on the rate of return on SHG credit. Here human capability is considered in the form of education and experience. As per the results of the analysis it was revealed that both education and experience have a negative but significant impact on credit productivity. This could be due to the low levels of each of these aspects of human capability. Further it was found that though education as a variable was relatively insignificant, higher levels of education had a greater effect on the rate of return from SHG credit.

The analysis provided low values for R^2 and adjusted R^2; however, this does not necessarily imply that the model is not a good fit. It is well known that the main objective of regression analysis is to obtain dependable estimates for the true population regression coefficients. As per our analysis we have got significant values for the coefficients of both education and experience. Thus in spite of low value for R^2 the presence of statistically significant values for the coefficients prove that the model is quite a good fit. This is further confirmed by the significant F value.

Concluding Remarks

Thus it is observed that participation in SHGs has resulted in distinct improvement in the status of the respondents in terms of family income, savings and utilisation of loans. Correspondingly there has been a definite empowerment of women as they have gained a measure of economic independence with better control over their own lives. However it is also a fact that low educational levels owing to high school dropout rates and

15

Self-Help Groups for Women Empowerment in Arunachal Pradesh: Result from the Primary Survey

Ram Krishna Mandal

Introduction

Micro-finance has evolved over the past quarter century across India into various operating forms and to a varying degree of success. Micro-finance is the term used for funding poor families with very small loans to improve their livelihoods but its activities grow more than providing small loans and it encompasses a broad range of services which includes credits, savings, insurance, etc. Since poor families are not accustomed to the traditionai form of financial institutions, they hesitate to approach and lack in financial support. Therefore, the task of micro-finance is very wide and highly essential for the development of poor families. Micro-finance refers to the provision of financial services to low-income clients including consumers and the self-employed. This is a type of banking service that provides financial support to unemployed or low-income individuals or groups who would otherwise have no other means of gaining financial services because ultimately the goal of microfinance is to give low income people an opportunity to become self-sufficient by providing a means of saving money and borrowing money (Sukanya, 2012).

Women development and their status depend on the level of their empowerment. The status of the women and their development is lagging on account of the fact that poverty is very acute among women than men.

For eradicating poverty from its roots, it requires sufficient financial and moral support from the part of the government at the centre and State in particular. One of the best ways of improving their status and empowering them is through micro-finance by forming self-help groups (hereafter SHGs). The present study is based on examining the role of SHGs in empowering women and thereby attaining development and poverty eradication. Duly recognizing the importance and involvement of women in participatory model of development, the Government of India in general and Kerala in particular has taken up the theme of women's empowerment as one of the main agenda items to tackle rural poverty and socio-economic issues. With over 700 million women living in poverty globally, micro-finance programmes are seen as an essential tool in poverty alleviation. In recent years, micro-finance programmes have been used not only as a tool for economic upliftment but also as an effective way to meet women's political and strategic needs.

Micro-Finance and SHGs Linkage for Rural Development

The philosophy of social work profession is to help people to help themselves. As put by Karmakar (1999) individual efforts are too inadequate to improve the fate of the poor thus making it necessary to organise them in a group so they get the benefit of collective perception, collective decision making and collective implementation of programmes for common benefits. Since formation of a group of the poor has shown better participation in a credit programme, savings and credit can be a good starting point for group formation called SHGs (Rajamani, 2011). Micro-finance as a tool for empowerment of the poorest of the poor was pioneered by Bangladesh's visionary banker Professor Muhammad Yunus, the founder of the Grameen Bank, an endeavour for which he was awarded the Nobel Peace Prize in 2006.

Lieten (1998) has rightly quoted Muhammad Yunus, "Small credits to individual families, mostly women, as members of a control group, are supposed to refer poverty back to the museum." A self-help group is a group that consists of about 10 to 20 persons of a homogeneous class who come together with a view to address common problems. Voluntary savings are collected on a regular basis and the pooled resources are used to make small interest bearing-loans to members. In the dark environment of credit indiscipline, women's thrift and credit societies have emerged as a torch bearer of thrift and self-reliance (Parthasarathy, 2003). In performing this function, they also emerged as training grounds for economic democracy of women. SHGs have become a powerful source for identification of problems and intervention. Regular meetings of the SHGs serve as a useful forum to women who otherwise live in isolation. Besides focusing on entrepreneurial development of the beneficiaries and the village as a whole, the groups undertake the responsibility of delivering non-credit services such as literacy. Adult education hopes to remedy the educational deprivation of the adult population in order to develop their full potential and make the development process sustainable. Women's SHGs are spreading a silent revolution in terms of economic and social empowerment across poverty-stricken swathes of rural India (Roy, 2006). Jawaharlal Nehru has rightly stated, "The greatest revolution in a country is one that affects the status and living conditions of its women". Remedios (2006) quotes Patankar-Mhaiskar who characterizes the SHG movement of tribal women as a revolution for advancement. The study substantiated the view that the normally submissive and weaker sections suddenly begin to feel empowered. Small economic activities may not even make a dent on the economy of the State but they work wonders for the rural woman who is otherwise at the mercy of her environment. SHGs are mostly informal groups of people where members pool in their savings and lend within the group on rotational basis, depending on consumption, production and investment needs. According to Fisher and Sriram (2002) these are autonomous organisations which are formed through the savings of the group members. Vatta (2003) puts it, SHGs are small, informal, and homogeneous groups of not more than 20 members wherein after its formation the group regularly collects a fixed amount of thrift from each member. It is the role of a bank which is managed by the people themselves and is called micro enterprises or affinity groups or MYRADA (Sarkar, 1987).

The basic rule concerning SHGs are a group size between 10 and 20 (preferably 15), three elected positions (President, Treasurers and Secretary), savings (frequently contributed by members), compulsory regular attendance, giving of loans and rules for repayment and finally documentation (keeping of documents like attendance register, proceedings register, savings and loan register, savings pass book, loan pass book, rules and regulations register). In an article on self-help groups and women empowerment, Rajamani (2011) pointed out that SHGs have engaged as a popular method of working with people in the recent years. Power to the people signifies a new social movement, which was probably born out of the realization that society's traditional arrangements can be used for solving their problems (Singh and Ram, 1987). The SHGs serve as a medium for the development of savings habit among women folk. It is a window for developing better technology and skill upgradation. The SHGs collective actions and solidarity are considered an important women empowerment mechanism and develops savings habit and mobilisation of resources among the women folk. Manimekalai and Rajeswari (2000) in their study of empowerment of women through SHGs attempts to find out the socio-economic conditions of SHG members and concluded that the SHG has contributed to women empowerment in decision making, starting micro enterprises and thereby increase in their income (Srilatha, 1994). Rajasekhar (2000) in his study on micro-finance programmes and women's empowerment in a study of two NGOs summarised that micro-finance is more successful in poverty alleviation and women's empowerment (Sushama, 1998). Kulkarni (2001) explored the issue of the changing status of women in households and the empowerment that is taking place through the SHG activity in his article, Empowerment of Women through Self-Help Groups. The study found that empowerment has taken place across caste/class and brought them together as women (Devi and Surendra, 2002). Anand (2002) valuates the performance of selected SHGs and NHGs identified the factors contributing to their success, examines the role of various promoting agencies in organizing and managing the SHGs and NHGs in her study of SHGs in empowering rural women. The study found that the members who earlier had some economic activity used the micro-credit effectively for expansion and modification and they reaped sustainable benefit by joining the group and the overall position is satisfactory (UNDP, Human Development Report, 1995). Sudha Rani *et al.* (2002) in their article, SHGs, Micro Credit and Empowerment, attempt to find out the difference in the self confidence, health consciousness, and house management and interaction styles of women members with development department officials before and after their participation in the SHGs. The study revealed that participation in the SHGs enriched the empowerment of women in four aspects such as self confidence, health consciousness, house management and interaction styles with officials (Vatta, 2003). Paramasivan, (2011) in his article on economic empowerment of women through SHG stated that empowerment as a social process has challenged the fundamental imbalances of power distribution and relations. It was the distribution of power within and between forties, society's process aiming at social equality which could be achieved through disempowering some structures, systems and institutions. Social empowerment has promoted sustainable rural structure for dissemination of knowledge about health, nutrition, literacy, education, freedom and opportunities of realizing women's potentialities and adoption of new agricultural practices. Also it has highlighted the participation of women in SHG function, awareness towards SHGs and motivation to join in the SHGs (Vijay, 2001).

Relevance, Objectives, Hypotheses Methodology

From the above discussion the researcher wants to investigate the benefits of SHGs in Arunachal Pradesh. This research will help in providing useful information for future researches. (1) The study is to examine the impact of SHGs as a poverty-alleviation tool; and (2) It aims at exploring the impact of SHGs on standard of living and family welfare.

As hypothesises of the study, SHGs play a vital role in women empowerment but it needs further support and encouragement for its development and growth. Of late, there is a paradigm shift in development process by incorporating the gender concerns as an important element of development strategy. Secondly, there is a considerable improvement in the lifestyle of the women after joining the SHG.

In order to examine the impact of SHGs on poverty alleviation, Papumpare district of Arunachal Pradesh was chosen. The improvement in employment, income, quality of diet, housing structure and female literacy, and children education through SHGs were explored. The primary data were collected through a scheduled questionnaire and followed by the interview based on the objectives of the study from the five SHGs selected in the district. The group consists of a combination of BPL (Below Poverty Line) and other women members. Secondary data were collected from relevant articles, Economic Surveys of India, Block Development Officers' records, Panchayat Samiti, NGOs' records and bank records. An extensive literature review, a series of discussions and a pilot visit were instrumental in preparing two detailed questionnaires. The first questionnaire was aimed at obtaining information about the SHG as a whole while the second one tried to obtain information about individual members. The questionnaire relating to individual members was divided into two parts. Part A dealt with the details of members before joining the SHG; and Part B with the details of respondents after joining the SHG. Primary data pertaining to SHGs was collected between October and December 2010.

Some Case Studies

In the study area, the Aryum, a SHG, in which maximum of the members are engaged in agricultural activities. Basically, they cultivate for their own consumption only. But vegetables and sweet potatoes they grow in the *jhum* paddy fields are for commercial purpose. In this way they could meet the cash requirement. Some members are engaged in petty trade and piggery. They take loans from the groups which engage in petty trade such as poultry, piggery, shop and petty contractual works. Though their life has improved significantly and moved from worse to better but is not moving from better to good or best. This means that they are not earning enough income to cross the poverty line. As per the cost of living prevalent in Itanagar, at least Rs. 5000 to 6000 income per month per family of 5 to 6 members is required to live the life of above poverty line. It may be possible by upgrading their skill of management and quantum of loan.

In a SHG, the Nit, there are five income generating activities. Two members were engaged in vegetable marketing, two members have grocery shop and one has wine shop. These members have taken a loan from the group corpus and ventured into these income generating activities. They are earning minimum net profit of Rs.1500 per month which is not enough to cross the poverty line. It is noticed that skill and quantum of loan is interrelated. The group members are not competent enough to venture into bigger income generating activities. Therefore, they took small dose of credit from their own group for their immediate family needs and for petty trades. They are bound to continue in the traditional sector due to lower skill because majority of them are illiterate. The few who are literate have only primary education or have studied up to middle school level. This makes them incompetent to deal with the banking agencies and other development agencies. Over a period of time increasing the quantum of loan per member is possible from their increasing corpus through saving and interest earned if their knowledge and skill are increased. However, for upgradation of skill, they have to outsource themselves to the other training institutions and if any government programme comes to impart the skill specific to the activities then they will be able to embark on skill based income generating activity.

Poum Poyi SHG, a group of 15 women from Laptap and nearby villages formed in January 2003 is one of the best SHGs in Sagalee in terms of its age, economic activities and functioning of group. This group is found to be doing the highest economic activities. They are:

> 1. Agro-Horticultural production; 2. An approximately 2½ hectares Orange Garden at Poum hill (Laptap) of about 350 number of orange trees with above 2000 plants nursery; 3. Crafts

making and handloom production; 4. Seasonal cash crops garden; 5. Fixed wages work, treated as social services amongst the group; 6. Participate in occasional exhibition/fairs for marketing of their products; 7. Food catering as and when opportunity comes; and 8. Community development work.

The above activities are in addition to their main activity, i.e., cultivation. Out of 15 members, eight members are engaged in handicrafts production, six members in weaving and one member is engaged in a grocery shop. They are maintaining separate directory for these each production. It is elicited from the information provided by the group and through observation that this SHG can be rated as best performing SHG under SGSY. Over the years of working experience with lots of economic activities besides their agriculture their empowerment level in terms of economic and social aspects have increased significantly. During the interview they are found to be quite confident of taking up any economic activities that benefits the group and its members. They are also found to be confident to intervene in the cases of gender discrimination. They have already solved many such cases in their village, i.e., child marriage, domestic and polygamy, the social issues in Nyishi society. Though the Nishi men want to uphold this practice as custom but for the Nyishi women it is an issue. It causes lot of problems in the family particularly women because discrimination often leads to domestic violence.

From the observation of the activities of Poum Poyi SHG, the way they perform and with data support given by them the level of education, confidence, awareness on gender discrimination, etc., have improved tremendously. The members of Poum Poyi SHG are empowered economically, socially and politically to a great extent.

In the same way, Karupu SHGs from Sagalee is also equally advanced. They understood the importance of collective power and, therefore, work together for the benefits of each member in all spheres, i.e. economic and social activities. Members are getting micro loan from group at 3 to 5 per cent per month. Members of the group are doing their economic activities such as agriculture, horticulture, handloom and handicrafts and grocery shops individually.

The study revealed the increase in economic, political, social and psychological empowerment of women. But still a lot of work has to be done to empower them fully. There are many problems confronted by SHG and its members. Women of Arunachal Pradesh are trapped in a typical traditional system. Women are the main agriculturist; from clearing forest to harvesting the produce, they are taking a lead role. Taking care of children and doing all household chores are the responsibility of women but they still don't have the right to take major decisions in the family. Women are the active and effective campaigner in the election but still their candidature in the election is discouraged. So to summarize, leadership role is discouraged for the women.

Level of Income of SHG Members

It is shown in the following Table 15.1 that incomes of the members are an increasing trend. 21 members out of 40 respondents are in the income group of Rs. 6000 and above. However, this income level is not sufficient to lead a decent life. They cannot fulfil the basic requirement in their daily life.

Table 15.1: SHG Members in Different Income Level

Income per month	*Total No. of SHG respondents*	*% of Members in the Income group*
Up to 2000	–	–
2000-2500	2	5.0
2500-3000	2	5.0
3000-3500	2	5.0
4000-4500	2	5.0
4500-5000	3	7.5
5000-5500	5	12.5
5500-6000	6	15.0
6000-6500	8	3.2
6500- and above	12	30.0
Total	**40**	

Source: Field Study.

Again, the remaining members out of 40 respondents earning below the income of Rs. 6000 have to lead lives hand to mouth. This is due to low level of literacy and lack of skills. Though the overall income level of all respondents is low, but level of earning shows upward trend. Before forming SHG, they are only family workers in their agricultural field. Their agricultural production was used only for self-consumption having no role of money transaction. At least after formation of SHG, they have come in the modern monetized market economy.

SHGs promote thrift mobilization considering it as an entry point activity by any SHG. In the first or second meeting, the groups unanimously decide the rate of saving per month or per week collectively. The entire sample group undertaken for study is saving monthly. Thrift and credit are the main activities of the group which is also the basis of group formation and its sustenance for longer duration. Rural poor and women are formed into a group mainly to access credit whenever required from pooled savings. SHGs play a tremendous role in creating saving habit amongst the women of Arunachal Pradesh. Here, the indigenous people do not have a saving habit. In emergency situation, community people come forward and share the crisis of that family. There were no banks in rural areas, therefore, the question of savings do not arise. With the opening of banks in the rural areas and opening of bank account by the SHGs, saving habits are developing now. As an individual, it is quite difficult for them to open an account and save regularly but as a group they are more capable. Keeping of money in the banks for unforeseen situation or reaping its benefits after certain period of time was not in their mind before joining the group. SHGs are effectively playing the role of mini micro finance institutions for the group. From the record of saving amount it is reflected that saving habits are already inculcated amongst the group members of the entire sample group.

Table 15.2: Savings/Corpus Fund of SHGs

Name of the group	*Total Savings fund*	*Average Savings per SHG*
Aryum SHG	190000	18.93
Nit	180000	17.93
Poum Poyi	317460	31.64
Numum	100000	9.97
Karupu	216000	21.53
Total	**1003460**	**100.00**

Source: Field Study.

The total saving till March 2009 of each group are presented in Table 15.2 and in Diagram 15.1. The diagram shows that the Poum Poyi SHG's shares highest in savings followed by Karupu. The Numum SHG shares lowest in saving being the youngest in time period.

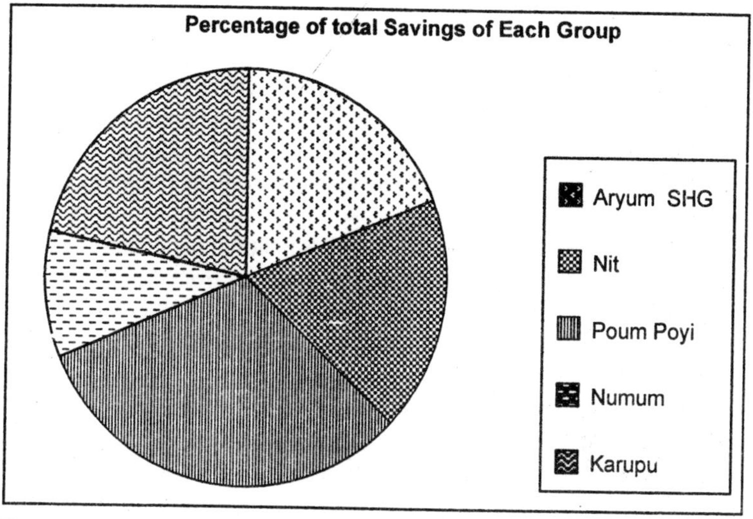

Fig. 15.1: Saving shared by the SHGs

Results and Discussion

The attempts of SHG approach are making its impact on the society especially among the women. The focus of the micro-finance projects are actually not successful in development of micro enterprises in the state, but successful in developing sustainable household livelihoods, decreasing household vulnerability and community development up to a great extent. The micro-finance has enabled women to make a greater contribution to household income, either through their own economic activity or by equally becoming a channel for loans to household activity. This contribution is recognized and valued by other household members and lead not only to increased household well-being, but women's increased role in decision-making and improved well-being for women themselves. This increased status in the household in itself in turn gives women the support they need to enable them together with men to bring about wider changes in gender inequality in the community.

In addition to the economic empowerment, social and political empowerment too has been attained. The group activities have given them a chance to come out to the mainstream, to realize the potentialities within themselves. This has led to a change in their outlook towards society. The status of being a woman is no more considered as a curse. All these, in fact, are looked upon as boon to bring them closer, to bind them closer and as a mean to lay the foundation of a new gender equity society. SHG has become an instrument to bridge the gap that exists in the society—the gender gap and the social gap between the rich and the poor. By contributing economically, women have gained a pivotal role in the decision making of the family. The inequality between the rich and the poor are also slowly decreasing.

This commonly used statement holds hundred per cent true that the "The transformation of any society has to begin from women, because women are the centre of a family—the foundation stone on which the family is built. When a woman is changed, the family is changed and a change in the family brings changes in the society." The impact of past fifty years of efforts by the State and the Central government to eradicate poverty from the society, in spite of the better educational, economic, political, cultural and social environment was minimal mainly because almost all the programmes failed to include women in it. It is in this decade the women empowerment policy (2001) has been introduced and women become integral part of the development strategy. Therefore, SHG is a silent revolution—a revolution that has all the potentiality of bridging the gender gap and building a world where poverty and gender discrimination with all its evils will be uprooted.

Awareness of benefits of SHGs, better self-awareness, decision making ability, ability to face problem has helped in personality development and influence the position of women in the family and the society. Hence, an attempt is made to analyze the extent of empowerment achieved by SHG members after joining SHGs or through SHGs. In order to measure the degree of empowerment, 10 variables were identified and analyzed. Table 15.3 revealed that SHG has contributed significantly to the members in awareness of benefits of SHGs, Better self-awareness, enhanced knowledge of enterprises and ability to sign. Since the respondents for all other variables, viz., decision making ability, ability to face problems, helped in personality development, leaderships quality, able to read and write lies between 12 to 25 in 'Yes' out of total 40 respondents, the degree of empowerment can be assumed as moderate.

To bring about gender equity in society it is important that any move to enforce laws must be accompanied by a movement to bring about an attitude change in our society. The existing laws and rights for women need to be strengthened and more vigorously implemented. Where policies and programmes do not serve the special needs of women, they need to be amended or recast. Where benefits do not reach our women in general

Table 15.3: Level of Empowerment

Variables	No. of SHG Members			Total Respondents
	Yes	To some extent	No	
1. Awareness of benefits of SHGs	40	-	—	40
2. Better Self Awareness	35	5	—	40
3. Decision making ability	20	20	—	40
4. Ability to face problems	19	21	—	40
5. Helped in personality development	25	15	—	40
6. Leadership Quality	12	28	—	40
7. Enhanced knowledge of enterprises	38	2	—	40
8. Enhance knowledge of rights & legal issues	30	10	—	40
9. Able to read & write	13	27	—	40
10. Able to sign	36	4	—	40

Source: Field Study.

and rural women in particular, there is a need for special intervention to enhance accessibility.

Though women have contributed significantly in every sphere of life, yet for various historical, social, religious and cultural reasons and in spite of many constitutional guarantees and legislative measures, women still remain backward and short of their rightful place in society. The findings of the National Status for Women Committee have revealed that the status of women has been declining steadily. This observation indicated that the initial recognition of women's rights, which emerged during the freedom struggle and was expressed in the Constitution, is actually not considered seriously. It is just there for knowledge sake not to be implemented. Our men-folk are failing to consider women as equal partner and place them in the same level. Sometimes, it is observed that they cannot think of women as equal human partner in their wildest dream. They want to continue to rule and dominate like the British were doing in India before independence. Though our country got independence in 1947, i.e., 60 years before but poverty is still the crux of the problem. It will be there till the attitude particularly of men, does not change.

Therefore, the inferences drawn from the analysis of the variables are that SHGs play a vital role in women empowerment but it needs further help for its development and growth. Of late, there is a paradigm shift in development process by incorporating the gender concerns as an important element of development strategy. There is a considerable improvement in the lifestyle of the women after joining the SHG and also in their attitudes. Therefore, both the hypothesis is proved.

Conclusion

Many programmes from *Garibi Hatao* to MGNREGA were started by the government enthusiastically but they were not able to achieve their objectives fully. The reason behind this is poor follow up, lack of management and participation from the government as well as the people. No programme can ever get its ultimate result until and unless there is a coordination and co-operation between the government and the beneficiaries. But micro-finance through SHGs has now become a modern economical weapon for empowerment to fight against poverty. The government of India in general and Arunachal Pradesh in particular has been vigorously pursuing the micro-finance agenda for empowering poor women. Many big and small institutions are taking part in this revolution of micro-finance vigorously. Still it has a long way to become a successful programme in the State. Necessary managerial, technical and marketing skills can be imparted to groups to enhance their livelihood opportunities.

Women play a pivotal role in poverty alleviation programmes because they use their income to meet the basic household needs. Marginalization of poor rural women with respect to credit was the prime factor behind the emergence of SHGs. Micro-credit is a significant tool to break the vicious cycle of poverty. It has contributed to building the self-esteem and self-reliance of poor rural women giving them the confidence and the economic means to move out of poverty into the threshold of survival and beyond. By creating self-employment opportunities it enhances the income level of women and raises family welfare. Thus credit targeted to women is more likely to benefit a whole family compared with credit to men which we see in our study in this district.

Therefore, SHGs serve as a useful forum to women for identification of problems and intervention. Self-help supplemented with mutual help can be powerful vehicle for socio-economic transition. The micro-credit programme for women is accepted by development agencies as an effective intervention with a positive impact on economic growth and improvement in the social status of women; Micro-credit schemes are potent agents of social change in impoverished settings where women are disadvantaged due to the lack of access to resources. Women SHGs can thereby turn the vicious circle of poverty into a virtuous one. The research needs more study to get a clear picture for the State as whole.

Government and non-government agencies can play a proactive role in mobilizing, organizing and sustaining SHGs. In order to promote entrepreneurship, it is necessary to provide guidance to potential entrepreneurs to develop ideas, organise resources and understand basic economic principles of supply and demand factors which influence price, common risks and problems likely to be encountered.

REFERENCES

Aziz, Abdul (1981). *Rural Poor: Problems and Prospects*. New Delhi: Ashish Publishing Company.

Anand (2001). *Micro Credit: Avenue for Sustainable Empowerment of Rural Women*. Champaign: IL University of Illinois, p.15.

Fisher, Thomas and M.S. Sriram. (2002). *Beyond Micro Credit: Putting Development Back into Micro Finance*. New Delhi: Vistaar Publications.

Anand, Jaya S. (2002). *Self Help Groups in Empowering Women: A Case Study of Selected SHGs and NHGs*. Discussion Paper No 38. Thiruvananthapuram: KRPLLD, CDS.

Karmakar, K.G. (1999). *Rural Credit and Self Help Groups: Micro Finance Needs and Concepts in India*. New Delhi: Sage Publication.

Lieten, G.K. (1998). *Microfinance Dissected. Economic and Political Weekly* 33(03):103.

Manimekalai, N. and G. Rajeswari (2000). *Empowerment of Women through Self Help Groups*, Margin 32(4).

Shaul, Marnie S. (1982). *The Status of Women in Local Governments*. An International Assessment, Public Administration Review, November – December.

Nair, K. Manoharan (2012). Self Help Groups: A New Paradigm Shift For Women Empowerment. *International Journal of Research in Commerce, Economics & Management* 2 (3):781-84.

Parthasarathy, G. (Ed.) (2003). *Economic Reforms and Rural Development in India*. New Delhi: Academic Foundation.

Rajamani, B. (2011). Self-Help Groups and Women Empowerment. *SELP Journal of Social Science*, 5:86-89.

Rajasekhar (2000). Micro Finance Programmes and Women's Empowerment: A study of Two NGOs from Kerala. *Journal of Social and Economic Development*. III (1).

Remedios, Flynn (2006). Media Should Highlight Rural Success Stories. *The Free Press Journal*, Mumbai.

Roy, Sudhir Kumar (2006). Shubhra Project: An Overview. Financing Agriculture —*A National Journal of Agriculture and Rural Development* 38(3). Mumbai: Agricultural Finance Corporation Limited (June-July).

Sarkar, D. C (1987). Integrating Women in Rural Development. *Kurukshetra*, XXXDV (4).

Singh and Ram Iqbal Singh (1987). Impact of rural development on Economic Status of Women in U.P. *Kurukshetra* , XXXV (16).

Batliwala, Srilatha (1994). *The Meaning of Women's Empowerment: New Concepts from Action* in Gita Sen, Andrienne Germain and Lincoln C. Chen (eds).

Rani, Sudha, Uma Devi and Surendra (2002). SHGs, Micro Credit and Empowerment. *Social Welfare* 48(11).

Sukanya, M (2012). Self Help Groups (SHGs): Impact on Welfare of Rural Women at IKP (Indira Kranthi Patham). *International Journal of Research in Commerce, Economics & Management*, Vol. 2 (3):76-78.

Sahay, Sushama (1998). *Women and Empowerment: Approaches and Strategies.* New Delhi: Discovery Publishing House.

UNDP, *Human Development Report* (1995). New Delhi: Oxford University Press. p. 36.

Vatta, Kamal (2003). Micro Finance and Poverty Alleviation. *Economic and Political Weekly* 38 (5):432-433.

Kulkarni, Vijay D. (2001). Empowerment of Women through Self Help Groups, *Ashwattha*, 3(4): March.

16

Poverty and Livelihood Promotion Programmes in Meghalaya: A Short Note

Natalie West Kharkongor

Introduction

Poverty is one of the socio-economic challenges which most countries of the world today struggle to overcome. According to the Food and Agriculture Organization (FAO), over one billion people in the world today do not get enough food to eat (Deborah, 2010). As on 31st October 2011, around 1.02 billion people were hungry everyday. Of this, the Asian and the Pacific shared the maximum of 642 million people, followed by Sub-Saharan Africa with 265 million, Latin America and the Caribbean with 53 million, Near East and North Africa with 42 million and Developed countries with 15 million (*ibid.*). The Central Intelligence Agency (CIA) *World Fact Book* stated that as on 1st January, 2011, Chad, Haiti, and Liberia recorded the highest poverty rate of 80 per cent each; India and China poverty rate at 25 per cent and 13.4 per cent respectively, and Taiwan recorded the lowest poverty rate of 1.16 per cent as on the same date (WFB, 2011).

Indian economy is growing at a rate of 6.5 per cent even after the recent global financial crisis, but poverty is still a major concern. Even after more than 60 years of independence, India still has the world's largest number of poor people. In 2011, altogether 32.7 per cent of Indians fall below the international poverty line of US$ 1.25 per day (PPP) while 68.7 per cent live on less than US$ 2 per day (GoI, 2011). India ranks 67 on the Global Hunger Index 2010 conducted by International Food Policy Research Institute among 88 nations (GoI, 2010). India is home to 42 per cent of the underweight children under the age of 5 years in the world. India is far worse than its neighbouring countries like Pakistan, Nepal and Sri Lanka (*Ibid.*). Slums population in India rose from 75.26 million in 2001 to 93.06 million in 2011 (GoI, 2011).

The North-Eastern Region comprises the States of Assam, Arunachal Pradesh, Manipur, Meghalaya, Mizoram, Nagaland, Tripura and Sikkim. According to the Tendulkar's Committee Recommendations, Manipur's poverty rate stood the highest at 47.1 per cent, followed by Assam at 37.9 per cent, Arunachal Pradesh at 25.9 per cent, Mizoram at 21.1 per cent, Nagaland at 20.9 per cent, Tripura at 17.4 per cent, Meghalaya at 17.1 per cent and the lowest poverty rate was recorded by Sikkim at 13.1 per cent (Debroy, 2012). Poverty among the rural tribals in the region stood at 47.4 per cent (Nayak, 2012).

Poverty Eradication

The United Nations has launched the eight Millennium Development Goals 2015. The first goal to end poverty and hunger consists of three targets. The first target is to halve the number of people whose income is less than $1 a day between 1990 and 2015. Target two is to achieve full and productive employment and decent work for all, including women and young people. Target three is to halve the proportion of people who suffer from hunger between 1990 and 2015 (UN, 2012a).

In India, eradication of poverty is a priority. The Government of India has launched a number of schemes to eradicate poverty and impoverishment. Mentioned can be made to the SGSY Scheme, MGNREGA, IGNOAPS, IAY, PMGSY, PURA, Rural Drinking Water, TSC, Watershed Development Programme and Employment and Social Security Programmes of other Ministries which have tremendously contributed to the upliftment of the standard of living of the people of the country (RHCSP, 2008).

In the North-East Region, the poverty alleviation programmes are financed by the Central as well as the State governments. In addition to the government sponsored schemes, there are other livelihood promotion programmes sponsored by North-Eastern Council (NEC), Department of North-Eastern Region (DoNER) and International Fund for Agriculture Development (IFAD).

The United Nations efforts to eradicate poverty get reflected in the report of the Department of Economics and Social Affairs (DESA). The DESA's Statistics Report 2012 revealed the gains in poverty reduction and access to safe drinking water, and an improvement in the lives of slum dwellers in urban areas. The Report also revealed the increase in gender parity, in primary education, a decline in levels of child mortality, tuberculosis, global malaria and deaths, and an expansion of treatment for HIV patients (UN, 2012b). No doubt, India too has adopted stringent measures to reduce poverty. The poor result is due to the mismanagement of financial resources.

Profile of Meghalaya

Meghalaya, the 'Abode of Clouds' with a population of 29,64,007 and 130.5 density of population per sq. km is predominantly an agrarian economy. Though recorded a poverty rate of 17.1 per cent, the second lowest among all the eight North-Eastern States, Meghalaya still has a huge number of people living below the poverty line. This is mainly because of the practice of *jhum* cultivation and low industrial development in the State. About half the people of Meghalaya live below the poverty line.

If Meghalaya has to achieve the Millennium Development Goal of halving the poverty level by 2015 and improving the basic services and welfare of the people residing in rural villages comprising of four lakh households, it is imperative to adopt a forward looking approach for making a productive and an optimum utilization of the State's natural resources. Committed to the eradication of poverty, Meghalaya has launched a number of livelihood promotion activities under different projects and programmes. The most important ones are explained below:

Integrated Basin Development and Livelihood Promotion Programme (IBDP)

The Government of Meghalaya has recently launched the flagship programme styled as the **IBDP** to be implemented during the Twelfth Plan Period (2012-2017). This has got its base on the term *Inclusive Growth*, highlighted by the Planning Commission of India in the Approach Paper for the Twelfth Plan. The mission of the programme is 'to promote an effective development and utilization of basin resources for ensuring livelihood security and inclusive growth, within the framework of sustainable development' (MBDA, 2012). The objectives are:

- To promote water, food and livelihood security, and to bridge critical gaps for leveraging;
- To provide knowledge-centric development;
- To evolve and promote climate change coping strategies and develop action plan;
- To promote the creation of physical infrastructure; and
- To promote modern and flexible institutions capable of triggering positive changes in the current paradigm of governance.

The key interventions of the programme are the Knowledge Management, the Natural Resource Management, the Enterprise/ Livelihood Promotion, the Institutions and the Governance. To achieve the objectives, a two pronged strategies will be adopted; the mission mode approach and the integrated approach. The former relates to the launching of independent missions for selective few sectors. The latter relates to the merger of the independent missions into the programme (*Ibid.*).

The positive outcomes of the programme are: integrated village development through sustainable natural resource management; reaching the unreached; developing human resources; entrepreneurial promotion; good governance and better quality of public services; avoidance of works' duplication; and sustainable growth (*Ibid.*).

The programme will be managed by the Basin Development Council, the Basin Development Authority, the Basin Development Unit, a district chapter of Basin Development Council, and the Village Councils. The sources of funds for the implementation of the programme are the State government, Central government, international and national institutions, beneficiaries, and other stakeholders. It will be monitored and evaluated by a competent authority (*Ibid.*).

Livelihoods Improvement Finance Company of Meghalaya

IFAD and Government of Meghalaya have jointly funded the Meghalaya Livelihood Project of the Himalayas (MLIPH) in the five project districts namely, East Khasi Hills, Ri Bhoi District, Jaintia Hills, East Garo Hills and South Garo Hills since 2004-05. The project is being implemented through Meghalaya Rural Development Society (MRDS). It has promoted a Livelihoods Improvement Finance Company of Meghalaya (LIFCOM), a social venture capital company under the Companies Act 1956, with the aim of promoting micro enterprises, small and medium enterprises and facilitating demand driven business development services in the Project Areas.

The LIFCOM would provide micro loan, patience capital, equity and near-equity financing along with other business development services for forward and backward linkage undertakings. The main motive behind LIPCOM is to assure the sustainability and economic viability of the livelihood activities undertaken at the household and community level under MLIPH. LIFCOM is based on a revenue earning model so that it attains operational sustainability by the end of project period 2012-13 (IFAD, 2006).

North-Eastern Region Community Resource Management Project

NERCORMP is a livelihood and rural development project which aims at transforming the lives of the poor and marginalized tribal families in the region. It is a joint livelihood project of IFAD, the Ministry of DONER, Government of India, and NEC. The main objective of the project is "to improve the livelihoods of vulnerable groups in a sustainable manner through improved management of their resource base in a way that contributes to the preservation and restoration of the environment" (IFAD, 2008).

The first phase was from 1998 to 2008 and the second phase from 2010 to 2016. A total amount of Rs. 159.70 crores was sanctioned for the first phase and an amount of Rs. 200 crores was sanctioned for the second phase. In Meghalaya, the project covers West Khasi Hills and West Garo Hills. During the first phase a total number of 354 villages and 13,970 households were covered. A total number of 1,306 SHGs and 419 NaRMGs were formed. In addition to this, 43 SHGs Federations and 45 NaRMGs Federations were formed during 1998 and 2008. From 2010 till date 151 villages and 7,246 households have been covered, 394 SHGs and 174 NaRGMs were formed (*Ibid.*).

The project carries two important components, the Economic Livelihood Activities and the Community Based Biodiversity Conservation. The objective of the first is 'to expand viable income earning activities for resource poor households in crops, horticulture, forestry, livestock, fish production and non-farm activities using sustainable environmentally sound practices' (Ibid.). The economic livelihood activities are to be achieved by addressing major sub-components *jhum* cultivation modification, horticulture/perennial crop development, minor irrigation, livestock and aquaculture/fishery development, production forestry, extension and technology transfer and development of non-farm enterprise. The objective of the second is 'to assist communities to conserve their unique and natural resource-based production systems; and to strengthen indigenous institutions and institutionalize new conservation practices'. These objectives are to be achieved through developing symbiotic relationship between the livelihood needs of the communities and biodiversity conservation programmes.

Economic Livelihood Activities

Conversion or transformation of *jhum* fallow forests into community conserved areas is the main focus of the project; about 64 per cent of the project villages adopted the interventions. Before the project implementation in the two districts, West Khasi Hills and West Garo Hills, 79 per cent of the households practiced *jhum* cultivation and after the project intervention the percentage declines to 57.5. The average *jhum* size per household stood at 2.05 acre before the intervention and 0.55 acre after the intervention. The percentage of project villages adopting agro-forestry/horticulture models stood at 50, the percentage of household who had given up *jhumming* entirely was 28.5, and the overall percentage reduction in *jhum* areas was 40 as on 2007 (*Ibid.*).

Home garden/kitchen garden is another focused area of the project. The percentage of project villages with home garden in the two districts as on 2007 stood at 80 per cent. The percentage of households with home garden stood at 75 per cent. An average number of 25 plant varieties are available for the farmers. The average income per household per year from home garden aggregated to Rs. 3,000 to Rs. 4,000 in West Khasi Hills and Rs. 1,500 to Rs. 2,000 in West Garo Hills. The number of villages in West Khasi Hills under the perennial mix crop model (arecanut + banana + pineapple) stood at 50 after the project execution which was 25 earlier, and the number of households increased from 1,288 to 2,260, an increase of 43 per cent (*Ibid.*).

By the end of the first phase of the project, 68 per cent of project villages in Meghalaya had terraced fields. The total area of terraced fields developed through project was 1,289 acres, and the total villages covered under new minor irrigation stood at 140 acres. The overall percentage increase in the food crop production was 42 per cent as on 2007 (*Ibid.*).

Community Based Biodiversity Conservation

By the end of the first phase of the project, almost 75 per cent of the project villages were covered under biodiversity conservation initiatives with a total area of 1,836 sq. km. In West Garo Hills, out of a total of 192 total project villages, 180 villages were sensitized with biodiversity conservation covering an area of 800 sq. km. In West Garo Hills, there were 11 villages with an area of 253 sq. km (NEC, 2011). The NaRGMs were trained on issues of biodiversity covering topics like NRM sensitization, land-use planning and management, NRM and livelihood linkages, biodiversity conservation, community forest management and conservation of crop biodiversity.

Micro Credit Initiatives

The project framed its policies, strategies, and activities for ensuring credit accessibility to community based organizations. Credit initiatives focused on SHGs and not NaRGMs though some of them availed credit from the project. Under the NERCORMP, many villages, households, families and individuals have benefited from the project. At the end of the first phase the number of families benefited from the project stood at 7,070 in West Garo Hills and 6,900 in West Khasi Hills. The total number of beneficiaries aggregated to 83,820 in the two districts. As on March 2008, the SHGs savings in West Garo Hills amounted to Rs. 1,46,39,528 and in West Khasi Hills amounted to Rs. 1,34,01,760. The amount of Revolving Fund to SHGs and NaRGMs as on the same date aggregated to Rs. 3,42,66,516 and Rs. 4,77,72,241 in West Garo Hills and West Khasi Hills respectively, whereas the amount of Facilitation Fund stood at Rs. 82,50,072 and Rs. 42,00,000 in the two districts respectively (*Ibid.*).

North-Eastern Council Projects

The NEC created in 1971 has been a source of finance for a number of livelihood promotion activities in Meghalaya. After its formation, it was decided that all central ministries will have to part 10 per cent of their budget for the development of the North-East region. The money is transferred to non-lapsable central pool of resources. Previously, the account was administered by the Planning Commission and now it is administered by the Ministry of DoNER. The projects taken up by the NEC for the development of Meghalaya during the 2011-2012 are appended below:

Kynshi Stage-II: H. E. P.

The project is to harness the power potential of about 150 MW. It will not cause submergence of any village or valuable land. The reservoir can be developed into tourist resort. The estimated cost of this project is Rs. 4.42 crores. An amount of Rs. 4.10 crores has been released towards this project by the NEC.

The other power projects approved and sanctioned by the NEC in the State are the construction of 132/33 KV, 2×20 MVA sub-station at Umiam at a cost of Rs. 480 lakhs; construction of 132 KV LILO of Sumer NEHU Line at 132/33 KV, 2×20 MVA Substation at Umiam at a cost of Rs. 494 lakhs; and the construction of 132/33 KV, 2×20 MVA sub-station at Mendipathar at a cost of Rs. 471 lakhs.

Health Care Projects

The Health and Family Welfare Department, Government of Meghalaya proposed for the establishment of six bedded Intensive Care Units each at Civil Hospital, Tura and Ganesh Das Hospital with an intention to provide emergency care. This will definitely lead to the saving of precious lives and addressing the critical health cases which require specialized care and treatment. An amount of Rs. 477.03 lakhs has been approved and sanctioned by the NEC during 2011-2012.

The State government has proposed to establish a Dialysis Unit, Endoscopic Unit, Major Operation Theatre upgradation and 10 bedded Emergency and Casuality Ward at Civil Hospital, Shillong. The project was approved at a total cost of Rs. 498.40 lakhs and an amount of Rs. 145 lakhs has already been sanctioned for implementation of the project by the NEC.

Governance

The NEC with a purpose to develop e-governance in the State has sanctioned an amount of Rs. 270 lakhs for the development of e-Governance Infrastructure and Applications in Meghalaya during 2011-2012. An amount of Rs. 245 lakhs has been released so far (GoM, 2012). The remaining amount will be released in the year 2012.

Centrally Sponsored Schemes and Central Sector Schemes

The Centrally Sponsored Schemes are schemes which are partly sponsored by the Central government and partly by the State government. The former includes agriculture, agriculture research and education, soil conservation, animal husbandry and veterinary, fisheries, corporation, land reforms, flood control, village and small scale industries, sericulture and weaving, forestry and wildlife, general and technical education, employment and training, arts and culture, medical and public health, water supply and sanitation, urban affairs, social security and welfare and nutrition. The latter includes agriculture, horticulture, cooperation, fisheries, forestry and wildlife, general education, technical education, sericulture and weaving.

The total outlay under the scheme for the year 2011-2012 stood at Rs. 63,334.99 lakhs. The share of the State in the distribution of the total outlay aggregated to Rs. 44,629.68 lakhs. An amount of Rs. 7834.49 is to be distributed to East, West Khasi Hills and Ri Bhoi District, an amount of Rs.7415.67 to East, West and South Garo Hills, and Rs. 3455.15 lakhs to Jaintia Hills. Under the Central Sector Schemes, the total outlay for the same year amounted to Rs. 2975.03 lakhs. Out of this, Rs. 2096.91 lakhs will go to the State, Rs. 618.17 lakhs to East, West Khasi Hills and Ri Bhoi District, Rs. 220.10 lakhs to East, West and South Garo Hills District, and Rs. 39.85 lakhs to Jaintia Hills.

Conclusion

This chapter has reflected the poverty level in Meghalaya and the attempts have been made to eradicate poverty and impoverishment. There is no denying the fact that the livelihood promotion programmes and projects adopted from time to time have significantly reduced the number of people living below the poverty line. However, this is not enough; a lot more has to be done by the countries and the world forums to further reduce the poverty level. Poverty is caused mainly because of mismanagement of resources and not because of lack of resources. Hence, proper evaluating and monitoring of the schemes, projects, and programmes is the need of the hour to prevent leakages. 'A rupee saved is a rupee earned'.

In Meghalaya, poverty can be reduced substantially if the agricultural sector is taken care of. Cultivation has to be practiced on modern lines with the adoption of advanced technology. Industrial investments have to pick up in the State by promoting industrial projects under the PPPP

(Private Public People Partnership) model. In this regard, State government has to volunteer playing the role of the main stakeholder since private players shy away from investing in the State due to militancy and insurgency problems. Meghalaya has to take forward the Look East Policy to build trading relationships with the neighbouring countries and thereby raising the State's income as well as the per capita income of the people in the State.

REFERENCES

Deborah Byrd (2010). *How Many Hungry in a World with 7 Billion. Earth Sky.* http://earthsky.org/human-world/how-many-people-in-the-world-today-are-hungry (Accessed 30 October 2011).

Debroy, Bibek (2011). *Poverty in North-East and UTs. The Economic Times.* http://blogs.economictimes.indiatimes.com/policypuzzles/entry/poverty-in-north-east-and-uts (*accessed 6 April 2012*)

Government of Meghalaya (2012). *Annual Plan 2011-12 of the Government of Meghalaya*, Shillong 2012.

Government of India (2011), 'The Census Report 2011'.

International Fund for Agricultural Development (2006). *Livelihood Improvement Finance Company of Meghalaya.* Government of Meghalaya, Shillong.

International Fund for Agricultural Development (2008). *NERCORMP, Process Documentation—Experiences and Lessons Learnt.* Government of Meghalaya.

Meghalaya Basin Development Authority (2012). *Integrated Basin Development Authority.* Government of Meghalaya, Shillong.

Nayak, C. K. (2012). *Poverty Up In Meghalaya: Plan Panel Report.* Indian Environmental Portal. www.indiaenvironmentportal.org.in › News (accessed 20 March 2012).

North Eastern Council (2011). *Annual Plan 2011-12 of the North-Eastern Council*, Shillong.

Rural Household Centered Strategy Paper (2008). *Poverty Eradication in India by 2015.* Ministry of Rural Development, Government of India. www.indiaenvironmentportal.org.in/files/Poverty_Eradication.pdf.

The Times of India (2010) 'India ranks below Pak, China on hunger index', International Food Policy Research Institute. articles.timesofindia.indiatimes.com ... Global Hunger Index (accessed 12 October 2010).

United Nations (2012a). *We Can End Poverty 2015 Millennium Development Goals.* UN System's Work on the MDGs. www.un.org/millenniumgoals/ (accessed 31 July 2012).

United Nations (2012b). *Millennium Development Goals Report 2012.*

Department of Economic and Social Affairs, www.un.org/en/development/desa/.../mdg-report-2012.html (accessed 2 July 2012).

World Fact Book (2011). *World Poverty.* Central Intelligence Agency, https://www.cia.gov/library/publications/the-world.../2046.html. (Accessed 10 June 2012).

17

Problems of NGO Sector in Manipur: A Short Note

N. Shanta Singh and *Damodar Nepram*

Introduction

A non-governmental organization (hereafter NGO) is a non-profit voluntary organization formed by a group of individuals with an objective to render certain humanitarian services to the people. The World Bank actively supports NGO participation in its projects and said "NGOs include a wide variety of groups and institutions that are entirely or largely independent of government and characterized primarily by humanitarian or cooperative, rather than commercial objectives."[1] A very popular definition is also given by Willets (2006) which defines NGO as "an independent voluntary association of people acting together on a continuous basis, for some common purpose, other than achieving government office, making illegal money or illegal activities". The NGOs have certain advantages over the government in providing various services to the people. To mention a few, they are able to work better at the grass root level, implement programme at a much cheaper cost, there is flexibility in their operations, etc. Understanding the importance of NGOs, the Planning Commission of India brought out a National Policy on the Voluntary Sector in 2007 which says that the "policy is a commitment to encourage, enable and empower an independent, creative and effective voluntary sector, with diversity in form and function, so that it can contribute to the social, cultural and economic advancement of the people of India."[2] It lays down the policy of the government towards the NGOs, how the government can help them and also the role they should be playing as partners in the developmental process of the country.

The NGO sector in Manipur has been gaining popularity and provides a variety of services to the people. The number of NGOs has also risen sharply and altogether there were 550 such organisations as on March 2007.[3] The sector can further grow as the State is facing a myriad of problems which is beyond the capacity of the government alone to solve them. Further, it can help to fill up the vacuum which has been created by the withdrawal of the government from many of the activities which it performed before liberalisation. Unfortunately, it is true to say that the NGOs working in the State face many problems and difficulties which really hamper their day-to-day functioning. The aim of this chapter is to highlight some of these problems based on the spot visits, interactions with the beneficiaries, government and NGO officials, review of literatures, etc.

Activities of NGOs towards Socio-Economic Development of Manipur

In order to understand the role played by the NGOs in Manipur, a preliminary study of the activities of eight NGOs, namely Wangjing Women and Girls Society (WWAGS), Citizen Volunteers Training Centre (CVTC), Volunteers for Village Development (VVD), Centre for Social Development (CSD), Rural Service Agency (RUSA), Rural Development Society (RDS), Rural Education and Action for Change - Manipur (REACH-M), and Rural Women Upliftment Society (RWUS) was made. In the course of the study it has come to light that many of the activities of these NGOs seem to be quite similar and, hence, in the present study a deeper analysis of the activities of only the first five NGOs is made. They have been chosen in such a manner that they are from both the hills and the plains regions of the State and their works cover most of the activities of the NGOs in Manipur.

The activities of the NGOs can be grouped under two categories (a) social activities and (b) economic activities. Prevention of HIV, supply of drinking water, running of old age homes, provision of training and loans for income generation, etc., are some important activities which have really benefited the local population. To mention a few such schemes, the water supply facilities created by CVTC around the village of Andro are still being used by the local people as a major source of drinking water. WWAGS has been fairly successful in its adult education programme and almost 90 per cent of the participants have become literates. CSD's main focus has been drug deaddiction and many have benefited from this facility and are leading a normal life. On the other hand, VVD operated mainly in Ukhrul district and especially in remote and distant places. It worked in promoting peaceful co-existence among various communities and in generating income and employment. Similarly, RUSA has been fairly successful in its effort to make local people aware of basic issues of health and hygiene. Its old aged homes have been appreciated by the local residents.

Problem facing the NGO Sector

As mentioned earlier, the NGO sector is facing many problems. They can be grouped into two (a) external, and (b) internal. External problems are those caused by factors which are beyond the control of the NGOs themselves while internal problems are caused by factors within their control. The latter can be termed as weaknesses which we shall discuss in the next section. Also, some of the external factors are briefly mentioned below.

Lack of Co-operation

The NGOs would have been even more successful if people had given more cooperation. Many a time the beneficiaries wanted help from the NGOs in terms of financial assistance or in terms of goods and other services but failed to do their duty on their part. For example, when the beneficiaries get loans from the NGOs under different schemes, they are diverted for personal use as a result of which recovery becomes a big problem.

Law and Order Problem

The law and order situation of a region (Manipur) influences the functioning of the NGOs. The situation in Manipur cannot be considered congenial as being reported by the local newspapers of the daily incidents like killings, bandhs and blockades, etc. A negative impression of the State is being created among the funding agencies which have affected the NGOs more than other factors. The Central ministries or the foreign agencies are reluctant to release funds to the NGOs which can lead to an abrupt end of projects. This would not only tarnish the image of the concerned NGO but lead to non-rendering of vital services to the people.

Infrastructural Problem

The infrastructural facilities in the State are very poor. Power supply in the non-rainy season is confined to few hours in a day even in the capital city of Imphal and the situation in rural areas can be easily imagined. Road conditions are extremely poor and many roads in the hill areas are non-motorable during the rainy season. All these factors hinder the working of the NGOs. For example, it was reported that an NGO took up poultry developmental programme in its working areas. The success of the programme was limited due to the irregular supply of electricity and consequent failure of the heating system.

NGO-Government Relationship

Many of the NGOs have given reservations on the working of some government departments which has not helped in their functioning. Even though funds for the NGOs are coming from the Central government, they are monitored by the local State government departments which according to them lack co-operation. Due to the incompetency and callous attitude of the government departments, the NGOs often could not utilise funds in time which hinders their functioning. There were times when various projects had to be interrupted in the middle of their implementation because of non-release of funds. On the other hand, the government does not feel comfortable in the functioning the NGOs. According to some government officials, many of the NGOs are one man organizations, managed by one person although they may appear to be more democratic and dedicated institutions. They allege that the necessary members exist only on papers with little association with the organization itself. They further claim that misutilisation of funds by the NGOs has also been a factor in weakening the relationship between the NGOs and the government.

Internal Problems : Weaknesses of the NGO Sector

The NGO sector suffers from many weaknesses some of which are given below. Correcting them will require skill, courage and spirit of voluntarism.

liberalisation where government is slowly moving away from various activities which it was earlier performing, it is high time from all sections of the society to encourage the NGOs to step in and take up many more people oriented developmental programmes.

NOTES

1. See Operational Directive 14.70 of the World Bank, 28 August 1989, (available at http://www.gdrc.org/ngo/wb-ngo-directive.html (accessed on 1 March 2010).
2. See Planning Commission of India (2007).
3. Information given by the NGO Forum, Manipur.

REFERENCES

Association of Voluntary Agencies for Rural Development, (1962). *An Introduction to Some Voluntary Organizations and Rural Development Programmes*. New Delhi: AVARD.

Centre for Social Development (CSD). *Various Reports,* Imphal.

Citizen Volunteers Training Centre (CVTC). *Various Reports,* Imphal.

Planning Commission of India, (2007). *National Policy on the Voluntary Sector,* Voluntary Action Cell.

Volunteers for Village Development (VVD), *Various Reports.* Ukhrul.

Wangjing Women and Girls Society (WWAGS), *Various Reports,* Wangjing.

Willets, Peter, (2006). What is a Non-Governmental Organisation?, Available at http.//www.staff.city.ac.uk/p.willets/cs-ntwks/ngo-art.htm (Accessed on 2 March 2010).

World Bank, (1998). The Bank's Relations with NGOs: Issues and Directions, *Social Development Papers* No. 28.

Part - V
Institutions and Rural Development

18

Public Sector Undertakings for Development of Rural Tripura : A Perspective of Corporate Social Responsibility

Bidhu Kanti Das

Introduction

Sustainability is one of the most pressing challenges worldwide today. Interest for social, environmental and ethical issues is increasing on a daily basis among different stakeholders, including general public, society, media, government, corporations and financial community. Sustainability is being researched in different fields and from different aspects, emphasizing its bold interdisciplinary character. The State like Tripura in India's North-Eastern Region where valuable resource, natural gas, is explored and exploited by the Public Sector Units (PSUs) of India needs to take care of the interest of different stakeholders especially local community and environment. These PSUs, viz., Oil and Natural Gas Corporation Limited (ONGC), Gas Authority of India Limited (GAIL) and Tripura Natural Gas Company Limited (TNGCL) are spending a substantial amount for the social upliftment of the weaker sections of the society.

Objectives and Methodology of the Study

The main objective of the study is to understand about the effect of Corporate Investment and Corporate Social Responsibility (CSR) with special reference to Oil and Gas sector industry. Further, an attempt has also been made to find out the extent of involvement in CSR with special reference to development of local community for their livelihood, employment generation and rural infrastructure by the Oil and Gas companies operating in Tripura.

The present study is based on both primary and secondary data. For Primary data, altogether 300 respondents were taken and analysed in certain parameters of CSR of Oil and Gas sectors PSUs in Tripura. Secondary data have been collected from company's annual reports, in house journals, magazines and websites. Some reputed journal and websites in the field of business ethics and corporate responsibility were also consulted.

Literatures on Social Development and CSR

The beginning of the debate on CSR is marked by a landmark study commissioned by the Federal Council of Churches of Christ in America, entitled "The Social Responsibility of Business Man" authored by Howard Bowen (1953). Yet, two years earlier, in May 1951, Frank Abrams, a top executive with Standard Oil, published a remarkable piece of reflection on "Management's Responsibilities in Complex World" in the Harvard Business Review, a title that seems even more topical today than almost sixty years ago. Abrams urged his fellow managers, i.e., businessmen, to think of themselves as professionals with an explicit sense of duty not just to shareholders, employees, and customers, but also to the public in general: "management must understand that the general public—man and women everywhere—have a very deep interest in, and are affected by, what is going on". He, thus, introduced an early stakeholder's perspective. Bowen's study (1953), in contrast, is concerned with detailing the specific social responsibilities of businessmen. He argued that businessmen must assume "a large measure of responsibilities if the economic system of free enterprise is to continue and prosper", appealing to enlightened self interest. And although Bowen addressed questions such as "what constitutes good citizenship for a business enterprise? How does a moral enterprise behave? Or what kind of business decisions promotes the end of modern society and what kinds detract?" His and Abrams' early contributions focus on the responsibilities of individuals within an enterprise or corporation. Thus, in hindsight the beginning of CSR is in fact marked by a discussion on individual responsibilities of managers *vis-à-vis* their constituencies and society in general. Put differently, CSR was more like "social responsibility (SR)"—and inextricably bound up with the responsibilities of executives.

The emergence of CSR as a development issue has to be seen in the context of the changing views of the development agencies on the main objectives of development and the best means of bringing it about. Over the past quarter century the view of development as being primarily about economic growth has become less dominant, with a much greater emphasis on the social dimensions of development as exemplified by the creation of the Human Development Index (HDI) by the United Nations Development Programme (UNDP). This shift culminated in the adoption of the UN Millennium Development Goals (MDGs), focused on eradicating poverty and hunger, achieving universal primary education, promoting gender equality, reducing mortality and improving health, and ensuring environmental sustainability.

In 2000, the United Nations launched the Global Compact, which involves business, labour, Non- Governmental Organizations (NGOs) and governments. Its original nine principles were derived from the Universal Declaration of Human Rights, the International Labour Organization's (ILO's) Fundamental Principles on Rights at Work and the Rio Declaration on Environment and Development. Critics have pointed to a tendency for the Global Compact Office to see the promotion of Foreign Direct Investment (FDI) in developing countries as an important objective and even to regard it as a manifestation of corporate responsibility.

Other development agencies have also recently emphasized the role of CSR in promoting social development. These include Ministry of Public Sector Enterprises, Ministry of Petroleum and Ministry of Heavy Industries in India. And set a target ranging from 0.5 per cent of their Net Profit of last financial year should be spent on CSR or social development purpose only depending on certain profit limits of the PSUs. The Indian Transnational Corporation, Tata, which has a high CSR profile in India, argues that if markets are to grow, "the poor must become consumers too".

Social Developmental Activities in Tripura

In Tripura, every company in the field of oil and gas sector has been incurring some expenditure for social overheads as a part of their Corporate Social Responsibility (CSR) policy. Despite overwhelming concern for getting more oil or gas, and make more profit on it, the corporate oil and gas sector has given top priority towards the upliftment of less privileged section of the society, education and employment generation in the areas where they operate. Though this sector is generating profits, it has a philosophy to contribute for well-being of the society to improve the quality of life of the people amongst whom it works, to the extent possible. It is also providing committed to provide safe working conditions to the employees and the maintaining high standard of environment stipulated by globally recognized standardizing authority in its operational activities. Special emphasis is given on pollution control and safety measures to prevent environmental degradation and accidents respectively. As it enters newer areas it ushers in hope and development for the people of these remote rural areas, connecting them with mainstream and helping them in realizing their dreams of a prosperous future.

Here, we will concentrate on the Corporate Social Responsibility action taken by the respective organization in Tripura and their performance in the field. The study is confined to Oil and Gas sector of Tripura only. And the companies included in the study are ONGC, GAIL TNGCL.

Oil and Natural Gas Corporation Limited (ONGC)

As a premier public sector undertaking in the country, focusing its activities towards exploration and production, it is also committed to the society at large, wherever it is operating. ONGC-Tripura Assets was started in 1970. By showing its social commitment, it has started social projects since long, nearly 30 years back at 1981 at the village of Khamtingbari, Baramura area, ONGC provided drinking water facility, which was renovated once again in the financial year 2010-11. Some of the major contributions of ONGC are:

1. ONGC launched its first PURA (Providing Urban Amenities in Rural Areas) project in 2005 at Maichara of East Kalabaria Panchayat in South Tripura district. The project was providing four components to the rural people, i.e., (a) Power Generation, (b) Community Kitchen, (c) Library and Computer Centre, and (d) Community Hall. The project envisages supplying power to the selected five villages benefiting 400 families under its fold. The project also includes model village, building village roads, health care facilities and vocational training institute, irrigation facilities for farmer. Unfortunately this project was closed by

the ONGC in 2010. Because ONGC has taken some other project like Nutrition Programme for poor women and children and discontinued PURA in national level.

2. In 2005-06 ONGC, has constructed houses for 90 BPL families in the village Vibekanda Colony, in Sarashima Gram Panchayat under the South Tripura district.
3. ONGC has played a vital role for the development of education in Tripura both school education as well as higher education, it has given fund for the establishment of Bhavans Science College which is one of the premier college for science and management education in the State. Apart from this, it is continuously supporting institutes like Ramkrishna Mission School, Pranabanada Vidhya Mandir, Vivekanda Sishu Mandir, Arabinda Bidhya Mandir, Ishanik Kola Kendra, Government College of Art and Craft, are few of them.
4. Till 2007, ONGC has constructed 200 km of road in remote areas of the State and still constructing road in different places for public use. ONGC ushers in improved connectivity and socio-economic development of the State.
5. Tripura is a State which is culturally very developed and its people love to learn and practice various forms of music and dance. Sangeet Gram is established for promoting this cause. ONGC has given approximately Rs. 2.5 crores for the establishment of this institute in the past and continuously supporting the organization.
6. Apart from it, ONGC is promoting entrepreneurship development programme, nutrition programme, rural development programme, and promoting arts and culture here in Agartala.

GAIL India Ltd.

GAIL is a Navaratna Company in India's Public Sector. The company was previously known as Gas Authority of India Ltd. It was set up by the Government of India in August 1984 to create gas sector infrastructure in the country and was renamed in the year 2002 as GAIL India Ltd. Its Agartala office was set up in 1990. It has undertaken its first CSR project in the financial year 1997-98 and spent Rs. 1,23,000 for various social programmes. GAIL is working for educational development and vocational training, creating rural infrastructure, literacy enhancement and women empowerment, and healthcare sector.

Some of the major contributions of GAIL are:

1. In the year 2001-02, the company spent Rs. 59.31 lakhs for implementing various social projects in Tripura.
2. In 2008-09, GAIL has spent Rs. 11.748 lakhs only for IGM Hospital. And the year 2007-08, it has given Rs. 11,73,800 to the IGM Hospital for creating infrastructure through Health Department, Government of Tripura.
3. For promoting health sector infrastructure in the suburban area of Agartala GAIL has constructed two OBB building of a new dispensary at old Agartala under Jirania Block, also given one ambulance, five beds and other medical instrument for the same dispensary by spending Rs. 10 lakhs in the financial year 2004-05.
4. Showing its social commitment GAIL has constructed Integrated Child Development Services (ICDS) centre in Radhanagar Gram Panchayat under Bishalghar Block.
5. By showing solidarity to the visually handicapped student, GAIL has constructed six numbers of classrooms in Narshinghar through Department of Social Welfare, Government of Tripura by spending Rs. 6.69 lakhs in the year 2001-02.
6. Gail has constructed school building, viz., Rajib Gandhi Junior Basic School and Sona Charan Thakur Para Junior Basic School under Mandai Block in the year 2001-02. Also, constructed school building at Kabiraj Tilla H.S. School at Rajlakshmi Nagar under Dukli Block in the year 2002-03.
7. Scholarship provided to the students of Ramthakur Pathsala High School under GAIL's scholarship to meritorious students for the economically deprived section of the society of Rs. 1,22,400 in the financial year 2003-04 and Rs. 1,25,000 for the financial year 2004-05.
8. Constructed a building for 'Anwesha' orphanage of Voluntary Health Association of Tripura and provided Rs. 5 lakh for creating other infrastructure in the financial year 2009-10.
9. GAIL has provided Rs. 10 lakhs to 'Ablamban' for upgrading infrastructure facilities, healthcare facilities and other basic amenities to benefit a large number of sick, aged and needy people residing in the old age home through the NGO 'APANGHAR'.

10. GAIL has done remarkable work for the employment generation of local people at different parts of the State. Few of them are; supported composite scheme on semi-intensive fish culture for Putia S.H.G of Putia Gram Panchayat under Boxanagar Block in the year 2003-04, GAIL has contributed Rs. 1,21,024 and supported composite scheme on Pig Flattery unit for the group 'Milam Badal S.H.G and Khumtia Badal SHG' of Dayal Para under Boxanagar Block in the year 2003-04 given a grant of Rs. 3,78,900.
11. GAIL has done very well in the rural infrastructure creation in the form of electrification and street lighting where State government was not able to lay electric line; GAIL has electrified through solar light. Among few of them are worthy to mention here;
    (a) Electrification of Baluchera Bazar of Boxanagar Block through solar light.
    (b) Installation of solar streetlight at Konabon Market under Bishalghar Block.
    (c) Electrification of Brajendra Colony, Prabhapur Mauza of Jampuijalla Block.

Tripura Natural Gas Company Limited (TNGCL)

TNGCL has been incorporated in July 1990 as a joint venture between Government of Tripura and Government of Assam and restructured in February 2005 on joining of GAIL. It is playing a very crucial role for promoting education, literacy, and by other social development programme. It has initiated social activity on and from 2008 before that it has done indirectly to reduce pressure on fire woods by providing piped gas to villagers at subsidies rate near their pipelines. TNGC has done following area so far its incorporation and generating profit from its business:

1. Has contributed Rs. 5 lakh to the Chief Ministers Relief Fund in the year 2008.
2. Given sponsorship for football tournament Rs. 1 lakh.
3. Given LCD TV for community hall and furnitures for the library of 14 Devotar Mandir at Khoirpur.
4. Sponsorship of Rs. 25 thousand for seminar on 'Photojurnalism' by Photo Journal Association of Tripura.

5. Sponsorship of Rs. 5,000 to the seminar organized by Indian Institute of Engineers, Tripura.
6. It is providing subsidies gas to Battala Samsan Ghat.
7. Apart from this TNGC is contributing fund to a number of NGOs in Agartala for the development programme in the nearby areas and for the plantation in the city area for increasing green coverage in the Agartala city area.

Findings and Observations

From the above discussion we can outline following findings and observations of the study:

1. The findings show that organization in the Oil and Gas PSUs operating in Tripura are spending a lot for the development of local community. ONGC is spending about Rs. 4 crores every year for various CSR programmes, education and SCs and STs component plans, GAIL is spending about Rs. 10 lakhs every year and TNGCL is spending nearly Rs. 2 lakhs for various programmes.
2. The Oil and Gas sector companies are helping for the development of entrepreneurial activity in the State among poor educated unemployed youth. They are conducting regular training for poultry, piggery, goatery, tailoring, driving light vehicle, beauty parlour, bamboo canning and other self-employment activity. Apart from the training they are helping for the setting up the business by providing initial grant to the beneficiary.
3. The sector has constructed large number of roads in rural and backward areas, electrified villages through solar light system in remote areas where electrification was not done by the government.
4. Oil PSUs are working hard for the social development of the people of Tripura by investing in various social projects like rural electrification, rural road, drinking water facility, health care, community hall, providing education facility by providing school buildings, libraries also providing community entertainment facility and communication facility to the remote villages in the States. This has created a better society with education, health, roads, and connectivity. This has definitely

benefited the society at large by reducing the gap between developed and less developed villages in the States.

5. People's perception about the companies who are implementing CSR projects for the social development is very good in Tripura. People were satisfied by the work done by PSUs in their locality or benefits driven by them from the CSR project implementing organizations.

Conclusion

Corporate social responsibility has become an increasingly significant phenomenon in today's business world. Public Sector Undertakings in the field of Oil and Gas sector aware of it and playing a vital role for the development of the State by investing in social development projects which create employment opportunities, increasing living standard, providing better healthcare facilities as well as rural infrastructure. It needs to be more proactive and go for a sustainable development projects in the areas like entrepreneurship development and agricultural development. This activity carried out by the PSUs like ONGC is appreciated by the people who are residing near the project area. This way every business organization should come forward and undertake activities relating to the social development. They should share shoulders with the Government of India and also State government in these novel activities.

REFERENCES

Abrams, F. W. (1951). Management Responsibilities in Complex World. *Harvard Business Review*, 29 (3), 29-34.

Bowen, H. R. (1953). *The Social Responsibility of Businessman.* New York: Harper & Row.

19

Rural Connectivity in North-Eastern Region of India: A Case of Prime Minister Gram Sadak Yojana

Pradip Chouhan, Pritam Bose and *Indraneel Bhowmik*

I. Introduction

Road connectivity is a facilitator of rural development as "it promotes access to economic and social services, thereby generating higher economic activities, agriculture and non-agriculture employment as well as non-agricultural productivity, which in turn expands rural growth opportunities and real income through which poverty can be reduced" (Mohapatra and Chandrasekhar, 2007). In a study by Binswanger, *et al.* (1993), consisting of 13 Indian States observed that investment in rural infrastructure reduces transportation cost, increases market access for farmers, thereby leading to agricultural expansion. The analysis of International Food Policy Research Institute (IFPRI) of the linkages between government expenditure and poverty in rural India observes that an investment worth Rs. 1 (one) crore on roads pushes 1,650 poor persons above the poverty line (Fan, *et al.*, 1999). Further, an analysis by Fan, *et al.* (2000), using a time series data from 1970 to 1993, explored that government expenditure on roads alleviates poverty in rural areas. People living within two kilometres of the all-weather road were found to be lesser poor. Study by Narayan, *et al.* (2000) also found through a household survey in Andhra Pradesh showed that apart from reduction in household poverty there is also decrease in the freight charges and increased in land under cultivation. Many of the poor communities are isolated by distance, bad road conditions, lack of or broken bridges and inadequate transport. These conditions make it difficult for people to get their goods to market and themselves to place of work, to handle health emergencies, to send children to school, and to obtain public services.

The state of rural roads in India is certainly not at the desirable level over the years. In this context, several programmes have been initiated by the Government of India. Rural roads were constructed under several schemes like the National Rural Employment Programme, Rural Landless Employment Guarantee Programme, Jawahar Rozgar Yojana, Prime Minister Gram Sadak Yojana, Employment Assurance Scheme, Mahatma Gandhi National Rural Employment Guarantee Scheme/Act and similar other schemes. Notable works have also been done under the Rural Infrastructure Development Fund scheme by National Bank for Agriculture and Rural Development (NABARD) in recent times. With more than 70 per cent of Indians living in the rural areas, the issue of rural connectivity and more precisely all-weather road connectivity has attained importance from the perspective of the government as well as the people. PMGSY was, thus, initiated in 2000 to facilitate better connectivity to the rural people so as to enhance their social and economic condition as well as provide them a better livelihood. It has two component—First, construction of new all-weather roads to unconnected habitations; and second, upgradation of the existing roads, so that it remains usable all the year round.

The assessment studies in nine states of the country on the socio-economic impact of PMGSY revealed that farmers find it easier to sell his crop as well as buy inputs like fertiliser and seeds following augmented market access. Activities like rearing of goats and sheep for commercial purpose has increased among households enjoying better connectivity. Moreover, the employment scenario has become better with wider job opportunities as villagers can travel to nearby cities and towns at lesser time. The PMGSY roads have contributed to the social issues also in a great earnest. Villagers can go to the nearby hospitals and health centres quickly as a result, decrease in infant mortality and child mortality rates were found in the country. In case of education as well, PMGSY indicates positive benefits in the form of increasing number of school-going girls and attendance of the teachers. Moreover, the construction of PMGSY roads have fostered the average household income in the connected areas and led to a declined in poverty as well (MoRD, 2004). Additionally, better connectivity has led to better governance in the form of greater visits of officials like Block Development Officers. Social relations have also improved with greater number of visits from and to the relatives as has the number of vehicles owned in the connected villages increased (Althaf, 2010).

The North-Eastern States of India, consisting of eight States (NER hereafter), share a commonality of poor infrastructure which is one of the major causes for the region's economic backwardness. Geographically, the region spreads along the hilly and rugged mountains and it makes the people of the region are restricted to access of minimum standards and facilities of the time. A dependable system of roads can lead to socio-economic transformation breaking the remoteness of village communities and eliminating the disparity between rural and urban population. PMGSY activities in the region have been in practice since 2000 and impact assessment studies from Assam and Mizoram indicate similar benefits like the rest of the country. Villages or habitations having the benefit of PMGSY roads were found to have increased accessibility to markets for agricultural products, increased usage of chemical fertilisers, changes in cropping pattern with a tinge towards cash crop, and growth of poultry and dairy sector. Employment opportunities for both on farm and off farm activities have increased. PMGSY roads have facilitated greater access to primary health centres by the people from their habitations as has the number of visits of health workers increased due to greater availability of public transport. There has been an increase in the number of school-going children. Moreover, better accessibility in the form of new and upgraded roads has led to a rise in land prices in both the States and conversion of houses from *kutcha* to *pucca* was also noticed (MoRD, 2004).

It is also true that the economic development of a region is not exclusively due to PMGSY activities but there are several other factors to influence it. Nevertheless, PMGSY roads have also played a part in the ongoing transformation. It is thus in this backdrop we undertake the present study with the broad objective to analyse the nature of activities occurring in the region under this scheme of the Union Government of India. It is obvious that there will be considerable differences among the States in absolute terms due to physiographic and demographic causes. Nevertheless, a supplementary objective is considered to check the nature of variation among the States in terms of average length and the cost of construction. The study is, therefore, exploratory in nature and focuses on comparable indicators like the average length, average expenditure, average sanction cost and per kilometre cost. In order to fulfil the stated goal, this chapter is structured in terms of four sections including the present introductory one. The second section specifies the methodology adopted while the third section provides the analysis and findings. The study is surmised in the final section.

II. Methodology and Data

The present study is exclusively made on the basis of secondary data and uses inputs from the PMGSY website (www.pmgsy.nic.in). Cumulative figures have been computed for the period April 2000 (the first month of the initial year) to September 2011 (first-six months of the current fiscal) to meet our specific needs to explore the extent of coverage, physical progress and financial progress. Physical progress of the scheme has been calculated on the basis of the ratio the length of completed projects against the length of total projects sanctioned as shown in Table 19.2 of Section III.

As mentioned in the previous section, we have used comparable indicators and, therefore, ignored the upgradation component of the scheme and have focussed only on new connectivity. Upgradation costs depend on the existing condition of the roads and are likely to vary much. Among the four comparable indicators, we have computed the first-three as below while the fourth (cost per km) is available at the source. Three computed indicators are:

- Average length = total length in the region ÷ total number of sanctioned projects.
- Average sanction cost = Sanctioned amount cleared by Government of India ÷ total number of sanctioned projects.
- Average expenditure = Total expenditure (pavement cost + cost of cross drainage + cost long span bridges) ÷ total number of sanctioned projects.

It should be noted here that the 'Cost per km' considers only the pavement component for new connectivity as it is given; we have ignored the costs for upgradation due to paucity of available data at the PMGSY website. Thus all figures in Table 19.4 of Section III relates to new roads. Additionally, to examine the nature of variation among the States in respect to length and construction cost, we undertake the testing of two hypotheses as stated below:

First Hypothesis

H_0: Average length of PMGSY roads in the NER States do not differ.
H_1: Average length of PMGSY roads in the NER States differ.

Second Hypothesis

H_0: Cost per km of pavement of PMGSY roads in the NER States are not similar.
H_1: Cost per km of pavement of PMGSY roads in the NER States are similar.

For the sake of testing the stated hypotheses, the standard statistical tool ANOVA along with its F-statistic is used for examining the existence of variation, if any. In the present context, the within group (State) variations were calculated on the basis of the data for the constituent 81 districts pertaining to the 8 States of the region.

III. PMGSY in North-Eastern Region

The present section attempts to explore the status of the PMGSY scheme in NER in terms of its spread, completed road projects and its length, financial involvements, etc. It should be noted here that in the NER, altogether 8,625 number of PMGSY projects have been implemented. Of which, 92 per cent are related to new connections while the remaining projects are related to upgradation of the old roads. On the other hand, a total of 34,684 km of road are being laid. Of which, around 2,467 km or 8 per cent of the total length are being upgraded, while the remaining 92 per cent are the sanctioned lengths for new roads. Interestingly, at the national level, we find that around 31 per cent of the PMGSY projects are for upgrading while the share of new projects is around 69 per cent which is much lower than that of the North-Eastern region. It can, therefore, be said that PMGSY roads in the region are more focussed in reaching new habitations. It should be noted here that habitations in the context of PMGSY are classified into four categories – (a) less than 250 population, (b) population between 250 to 499 population, (c) between 500 to 999 population, and (d) population above 1000.

The Table 19.1 shows that the NER States account for 4.92 per cent of the total 9,49,445 rural habitations of India and among the 46,734 habitations of the region. Of the total, 63.60 per cent were unconnected

Table 19.1: Spread of PMGSY Habitations

States	*Total Habitations*	*Unconnected (01-04-2000)*	*Unconnected (30-09-2011)*
Arunachal Pradesh	3880	2670	2227
	(100)	(68.81)	(57.40)
Assam	23182	17955	12765
	(100)	(77.45)	(55.06)
Manipur	3406	1661	1392
	(100)	(48.77)	(40.87)
Meghalaya	5355	2749	2579
	(100)	(51.34)	(48.16)
Mizoram	795	363	230
	(100)	(45.66)	(28.93)
Nagaland	1083	145	47
	(100)	(13.39)	(4.34)
Sikkim	901	410	242
	(100)	(45.50)	(26.86)
Tripura	8132	3772	1663
	(100)	(46.38)	(20.45)
NER	46734	29725	21145
	(100)	(63.60)	(45.25)
India	949445	353182	276500
	(100)	(37.20)	(29.12)

Source: Computed from http://pmgsyonline.nic.in/aspnet/citizens/NAT/01NCH/Habsreportlocalization accessed on 30/11/11

Notes: Figures in the parentheses indicate percentage of total habitation.

with all-weather roads prior to the Pradhan Mantri Gram Sadak Yojana (2000) while the national unconnected proportion was 37.20 per cent at that time. In a span of little above ten years, 8,580 habitations have been brought under all-weather roads, yet 45.25 per cent habitations in the region are still unconnected by road in 2011. As is obvious the largest State in the region Assam had the highest number of habitations, almost 50 per cent of the region's aggregate, followed by Tripura at *quite* a distance. The number of habitations was lowest in Mizoram because of the higher rates of urbanisation. Among the States, in 2000, all-weather roads were available at 86 per cent of the habitations of Nagaland as only 145 habitations were targeted under PMGSY. On the contrary, the situation was worst for Assam with 77.45 per cent of the habitations reporting unconnected status. After more than 10 years of PMGSY, it is seen that unconnected habitations have declined for all the States in the region and the improved condition appears to be most visible for Tripura with new connectivity spreading to about 26 per cent of the habitations during the period. The progress has been relatively lower for Arunachal Pradesh because still 57 per cent of the habitations remained unconnected in 2011. The data for Meghalaya also appears to be unimpressive, with only 3 per cent of the unconnected habitations being brought under new roads. Among the NER States, only Nagaland appears to have a very good proportion of connected habitations, with almost 96 per cent.

Table 19.2: Financial Progress of PMGSY in NER States

Name of State	*Sanctioned Amount [Rs. Crores]*	*Release Amount [Rs. Crores]*	*Payment Made [Rs. Crores]*	*Value of work done [Rs. Crores]*
Arunachal Pradesh	2076.07	1094.07 [52.70]	1060.41 [51.08]	1030.76 [49.65]
Assam	8801.8	5982.68 [67.97]	5259.53 [59.76]	5392.25 [61.26]
Meghalaya	302.03	223.14 [73.88]	212.92 [70.50]	241.51 [79.96]
Manipur	886.97	494.64 [55.77]	600.4 [67.69]	647.29 [72.98]
Mizoram	708.02	467.06 [65.97]	485.7 [68.60]	559.13 [78.97]
Nagaland	375.27	349.93 [93.25]	339.72 [90.53]	347.03 [92.47]
Sikkim	766.5	521.25 [68.00]	480.69 [62.71]	480.69 [62.71]
Tripura	1555.09	1071.27 [68.89]	1101.06 [70.80]	1185.32 [76.22]
NER	15471.75	10204.04 [65.95]	9540.43 [61.66]	9883.98 [63.88]
India	114417	85929.28 [75.10]	77581.62 [67.81]	78759.35 [68.84]

Source: http://pmgsyonline.nic.in/aspnet/citizens/NAT/07NFP/FinancialProgressReportStateLocalization accessed on 30/09/12.

Notes: Figures in the parentheses indicate percentage of release amount, payment made in and value of work done respectively of the last-three columns, in terms of sanctioned cost.

From Table 19.2 we find that the sanctioned amount for NER under PMGSY was almost 13.52 per cent of the total all-India level. Within the region the amount is highest for Assam followed by Arunachal Pradesh and Tripura. In absolute terms, the sanctioned amount is least for

Meghalaya. However, in terms of amount released for the scheme, we find that for India 75.10 per cent of the sanctioned amount has been released, while for NER only 65.95 per cent have been released. Nagaland has had the highest proportion of release, while Arunachal Pradesh has the lowest proportion. On the other hand, Manipur, Mizoram and Tripura have made payment beyond the released amount with the expectation of later realisation of funds. In terms of the value of work done, it is seen that 63.88 per cent, worth almost Rs. 10,000 crores, has been completed in the region with Arunachal Pradesh, Assam and Sikkim exhibiting even lower rate. Moreover, for all States except Arunachal Pradesh, value of work is higher than the payment made.

Physical progress has been defined as the proportion of completed road length in respect to the sanctioned road length. Table 19.3 shows that 4,202 new projects have been constructed with 16583.84 km of all-weather roads in the region. Additionally, almost 1,900 km of roads have been relaid or upgraded. It is further seen that the physical progress has been highest for Nagaland, 97.92 per cent, and least in Meghalaya, 39.77 per cent. It should be noted that Mizoram and Tripura are the two other States which have had higher physical progress as compared to region's average. It is interesting to see that within the NER States; the number of completed upgraded projects has been highest for Sikkim with 267, while in terms of road length, Nagaland leads in the region. Assam, though, has the highest number of completed projects, 2,189, as well as road length of 7115.44 km, the State has achieved only 44.93 per cent of its target.

Table 19.3: Physical Progress of Work (Completed Works as on September 30, 2011)

States	*New Connectivity*		*Upgradation*		*Physical Progress (%)*
	Nos.	*Length*	*Nos.*	*Length*	
Arunachal Pradesh	498	1934.25	0	0	44.20
Assam	2189	7115.44	6	32.49	44.93
Meghalaya	355	450.77	0	0	39.77
Manipur	153	1218.45	100	541.05	53.23
Mizoram	134	1740.35	9	73.5	72.93
Nagaland	165	1868.3	71	745.21	97.92
Sikkim	144	592.94	267	242.63	46.29
Tripura	564	1663.34	145	264.67	64.21
NER	4202	16583.84	598	1899.55	53.29
India	52093	166646.6	27916	8396.16	69.42

Source: http://pmgsyonline.nic.in/aspnet/citizens/NAT/06NPW/SPWLocalization accessed on 30/11/11

Interestingly, none of the upgradation projects in Arunachal Pradesh and Meghalaya has completed till the considered period.

As stated in the previous sections we have used few comparable indicators like average length, average expenditure, and average sanction cost for analysing the nature of PMGSY activities among the States along with the per km cost. Table 19.4 shows that the average length under PMGSY is highest in Mizoram with 13.02 km, while Nagaland follows with 10.76 km. The average road length in the region was 3.73 km, which is higher than the average length of the four States, namely, Assam, Meghalaya, Sikkim and Tripura. The State of Meghalaya appears to have the lowest average length under PMGSY.

Table 19.4: Extent of PMGSY in NER States

State	*Average length (in km)*	*Average Sanction Cost (Rs in lakh)*	*Average expenditure (Rs in lakh)*	*Cost/km (Rs in lakh)*
Arunachal Pradesh	5.97	283.23	240.14	40.23
Assam	3.42	189.37	175.84	51.38
Manipur	3.88	104.23	91.52	23.57
Meghalaya	2.84	75.70	42.08	14.81
Mizoram	13.02	370.69	247.83	19.03
Nagaland	10.76	151.32	148.67	13.81
Sikkim	3.02	128.39	71.21	23.55
Tripura	3.13	162.33	145.79	46.52
NER	**3.73**	**179.38**	**157.03**	**42.06**

Source: Computed from www.pmgsy.nic.in

On the other hand, the average sanction cost for each project was highest for Mizoram and lowest for Meghalaya, understandably for greater length and the smallest length respectively. But the surprising case is for Nagaland, which is much below than many other States even though the length was higher. The average expenditures for the projects (roads) are mostly in tune with the sanction cost, though we find a sizeable difference between the two for Mizoram in absolute terms, Rs. 123 lakhs approx, and for Meghalaya and Sikkim in proportional terms, around 55 per cent. In case of per km cost, we find that Assam (51.38 lakh) has the highest expenditure followed by Tripura (46.52 lakh) and Arunachal Pradesh (40.23 lakh). Nagaland (13.81 lakh) exhibits the lowest in this category followed by Meghalaya (14.81 lakh), Mizoram (19.03 lakh). The region's average tilts towards Rs. 42.06 lakh per km due to the pull from Assam and Tripura for having the highest length. Table 19.4 helps us to understand the cause of higher aggregate sanctions for these States apart from the fact that the two top States has the highest number of habitation and length to be covered as well.

Results of Hypotheses

The NER has 81 districts and the data on average length and pavement cost per km of all the districts have been used for the testing of two hypotheses.

First Hypothesis

Table 19.5 shows that the calculated *F* statistic, 43.41, is significant at 1 per cent level, suggesting the rejection of the Null Hypothesis and accepting the alternative Hypothesis. Thus one can infer that average lengths of road in the region are unevenly distributed, and there is significant variation among the lengths of roads constructed under PMGSY among the various States. The difference in the average length of the roads occurs mostly due to spread of the habitations, which appear to be far-off particularly for Nagaland and Mizoram.

Table 19.5: Analysis of Variance for Average Length of PMGSY Roads

Length	*Sum of Squares*	*df*	*Mean Square*	*F*	*Sig.*
Between Groups	912.74	7	130.39	43.41	0.00
Within Groups	219.29	73	3.00	—	—
Total	**1132.04**	**80**	—	—	—

Source: Computed from www.pmgsy.nic.in

Second Hypothesis

In terms of cost per km at different States, we find from Table 19.6 that the calculated *F* value is 7.59, which is statistically significant at 1 per cent level. Thus, our Null Hypothesis is rejected and the alternative hypotheses may be accepted. In other words, we say that per km cost of new pavements for PMGSY activities varies significantly between the states. The variation in the cost of roads is probably due to the nature of roads and the cost of materials. It is likely that in Mizoram and Nagaland, the input costs of roads are less due to greater use of stones, while in States like Tripura and Assam, PMGSY roads are made of brick and also involves a lot of manual labour/input for land development. However, for any other reasons for variation a field level study can only help.

Table 19.6: Analysis of Variance for per km Cost of PMGSY Roads

Length	*Sum of Squares*	*df*	*Mean Square*	*F*	*Sig.*
Between Groups	10257.67	7	1465.38	7.59	0.00
Within Groups	14092.17	73	193.04		
Total	**24349.84**	**80**	—	—	—

Source: Computed from www.pmgsy.nic.in

Thus, it can be said that though all the NER States have undertaken PMGSY activities, the magnitude or the scale of work is different resulting in variation in average length, sanction cost, and unit cost of construction. Moreover, the rate of progress also varies among the States.

IV. Conclusion

It is evident that the extent of connectivity in the North-Eastern region is much less than the national average and had been much worse prior to the PMGSY. Moreover, in terms of financial parameters, the release of funds for the region has been much less than that of the national average even though the gap between the released and value of work done has been much higher in States belonging to other parts of the country. However, it is true that in terms of physical progress also, most of the NER States lag behind the national level. The lack of uniformity in the cost of pavement construction could have been due to a host of factors like—physiographic, input cost, technique of production. One cannot ignore the possibility of the existence of some localised and unexplained issues also. The cause for deficiency in implementation is beyond the scope of the present study. Nonetheless, the partial achievements do generate a lot of facilities for the benefactors of the connected habitation. It is obvious that a lot of the sanctioned projects in the region are yet to be completed and if it is completed, obviously the benefits accruing from PMGSY would increase manifold. Moreover, the spread of the PMGSY network among the hinterlands of the NER can give a fillip to economic activities within the country as well as the region with the East and

South- East Asian countries. Therefore, the government should take special initiative to ensure the proper and timely release of funds so that the targeted goal can be achieved at the right earnest as it will be a concrete step in bringing about urban-rural integration and finally for national integration.

REFERENCES

Althaf, S. (2010). *Socio-Economic Impact Evaluation of Pradhan Mantri Gram Sadak Yojana The "Clarion" call for a good tomorrow for Rural Madhya Pradesh.* http://96.0.26.98/attachments/article/52/PMGSY%20MP%20Althaf%20IIT%20Madras.pdf (accessed on 29 September 2011)

APERP (1997). *Rural Transport Survey 1997—Andhra Pradesh Economic Restructuring Project*, World Bank, Washington D.C.

Bhattacharjee, Rajarishi (2010). *An Exploratory Study on the Pradhan Mantri Gram Sadak Yojana in Tripura.* Dissertation submitted in the Department of Economics, Tripura University.

Binswanger, Hans P. Shahidur R. Khandker and Mark R. Rosenzweig (1993). *How Infrastructure and Financial Institutions affect Agricultural Output and Investment in India.* http://www-wds.worldbank.org/servlet/WDSContentServer/WDSP/IB/1989/03/01/000009265_3960927171152/Rendered/PDF/multi_page.pdf (accessed on 12 August 2011)

Fan, Shenggen; Peter B.R. Hazell; and Sukhdeo Thorat (1999). 'Linkages between Government Spending, Growth, and Poverty in Rural India,' Research reports 110, International Food Policy Research Institute (IFPRI), Washington DC http://ageconsearch.umn.edu/bitstream/37898/2/rr110.pdf (accessed on 22 August 2011)

Fan, Shenggen; B.R. Peter Hazell and T. Haque (2000). *Targeting Public Investments by Agro-Economic Zone to Achieve Growth and Poverty Alleviation in Rural India.* Food Policy, 25(4): 411-428 http://202.114.32.103/ctdb/UserFile/Inspect/2011061204020771.pdf (accessed on 20 August, 2011)

Mohapatra and Chandrasekhar (2007). '*Rural Roads*', '*India Infrastructure Report.*' http://www.iitk.ac.in/3inetwork/html/reports/IIR2007/05-Rural%20Roads.pdf (accessed on 20 August 2011)

MoRD (2005). *Rural Roads Development Plan: Vision—2025* (Draft), Ministry of Rural Development, Government of India, New Delhi.

MoRD (2004). *Impact Assessment of Pradhan Mantri Gram Sadak Yojana-PMGSY.* Ministry of Rural Development, 2004 at http://pmgsy.nic.in/downloads/ImpAsses-Eng.pdf (accessed on 23 August 2011)

Narayan; Deepa Raj Patel; K. Shafft; A. Rademacher and S. Koch-Schulte (2000).

Voices of the Poor. Crying Out for Change, The World Bank, Oxford University Press.

Planning Commission (2008). *Summary of A Quick Concurrent Evaluation of PMGSY*. http://planningcommission.nic.in/reports/peoreport/peoevalu/peo_pmgsy.pdf (accessed on 11 October 2011)

Sarkar, A. (2007). *Impact of PMGSY Roads on the Traffic Safety of School Going Children in Rural Areas*. http://www4.worldbank.org/afr/ ssatp/Resources/ConferenceWorkshopMaterials/RoadSafetyConf2007/DayTwo/IFRTD/ifrtd-IndiaQuantitative Accident Exposure.pdf (accessed on 12 August 2011)

www.pmgsy.nic.in

20

Credit for Agriculture Sector in Mizoram: A Study of Mizoram Rural Bank

C. Vanlalkulhpuia and *Elangbam Nixon Singh*

Introduction

Agriculture sector, world over, has experienced a phenomenal growth since the mid-twentieth century. Since the mid 1960s, a veritable revolution took place in India with the traditional agricultural practices gradually being replaced by modern technology and farm practices. The new technology was tried in 1960-61 as pilot project in seven districts and was called Intensive Agricultural District Programme (IADP). The seven districts were: Thanjavur (Tamil Nadu), West Godavari (Andhra Pradesh), Shahabad (Bihar), Raipur (Madhya Pradesh), Aligarh (Uttar Pradesh), Ludhiana (Punjab) and Pali (Rajasthan). Later High Yielding Variety Programme (HYVP) was added and was extended to cover the entire country. This strategy was popularly known as 'Green Revolution' (Mohanty, 2010: 5).

The growth, driven by the green revolution technology, has made a significant dent on aggregate supply of foodgrain, ensuring food security to the growing population. The next stage of agricultural growth, however, faces serious challenges in terms of sustainability. Whereas the main problem faced by the developing countries pertaining to sustainability of resource use is the challenges that have been the overuse of chemical input in agriculture by the developed countries/economies during the green revolution phase, to sustainable farming in different parts of the world

(Jeyakumar, 2011: 26). In the post-green revolution period, agricultural production has increased four times, from 51 million tonnes in 1950-51 to 211 million tonnes in 2001-02 whereas, the fertilizer consumption has increased 250 times from 69,000 tonnes during 1950-51 to 17.4 million tonnes in 2001-02 (Singh, 2009: 3).

Indian agriculture, in spite of its declining share in the total GDP, has remained the backbone of the country's economy. The contour of Indian agriculture started in the mid 1960s with the introduction of high yielding varieties (HYV) and the growing emphasis on the development of agro-infrastructure like irrigation, input supply, storage marketing and distribution of foodgrains. The revolution, however, was biased toward irrigated regions and benefits from this were not shared equally amongst all stakeholders across the country. Notwithstanding India's journey of economic reforms since 1991 lack of availability of quality inputs coupled with less vibrant and deficient institutional reforms have continued to plague the Indian agriculture (Tripathy, 2011: 3). Agriculture in India has a significant history. Today, India ranks second in the world in farm output. Agriculture and allied sectors like forestry and fisheries accounted for 16.6 per cent of the GDP in 2009, about 50 per cent of the total workforce. The economic contribution of agriculture to India's GDP is steadily declining with the country's broad-based economic growth. Still, agriculture is demographically the broadest economic sector and plays a significant role in the overall socio-economic fabric of India. In Indian economy, rural sector plays a very important role and also affects directly or indirectly almost all the economic activities through their agricultural outputs. The credit is a basic input for any development programme especially to agricultural sector. This is particularly true for agricultural development, whose goal is to improve the standards of living as well as to increase agricultural productivity. Finance is an essential requirement for almost every activity. If required finance is not available out of one's own income then one needs credit (Sivachithappa and Thammaiya, 2010: 2-3).

Mizoram lags behind economically within India with little development due to its difficult terrain and lack of markets and raw materials. Cottage and other small-scale industries play an important role in the economy. Forest produces are being encouraged and the Ninth Five Year Plan (1997-2002) gave priority to "agro-based industries." Around 70 per cent of the population is engaged in agriculture. The small and marginal farmers in Mizoram find it difficult to make investment on modern inputs like high yielding varieties of seeds, chemical fertilizers, purchase of raw materials, etc., as they do not have sufficient funds of their own for investment purpose. Hence, Mizoram Rural Bank, the only regional rural bank in the State, plays an important role in covering all the districts of the State.

The agro-climatic conditions of Mizoram having both temperate and semi-tropical climates with tropic and temperate zones, is conducive to a wide variety of crops. Mizoram has well-distributed rainfall of 1900 mm to 3000 mm (75 to 118 inches) spread over eight to ten months in the year and agriculture is the mainstay of the people. More than 70 per cent of the total population is engaged in some form of agriculture. The age-old practice of *jhum* cultivation is conducted by most people living in rural areas. Recently, Godrej Agrovet Limited has entered into a new venture wherein Oil Palm and Jatropha cultivation, for bio-fuels is being promoted. A low calorie sugar substitute, *Stevia rebaudiana*, known as 'sweet leaf', has also recently been grown to improve economic condition and agricultural diversity.

Literature Review

Garg, *et al.* (1956), from their study on agriculture financing by Regional Rural Banks (RRBs) concluded that small and marginal farmers are much in need of financial assistance. The analysis of the purpose-wise advances revealed that there was an increasing demand for term-loans, particularly for the development of irrigation, dairying, and poultry. Ravindran (1986), analysed the problem of agricultural credit and recovery of North Malabar Grameen Bank (NMGB) in Kerala. It was found that the quantum of financial assistance for agricultural and allied activities had steadily increased over the year. It also revealed that the bank was lacking ample interest in the upliftment of Scheduled Castes and Scheduled Tribes and the bank finance has reduced the dependence on moneylenders by the sample borrowers. But on the recovery front, the bank provides a dismal picture.

Ghosh (2006) in her study, focused programme for making the RRBs more viable and more able to concentrate on their social and developmental functions and mentioned that the number of rural branches should be increased rather than reduced; they should be encouraged to develop more sophisticated methods of credit delivery to meet the changing needs of farming; and most of all, there should be greater coordination between district planning authorities, Panchayati Raj institutions and the banks operating in rural areas. Only then will the RRBs fulfil the promise that is so essential for rural development.

Roy (2007) in his case study observed that the RRBs have experienced high rate of growth of deposits on their savings bank accounts. But, there still seems to be further scope of mobilisation of savings with regard to the agricultural working population of the area of operation of RRBs. He suggested that the loan-able funds should be more liberally augmented by borrowings from the Reserve Bank of India, sponsoring banks, National Bank for Agriculture and Rural Development (NABARD) to stimulate growth of savings bank deposits of the RRBs as well as their loaning operations. He also suggested that strong monitoring and supervision of the activities of the recipients of credit should be made since the most problem of the RRBs is poor recovery of loans.

Objective and Methodology of the Study

Here there is an attempt to analyse the role of Mizoram Rural Bank (MRB) on agricultural development in the State of Mizoram. It also comes up with the problems faced by MRB in financing for agricultural development and concludes with some suggestions for the betterment of the role played by MRB in agricultural development. This chapter has the following specific objectives:

1. To highlight and examine the agricultural scenario of Mizoram;
2. To study the working and performance of MRB on agricultural development; and
3. To highlight the problems and give suitable suggestions to improve the functioning of MRB to develop agricultural sector in the State.

This chapter is based on secondary data which were collected and analysed from various reports and publications of the Department of Agriculture and Department of Economic and Statistics of the Government of Mizoram, scholarly literatures and media reports.

Agricultural Development in Mizoram

Before 1947, the agricultural system of India was traditional and stagnant in different respects. It was characterised by feudal land relations, primitive technology and the resultant law productivity per hectare. During the pre-independent period, a large proportion of population (about three-fourth) depended on agriculture which was a subsistence occupation. Agricultural activities were mainly devoted to food crops like paddy, wheat and millets. Most of the food produced in the villages was consumed by the village population itself. The raw materials produced fed the handicraft. Over the vast areas in the country has contributed to be traditional in character, resulting in low yields, limited income and lack of capacity to invest as compared to the levels in developed countries, some notable developments have occurred over the year since independence (Prasad, 2009: 3-4).

The National Development Council has set the goal of 4 per cent growth in the Eleventh Plan by reorienting strategies of agricultural development towards meeting the needs of farmers and appropriate use of natural resources. The State governments are motivated to concentrate on finding and evolving suitable strategies with innovative technologies and projects for rejuvenation of agriculture in the country. The need for integrated local area plans, based on specific endowments and needs of each area, was stressed from the beginning of planned development. However, despite several reports and studies, only sporadic efforts and isolated cases of such planning could be located. It has, therefore, been decided by the Government of India that the 'District Plan Process' should be an integral part of the process of preparation of the State. The Government of India introduced new additional central assistance scheme to incentivize States to draw up plans for their agriculture sector more comprehensively, taking agro-climatic conditions, natural resource issues and technology into account, and integrating livestock, poultry and fisheries more fully.

Specifically, agriculture occupies a very important place in the economy of Mizoram. As per Economic Classification of Workers 2001 Census, about 60 per cent of the total workers are engaged in agricultural and allied sector. The State is deficient in foodgrain production; the production of rice is 46,000 MT against the requirement of 1,80,000 MT a year which could meet only 20 per cent of the requirement of the State (NEDFi Databank, 2011).

Cropped Area, Production and Productivity

Mizoram has a total geographical area of 21,08,700 hectares with forests covering about 75 per cent of the total area. The gross cropped area of the State is 1,33,226 hectares which is only 6.31 per cent of the total area. Due to hilly terrain, potential area for Wet Rice Cultivation (WRC) is very limited. It is estimated that there are 74,644 hectare of area having a slope of 0-25 per cent out of this; only 11,198 hectares are currently under cultivation, and the rémaining 85 per cent of land needs to be exploited for increased production and productivity (NEDFi Databank, 2011).

The area under *jhum* cultivation has decreased from 44,947 hectares at the beginning of Eleventh Plan to 28,735 hectares during 2010-20 11. The reduction in *jhum* cultivation area is mainly due to the implementation of Watershed Development Programme for Shifting Cultivation Areas and Oil Palm Development Programme and Sugarcane Cultivation Programme. On the other hand, marginal increase in WRC area has been recorded from 9,446 hectares at the beginning of Eleventh Plan to 11,937 hectares till date. The productivity of rice under WRC has risen to 1.7 MT per hectare from the level of 1.5 MT per hectare at the beginning of Eleventh Five Year Plan. Increase in productivity per hectare may be attributed to the increase in availability of Farm Power through the heavy subsidy of Power Tillers and Tractors (NEDFi databank, 2011).

From the Table 20.1, we can observed that the area and production and yiėld of major agricultural crops during the period 2007 to 2010. Paddy is the main and more productive in the State till date. The area covered for cultivating paddy during 2007 is highest as compared with the other crops like maize, pulse, etc., and also paddy productions per area in hectare are very high as compared with the other crops. In 2007-08, altogether 54,541 ha of areas were cultivated and out of it, 15,688 MT of paddy was produced but it gradually decreases due to decreased in area of cultivated land. In the year 2009-10, only 47,205 ha was cultivated and produced only 66,132 MT. The production of maize gets a good picture, even though the total production per ha, and yield in MT per ha is not higher than paddy produced. The production per ha and yield is increasing from the year 2007-08 to 2009-10. Potato is one of the lowest crops produced in the State till the year 2010.

Economic Activities

The target for distribution of quality seeds and high yielding varieties of rice, maize, oilseeds and pulses has been achieved coupled with the fund received under Macro Management of Agriculture (**centrally sponsored schemes**). Under Oil Seed Sector, cultivation of oil palm has been taken up with a target area of 16,566 ha during the Eleventh Plan Period. However,

Table 20.1: Area and Production and Yield of Major Agricultural Crops

Sl. No	Name of Crop	2007-08			2008-09			2009-10		
		Area in Ha	*Production MT*	*Yield (MT/Ha)*	*Area in Ha*	*Production MT*	*Yield (MT/Ha)*	*Area in Ha*	*Production MT*	*Yield (MT/Ha)*
	1	2	3	4	5	6	7	8	9	10
1.	Paddy	54541	15688	0.29	51990	68917	1.32	47204	66132	1.40
	(a) Kharif	54393	15501	0.28	51859	68637	1.32	47085	65894	1.40
	(b) Rabi	148	187	1.26	131	280	2.13	119	238	2.00
2.	Maize	7328	729	0.09	9558	9318	0.97	8551	11510	1.35
3.	Pulses	5048	2632	0.52	3931	3646	0.93	3920	6479	1.65
4.	Oilseeds	8485	748	0.08	3275	2514	0.76	2741	2988	1.09
5.	Sugarcane	883	828	0.93	1342	13696	10.20	1434	12368	6.82
6.	Potato	330	1158	3.51	269	1569	5.83	285	2235	7.80

Source: Statistical Handbook of Mizoram, 2007-2010.

Table 20.2: Gross State Domestic Product (GSDP) at Factor Cost by Industry of Origin in Mizoram, [(At Constant 2004-05 Prices) (2004-2005 to 2009-2010)]

(*in Lakh*)

Industry	2004-05		2005-2006		2006-07		2007-08		2008-09		2009-10	
	GSDP	%share to GSDP	GSDP	%share to GSDP	GSDP	%share to GSDP	GSDP	%share to GSDP	GSDP	%share to GSDP	GSDP	%share to GSD
						Agriculture & Allied Sector						
Agriculture	36138	13.47	37848	12.74	40782	12.4	52208	13.68	74001	15.88	91116	16.17
Forestry & logging	23867	8.9	23866	8.03	24608	7.48	25800	6.76	26923	5.78	28799	5.11
Fishing	3020	1.13	3073	1.03	3175	0.97	2101	0.55	2145	0.46	268	5.11
Total	**63025**	**23.5**	**64787**	**21.8**	**68565**	**20.85**	**80109**	**20.99**	**103069**	**22.12**	**120183**	**26.39**

Source: Statistical Handbook of Mizoram (2010).

8,261 hectares is under cultivation which account for 50 per cent achievement of the target. Due to the gregarious flowering of bamboo coupled with constraint of funds for state matching share, desired level of target may not be achieved. For carrying out the scheme of 'Farm Mechanization', a total of 413 numbers of Power Tillers, 55 numbers of Tractors, about 50 numbers of Mini Power Tillers, and about 1,000 numbers of Water Pump sets were distributed to farmers at subsidized rate.

Table 20.2 clearly shows that the Gross State Domestic Product at factor cost by industry of origin in the State under agricultural and allied sector was improved from 2004 at Rs. 63,025 lakhs to Rs. 1,20,183 in the year 2010. Among the three sectors, agriculture contributed to the highest rate of GSDP in comparison to forestry, logging and fishing.

Table 20.3: Percentage Share to GSDP at Factor Cost by Industry of Origin in Mizoram

Sectors	*2004-05*	*2005-06*	*2006-07*	*2007-08*	*2008-09*	*2009-10*
	%share to GSDP	*%share to GSDP*	*%share to GSDP*	*%share to GSDP*	*%share to GSDP*	*%share to GSDP*
Agriculture & Allied Sector	23.5	21.8	20.85	20.99	22.12	26.39
Industry	16.6	20.14	19.52	20.01	19.46	19.71
Service Sector	59.9	57.74	59.4	58.46	57.49	57.59

Source: Statistical Handbook of Mizoram (2010).

Further, Table 20.3 clearly shows that, the percentage share to gross domestic product at factor cost by industry of origin in Mizoram like agriculture and allied sector, industry and service sector are not much good in picture. But only agriculture and industry have an increasing trend during the period of 2004-2010. The percentage share to GSDP by agriculture and allied sectors increases from 23.5 per cent in the year 2004-05 to 26.39 per cent in 2009-2010, and also 16.6 per cent contributed by industrial sector during 2004-05, it is also increased to 19.71 per cent in 2009-2010, while the percentage share to GSDP of service sector decreases form 59.9 per cent in 2004-05 to 57.59 per cent in 2009-10.

Working and Performance of MRB on Agricultural Development

All India Rural Credit Committee (1969) pointed out that over large parts of the country the small farmers have been handicapped in having access to the co-operative credit both for current inputs and investment. Therefore, a need arose for the establishment of institutional agencies. This led to the first spell of nationalization of the banks with greater expectations. Though they did add to the institutions structure and simultaneously created some problems too.

The first RRB in Mizoram was set up in September 1983 under the Regional Rural Bank Act 1975. It is perhaps the only RRB in the country to be spread out in all the districts and Blocks of the State. It covers eight districts and 25 Rural Development Blocks including one urban and 11 semi-urban centre. It is the second largest bank in the State next to the State Bank of India which is also the sponsoring small credit to the small and marginal farmers. It has a market share of 8.55 per cent in deposits and 17.64 per cent in advances (MRB Annual Reports 2000-10). The paid-up share capital of Rs 602.76 lakhs is contributed by all the share holders, Government of India, Government of Mizoram and State Bank of India was in the ratio of 50 : 35 : 15. In addition to this, an additional equity share capital of Rs. 301.06 lakhs towards equity support for the purpose of cleansing of the balance sheet has been received from the shareholders.

Table 20.4: Total Loans and Advances Distribution to Priority Sectors (2000-2010

(*Rs. in Lakhs*)

No. of Years	Agriculture	Industries	Services
2000-01	71.74	45.37	357.22
2001-02	93.64	54.19	706.59
2002-03	76.17	40.81	530.49
2003-04	122.49	81.28	1533.14
2004-05	869..89	206.83	1912.83
2005-06	1356..80	398.56	255.26
2006-07	1208.30	969.61	1075.45
2007-08	1861.78	1638.62	591.90
2008-09	2318.22	424.59	3279.90
2009-10	2361.58	601.44	4585.80
Total	**10340.61**	**4461.30**	**14828.58**

Source: MRB Annual Report 2000-10.

Table 20.4 tries to give a clear picture of MRB in terms of loans and advances given to priority sector in the State. It can be observed that total loans and advances disbursed by MRB to different sectors like agriculture up to Rs. 10340.61 lakhs, industries up to Rs. 4461.30 lakhs and services up to Rs. 14828.58 lakhs in the last ten years (2000-2010). The increases of loans and advances from 2008-2009 in agricultural sector and services are Rs. 43.36 lakhs and Rs. 1305.90 lakhs. From this table we can assume that total loans and advances issued by the MRB gradually increases year by year.

Problems with Agricultural Finance by MRB

1. Customers themselves are a big problem because, some of them are illiterate and they do not know how to save their money.
2. Lack of trained staffs in the rural branches. Some of the rural branches staff never give attention to their customers and also cannot tell them the rules and regulations about the scheme.
3. Lack of competition among financial institutions: MRB is the bank that covers all the districts and almost all the rural areas of Mizoram with 61 branches, 31 branches are opened in rural areas while other commercial banks does not open their branches and hence does not have competitor in the rural areas. Since, MRB cannot improve their performance in different way.
4. MRB is found to be giving a higher priority to services sector, due to long waiting period of loan, people in rural areas face the problem for taking loan for their agricultural need. Since rural people are poor, they do not have enough fund for their day-to-day requirements, they are dependent on financial institutions like MRB the bank only reaching rural areas in the State. In this situation, people in rural areas faced a problem that they do not receive loans while they need more.
5. Utilization of loan for non-agriculture purpose is one of the main causes of repayment problem of loan. Other debts like, family expenditure and children education were the important non-agricultural purposes for which the loans were diverted.
6. The above mentioned three purposes are the pressing needs which require immediate attention and hence this might be possible reason for the diversion of bank loans from the right purpose to these non-agricultural purposes.

Conclusion and Suggestions

Thus, during these initial years, MRB was mainly engaged in building up the necessary expertise for handling problems relating to agricultural credit and the cooperative movement. In its statutory report the bank endeavoured to State, in broad terms, the salient features of agricultural finance in India and the scope of action which the bank could undertake to begin with. The bank made efforts towards an enlarged flow of agricultural credit through the agency of the moneylender and to bring the indigenous banker within the ambit of organised banking, though these efforts met with little success. Modest as these activities of the bank were in the sphere of agricultural credit, they prepared the ground for a more active role in later years. In Mizoram, MRB plays an important role in developing and granting loan to agricultural sectors as compared with the other commercial banks. But there is more need to improvement for MRB to increase their performance for the agricultural development in Mizoram.

So far as financing agricultural sector by the MRB is concerned, the participation taken by MRB is still quite commendable.[1] However, there exists many shortcomings. Banks have to go a long way to be the leader in rural financial sector by ensuring flow of adequate financial resources to the agricultural sector. To conclude:

- More credit should be provided to agricultural sectors. If MRB provide more credit to the agricultural sectors, the availability of loan for agricultural sector increases and the people who are engaged in this sector can take more loans from the bank. This will effect agricultural development.
- MRB should mobilize new and young trained people to attain credit facilities.
- MRB should give more grant loans and advances to agricultural sectors. As of now MRB disburses more credit to service sector due to the certainty of repayment of loan. This implies that people engage in the agricultural sector have been neglected even though they are much more in need of financial assistance for their sustenance.
- New and operative areas of operation must be developed. As of now it seems that MRB opens more branches in many areas without proper functioning due to shortage of trained staffs. Most of the branches in rural areas exist only in name.
- More awareness to the beneficiaries should be organized. Since the beneficiaries of MRB in rural areas spend their loan to non-agricultural sectors like family expenditure, etc. If the bank

officials provide more information and awareness it will reduce the problem faced in repayment of loan.

NOTE

1. Vanlalkulhpuia, C. & Singh, Nixon. (2011) 'Mizoram Rural Bank (MRB) and Financial Inclusion: An Analysis'. Paper presented at the National Conference on "Financial Inclusion: Issues and Challenges" Organized by Department of Economic, Mizoram University, Aizawl (22-23 November).

REFERENCES

Garg, J.S.; Singh, G.N. and R.N. Tripathi (1956). An Analysis of Agricultural Financing by Regional Rural Banks in Moradabad District of Uttar Pradesh'. *Journal of Agricultural Economics*, 23(24): 31-36.

Ghosh, Jayati (2006). Saving the Regional Rural Banks. *Frontline*, 23(03):11-24.

Government of Mizoram, *Statistical Handbook of Mizoram* (2006-2010), Aizawl.

Jeyakumar, S. (2011). Sustainable Agriculture in India: An Overview. *Kurukshetra: A Journal on Rural Development* 51(9):26-30.

Mizoram Rural Bank (2000-2010) Annual Reports.

Mohanty, B.K. (2010). *Agriculture Growth: It's Time for Gene Revolution.* Kurukshetra: A Journal on Rural Development 58(9):3-7, July.

NEDFi Databank (2011). http://databank.nedfi.com/content/north-east-india (accessed on 15 April, 2012).

Prasad, Chandra Shekhar (2009). *Agriculture and Rural Development in India since 1947.* New Delhi: New Century Publications: 3-4.

Ravindran (1986). *Agricultural Credit and Recovery Problem* (A Study with Special Reference to North Malabar Grameen Bank Kerala'. University of Madras: Unpublished M. Phil. Dissertation.

Roy, B.S. (2007) *Rural Banking and Poverty Alleviation*, Delhi: Abhijeet Publications, 2/46 Tukhmeerpur Extension.

Sivachithappa, K. and T.D. Thammaiya (2010). *Banking in Rural Areas and Agricultural Development: A Regional Perspective.* New Delhi: Adhyayan Publishers & Distributors.

Singh, Sukhjinder (2009). Boosting Agriculture Productivity. *Kurukshetra: A Journal on Rural Development* 57(7):3-5, May.

Tripathy, K.K. (2011). Indian Agricultural Growth and Stagnation: A Review. *Kurukshetra: A Journal on Rural Development*, 60(2), December.

21

Ecotourism Development in a Hilly State: A Study of Arunachal Pradesh

Maila Lama

Introduction

Tourism is one of the world's largest industries and for many developing countries it has become a prime source of foreign exchange earnings (Wunder, 1999). Of which, ecotourism is the fastest growing segment of the industry (Whelan, 1991). An estimate made by the World Tourism Organization (WTO) shows that the global spending on ecotourism increased by 20 per cent per year, about five times the average rate of growth in tourism industry as a whole (Vijayakumar, 2005). This is because people all over the world are turning to nature for peace, happiness and enjoyment. The term ecotourism is used to describe nature based travel to undisturbed areas having educative value. A variety of definition exists for the term ecotourism. However, the earliest and the most widely used definition of ecotourism was given by Hector Ceballos-Lascurain in 1983 who defined it as, "Tourism that involves travelling to relatively undisturbed or uncontaminated natural areas with the specific objective of studying, admiring and enjoying the scenery and its wild plants and animals as well as any existing cultural manifestations (both past and present) found in these areas".

Ecotourism has emerged as an attractive alternative to promote development mainly because of its potential to conserve environment and produce economic benefits. Ecotourism can contribute to safeguard biodiversity and ecosystem functions in developing countries (Gossling, 1999). It is appealing because it can significantly contribute to the conservation of biodiversity and the sustainable use of natural resources. Ecotourism has a generally low negative impact on the environment compared to other productive sectors such as agriculture, cattle ranching and mining as it is based on the use of natural resources for non-consumptive purposes. It is regarded as a potential means to promote conservation of biological resources and an attractive sustainable development alternative (Hvenegaard, 1994). An important aspect of ecotourism is that local residents at the sites should receive substantial economic benefits which serve both to raise local living standards and as an enhanced incentives for nature conservation (Wunder, 1999).

Arunachal Pradesh, the easternmost State of India, is situated in the eastern Himalayas between latitude 26° 28′N and 29° 33′N and longitude 91° 31′E and 97° 30′E. It is a hilly State spread over 83,743 sq km. The State, due to its geographical location, is highly rich in biodiversity and forest resources. The State has about 80.50 per cent of its total geographical area under forest cover which is one of the highest among the States of India (State of Forest Reports, 2011). In its vast and varied forests it houses diverse species of flora and fauna, some of which are rare and endangered. The State is highly rich in biodiversity and it falls under Indo-Burma biodiversity "hotspot" which is one of the mega-diversity hotspots in the world (Chatterjee, *et al.,* 2006). The State accounts for 20 per cent species of country's fauna. There are two national parks, eight wild life sanctuaries, orchid sanctuary in the State which are home of various species of plants, animals and orchids. At the same time, the State is one of the most picturesque and beautiful places on the earth with the presence of snow capped mountain peaks, passes, lakes, waterfalls, river valleys. It shows that the State has a tremendous potential for development of ecotourism.

However, the State's forest resources and rich biodiversity are under severe threat due to growing population and adoption of unsustainable development practices. The State has been receiving increasing number of illegal migrant population who settle down in the fringes of forest areas and are reported to be involved in illegal felling of trees. Shifting cultivation which is widely practised by the tribes of the State in hilly slopes has also resulted in huge losses of forest cover and biodiversity. At the same time, the recent hydropower development strategy of the State government can have severe environmental consequences. In this background, development of ecotourism appears to be one of the best routes for this State to enhance economic development and conserve its rich biodiversity. Here it is an attempt to explore ecotourism potentials of Arunachal Pradesh and to examine nature of tourist demand. It is based on both primary and secondary sources of data.

Ecotourism Potential

Ecotourism is depended on natural environments (both living and non-living) and with any indigenous cultures closely connected to such environments (Tisdell, 1998). Arunachal Pradesh, the land of dawn-lit mountains, is known for its pristine natural beauty. Blessed with abundant natural as well as cultural resources, it is an excellent ecotourism destination. The State's richness in natural and cultural resources for promotion of ecotourism is discussed as below:

Natural Beauty

Arunachal Pradesh is well known for its scenic natural beauty. Its landscape is quite fascinating due to uneven topography, dense forest, flora and fauna, river valley, snow covered peaks, passes, lakes, waterfalls. Snowfall which occurs during December and January in high altitude tourist spots like Bomdila, Tawang and Mechuka are an added attraction for the tourists. There are numerous mountain peaks. The most important peaks are Kangte in West Kameng district and Gorichen in Tawang district. The important passes are Bomdila Pass, Sela Pass, and Lumla Pass. The major lakes are Sangester Lake and Sela Lake in Tawang district, Ganga Lake in Itanagar, Mehao Lake and Sally Lake in Lower Dibang valley. The major rivers are Siang, Kameng, Subansiri, Lohit, etc. This makes the State an ideal destination for adventure tourism. Adventure sports like rock climbing; trekking, paragliding, river rafting and boating can be well developed to attract adventure lovers from all over the world.

Forest Resources

Arunachal Pradesh is highly rich in forest resources. In terms of forest covers, it (with forest covers of 67,410 sq km) is ranked second among the States of India. The forest covers in the State account for about 80.50 per cent of its total geographical area which is one of the highest among the States of India (State of Forest Reports, 2011). The important forest species found are tropical, evergreen, semi-evergreen, deciduous, pine, temperate, alpine and grassland. The forest of the State is an important attraction for tourists as it houses diverse species of flora and fauna. Some of the species of plants and animals found are rare and endemic.

Biodiversity

Arunachal Pradesh, due to its location in the Eastern Himalayas, is highly rich in biodiversity. The State falls under Indo-Burma biodiversity "hotspot" which is recognized as one of the mega biodiversity hotspots of the world (Chatterjee *et al.*, 2006). The State houses a number of diverse and rare species of flora and fauna. The State possesses over 5000 species of flowering plants, various species of medicinal plants and more than 545 species of orchids which is perhaps the highest number of species of orchids known from any single State of India. The State is equally rich in fauna. There are about 85 terrestrial mammals, over 650 birds, and a large number of butterflies, insects and reptiles. Out of 16 primates in the world, seven are found in this State. In fact it accounts for about 20 per cent of fauna and around 50 per cent of the species of orchids found in the entire country. Its richness in biodiversity clearly reveals its prospects of developing ecotourism.

Wildlife

The State has a huge potential for wildlife-based tourism. It is a home to animals like, elephant, tiger, leopard, jungle, cat, red pandas, musk deer, mithun, etc. There are two National Parks namely, Namdapha National Park and Mouling National Park and eight wildlife sanctuaries and orchid sanctuary. These parks and sanctuaries are home to a number of diverse species of animals, birds and plants some of which are rare and endangered (Table 21.1). Hence, viewing wildlife can be a satisfying experience for tourists.

Cultural Diversity

Arunachal Pradesh is equally rich in cultural resources. It is a land of cultural diversity. It is inhabited by twenty six major tribes and one hundred and ten sub-tribes. It is regarded as one of the most culturally diverse and multi-lingual tribal areas of the world. Each tribe in the State has their own tradition, culture and local dialects. Different culture, language,

Table 21.1: Wildlife Resources in Arunachal Pradesh

Name of National Park	*District*	*Area (Sq. Km)*	*Major Animals*
Namdapha National Park	Changlang	1985.23	Tiger, Leopard, Snow-Leopard, Clouded Leopard, Hoolock Gibbon, Red Panda, Takin, Musk Deer, rare birds etc.
Mouling National Park	Upper Siang	483.0	Takin, Serow, Goral, Clouded Leopard, Black Bear, Leopard, Red Panda, Pheasants, etc.

Source: Directorate of Tourism, Government of Arunachal Pradesh.

colourful festivals, music and dances of tribal groups are an added attraction for tourists. It can attract researchers from all over the world.

Trend and Growth in Tourist Arrivals

Arunachal Pradesh is in the initial stage of tourism development. Although the State has tremendous potential to attract tourists from various parts of the country as well as from different countries yet the number of tourist arrivals is found to be comparatively less but growing at a faster rate (Figure 21.1).

Table 21.2: Tourist Arrivals in Arunachal Pradesh

Year	*Domestic*	*Foreign*	*Total*
2004	39767 (99.19)	321 (0.81)	40088
2005	50560 (99.38)	313 (0.62)	50873
2006	80137 (99.13)	706 (0.87)	80843
2007	91100 (97.63)	2212 (2.37)	93312
2008	149292 (98.02)	3020 (1.98)	152312
2009	195147 (98.02)	3945 (1.98)	199092
2010	227857 (98.53)	3395 (1.47)	231252

Source: Directorate of Tourism, Government of Arunachal Pradesh.

Note: Figures in the bracket indicate percentage of total tourist.

Table 21.2 shows that the number of tourist arrivals in Arunachal Pradesh from 2004 onwards. It is observed that the number of tourist arrivals has increased rapidly after 2004. The number of tourist arrivals increased from 40,088 to 93,312 in 2007. It increased substantially to 1,99,092 in 2009 and further increased to 2,31,252 in 2010 marking 16.15 per cent growth over the previous year (Table 21.2). It is important to note that domestic tourists constitute a very large proportion of total tourist arrivals in the State. The share of foreign tourists in the total tourist arrivals has been very less. It was 0.81 per cent in 2004 which significantly increased to 2.37 per cent in 2007. But it came down to 1.47 per cent in 2010. In absolute term, number of foreign tourist arrivals in the state has increased from 321 in 2004 to 3,945 in 2009. In 2010 foreign tourist arrival in the State had declined to 3,395.

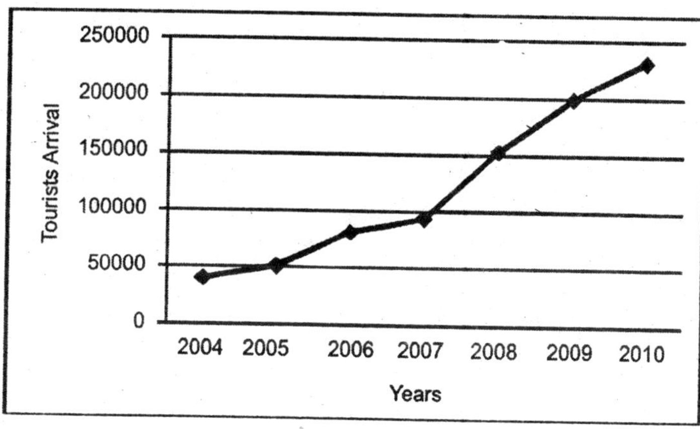

Fig. 21.1: Tourists Arrival in Arunachal Pradesh during 2004 to 2010.

Relatively small proportion of foreign tourists arrivals in the State can be attributed to its remote location, inaccessibility and entry formality. Foreign tourists are required to obtain Protected Area Permit (PAP) to visit the State. The procedure for obtaining PAP is reported to be complex and time consuming. This act as a disincentive for potential foreign tourists to visit the State (Mitra, 1998).

Arunachal Pradesh, despite having tremendous potential for ecotourism development accounts for relatively small share in tourist arrivals of the North-East region of India. However, it is observed that its share has been improving over the years. The State accounted for only 2.02 per cent of the total domestic tourist arrivals in the North-East region.

Its share improved significantly to 3.42 per cent in 2009 and further improved to 3.70 per cent in 2010. In case of foreign tourists arrivals in the region, the share of the State significantly increased from just 1.83 per cent in 2006 to 6.35 per cent in 2008 (Indian Tourism Statistics, 2010). The improvement in share of the State in tourist arrivals in the region is due to high growth of tourist arrivals in the State during the period 2006 to 2010. During this period domestic tourist arrivals in the State grew at an annual average growth rate of 46.08 per cent followed by Sikkim which recorded 34.83 per cent annual average growth rate. In terms of share in total domestic tourist arrivals in the region in 2010, Arunachal Pradesh is ranked fifth among the eight States of the region. Assam with its share of 65.59 per cent is ranked first followed by Sikkim (11.35%).

Nature of Tourist Demand and Related Issues

An attempt has been made to examine the nature of tourist demand in the State and related issues as the number of tourist arrivals has been growing rapidly. The analysis of the survey data revealed that most of the tourists came to enjoy natural beauty. It was found that 67.31 per cent of the surveyed tourists came to enjoy natural beauty followed by people who wanted to know their culture (19.09%). As the State has a huge potential for adventure tourist activities such as trekking, river rafting, boating, angling, paragliding it was considered important to know tourists' willingness to participate in adventure activities. It was found that a high percentage of surveyed tourists were interested to participate in adventure activities. The survey data showed that 56.60 per cent of the surveyed domestic tourists and 61.30 per cent of the surveyed foreign tourists expressed their willingness to participate in adventure activities. Hence, it calls for developing facilities for adventure tourism activities.

An attempt was also made to examine the types of accommodation availed by the surveyed tourists in the State. It was found that majority of the surveyed tourists (83.82%) stayed in hotels followed by tourist lodge (10.36%). As far as the tourists' satisfaction is concerned it was found that 43.90 per cent of the surveyed domestic tourists were satisfied with accommodation facilities. However, a good percentage of surveyed foreign tourists (35.50%) opined for the improvement of accommodation facilities. As far as quality of food is concerned a good percentage of surveyed domestic tourists (29.90%) were of the opinion that it is needed to be improved.

The principle mode of transport to visit tourist spots is roadways. However, most of the surveyed tourists were not at all satisfied with condition of roads and transport facilities and suggested for its improvement. The analysis of data showed that 72.70 per cent of the surveyed domestic tourists and 42 per cent of the surveyed foreign tourists suggested for improving transport and road condition. In fact, a high percentage of surveyed tourists opined that the first and the foremost requirement were to improve transport facilities and road condition for development of tourism in the State.

Despite poor road condition and absence of better means of transport facilities, a very high percentage of the surveyed tourists (95.15%) were willing to visit the State again. However, they suggested for improving the condition of roads and means of transportation. At the same time a very high percentage of the surveyed domestic tourists (96.40%) and foreign tourists (93.50%) stated that they would advice their friends and relatives to visit tourist spots in the study area. These facts are a clear manifestation of ecotourism potential of the State.

Policy Implications

On the basis of the above discussion and findings, the following suggestions have been extended for development of ecotourism in Arunachal Pradesh:

- Ecotourism is based on natural environment. It may cause damage to nature. Hence, there is a need to formulate proper guidelines for tour operators, hotels and resorts, transport operators and architectural guidelines for effective implementation of the policy and to conserve natural environment.
- The State government must formulate guidelines for each destination and also estimate carrying capacity of each destination so that with the growth of tourists, ecology of the destination does not suffer and damages to environment are avoided.
- Eco-tourists are nature lovers and their desire is to have a close association with nature. Hence, it is also important to build accommodation facilities using locally available resources in such a location so as to provide unique experience to the tourists. The participation of local people should be encouraged so that they receive the benefit of ecotourism. One of the best ways is to

22

Public Funded Programmes for Inclusive Agricultural Growth in Mizoram: A Study of NLUP

R.K.P.G. Singha

Introduction

Development has become one of the burning topics in academic research, public policy meeting, seminars, and in many other forums at the present context. India is completing the Eleventh Plan period (2007-2012) with a slow record of economic growth. After a lacklustre performance in the Ninth Plan Period (1997-98 to 2001-02) with a Gross Domestic Product (GDP) growth at only 5.5 per cent per annum, the economy got accelerated in the Tenth Plan period (2002-03 to 2006-07) to record an average growth of 7.7 per cent of GDP, the highest in any plan period so far. Notwithstanding this growth, a major weakness in the economy is that growth is not perceived as being sufficiently inclusive for many groups, especially Scheduled Castes (SCs), Scheduled Tribes (STs), and minorities. So, the most pressing challenge before the country today is to eradicate poverty, which continues to assume new dimensions.

Despite India's recent high economic growth rate, around 350 million people are still living on less than one dollar a day. About 72 per cent of India's poor are living in rural areas; primarily depend on agriculture and natural resources for their sustenance. The growth is so far exclusive in nature. Inclusive growth is the need of the hour. Inclusive growth highlights on economic growth which is a necessary and essential condition for poverty reduction. Inclusive growth assumes a long term outlook and is concerned with sustained growth. For long run growth and to sustain, it should be broad-based across the sector. Emphasis of inclusive growth is given on productive employment rather than income redistribution. Therefore, the focus of this study is not only on employment growth but also on productivity growth. The most realistic approach to improving livelihoods for inclusive growth is to mobilize local resources and build capacity of the rural and urban poor.

In Mizoram about 63 per cent of the total crop area is under *jhum* or shifting cultivation. About 90 per cent of farmers still depend on shifting cultivation. Being a hilly State, earning a sustainable livelihood has been difficult for the poor farmers. Government of Mizoram has now implemented the much-awaited *New Land Use Policy* (NLUP), to help the farmers to move away from the traditional shifting cultivation to more sustainable land-based means of livelihood. The objective of NLUP is to switch over from the poor traditional system of livelihood to permanent and sustainable livelihood activities with higher income. The policy is expected to be a new horizon for the poor farmer for inclusive growth in the State. With the inception of the policy, the present study tries to look into the following objectives:

- To study the importance and expected benefits of NLUP in Mizoram for the farmers;
- To examine implementation of NLUP and inclusive growth for farmers/jhumias; and
- To recommend some possible suggestions for successful implementation of NLUP.

Brief Profile of Mizoram

Mizoram is a hilly and undeveloped State, which was originally a district of Assam. It was accorded the status of Union Territory in 1972 and it became the 23rd State of India. Mizoram is situated at the southern corner of the north-eastern region, sandwiched between two countries and three States of India; it lays between 92°15′ and 93°29′ East Longitudes and 21°58′ and 24°35′ North Latitudes. Its length north to south is 277 km and east to west is 121 km, covering an area of 21,087 sq km. It shares a common international boundary of 404 km with Myanmar and 318 km with Bangladesh; besides it shares a common national inter-State boundary with Assam, Tripura and Manipur. It has a total population of 10,91,014 (2011 Census). The decadal growth rate (2001-2011) had been 22.78 per cent. There are more than 1.76 lakh households. Vast majority of the population are Scheduled Tribes. About 63 per cent of the total crop area of Mizoram comes under *jhum* cultivation. *Jhum* cultivation, a major form of livelihood for farming community and it was a viable proposition in the past. But increased population growth, changes in the land-use pattern, resulting in loss of soil fertility, natural forest and shrinkage of *jhum* cycles have rendered *jhum* practices unsustainable leading to the problems of food security and increased poverty. In the absence of viable alternative livelihood option, about 3 lakh work forces are engaged in low productivity practices eking out a subsistence or distress living. Long term impact on economy will be still more disastrous owing to destruction of rain forest of 1.5 lakh acres of land every year, heavy soil erosion and resultant ecological imbalance.

Any developmental initiative in the State needs to address the problems of *jhum* practices on a priority basis and the solution lies in providing viable alternative livelihood opportunities to *jhumia* families. Development process in the context of Mizoram started as late as Seventh Plan, and it did not address the problems of *jhum* practices effectively. Therefore, stagnation in rural economy persists with increasing incidence of poverty and deprivation. The present State government, on assuming office in December 2008 adopted a programme called *New Land Use Policy* (hereafter NLUP) to devise a policy for the *jhumia* families from destructive *jhum* practices and open opportunities for more productive and sustainable livelihood options.

Occupational Structure and Land Use Pattern in Mizoram

Agriculture is the mainstay of the people; more than 70 per cent of the total population is engaged in some form of agriculture. Cultivators and agricultural labourers constitute 60.66 per cent of the total work force and are engaged in the primary sector of the economy (refer to Table 22.1), only 1.5 per cent of the workforce are engaged in small scale household industries (the only industrial sector in the State), which reveals the industrial backwardness of Mizoram's economy. The age-old practice of *jhum* cultivation is carried out annually by a large number of people living in rural areas.

Table 22.1: Occupational Structure of Mizoram (as per 2001 Census)

Category	*Number*	*Percentage*
Total population	888573	100
Number of workers (total workforce)	467159	52.6
Cultivators	256332	54.9
Agricultural labourer	26783	5.7
Household industrial workers	7100	1.5
Other workers	176944	37.9

Source: Directorate of Census Operations, Government of India. Aizawl.

The climatic conditions of the State, its location in the tropic and temperate zones, and its various soil types along with well-distributed rainfall spread over eight to ten months in the year, have all contributed to a wide spectrum of rich and varied flora and fauna in Mizoram. These natural features and resources also offer opportunities for growing a variety of horticultural crops. But due to the geographical disadvantage only

Table 22.2: Land-use Pattern in Mizoram

('000 ha)

	Land-Use	*2006-07*	*2007-08*	*Percentage*
1.	Total Geographical area	2108.700	2108.700	—
2.	Reporting area of land utilization	2108.700	2108.700	100
3.	Not available for cultivation (a+b)	134.040	130.050	6.89
	a) Land put to non-agricultural use	125.420	125.430	—
	(b) Barren and Uncultivable Land	8.620	8.620	—
4.	Other Uncultivated Land Excluding Fallow Land a+b+c	79.230	77.209	—
	(a) Permanent Pastures and Other Gazing Land	5.235	5.230	0.26
	(b) Land under Miscellaneous Tree-Crops and Groves not Included in Net Area Sown	68.765	66.749	0.51
	(c) Cultivable Waste	5.230	5.230	0.26
5.	Fallow Lands (a+b)	207.543	210.928	4.21
	(a) Fallow Lands Other than Current Fallows	166.078	165.981	—
	(b) Current Fallows	41.465	44.947	1.23
6.	Net sown area	94.187	92.813	4.73
7.	Total Crop Area	105.575	102.903	—
8.	Area Sown More than Once	5.000	1.437	—
	Total Irrigation Area	16.360	14.169	—
	Area Irrigated for the year	11.388	9.446	—

Source: Statistical Handbook of Mizoram (2008).

4.73 per cent of the utilized land area (refer Table 22.2) is used for cultivation (net sown area), the contribution of this sector to SDP is a meagre 16.00 per cent and the State is far away from self sufficiency in foodgrain production.

NLUP for Inclusive Growth in Mizoram

The much awaited NLUP, a flagship programme of Mizoram government launched recently to help the poor farmers to move away from the traditional *jhum* cultivation to more sustainable land-based means of livelihood. NLUP is a programme which can change in the management of two critical resources–land and water and its main objective is to attain inclusive growth for all. If this is successful it can be a unique model for inclusive growth in the North-East region and can be adopted in other parts of the country also.

The project aims at benefiting immensely poor families. It is expected that the project will benefit about 1,20,000 families out of 2,06,365 families in Mizoram with average assistance of more than Rs 1,00,000 per family in the first five years for various livelihood activities, and about 19,640 families to be covered on a pilot basis. Under this scheme the following departments have been identified for implementation. They are agriculture, horticulture, sericulture, fishery, soil conservation, animal husbandry, forest, and industry development. NLUP will give priority attention to preserve and regenerate natural resources particularly forests and biodiversity.

The primary objective is to change the traditional method of shifting cultivation with a new form of land-use, empowerment of people, conservation of the environment, adoption of effective water harvesting measures and commercial utilization of abundant local resources and planned marketing of agricultural products.

The NLUP formally took off with great enthusiasm across the State in January 2011. At the launch of the scheme, the Chief Minister Lalthanhawla gave away the first instalment of funds amounting to Rs. 20,000 each to 400 beneficiaries. Introducing the policy, the Chief Minister maintained that "Insurgency played havoc with the livelihood of the Mizos, but today NLUP brings the beacon of hope for those who are ready to put in sincere hard work and are determined to change their lives. The governments, on its part, is doing its best to provide sufficient power and better roads at the earliest in order to make a success. We must work together to make a better and more progressive Mizoram".

With the launch of this project, Mizoram is projected to be changed socially and economically. Majority of *jhumia* families will slowly but surely shift over to enduring and sustainable means of livelihood and thus income levels of those involved in agriculture and allied sectors will improve radically. The overall growth of the economy of the State is projected to increase from 8 per cent during the past decade to 16 per cent in the next 8 to 10 years. After 10 years the per capita income is also likely to increase from Rs 32,634 in 2008-09 to Rs. 51,846.

The overall objectives will be to improve the livelihood of vulnerable groups mainly *jhumia* families in a sustainable manner through improved management of their resource base in a way that contributes to protecting and restoring environment. The specific objectives are:

1. It aims at keeping 60 per cent of Mizoram under rain forests. Deforestation and *jhum* burning go together. *Jhum* burning accounts for a very high percentage of greenhouse gas emissions when every year almost 2 lakh acres of land in rain forest are cut down and burnt. The State government through the NLUP now committed to respond to the crying demand to stop the *jhuming* practice. Mizoram has 52 lakh acres of land area. There are still about 1 lakh *jhumia* families. Under the NLUP family oriented programmes will be prepared for every *jhumia* family in a wide range of sectors. On an average 7 acres of land will be allotted to one family for agriculture, horticulture and allied activities. Thus only about 12 per cent of the total land area in Mizoram will be required or utilized.
2. The entire workforce hitherto engaged in *jhuming* will henceforth be employed in sustainable economic venture to create productive assets for each family. Projects will be prepared for each family to enable him/her to increase productivity at least five times from the level under the *jhum* system. A large number of educated unemployed will be covered under the NLUP. The programme will check the present discontent of thousands of educated people as well as the poor people. The government is fully aware of the urgency for action. Fortunately there is still enough land in Mizoram for the permanent residents who wish to avail the programmes under the NLUP. The major problem is lack of financial resources.
3. Promoting a sensitive approach to the design and implementation of development intervention.

4. Increase income through development of sustainable farming system, Micro enterprises including promotion and modernization of small scale and cottage industries.
5. Reclaiming land having potential for wet rice cultivation and providing minor irrigation so as to encourage settled cultivation in valleys and terraced rice cultivation on slopes.
6. Promotion/cultivation of suitable horticulture crops including medicinal and herbal plants and value addition locally.
7. Search and research of markets as would ensure remunerative prices of produces to farmers.
8. Access to basic service like power, telecommunication, and road network including agro link roads.
9. Providing housing assistance to the extremely poor families.

Table 22.3 highlights the proposal for NLUP livelihood activities for 5 years from 2009-10 to 2013-14 with Physical and Financial Target. A critical analysis of the Table shows that number of household involved in agricultural activities ranked highest, followed by horticulture and animal husbandry respectively and fishery and handloom ranked last.

Table 22.3: NLUP Livelihood Activities of Five Years with Physical and Financial Target (2009-10 to 2013-14)

Sl No.	*Name of Activity*	*1st year 2009-2010*		*For 5 year 2009-2014*		*Rank of activity and house-hold*
		Phy/No of households	*Financial (in lakh)*	*Phy/No of house-holds*	*Financial (in lakh)*	
1.	Agriculture	5920	7040.00	31600	37600.00	1
2.	Horticulture	5760	5370.00	28800	26850.00	2
3.	Sericulture	500	500.00	8500	8500.00	6
4.	Fishery	600	1270.00	3000	6352.00	8
5.	Animal Husbandry	2060	1673.00	18860	15282.00	3
6.	Soil & Water Con.	1700	655.00	9000	8405.00	5
7.	Micro Enterprises	500	400.00	6500	5200.00	7
8.	Handloom	600	480.00	3000	2400.00	8
9.	Forest (Bamboo)	2000	3053.00	10740	16393.00	4
	Total	**19640**	**20441.00**	**120000**	**126982.00**	—

Source: Government of Mizoram.

Further, Table 22.4 shows the district-wise targeted number of families to be assisted under NLUP for the first year, i.e., 2010-11. It can be observed from the table that Aizawl district got the highest number of families to be assisted (13,221 *jhumias*), followed by Lunglei district (7,103) and Lawngtlai district (5,921) during the year 2010-11 and at the same time the total number of families to be assisted for the whole programme also, Aizawl district has the highest number being 35,149.

Table 22.4: District-wise Target Number of Families to be assisted by NLUP

Sl. No.	*Name of District*	*No. of Families Surveyed*	*No. of Families Eligible*	*No. of Families to be Assisted*	*No. of Families to be Assisted for (1st years-2010-11)*
1.	Mamit	15302	13686	10288	3870
2.	Kolasib	16182	13476	10133	3813
3.	Aizawl	72366	46743	35149	13221
4.	Champhai	24278	20799	15651	5887
5.	Serchhip	13365	10791	8120	3055
6.	Lunglei	31813	25096	18886	7103
7.	Lawngtlai	24318	20925	15741	5921
8.	Saiha	10487	8012	6032	2269
	Grand Total	**208111**	**159528**	**120000**	**45139**

Source: NLUP Board, Government of Mizoram.

Further, an attempt has been made here to assess the projected funds necessary for implementation of NLUP (Table 22.5). The funds required for implementation of the policy shall be convergent with funds flow from centrally sponsored schemes (CSS) like MNREGA (Mahatma Gandhi National Rural Employment Guaranteed Act), Technology Mission and National Mission for Medicinal Plants, IWDP (Integrated Wasteland Development Programme), BADP (Border Area Development Programme) and BRGF (Backward Regions Grant Fund). 52 per cent of the projected amount of the policy fund comes from MNREGA. Another 26 per cent is coming from Bamboo Mission, followed by 18.3 per cent (BADP & BRGF) and 17 per cent (Technology Mission and National Mission for Medicinal Plants).

Future Goal of NLUP

- It is projected that NLUP programme as intended will gradually wean away farmers to alternative livelihood activities. Moreover the farming community with the benefit of plan intervention will

Table 22.5: Projected Funds flow from CSS *vis-à-vis* Convergence with NLUP

(Rs. in crores)

Sl. No.	*Name of CSS*	*Projected CSS funds flow 2009-10 to 2013-14*	*Proposed Convergence with NLUP during 2009-10 to 2013-14*	*% of the Projected Amount*	*Balance (Non-NLUP)*
1.	MNREGA	1831.50	966.68	52%	864.82
2.	Technology Mission and National Mission for Medicinal Plants	240.60	42.00	17%	198.6
3.	Bamboo Mission	67.00	17.45	26%	4.45
4.	IWDP	183.00	8.6	4.7%	174.40
5.	BADP & BRGF	152.6	27.90	18.3%	124.7
Total		**2420.7**	**1062.63**	**43.9%**	**1366.97**

Source: NLUP Board, Government of Mizoram.

be able to increase their income significantly in view of increased productivity, economics of scale and availability of markets. The project visualizes creating sustained livelihood activities to an estimate of 1,20,000 households over next five years.

- NLUP programme focused on increased production of essential items like paddy, pulses, oil seeds, vegetables, fruits, livestock, fisheries, etc., for food security and progressively attaining self-sufficiency for many items which have potentials for local propagation and production.
- NLUP is aiming at commercial production of agri-horticultural produces on commercial scale for which Mizoram has a great potential. Sustained efforts in this direction are bound to yield results.
- Apart from generating livelihood opportunities in rural areas, NLUP will also promise micro enterprises in cottage and small scale industries which would generate employment opportunities in non-farm sector. Commutative impact of such micro enterprises is expected to generate employment for 6,500 families.

- Increase production in agro-horticultural crops and spices like ginger, turmeric, etc. could facilitate agro-based industries generating income and employment and thereby heralding economic development. The existing processing unit at Chhingchhip may operate full time with increased availability of raw materials and further necessitating setting up of more such processing units in the near future.
- If NLUP is successfully implemented, it is expected that poverty in Mizoram will be eradicated within 10 years which would be a great achievement for government.

Conclusion and Suggestion

In view of the above, it is observed that at the present context, many States of the North-East region are facing various problems like insurgency, law and order problems which are not conducive to implement many centrally funded programmes. But in case of Mizoram, situation is opposite and considered as one of peaceful States in the country. So, the implementation of developmental project like NLUP is not a problem. State government should give emphasis on good governance as well as improve the work culture and should implement the policy in such a manner that reaches the intended and selected household beneficiaries for whom the policy was initiated. As the overall objectives of NLUP are to improve the livelihood of vulnerable groups mainly *jhumia* families in a sustainable manner through improved management of their resource-base in a way that contributes to protecting and restoring environment, it is necessary to set a well structure regulation in this context. It is also projected that by the end of the next three years around onc lakh families in the State will have permanent occupation, provided they judiciously utilize the money they received from this programme. There is enough fund to cover 1,20,000 families in five years. The farmers will have permanent occupation of their own choice, and will do away with the age-old shifting cultivation. Recently NABARD has also sanctioned Rs. 5 lakh for construction of the rural *haat* meant for the rural farmers to sell their agricultural produce. NABARD has constructed such rural *haats* in different places of the State.

Further, the successful implementation of NLUP shall largely depend on how far the funds meant for this policy is utilized properly. It is very crucial that transparency should be maintained as far as the policy funds are concerned. The funds required for implementation of the policy shall be convergent with funds flow from centrally sponsored schemes.

The success or failure of this policy will also largely depend on whether these beneficiaries have been selected impartially or not. As for the suggestion, it is presumed that these beneficiaries have been selected impartially and it is also a fact that they should be selected impartially irrespective of their political or whatever considerations. Then only, its objectives may be fulfilled.

The other important aspect which is of vital importance for the effective implementation of the policy is the proper monitoring. At different levels, district as well as village level, there must be effective monitoring of the policy. In the policy itself, there is provision for release of funds by instalment basis so that no money is spent for the purpose for which there is no provision in the policy.

It may be mentioned that in the NLUP itself there is provision for the social audit, particularly by the NGOs. Regarding NGOs, YMA (Young Mizo Association), MHIP (a Mizo Women's Society), etc., can take an active part in the effective implementation of the policy. Without social auditing, there cannot be a successful NLUP in the State.

The stakeholders' participation in the overall implementation of the policy is also very crucial. The society at large required taking active participation in this policy as it is going to be an ambitious project for a paradigm shift in the management of land and to attain inclusive growth for all. With the proper implementation of the policy, the State is expected to be transformed socially and economically. It is expected that all *jhuming* families will gradually switch over to permanent and sustainable livelihood activities; hence income levels of those involved in agriculture and allied sectors will increase drastically and it will lead to inclusive growth and for overall socio-economic development for Mizoram in future.

23

Small Scale Tea Cultivation in Assam

P. Guha

Introduction

Tropical plantation crop like tea, coffee, rubber are profitably grown in peripheral or semi-peripheral region (southern part of the world) and is widely consumed in northern part of the world (Talbot, 2002). To the cultivating nations, they have meant employment, foreign exchange, widespread use of unproductive land, industrial raw materials, export, etc. Tea is ranked prominently amongst other plantation crop for its global preference and mass consumption (Mitra, 1991). Tea production involves partially agricultural and manufacturing stages while larger percentage of it belongs to agriculture and the rest to manufacturing process.

India is the second largest producer, largest consumer and the fourth largest exporter of tea in the world (Kumar *et al.* 2008). Four countries, viz., India, China, Kenya and Sri Lanka produced about 69 per cent of the global tea output. Another two countries, viz., Turkey and Indonesia produced 5 per cent each and the rest 21 per cent was produced by other countries, viz., Bangladesh, Taiwan, Japan, Vietnam, Papua and New Guinea, Iran, Russia, Uganda, Tanzania, Malawi, Mozambique, Zaire, Mauritius, Rwanda, Burundi, Cameroon, Argentina, Brazil, Peru, Ecuador, Zimbabwe, Myanmar, Thailand, Malaysia, South Africa, Ethiopia, Australia as recorded in 2003.

Discovery of indigenous tea plants growing wild in Assam in 1823 and the end of British monopoly of tea trade with China in 1833 resulted in the expansion of tea sector in the country. Apart from earning valuable foreign exchange, the tea sector directly employs one million people and another two million indirectly. Although tea export earning has decreased, yet India maintains a major stake in tea as a net substantial foreign exchange earner for India (Guha, 2012). In India, tea growing regions are located in the monsoon belt—Assam, West Bengal, Tripura, Bihar, Himachal Pradesh, Manipur, Sikkim, Arunachal Pradesh, Nagaland, Meghalaya, Mizoram and Tamil Nadu, Kerala and Karnataka in South India.

Over the years, the tea sector of the country has experienced changes in several dimensions like export, consumption, area expansion, marketing, etc. Indian tea sector has exhibited significant change in the level of export over the past five decades since independence, registered 45 per cent in 1951, 38 per cent in 1961, 30 per cent in 1971, 28 per cent in 1981, 19 per cent in 1991 and further to 14 per cent in 2002 with 201 million kilogram (mkg) of exports out of 1,431 mkg of world export (Gogoi, 2007). The decline in export level continued in the recent past also. The exported tea was 218.7 mkg in 2006 dropped to 156.7 mkg in 2007. In 2006, around 98.81 mkg of tea was exported from North India and the figure came down to 84.05 mkg in 2007. Similarly, around 119 mkg of South Indian tea was exported in 2006 and the figure dropped to 72.65 mkg in 2007. The overall decline in export has posed major threat to the tea sector of Assam which produces more than 50 per cent of tea produced by the country (Choudhury, 2008).The global competition from other tea producing nations particularly Kenya, Sri Lanka, China and Vietnam and turning out quality of indigenous tea can be traced as responsible for fall in Indian export of tea towards the world.

The Tea Economy and Small Tea Growers of Assam

The economy of Assam is largely agricultural. Nature gifted climatic geographical condition is favourable for agro-economic sectors. Tea cultivation in Assam is done in a valley 8 to 9 miles on either side of the mighty Brahmaputra and Barak rivers at mean latitude of 26 degree N bounded in the North by the Himalayas and in the South by Mizoram and Nagaland. It is the only region in the world where such huge tracts of tea are grown at an altitude of below 150 metres where roots go down only to three feet (Bedi, 2008). The Brahmaputra valley and Barak valley are ideal for tea cultivation in the State. Out of all-India acreage, Assam tea cultivation covers 52.07 per cent of area that is 2.70 lakh hectares as per

2002 statistics. Tea sector of Assam is the mainstay of the State's economy, with a turnover of Rs 2,030 crore annually. The agro-based plantation sector (tea) provides livelihood to over 6 lakh persons directly and 18 lakh persons indirectly. There are more than 800 commercial tea estates in Assam (Gogoi, 2007).

The organized tea sector of Assam experienced most significant development at the end of the last century as a result of participation of unemployed youths as small tea growers and thereby resulting quantitative increase in tea output of the State influencing socio-economic sphere of Assam. The small-scale tea cultivation in Assam is rather in an infant stage considering the 180 years age of Indian tea sector. As per the available records, the first commercial small tea garden was established in Golaghat district in 1978. However, the profession becomes popular in upper Assam since 1990. The history of small tea cultivation was the interest of some paddy farmers in few districts (Golaghat, Jorhat, Sivsagar and Dibrugarh) of upper Assam initiated cultivation in their small holding ranging from 0.13 hectares to 3 hectares. There were only 21 small holdings in 1987 increased to 4,028 in 1992-93 further to 21,348 in 1997-98. In the past three decade more than 38,000 farmers have entered into the small scale tea cultivation covering 57,000 hectares area. As per 2004 statistics there were 38,393 small tea growers were producing an estimated 85 million kg (18 per cent of total tea output of Assam) and employed 2.4 lakh persons of Assam (Gogoi, 2007).

In the early years of its development, the green leaf produced by the small growers was purchased by the factories of large planters. As a result of quantities increase of green leaf, there was an urgency to establish Bought Leaf Factories (BLF). In 2002, there were more than 138 BLF in Assam to cater to the need of the small tea growers producing 46.82 mkg of tea (Baruah, 2008). Major BLF was located in the five districts of upper Assam, viz., Tinsukia (65), Dibrugarh (34), Sivsagar (25), Jorhat (10), Golaghat (12) and others (1).

All Assam Small Tea Growers' Association (AASTGA) has claimed that the actual number of small tea growers in Assam could be more than 35,000. These small tea gardens have given self-employment to large number of people including unemployed youths and over 5,000 have been employed in clerical and other jobs (Baruah, 2008). The growth of small tea cultivation was very conspicuous in the five districts of upper Assam as mentioned that accounted for 90 per cent of small tea growers and 10 per cent growers spread over remaining 16 districts of Assam.

$$Y_t = \theta_0 + \theta_1 Z_{1t} + \theta_2 Z_{2t} + u_t \qquad ...(ii)$$

where, Z_{1t} is total area under tea cultivation[1] (hectare)

Z_{2t} is Average Daily Number of Labour employed in Tea (small & large) in total, θ_0, θ_1, θ_2 are being non-negative.

District Level Density of Small Tea Grower and Area in Assam

Refer to Table 23.1, it can be observed that density of small tea cultivators in number and area under small tea cultivation is restricted to few districts

Table 23.1: Small Tea Growers of Assam Registered with the Tea Board of India

(up to 31st March, 2007)

Sl. No.	District	Number of Small Tea Growers	Rank	Registered Area (in hectares)	Rank
1.	Dhubri	1	—	1.04	—
2.	Kokrajhar	9	—	46.65	—
3.	Bongaigaon	35	—	93.01	—
4.	Goalpara	1	—	6.25	—
5.	Barpeta	1	—	1.51	—
6.	Nalbari	8	—	29.42	—
7..	Kamrup	7	—	26.95	—
8.	Darrang	162	7	476.07	6
9.	Sonitpur	604	2	1209.93	3
10.	Lakhimpur	185	6	351.45	7
11.	Dhemaji	58	—	117.16	—
12.	Morigaon	7	—	7.35	—
13.	Nagaon	122	10	305.32	9
14.	Golaghat	938	1	2102.31	1
15.	Jorhat	147	8	296.93	10
16.	Sibsagar	127	9	347.41	8
17.	Dibrugarh	199	5	501.17	5
18.	Tinsukia	223	4	502.99	4
19.	Karbi Anglong	302	3	2058.39	2
20.	N.C. Hills	1	—	4.68	—
21.	Karimganj	7	—	36.28	—
22.	Hailakandi	4	—	23.84	—
23.	Cachar	31	—	127.70	—
24.	Baksa	1	—	3.22	—
25.	Udalguri	7	—	16.39	—
Grand Total		**3187**		**8693.42**	

Source: Tea Board of India, Zonal Office, Guwahati.

only. As per Tea Board Statistics till March 2007, there were 25 districts where 3,187 registered small tea gardens were cultivating tea on 8693.42 hectares of land in Assam. In the table, it also reveals that Golaghat district has 938 small tea growers ranked first among the districts, followed by Sonitpur district in second position, Karbi Anglong at third position. Other districts having good number of small tea growers are such as Tinsukia, Dibrugarh, Lkhimpur, Darrang, Jorhat, Sibsagar and Nagaon. Again in terms of registered Tea growing area (in hectares) are also shown in the table, Golaghat district ranked first in terms of area of tea plantation, followed by Karbi Anglong and Sonitpur districts as second and third position respectively.

Thus it is observed that small tea cultivation in terms of density and area under cultivation is restricted to few districts only. Other districts (for example Dhubri, Barpeta, Goalpara, Baksa, N.C. Hills) have started up small tea cultivation but very less in number and even the area under cultivation in such districts is very insignificant.

The results for the fitted production function post-estimation being presented in Table 23.2. From the Table 23.2, we can observe that the model (i) gives good fit to the sampled data in terms of R^2 value. About 86 per cent variation in total tea output (in '000 kg) in Assam is explained by registered area under small tea cuitivation (in hectare) and number of small tea growers in the State. Individually X_{1t} has not been observed to be statistically significant while X_{2t} have been remarked to be weakly significant at 90 per cent level. Thus a unit increase in number of small

Table 23.2: Estimated Production Function of Assam Tea Sector

Constant/ Explanatory Variable	*Estimated Coefficients of the Models*	
	Model (i)	*Model (ii)*
β_0 and θ_0	34458.17	77.08
X_{1t}	–53.64	NA
X_{2t}	273.86***	NA
Z_{1t}	NA	1.73*
Z_{2t}	NA	–0.057
R^2	0.86	0.99
Adjusted R^2	0.82	0.95

Note: *Significant at 1% level, ** Significant at 5% level, *** Significant at 10% level

Source: Author's own computation based on Statistical Handbook of Assam, 2007.

tea growers in Assam has helped 273.86 per cent increase in tea output of the State. The adjusted R^2 for the model (i) has been observed to be high.

Again the Coefficient of determination for the model (ii) has been observed to be satisfactory implying 99 per cent variation in total tea output (in'000 kg) in Assam is due to total area under tea cultivation (hectare) and average daily number of labour employed in tea sector (small and large) in total. Individually area under tea cultivation (hectare) has been remarked to be highly significant while average daily number of labour employed in tea sector (small and large) in total not being observed to be statistically insignificant in model. Thus, a unit change in total area under tea cultivation (hectare) has resulted 1.73 per cent increase in total tea output (in'000 kg) of Assam. The adjusted R^2 has also been observed to be satisfactory for model (ii). Model (ii) is more preferred than model (i) on the basis of value of adjusted R^2.

Observations of the Study

The small tea cultivation in Assam in terms of density and area under cultivation is restricted to few districts only. Emergence of small tea grower since late eighties has significantly influenced tea output of the State. The overall tea output level in Assam has experienced a steep rise during 2004 due to the initiation of tea cultivation by small tea grower in large number. However, acreage expansion due to expansion of registered area under small tea cultivation has unable to significantly influence the overall output level of the State till 2004. Total area under tea cultivation has been observed to be significant determinant of gross tea output of the State. However, the average number of daily labour employed in tea plantation has not brought any significant improvement in the tea output of the State. One may assume low productivity of tea labourer as a reason for it. Studies have claimed that productivity of tea labour in South Indian plantation is higher than Assam and North Bengal (Sunny and Chattopadhyaya, 2008).

Conclusion

No doubt, small tea growers are large in number. But, most of the small tea grower lacks formal ownership of land under tea cultivation except a minority section. Moreover, many small tea growers in Assam are unable to qualify for registration with Tea Board of India. The registered land under small tea cultivation is relatively insignificant compared with the

180 years old organised tea sector of Assam. Hence, area expansion due to small scale tea cultivation has not able to influence the overall output level of the State.

Proper reorganization of small tea grower is the need of the hour though admittedly is not an easy task. Efficient technical support to the small tea grower in the form of field level training and advisory services may be helpful for raising the output level. Initiative from Tea Board of India about support price towards the small tea grower may be helpful in minimizing their problems. The encouragement is necessary from NGOs and self-help groups towards small tea grower to develop their entrepreneurial ability.

NOTE

1. Includes Small Tea Grower as well as large tea grower.

REFERENCES

Baruah, P. (2008). *The Tea Industry of Assam Origin and Development,* EBH Publisher (India), Guwahati.

Baruah, S. (2007). *Small Scale Tea Cultivation in Assam—Its Sustainability and Export Acceptability*. In S. Borbora and J. K. Gogoi (eds.), *Development Issue in the North-East in the turn of the Century*, Papyrus, Guawahati.

Baruah, S. and M. Taparia (2004). *The Small Tea Growers of Assam: Status and Strategies*. Seminar paper presented in Dibrugarh University, February 10-11.

Bedi, C.S. (2007-2008). *Assam Tea: A Unique Proposition*. Contemporary Tea Time (December-February), Samar Sircar, Kolkata, Vol. XVI No.4, p.29.

Choudhury, R. Dutta (2008). Tea Exports come down drastically, *The Assam Tribune*, February 10.

Gogoi, Jayanta. Kr. (2007). Tea Industry of India with Special Reference to Assam, In Borbora, S., Gogoi, J.K. (eds.), *Development Issue in the North East in the Turn of the Century*, Papyrus, Guwahati.

Government of Assam, *Statistical Handbook of Assam* (2007), Directorate of Economics and Statistics, Guwahati.

Guha, P. (2012). Period of Indian Economic Structural Adjustment and Assam Tea Sector, *The IUP Journal of Agricultural Economics*, Vol. 9, No. 1.

Kumar, P; P. S. Badal; N. P. Singh and Singh R. P. (2008), "Tea Industry in India: Problems and Prospects", *Indian Journal of Agricultural Economics*, Vol. 63, No. 1, pp. 84-96.

Mitra, N. (1991). Indian Tea Industry: Problems and Policies, *Economic and Political Weekly*, Vol. 26, No. 48, November 30.

Sunny, K. P. and A. Chattopadhyay (2008). *Impact of Trade and Globalisation on Gender in India*. Presentation During Session-I of International Conference on Moving Towards Gender Sensitisation of Trade Policy, February 25, p. 73, pp. 66-76, pp. 237-241, New Delhi.

Talbot, John M. (2002). Tropical Commodity Chains, Forward Integration Strategies and International Inequality: Coffee, Cocoa and Tea. *Review of International Political Economy*, Vol.9, No.4, November, pp. 701-734.

Tea Statistics, Tea Board of India (Zonal Office), Guwahati, Assam.

Index